Union "Tales of the War" in the Trans-Mississippi Part One

UNWRITTEN CHAPTERS OF
THE CIVIL WAR
WEST OF THE RIVER

VOLUME VIII

Union
"Tales of the War"
In the Trans-Mississippi
Part One: 1861

Author/Editor Michael E. Banasik

Camp Pope Publishing
2024

Library of Congress Control Number: 2024901426

ISBN: 978-1-929919-95-6

Camp Pope Publishing
P.O. Box 2232
Iowa City, Iowa 52244
www.camppope.com

Series Dedication:

Dedicated to the forgotten soldiers of both North and South, who fought in the American Civil War west of the Mississippi River; their deeds of perseverance and valor shall not be lost through the ravages of time, but rather recorded for all to remember.

Volume VIII, Part One Dedication:

To my wife of 47 years, Brenda. You are the best thing that has ever happened to me.

CONTENTS

Chapter 1—Missouri's Path to Civil War (January—July 1861) 1

Securing the St. Louis Arsenal and U. S. Sub-Treasury in early 1861, by Isaac H. Sturgeon, Assistant Treasure of the United States 1

Arrival of Nathaniel Lyon in St. Louis, in the Spring of 1861, and comments on Lyon, by General Justus McKinstry. 21

Governor Claiborne F. Jackson, the Missouri Legislature and the Secession Crisis, by General Justus McKinstry. 27

Recruitment for Missouri troops in April 1861, by Colonel David Murphy. 35

Camp Jackson, Missouri, May 10, 1861 by Captain Otto C. Lademann, Late Captain Third Missouri Volunteers. 42

Operations against General Thomas Harris, near Florida, Missouri on July 17, 1861, by General U. S. Grant and Mark Twain or Samuel Clemens. 59

Chapter 2—Battles of Carthage and Wilson's Creek **62**

Battle of Carthage, Missouri (July 5, 1861), by Otto C. Lademann, late captain 3rd Missouri Volunteers. 62

The Battle of Wilson's Creek (August 10, 1861), by Otto C. Lademann, late captain 3rd Missouri Volunteers. 82

Sigel's retreat from Wilson's Creek., by Otto C. Lademann, late captain 3rd Missouri Volunteers 102

The aftermath of the Battle of Wilson's Creek and the retreat to Rolla, by Michael E. Banasik 114

Incident from the Battle of Wilson's Creek–The death of General Lyon at Wilson's Creek, by Alexander Becher. 122

Incident from the Battle of Wilson's Creek–The Union rebuttal to the final actions at Wilson's Creek by the 3rd Texas Cavalry, by R. I. Holcombe.... 124

Incident from the Battle of Wilson's Creek–General N. Lyon's Burial, by J. Coleman Gardner. 126

Chapter 3—Fall Campaign (September–November 1861) **128**

Use of hemp bales at the siege of Lexington, Missouri, September 13–20, 1861, by unknown, though a Union supporter labeled "Chicago Comrade." 128

Battle of Belmont (November 7, 1861), by Charles M. Scott, Pilot of the *Belle Memphis.* 131

Appendix A: Assorted Official Documents, Letters and Correspondence.... 142

Appendix B: Selected Biographies 164

James Buchanan Eads 164
Thomas Clement Fletcher 165
Hamilton Rowan Gamble... 166
John William Reid... 168
Thomas Caute Reynolds 169
Charles E. Salomon... 171
Joseph Wofford Tucker... 172

Appendix C: Extended Comments... 175

Appendix D: Various Orders of Battle... 198

Bibliography.. 236

Credits... 255

Index.. 256

Photos and Illustrations

"Tales of the War" nameplate..xii
James B. Clay.. 4
George D. Prentice 5
Henry S. Geyer.. 5
Brigadier General Nathaniel Lyon 18
Claiborne F. Jackson 20
Colonel David Murphy 36
Brigadier General Franz Sigel... 45
General Daniel M. Frost... 47
General James S. Rains 68
General Sterling Price 108
James B. Eads.. 164
Thomas C. Fletcher 165
Captain James Totten 181
Brigadier General John M. Schofield.. 184

Maps

Camp Jackson.. 51
Battle of Dry Fork 70
Battle of Wilson's Creek 94
Battle of Belmont 135

Series Introduction

The Civil War in the Trans-Mississippi region provides a fascinating study of Nineteenth Century warfare under the most severe conditions. Soldiers serving in the region faced an almost complete lack of a railroad net, a decrepit road system, and terrain that varied from arid deserts to rugged mountains. Battles were few, but the constant strain of living under less than ideal conditions wore heavily upon the soldiers serving west of the Mississippi River. Often the stories told by the frontier soldiers were not of great engagements but of long marches, poor living conditions, or simply one of survival. And for each story told there was always two parts; one told by a man in gray or one who wore the blue. This is one of their stories.

Michael E. Banasik

Introduction to Volume VIII, Part One

This latest volume of my series comprises an extensive group of reminiscences published by *The Missouri Republican* between 1885 and 1887. These pieces were written by the participants in the Civil War and cover the entire conflict from the firing of the first guns until the surrender of the Confederacy in 1865. The first issue appeared on July 4, 1885 and the last one, that I discovered, occurred on July 2, 1887—in all 95 issues were published. (A previously unknown newspaper has been added to the number of issues that are part of this series and has been incorporated into these accounts.)

Typically, in each Saturday issue, the *Republican* published assorted pieces from the lowliest private to the exalted general, all veterans of the war and covering the Civil War from every aspect; both North and South and from every front of the action, including the high-seas. For this volume, only those pieces not previously published and dealing with the Trans-Mississippi will be presented.

As to why these articles were published, the *Missouri Republican* wrote the following concerning its first issue:

> The publication of the official orders and correspondence of the war of the rebellion made it comparatively easy for military writers to get at the exact facts of many disputed questions, and all the campaigns have been discussed by the record in recent years by competent officers of both the contending armies. Probably it is the publication of these numerous volumes, which, as much as anything else, has aroused a renewed interest in all manner of literature based on the incidents of the civil war. In response to what seems a public desire the REPUBLICAN will hereafter publish in its Saturday edition a series of war papers, either original or selected from the best current sketches in contemporary publications.
>
> It is not desired to make this department especially a medium for

criticism of military operations. The incidents of camp life and the experiences of the private soldier will find as ready access to these columns as the history of great campaigns. What ever war reminiscences will interest the thousands of old soldiers and the greater thousands of their children, will gladly be published in the full ballet that these chronicles of personal experiences from both sides, while reviving the memories, will at the same time aid in obliterating the animosities of the great struggle."[1]

The 1861 portion of the Union "Tales of the War," covers the events in Missouri that led up to Missouri reluctantly entering the Civil War, including the war preparations in St. Louis, the arrival of Nathaniel Lyon in St. Louis and the role he played in preparing the Union side for the eventual conflict in Missouri. Also included you will be introduced to the Missouri secession crisis and the capture of Camp Jackson on May 10, 1861, which propelled Missouri into the Civil War. Other events in the 1861 volume of this series, the reader will find an extensive accounts on the Battles of Carthage (July 5, 1861), Wilson's Creek (August 10, 1861), and, to a lesser extent the Battle of Belmont on November 7, 1861, as related by the pilot of General Grant's headquarters vessel, the *Belle Memphis*. This volume also includes several appendices covering official correspondence, various biographies and extensive Order of Battles for the major engagement in 1861 Missouri.

I hope you find these pieces as fascinating as I did in researching and preparing them for your reading pleasure.

Michael E. Banasik

1. Editorial Comment, *The Missouri Republican* (St. Louis, Missouri), July 4, 1885.

Nameplate which appeared ahead of most of the "Tales of the War" in the *Republican*.

Union "Tales of the War"
In the Trans-Mississippi
Part One

Chapter 1

Missouri's Path to Civil War (January—July 1861)

Item: Securing the St. Louis Arsenal and U. S. Sub-Treasury in early 1861, by Isaac H. Sturgeon, Assistant Treasure of the United States.[1]
Published: January 9, 1886.

The Crisis of 1850 and 1861

The *Republican*, knowing that Hon. Isaac H. Sturgeon had some interesting letters bearing upon the early history of those events which culminated in the war of the rebellion, solicited the privilege of publishing them in these columns, and obtained from him not only the letters themselves, but also an outline of the circumstances under which they were written, with the following account of his own connection with public affairs at two important crisis of the nation's history.

At the assembling of Congress in 1849—50 the slavery agitation had assumed alarming proportions and the greatest apprehension prevailed in regard to the safety of the Union. A committee of thirteen was appointed with the Hon. Henry

---

1. Isaac H. Sturgeon was born in Kentucky, moved to Missouri, and was a long-time resident of St. Louis by the beginning of the Civil War. With the election of Franklin Pierce, as President in 1854, Sturgeon was appointed to his treasury position. In the election of 1856, he supported James Buchanan for President and was subsequently re-appointed to the treasury position in St. Louis. Prior to the war, Sturgeon supported the Preston Blair family of St. Louis, but when Blair joined the Republican Party, Sturgeon considered it a "traitorous" act, disavowing him. During the Presidential election of 1860, Sturgeon supported John Bell for President, leading many to believe that he was a "cunning secessionist"; however Sturgeon would prove otherwise. Thomas L. Snead knew Sturgeon as a "Southern Rights" man, one who was "active, shrewd, and a cunning politician." He was one of seven candidates for Missouri Governor in 1860, but lost to Claiborne F. Jackson. After the election of President Lincoln, Sturgeon left his position in the Treasury Department and became the President of the Mexico Railroad. As the war progressed Sturgeon became the President and Superintendent of the North Missouri Railroad Company, a position he held until the end of the war. United States War Department, *The War of the Rebellion: A Compilation of the Official Records of the Union and Confederate Armies,* 70 vols. in 128 (Washington, DC, 1880–1901), vol. 22, pt. 2: 256, vol. 34, pt. 4: 548–549, vol. 41, pt. 2:539, 560, vol. 48, pt. 1:1116, hereafter cited as *O.R.* All citations of *O.R.* refer to Series 1 unless indicated otherwise; Louis S. Gerteis, *Civil War St. Louis* (Lawrence, KS, 2001), 83, hereafter cited as Gerteis, *St. Louis*; John McElroy, *The Struggle For Missouri* (Washington, 1909), 41, hereafter cited as McElroy; Walter Harrington Ryle *Missouri: Union or Secession* (Nashville, TN, 1931), 141, hereafter cited as Ryle; William Ernest Smith, *The Francis Preston Blair Family in Politics,* 2 vols. (New York, 1933), vol. 1: 429, vol. 2: 33, hereafter cited as Smith, *Blair Family*; Thomas L. Snead, *The Fight for Missouri From the Election of Lincoln to the Death of Lyons* (New York, 1866), 101–102, hereafter cited as Snead, *Fight for Missouri*.

Clay as chairman to prepare measures to be adopted by Congress in the hope of pacificating the country.[2] After long deliberation, Mr. Clay introduced as the result of the labors of the committee what was termed as the compromise measure in one bill known as "Omnibus Bill."[3] The bill was antagonized by Col. [Thomas H.] Benton and others, as the debate will show, but by Col. Benton mainly on the grounds that it was bad legislation to put all the measures in one bill, making good measures carry through bad ones.[4] That there were some things in the bill

2. Henry Clay was born on April 12, 1777, in Virginia, moved to Lexington, Kentucky, in 1798. A lawyer by profession, he entered politics in 1803, and was appointed a U.S. Senator in 1806. Leaving the Senate, Clay was elected to the U.S. House of Representatives, served as Speaker of the House for 15 years, and was "instrumental in securing the passage of the Missouri Compromise in 1820." With the election of John Quincy Adams, as President, Clay was appointed Secretary of State. Returning to the Senate in 1831, Clay ran for the Whig Party nomination for President in 1832, but lost to Andrew Jackson. After several failed attempts at the Presidency, Clay returned to the Senate for the final time in 1849. Crafting what was popularly known as the Compromise of 1850, with the assistance of the Senate Committee of Thirteen, Clay never finished his product, leaving it to Stephen A. Douglas to complete the "Omnibus Bill," which embraced all the parts of Clay's last great compromise. He died on June 29, 1852, believing that the Compromise of 1850 would "quell the slavery debate for another thirty years." William L. Barney, *The Oxford Encyclopedia of the Civil War* (New York, 2001), 80–81, hereafter cited as Barney; David S. Heidler and Jeanne T. Heidler, eds., "Clay, Henry," in *Encyclopedia of the American Civil War*, 451–452, hereafter cited as *Encyclopedia of the Civil War*.
3. In April 1850, Henry Clay was appointed Chairman of a Senate "Select Committee of Thirteen," to consider Clay's proposals to settle the question of slavery in the new territories acquired as a result of the Mexican War. The Omnibus Bill, the product of that committee, was largely defeated on July 31, all except the organizing of Utah Territory, which could enter the "Union with or without slavery as its constitution may prescribe at the time of its admission"; however, Stephen A. Douglas, with the consent of Clay, took over the process of passing the remaining parts of the compromise. By dividing the Omnibus Bill into its several parts, Douglas succeeded in passing the bill, which was also known as the Compromise of 1850. Passed on September 17,1850, the bill was subsequently signed into law by President Millard Fillmore. There were five components to the Omnibus Bill not previously passed; The Texas-New Mexico border dispute awarded more land to Texas; California was admitted as a Free State; New Mexico Territory was organized; The Fugitive Slave Act was enacted; and Slave trade was prohibited in the District of Columbia. Avery O. Craven, *The Growth of Southern Nationalism 1848–1861* (Baton Rouge, LA, 1953), 98, 102, hereafter cited as Craven; Clement A. Evans, gen. ed. *Confederate Military History*, 13 vols. (Atlanta, 1899; reprint ed., Secaucus, NJ, 1974), vol 1: *Secession and the Civil War* by Clement A. Evans, 272–273, hereafter cited as Evans, *Secession and the Civil War, Confederate Military History*; David S. Heidler, *Pulling the Temple Down: The Fire-Eaters and the Destruction of the Union* (Mechanicsburg, PA, 1994), 61–63, hereafter cited a Heidler, *Pulling the Temple Down*; David M. Potter, *The Impending Crisis 1848–1861* (Don E. Fehrenbacher, ed., New York, 1976), 103,107–108, 111–112., hereafter cited as Potter, *Impending Crisis*.
4. Thomas Hart Benton was born in North Carolina in 1782, moved to Tennessee, and was elected a senator in the Tennessee Legislature. A lawyer by profession, Benton next moved to St. Louis in 1815, where he became the editor of the *Missouri Enquirer*. Elected as one of Missouri's first senators (1820–1850), Benton championed western causes like free navigation of the Mississippi River and a national road to New Mexico. A tacit supporter of slavery, Benton was defeated for office in 1850, won a U.S. House of Representatives seat in 1856, and died of cancer on April 10, 1858. James Neal Primm, *Lion of the Valley St. Louis, Missouri* (Boulder, CO, 1981), 113–114, 116–117, 120, hereafter cited as Primm; James M. Volo and Dorothy Denneen Volo, *Encyclopedia of the Antebellum South* (Westport, CT, 2000), 30–31.

that members could vote for others they could not, and that the measures in the "Omnibus Bill," as it was termed,, should be presented in separate bills so that each should stand on its own merits. The idea of embracing all the measures in one bill was that each interest should know exactly what it would get, and that no one should be deceived. The discussion was long and acrimonious over the bill, and it was during the debate that Sen. [Henry S.] Foote of Mississippi drew his pistol on Sen. Benton in the Senate chamber.[5] Mr. Isaac. H. Sturgeon of the city was in Washington during the debate, and, although a young man and a Democrat at the time, he warmly espoused the compromise measures and visited Mr. Clay almost daily

At His Rooms

at the National hotel in Washington after he would come from the Senate. He knew Mr. Clay well, having traveled with him, and his Hon James B. Clay, having married the sister of his aunt.[6] On one of the calls on Mr. Clay he suggested

---

5. Henry Stuart Foote was born on February 28, 1804, in Virginia, became a lawyer with an office in Richmond, before moving to Alabama, where he established a law practice and edited a newspaper. Following a duel, that Foote instigated, he was barred from practicing law in Alabama and subsequently moved to Mississippi, where he eventually settled in Jackson. In the 1840's Foote entered the political arena, being appointed a U.S. Senator in 1847. While in the Senate, not only did Foote pull a pistol on Senator Benton he came to fisticuffs with his fellow Senator from Mississippi–Jefferson Davis. Foote was a rabid Unionist and supported the Compromise of 1850. The Mississippi Legislature later censured Foote for his support of the compromise; Foote in turn ran for Governor of Mississippi, narrowly beating Jefferson Davis. Resigning from officer in 1854, Foote moved briefly to California, where he lost a bid for the U.S. Senate. Returning to Mississippi in 1858, Foote relocated to Nashville, where he was located at the beginning of the Civil War. During the war, Foote served in the Confederate Congress, being essentially an anti-war Congressman throughout the conflict and opposing virtually everything that Jefferson Davis advocated. Foote went so far as to institute "no fewer than 30 inquiries into fraud in the commissary and quartermasters departments." Peace talks having failed in early 1865, Foote decided to institute his own peace initiative, but failed. Following the war Foote relocated briefly to Canada and Europe before settling in Washington, DC, where he befriended U.S. Grant, who appointed him Superintendent of the New Orleans Mint. Foote died in New Orleans on May 19 or 20, 1880. Among his post war activities, Foote wrote numerous articles and books, including *War of the Rebellion* (1866). Mark Mayo Boatner III, *The Civil War Dictionary* (New York, 1959), 287, hereafter cited as Boatner; Patricia L. Faust, ed., *Historical Times Illustrated Encyclopedia of the Civil War* (New York, 1986), 266, hereafter cited as Faust; Ben Wynne, "Foote, Henry Stuart," in *Encyclopedia of the Civil War*, 714.

6. Judge James Brown Clay, was born on November 9, 1817, graduated from Transylvania University, was a lawyer by profession and served in the U.S. Congress (1857–1859). At the beginning of the Civil War, Clay a decided secessionist, resided at Ashland Plantation (Henry Clay estate), in Clark County near Lexington, Kentucky. He was captured on September 24, 1861, with a group of fourteen men while heading to join the Confederate Army; however, Clay posted a bond and was released. As the war progressed Clay was forced into exile, departing for Cuba, from Charleston in early 1863. Fleeing to Canada, Clay died in Montreal on January 26, 1864. *O.R.*, Series 2, vol. 2: 844, 886, 890; *O.R.*, Series 4, vol. 2: 391; R. A. Brock, ed., *Southern Historical Society Papers*, 52 vols. (Richmond, VA, 1876–1959; reprint ed., Wilmington, NC, 1990–1992), vol. 9: 292, hereafter cited as Brock, *SHSP*; "James Brown Clay," in Wikipedia.org.

James B. Clay

to Mr. Clay whether he did not think it would strengthen his bill to get up Union meetings over the country in favor of it. Mr. Sturgeon said to him that he thought if such meetings were held it would make those who were necessitating as to their course certain for the bill, as what they desired to feel assured of was that the constituency behind them would sustain their action. Mr. Clay approved the holdings of such meeting, but said he was so worn and pressed with the debate that he had daily to sustain, that he could not find the time to write the necessary letters for the purpose. Mr. Sturgeon asked if he would have the right to use Mr. Clay's name in letters to friends in Louisville, Ky., and St. Louis, Mo., as appropriate and desiring such meeting to be held. Mr. Clay consented and Mr. Sturgeon at once wrote to the Hon. James Guthrie, the leader of the Democracy of Kentucky and law partner of his uncle, Robert Tyler, afterwards United States secretary of the treasury under President Pierce, and also to George D Prentice, editor of the Louisville *Journal*, advising them of the action that would meet the approval of Mr. Clay.[7] Mr. Prentice, although a Whig was a warm personal friend of Mr. Sturgeon and published his letter, saying in an editorial in his paper that it was from a young Democrat, but a patriot.[8] Mr. Sturgeon at the same time wrote to St. Louis. Steps were at once

7. James Guthrie was born on December 5, 1792, near Bardstown, Kentucky, educated locally and was admitted to the Kentucky bar in 1817. At the age of 41, he was appointed the state's Attorney General and moved to Louisville. Guthrie served in both the Kentucky House and Senate (1827–1840) and in 1853, upon the recommendation of Thomas Benton, Guthrie was appointed Franklin Pierce's Secretary of the Treasury. Returning to Louisville in 1855, Guthrie was first appointed vice president and then president of the *Louisville & Nashville Railroad*, a position he held until 1868. Guthrie ran for the Democratic nomination for President in 1860, but lost to Stephen A. Douglas. Later, with the secession crisis in full bloom, Guthrie represented Kentucky at the Washington Peace Conference in February 1861, being appointed Chairman of the Compromise Committee. The Peace Conference completed their recommendations, on February 27. Known as the "Guthrie Plan," the committee recommended seven Constitutional Amendments which were rejected by all parties. During the war Guthrie supported the Union, being elected a Kentucky Senator in 1865. Resigning from the Senate in February 1868, because of health, Guthrie died on March 13, 1869. Brock, "Efforts to Establish a Central Confederacy In 1861," in SHSP, vol. 28: 146; "James Gutherie," in Wikipedia.org; Randolph Hollingsworth, "Guthrie, James," in *Encyclopedia of the Civil War*, 903–904; Potter, *Impending Crisis*, 411; Smith, *Blair Family*, vol. 1: 287.
8. George D. Prentice was born on December 18, 1802, in Connecticut, attended Brown University in Rhode Island and later moved to Louisville, Kentucky. He became the editor of the *Louisville Journal* in 1830, writing a biography on Henry Clay the same year. Prentice married in 1835, and had four children. Known for his "militant editorials," Prentice sparked the 1855 Election Riots, in

taken to get mass Union meeting in favor of Mr. Clay's compromise measure in both cities. The meeting in Louisville Kentucky was a monster-one and was presided over by Hon. James Guthrie, a Democrat. That in St. Louis was presided over by Hon. Henry S Geyer, a Whig, while Gen. Nathan Ranney, a Democrat, acted as secretary.[9] Thus it may be said that Isaac H. Sturgeon was the instigator of the

---

Louisville, on August 6, 1855. Dubbed "Bloody Monday" 22 were killed. A slave owner, Prentice had two sons who joined the Confederate Army, while he appeared to support the Union cause. As the war progressed he lost one son while the other, Major Clarence J. Prentice was captured while visiting his family in Louisville in 1863, and later exchanged following an appeal to President Lincoln. Despite his professed Union sentiment, Prentice appears to have actually supported the Confederacy. In 1864, a former POW from Sterling Price's Confederate Army reported that Prentice was "one of the best rebels in Kentucky," supplying funds to purchase arms for the rebels as well as monies to support General M. Jeff Thompson, and others while on parole in St. Louis. An "exceedingly shrewd and wary" individual, Prentice seemed to have fooled Union authorities as to his true nature. In late 1864, with the permission of Union officials, Prentice visited Richmond, Virginia, to see his son, Clarence, who had been indited for murder; however, the young Prentice was later released, survived the war and returned to Kentucky. Meanwhile, in Richmond, Prentice supplied valuable information to the Confederacy on the state of affairs in Kentucky as well informing them of his help for rebel POWs. Returning to Kentucky, Prentice famously branded a local guerrilla, Marcellus J. Clarke, as "Sue Mundy," in his "'noosepaper,'" to irk General Stephen Burbridge, who failed to capture the elusive guerrilla. Clarke was eventually caught and hung under Burbridge's successor, John M. Palmer. Following the war George continued as editor of the *Louisville Journal*, until his death on January 22, 1870. *O.R.*, vol. 4: 187, vol. 45, pt. 2: 503–505, vol. 49, pt. 2: 581–582; *O.R.*, Series 2, vol. 5: 520, 527–529; *O.R.*, Series 2, vol. 7: 264–265; "George D. Prentice,"in Wikipedia.org; Stewart Sifakis, *Who Was Who in the Union: A Comprehensive, Illustrated Biographical Reference to More Than 1,500 of the Principal Union Participants in the Civil War* (New York, 1988.) 321, hereafter cited as Sifakis, *Who Was Who in the Union.*

George D. Prentice

9. Henry S. Geyer was born in Maryland, on December 9, 1790, fought in the War of 1812, as a 1st lieutenant. after which he moved to Missouri, settling in St. Louis. A lawyer by profession, Geyer became the editor of the *St. Louis Times* in 1833, and married in 1835. He was a pro-slavery Whig, served three terms in the Missouri Territorial Legislature, was elected to the Missouri House (1834–1835) and in 1850 defeated Thomas Benton for the U.S. Senate (1851–1857) on the fortieth ballot with a vote of 80 to 55. Geyer served one term, being replaced by Trusten Polk after his term expired. During the Dred Scott case, Geyer was one of two lawyers, who represented John Sanford in the case, having volunteered to serve on the case with Reverdy Johnson, a former member of Zachary Taylor's cabinet and Maryland resident. By the time of his death on March 5, 1859, Geyer had been

Henry S. Geyer

First Union Meeting

ever deemed necessary to be held in this country. Following close on the heels of the Louisville and St. Louis meetings a monster meeting was held in Philadelphia and these intense meetings were held all over the country in favor of Mr. Clay's compromise measure.

After debate was closed and the vote was taken on the Omnibus Bill but it was defeated.; but at once the various measures in Omnibus Bill were formulated into separate bills and all were passed and became laws.

Upon the passage of these measures an address was issued to the country by those who had voted for them, deprecating all further agitation of the slavery question and counseling that these measures should be regarded as a final adjustment of the slavery question.[10]

As matters rested for a time, when a proposition was introduced into Congress to repeal the Missouri Compromise. This proposition rekindle the agitation of the slavery question, which continued, increasing in intensity ((illegible)) and between the North in the South and culminated in the election of Abraham Lincoln as president of the United States.[11]

---

married three times and fathered three children. Gerteis, *St. Louis*, 23, 58, 60; "Henry S. Geyer," in Wikipedia.org; Potter, *Impending Crisis*, 269; Smith, *Blair Family*, vol. 1: 267, 387.

10. On December 2, 1850, President Millard Fillmore sent a message to Congress announcing the success of the Compromise of 1850 calling "'its character final and irrevocable.'" Stephen A. Douglas, the final architect of the compromise, labeled it the "'final settlement'" of the slavery question and that all parties should "'stop the debate, and drop the subject'"; but such was not the case. According to Clement Evens, "The settlement was not wholly satisfactory to the minority North and South." The slavery issue in the territories had not been settled, spawning increased activity of "fire-eaters," in the South, who preached dissolving the Union. In the North, the Fugitive Slave Law "inflamed" many of the prominent men, including Horace Greely, who wrote of the compromise: "The net product was a corrupt monstrosity in Legislation and morals which even the great name of [Henry] Clay should not shield from lasting opposition." Ultimately the success or failure of the Compromise of 1850 rested on what one Southern commentator penned to the *Southern Literary Messenger*—"the full and faithful execution of the Fugitive Slave Bill.'" Craven, 103; Evans, *Secession and Civil War, Confederate Military History,* 275–277; Heidler, *Pulling the Temple Down*, 68; Potter, *Impending Crisis*, 121–122, 124–125.

11. On December 13, 1853, Senator Augustus C. Dodge, of Iowa, introduced a measure in Congress to organize the Nebraska Territory, while a similar measure was introduced in the House of Representatives by John G, Miller, also of Iowa. Senator David Atchinson, from Missouri, upon hearing of the proposal, cautioned that admitting Nebraska as a potential Free State would not be acceptable to the Southern States. Stephen A. Douglas, Chairman of the Committee of Territories, wanted to see the country expand, accepted the new bill on January 4; however, Atchinson suggested that Southerners would not support the bill unless slave owners were allowed into the territory with their property. On January 16, Senator Archabald Dixon, of Kentucky, proposed repealing the prohibition as contained in the Missouri Compromise of 1820, which limited slavery to south of 36* 30'. In the end Douglas created the Kansas-Nebraska Bill, which would allow the two new territories to determine their course on slavery, much the same as Utah in the Compromise of 1850. However, in order to pass the bill, Douglas needed President Franklin Pierce approval, as well as the support key Southerners, to repeal the Missouri Compromise. With Pierce's consent, Douglas proposed the new bill on January 23, 1854, thus reopening the slavery question

Immediately after the election of Mr. Lincoln, Mr. Sturgeon wrote letters, which were published in two different papers in Missouri, taking the ground that his election was no justification for an attempt to break up the Union, and in his humble sphere he labored to bring about a peaceful solution of our troubles and save the Union. He was at this time the assistant treasurer of the United States, having held the position under the administration's of Presidents Pierce and Buchanan.[12]

On the second day of February, 1861, there appeared in the *St. Louis Democrat* of the city the following editorial:[13]

Federal Officers in Missouri

The office holders in this state are among the most malignant disunionists. They eat the head of the government they are plotting to destroy. They call themselves, the 'chivalry,' and we don't know but they are as good specimens as any that could be found. The clerk of the United States District Court is the head devil—the physician at the Marine Hospital is another. The postmaster and the surveyor of the port—the clerks of the latter being the principal source from which the ranks of the 'minute men' are recruited, enter into the same category. The gentleman who fills office of the assistant treasurer is only one who has the decency to regard spirit of the oath by which their fidelity's pledge to the government which employs and feeds them.

Maj. [William H.] Hall [Bell] was in charge of the United States arsenal

---

yet again. "Popular Sovereignty" was thus proposed for the two new territories, negating the Missouri Compromise. For the next three and a half months the debate continued in the U.S. Congress. Southerners, with few reservations, readily accepted the new concept, believing that it offered new opportunities for the expansion of slavery. Northerners objected, according to David Potter, "on moral absolutes: the Missouri Compromise was not just an act of Congress; it was a sacred pledge" to limit the expansion of slavery. Simply put, Salmon P. Chase, Senator from Ohio, and other Northern Democrats, saw the passage of the bill as a "betrayal"of their beliefs by allowing the uncontrolled spread of slavery. The Senate passed the bill on March 3, while the House continued the rancorous debate until May 22, when they finally passed the bill. Pierce signed the bill on May 30, which ushered in the saga of "Bleeding Kansas." But by far, the greatest impact of the Kansas-Nebraska Bill was the splitting of the Democratic Party, which in turn would lead to the election of Abraham Lincoln and the American Civil War. Craven, 179–181; Nicole Etcheson, *Bleeding Kansas: Contested Liberty in the Civil War Era* (Lawrence, KS, 2004), 10–15, hereafter cited as Etcheson; Potter, *Impending Crisis*, 158, 160, 164–167.

12. Franklin Pierce was the fourteenth President of the United States (1853–1856). James Buchanan was the fifteenth President of the United States (1857–1860).

13. The *Daily Missouri Democrat* began publishing in 1843, under the title of the *Old School Democrat and St. Louis Herald*. In 1844, it became the *St. Louis Democrat* and in 1852, it received its Civil War title, the *Daily Missouri Democrat*. After the war the paper underwent several name changes and merged with the *St. Louis Daily* to form the *St. Louis Globe-Democrat*. The newspaper went out of business in the 1990's. Library of Congress, *Newspapers in Microform*, 1:563–565, hereafter cited as *Newspapers in Microform*.

in St. Louis in January, 1861.[14] His account as disbursing officer of the United States was kept with Mr. Sturgeon as assistant treasurer of the United States. He was frequently in the office of the assistant treasurer, and, being in the office about January, 1861, Mr. Sturgeon inquired of him in a casual way, what quantity of munitions of war were stored at the arsenal, and, he thinks, he stated that there were 60,000 stands of arms, 200 barrels of powder, cannon, cartridges, ball, etc..[15]

Mr. Sturgeon feeling apprehension from what was taking place in the South that an effort might be made to seize the arsenal and the money in his charge as assistant treasurer felt it his duty to advise President Buchanan of his apprehensions, which he did in the following

Personal Letter

St. Louis, Jan. 5, 1861.—His Excellency James Buchanan, President of the United States: Dear Sir—in the present excited condition of the country I cannot help feeling concerned in regard to the safety of the government funds in my hands, and its arms and munitions of war which are in the arsenal, which is within the limits of the city.

I am satisfied that if either the Republicans or the secessionists should attempt to seize the arsenal war would at once begin in this section, as neither would submit to the possession of the other peacefully.

I have not over $400,000 of government money on hand which might be seized, and I have thought proper under all circumstances to submit to you whether it is not advisable without delay to concentrate troops at the arsenal for the protection of government property there, which I think is very large, and the treasure in my care, if it should become necessary. I am

14. Major William H. Bell was in charge of the St. Luis Arsenal in January 1861, not a Major Hall. Bell was born in North Carolina, attended West Point, graduating in 1816 (number 4), being commissioned an ordnance lieutenant. He was promoted to captain on May 30, 1832, and major on March 25, 1848. As an ordnance officer, Bell was frequently stationed in St. Louis and eventually established a residence in the area. Amassing a "considerable fortune" in Missouri, Bell was none the less labeled "a capable officer," by Thomas Snead, "and bore a high character both in the army and among friends in civil life." For his part Bell believed that since the arsenal was in Missouri, it belonged to Missouri and "'Missouri had, whenever the time came, a right too claim it.'" Frank Blair did not trust Bell and arranged for him to be relieved of command, through his brother Montgomery, Lincoln's Postmaster General. Bell was ordered back East; however, instead of complying, he resigned his commission on May 28, 1861, and retired to his farm in St. Charles, where he died on December 20, 1865. The new commander of the arsenal was Major Peter V. Hagner. Gerteis, *St. Louis*, 82–83, 348 n. 40; Francis B. Heitman, *Historical Register and Dictionary of the United States Army, From its Organization, September 29, 1789, to March 2, 1903*, 2 vols. (Washington, 1903), vol. 1:208, hereafter cited as Heitman; McElroy, 36–37, 40; Smith, *Blair Family*, vol. 2: 31, 33; Snead, *Fight for Missouri*, 101, 114–115; William C. Winter, *The Civil War in St. Louis: A Guided Tour* (St. Louis, 1994), 39, hereafter cited as Winter.
15. In addition to the 60,000 muskets, the arsenal contained 90,000 pounds of powder, 1,500,000 cartridges, 40 cannon "and equipment for the manufacture of arms." Winter, 39.

satisfied that both sides here have their eyes fixed upon these two points, the arsenal and the treasury, and that taking possession of them by either of them will lead to conflict, and it therefore seems to me that the sooner provision is made to guard them the better. A little later and the excitement may arrive at the point here that any suggestion of a force here for their protection would precipitate the seizure of them.

I wish very much that the amount of this place to the credited of disbursing officers, the United States treasury and Post Office Department could be placed at a point where there would be less danger of its seizure. There may be none, but I fear there is–I fear we are arriving at a point in our troubles that there is danger of a conflict here.

I should be glad if you would advise me, if there should seem to be imminent danger, what course to pursue and what office to apply to for protection.

I sympathize most deeply with you in the trying and delicate position in which you are placed, and nothing shall be wanting on my part to render you all the aid in my power here or elsewhere.

I am most respectfully and truly yours,

Isaac H. Sturgeon
Assistant Treasurer U. S.. St. Louis, Mo.

At the Time of the Writing

the foregoing letter Maj. Bell was in charge of arsenal with its large store of arms and munitions of war, and had started to Mr. Sturgeon that the only guard he had was one man to patrol the ground from trespassers.

In response to Mr. Sturgeon letter to President Buchanan the President at once ordered a force of forty men under command of Lieut. [William G.] Robinson to be placed at the disposal of the assistant treasurer of the United States, Mr. Sturgeon.[16] Gen. Justus McKinstry (then Maj. McKinstry) called upon Mr. Stur-

---

16. William G. Robinson was born in Quebec, Canada, moved to Goldsboro, North Carolina, where his father owned a local newspaper. Robinson graduated from West Point in 1859 (number 25) and was commissioned a 2nd Lieutenant in the 7th U.S. Infantry. He was dispatched from Newport Barracks, Kentucky, and arrived by train on January 11. After the capture of Camp Jackson, Robinson resigned his commission on May 17, 1861. He later entered the Confederate Army, rising to the rank of colonel commanding the 19th North Carolina Infantry. He survived the war, having served his entire service in the East. He died on December 1, 1893. NOTE: Louis Gerteis says it was W. J. Robinson, a St Louisian, who commanded the troops; however there was no W. J. Robinson found in the *Historical Record*. Bruce S. Allardice, *Confederate Colonels A Biographical Register*. (Columbia, MO, 2008), 325, hereafter cited as Allardice, *Confederate Colonels*; William Riley Brooksher, *Bloody Hill: The Civil War Battle of Wilson's Creek* (Washington, DC, 1995), 32, hereafter cited as Brooksher; Gerteis, *St. Louis*, 84; Heitman, vol. 1: 839; Christopher Phillips, *Damned Yankee: The Life of General Nathaniel Lyon* (Columbia, MO, 1990), 139, hereafter cited as Phillips, *Damned Yankee; The Union Army A History of Military Affairs in the Loyal United States 1861–1865—Records of the Regiments in the Union Army—Cyclopedia of*

geon to inform him of the order of the president, and a conference ensued as too whether they should be placed at the arsenal or in the old custom-house on Third Street.[17] Gen. McKinstry thought they should be quartered in the custom-house. Mr. Sturgeon did not comprehend at the time that he had any discretion as to where they should be placed, and deferred entirely to Gen. McKinstry. The matter being settled as to where the troops would be quartered Mr. Sturgeon was called into the country, and suffering with sickness did not return to his office, but went at once to his residence at the corner of Eleventh and Olive streets. About 3 o'clock on that day Lieut. Robinson in company with Mr. Nathaniel Paschall, then editor of the St. Louis REPUBLICAN, called on Mr. Sturgeon and stated that the greatest excitement had been created in the city by quartering troops in the custom-house, and asked Mr. Sturgeon whether they could not be removed to the arsenal, which would allay the excitement.[18] Mr. Sturgeon did not comprehend that he had any authority to dictate where they should be placed, but being advised that he had, readily

Consented to Their Removal

to the arsenal, deeming it best that they should be there to protect the large quan-

Battles—Memoirs of Commanders and Soldiers, 8 vols. (New York, 1908; reprint ed., Wilmington, NC, 1998), vol. 4: 239, hereafter cited as Union Army.

17. Justus McKinstry was born on July 6, 1814, in New York state, moved to Michigan, and received an appointment to West Point in 1834. He graduated in 1838 (number 40 of 45), fought in the Mexican War, where he was breveted a major for bravery. Following the war, McKinstry served in various Quartermaster positions and was serving in St. Louis as Quartermaster of the Department of the West, when the Civil War began. Under John C. Frémont, McKinstry also served as the Provost Marshal of St. Louis and on September 2, 1861, he was promoted to brigadier general. McKinstry commanded a division under Frémont, while still maintaining his position of Quartermaster for the department. Within days of Frémont's departure, General David Hunter arrested McKinstry on November 11, 1861, and in October of 1862, McKinstry was court-martialed for graft and corruption. Convicted, McKinstry was dismissed from the service on January 28, 1863, being the "only Union general officer cashiered for violation of his duty." Moving to New York, for a time, McKinstry became a stock broker, but later returned to Rolla, Missouri, where he was a land agent. He died in St. Louis on December 11, 1897. See Missouri in 1861, of this series, for a complete biography and photograph of McKinstry. Michael E. Banasik, Missouri in 1861: The Civil War Letters of Franc B. Wilkie, Newspaper Correspondent. Unwritten Chapters of the Civil War West of the River Volume IV (Iowa City. IA, 2001) 358–359, hereafter cited as Banasik, Missouri in 1861.

18. Nathaniel Paschall, was the co-editor of the Missouri Republican, in 1855, with John Knapp, both of whom were Conditional Unionists, and supported slavery but not secession. He was described as "a man of mature age, great experience, strong intellect and consummate common sense." An advocate for public support of the railroads, Paschall supported Claiborne F. Jackson for Missouri Governor in 1860, but only after Jackson declared his support for Stephen A. Douglas for President. Paschall survived the war, but died in 1866. Gerteis, St. Louis, 81, 102; Frederick A. Hodes, A Divided City: A History of St. Louis 1851 to 1876 (n. c., 2015), 272–274, 337, 694, hereafter cited as Hodes; William H. Lyon, "Claiborne Fox Jackson and the Secession Crisis In Missouri," 58 Missouri Historical Review (July, 1964), 423, hereafter cited as Lyon; Ryle, 93 n. 136, 143–144, 147; Snead, Fight for Missouri, 54–55.

tity of arms and other munitions of war, and they were at once removed that afternoon to the arsenal. During the next day Lieut. Robinson called upon Mr. Sturgeon at his office to learn if there was any armed loyal man in the city, on whom he could rely to come to his rescue in case of an attack. Mr. Sturgeon stated that he knew of no such body of men, but that during the presidential canvass there was an organization of Germans, called "Black Jaegers," a Republican organization, who were said to be armed and that if Lieut. Robinson would call at 11 o'clock the next day, he would get the information and put in communication with them if armed.[19] Mr. Sturgeon at once sent for the honorable, afterwards Maj. Gen. F. P. Blair, Jr., explained all to him and asked if this organization was armed and Gen. Blair replied that he was ignorant of the fact whether they were armed or not, but would ascertain, and meet Lieut. Robinson at Mr. Sturgeon's office the next day to inform him.[20] The meeting was held and Lieut. Robinson was informed that they were armed, and Gen. Blair placed him in communication with the officers. Gen. Blair, in a subsequent conversation in response to an inquiry of Mr. Sturgeon as to what was to be the end of this matter, said that rather than this Union should be broken up it would be better that every rebel in the South should perish, and repeople those states anew with a loyal element, and that in his opinion within ten years of this time, there would not be a slave in the United States. His prediction at this early day in the troubles were verified sooner than he anticipated.

At the time this step was taken Lieut. Gov. [Thomas C.] Reynolds had returned from the South and published a letter in harmony with the views of the southern states, and Gov. [Claiborne F.] Jackson had delivered his

---

19. The Black Jaegers or Black Rifles were one of several German companies secretly organized and commanded by Frank Blair, in January 1861, to counter the Southern leaning Minutemen. The unit had its roots in the recently disbanded "Wide Awakes" and was part of the ten-company Union Legion. Their basic mission was to come to the aid of the St. Louis Arsenal if there was ever an attempt to capture the facility. Michael Priester captained the unit which contained 50 rank and file. James Peckham, *Gen. Nathaniel Lyon, Missouri in 1861, A Monograph of the Great Rebellion* (New York, 1866), 36, 55, 433, 445, hereafter cited as Peckham.

20. Francis "Frank" Preston Blair, Jr., was born on February 19, 1821, in Lexington, Kentucky, educated at Princeton and Transylvania Universities. He moved to St. Louis, Missouri, in 1843, where he practiced law, moved west for a time, and joined the Mexican War as a private. After the war, Blair founded the Free Soil Party in Missouri, was a member of the Missouri Legislature in 1852, founded the *St. Louis Democrat* newspaper with B. Gratz Brown and was elected to the U.S. Congress in 1856. Elected colonel of the 1st Missouri Infantry (Three months), at the beginning of the Civil War, Blair served throughout the war, attaining the rank of major general. After the war, Blair returned to Missouri, was the Democratic Party vice-presidential nominee in 1868, but lost, and served in the U.S. Senate from 1871–1873. Suffering a stroke in 1873, Blair never recovered and died on July 9, 1875. Boatner, 67; Elbert B. Smith, "Blair, Francis Preston, Jr.," in *Encyclopedia of the Civil War*, 238–239; Thomas L. Snead, "The First Year of the War In Missouri," 4 vols. *Battles and Leaders of the Civil War* (New York, 1887–1888), vol. 1: 263, hereafter cited as Snead, "First Year in Missouri."

Secession Inaugural,

message to the legislature.[21]

There seemed evidence satisfactory to the mind of Mr. Sturgeon that the "min-ute men" and their allies were meditating the seizure of arsenal and he was equally well satisfied that if attempted it would be resisted by the "Wide-a-awakes" and the loyal citizens.[22] Mr. Sturgeon was anxious to prevent this conflict in the city

21. Thomas C. Reynolds was born in Charleston, South Carolina, on October 11, 1821, moved to Virginia, where he graduated from the University of Virginia in 1842. After traveling abroad, Reynolds eventually settled in St. Louis, where he opened a law office. Proud of his South Caro-linian heritage, Reynolds boasted of his birth place for its "origin and the aristocracy," despite his new surroundings in Missouri. By the time of the Civil War, Reynolds was a "hardline secessionist Democrat" and the "leading spirit of the secession cause in Missouri." He was elected lieutenant governor in 1860, and upon the death on Governor Claiborne F. Jackson, in late 1862, became the Confederate Governor of Missouri in exile. Following the war, Reynolds fled to Mexico, but returned to Missouri, in 1868, settling in St. Louis. He died on March 30, 1887. See **Appendix B** for a complete biography. Governor Jackson will be covered below. Faust, 626–627; *History of Audrain County, Missouri, Written and Compiled from the Most Authentic Official and Private Sources Including a History of Its Townships, Towns and Villages* (St. Louis, 1884), 38, hereafter cited as *History of Audrain County*; Peckham, 27.

22. Of the two organizations, the St. Louis Wide Awakes were organized first, in July 1860, by Frank Blair. They consisted primarily of the German population and were present at all of Blair's political gatherings to prevent disruption of the event. The Wide Awakes would eventually be disbanded in favor of Union Clubs or Home Guards, in a large part, according to Sceva Laughlin, because "the name Republican was so repulsive to other Unionists." Ultimately the Wide Awakes, like the Black Jaegers, were formed to counter the formation of the Southern Minutemen. On January 8, 1861 (Gerteis says it was January 7), Thomas C. Reynolds "instigated" a "meeting in St. Louis for the purpose of organizing the pro-slavery sentiment of the city." Thus was born the "Minuet Men," led by Bazil Duke, Colton Greene and J. R. "Rock" Champion. The Minuet Men headquarters was located in the Berthold Mansion and proudly flew the "Rebel Flag," according to most sources; however William Bull, one of the Minuet Men, recorded that the flag was "of the 'Sons of Malta'–a secret, humorous, fun-making order which existed before the war." However, a Union man wrote in 1862, that it was a"large Palmetto Flag," which was normally associated with South Carolina, the first state to secede The Minuet Men "in a spirit of deviltry hung the flag out from their headquarters." Their stated purpose was to "pledge Missouri to a hearty co-operation with our sister Southern states, in such measures as shall be deemed necessary for our mutual protection against the encroachment of Northern fanaticism and the coercion of the Federal Gov-ernment." The day after the Minuet Men organized, Blair set in motion the organization of what became the Union Home Guards. The Minuet Men were eventually legalized under state law, on February13, 1861, as a five company battalion, numbering about 300 men (Gerteis says 400), commanded by James R. Shaler, while Blair's Wide Awakes/Home Guards initially counted 500 members (Smith says 750), but would grow into the thousands by Camp Jackson in May 1861. Michael E. Banasik, *Missouri Brothers in Gray: The Reminiscences and Letters of William J. Bull and John P. Bull. Unwritten Chapters of the Civil War West of the River Volume I* (Iowa City, IA, 1998), 9, hereafter cited as Banasik. *Missouri Brothers in Gray*; John Coleman, "The Riots of St. Louis, Missouri, 1861," Camp Jackson Papers, Missouri Historical Society (St. Louis), 2, hereaf-ter cited as Coleman; Gerteis, *St. Louis*, 79, 87; Sceva Bright Laughlin,."Missouri Politics During the Civil War.," *Missouri Historical Review* 23 (July, 1929), 590, hereafter cited as Laughlin; William E. Parrish, *Frank Blair Lincoln's Conservative* (Columbia, MO, 1998), 85, 90, hereafter cited as Parrish, *Frank Blair*; Peckham, 30; Ryle, 185–187; Smith, *Blair Family*, vol. 2: 31–32; Snead, *Fight for Missouri*, 109–111; *Union Army*, vol. 4: 230.

and adopted the course would seem to him wisest to prevent it and save the city from the consequences of such a struggle.

About this time the Hon. Thos. C Johnson, state senator from St. Louis, introduced a bill in the legislature to take from the mayor of the city the power to call out the police force to suppress riots placing the power in the hands of the governor, with power on his part to delegated.[23]

Mr. Johnson in a letter to the St. Louis REPUBLICAN assigned as a reason for the introduction of this bill that he apprehended that the "Wide-a-wakes" were preparing to seize the arsenal: and they were being identified with the Republican party, to which the mayor belonged, and he could not be relied upon to do his duty as he should under such circumstances.[24]

With Lieut. Robinson and his forty man inside arsenal walls and three or four hundred troops at Jefferson barracks, matters rested for a time.[25]

The Result Reported

on 12 January, 1861, Mr. Sturgeon addressed Pres. Buchanan the following letter:

St. Louis, Jan. 12, 1861.—His Excellency, James Buchanan, President of the United States: Dear Sir—Forty men, under command of Lieut. Robinson, arrived here yesterday morning, and on the advice of Maj. McKinstry were temporarily placed in some vacant rooms at the customhouse. In consulting with Lieut. Robinson in the afternoon, we deemed it best for them to take up their quarters at the arsenal, which in some two miles from the office of the assistant treasurer of the United States.

The session paper of this city and those who follow it seem to think

---

23. The bill was called An Act Creating a Board of Police Commissioners. It was introduced on January 5, two days after the inauguration of Governor C. F. Jackson. The bill was the brain child of Lieutenant Governor Thomas C. Reynolds, and meant to curb the power of the Unionists in St. Louis, represented by Frank Blair. The bill was passed and signed into law on January 14, 1861. Ryle, 181–182

24. In early 1861 the mayor of St. Louis was Oliver D. Filley, who had came to St. Louis in 1829, from Connecticut, and was elected for a two year term, as mayor, in 1859. Filley was replaced as mayor on April 1, 1861 by Daniel G. Taylor. Gerteis, *St. Louis*, 41; Leo Rassieur, *Civil War Regiments From Missouri* (Washinton, DC,1908; reprint ed., Pensacola, FL, 2007), 17, hereafter cited as Rassieur;

25. Jefferson Barracks was established in what would be south St. Louis County on October 23, 1826, by Colonel Henry Atkinson; the barracks was about eight mile south of Civil War St. Louis. Establish to protect settlers from Indians, the post participated in the Black War in 1832, and the Mexican War in 1846. Prior to the Civil War numerous personalities were stationed at the barracks including William Harney, Robert E. Lee, Winfield Hancock, A.S. Johnston, Joseph E. Johnston, Nathaniel Lyon and Braxton Bragg to name a few. During the war Jefferson Barracks served as a rendezvous point for troops in the Western Theater, and, as the war progressed, a military hospital run by the Western Sanitary Commission. In 1863, the Barracks were designated a national cemetery, which still exists today. Winter, 4–7, 144.

it highly improper that the government should send troops here to guard public property from seizure.[26]

All the Union men whom I have seen today are gratified that the government has taken this precautionary measure. I wish it was about two hundred instead of forty men. I give no explanation in regard to the matter except that they were sent to be placed at the arsenal for the protection of public property.

There was a tremendous Union meeting here to-day.[27] I observed that I was made one of vice presidents, was not able to get to the meeting by reason of engagements until it had been underway for an hour and the resolutions adopted, which I had not the opportunity to read until published. I enclosed a copy of them. They seem well enough. The tenth resolution, as I understand it, is merely an appeal to avoid shedding of blood if possible. May heaven grant us a peaceful solution of our troubles. With high regard, your obedient servant,

Isaac H. Sturgeon,
Assistant Treasurer United States, St. Louis Mo.

Calls for More Men

on the same day Mr. Sturgeon wrote Gen. Winfield Scott as follows:[28]

---

26. The *St. Louis Bulletin*, the secessionist newspaper in St. Louis, "was ultra-Southern, but it was newly established" during the secession crisis, having "a limited circulation and influence." The newspaper was also a "short-lived" periodical, with no record listed in the *Newspapers in Microform*. Thomas L. Snead was the newspaper's editor. *Confederate Military History*, vol. 9: *Missouri*, by John C. Moore, 9, hereafter cited as Moore, *Missouri, Confederate Military History*; *Newspapers in Microform*, passim; Ryle, 171, 208.

27. The Democratic meeting of Conditional Unionists that Sturgeon referred too, took place on Saturday evening, January 12, in the "East Front of the Courthouse, " with 1,500 to 2,000 people being present (The Union Army misstated the number as 15,000 to 20,000 as did Christopher Phillips.). Those attending the meting believed "that the rights and property of all sections of the country could be better protected within the American Union." It was instituted by "such staunch loyalists as Nathaniel Paschall, Hamilton R. Gamble, James Yeatman and Robert Campbell"; however, Blair and the Republicans generally boycotted the meeting because it "was expected to adopt the Crittenden Compromise resolutions as the basis of settlement of the pending" crisis. As proposed, the Crittenden Compromise had six resolutions that were meant to define the Federal government's actions concerning slavery and ensure the existence of slavery in those states that so chose to allow the practice. When the meeting adjourned they did indeed adopt the Crittenden Compromise. See **Appendix A** for the principle amendments, as recorded by Thomas Snead, in support of the Crittenden Compromise. Faust, 193; Gerteis, *St. Louis*, 73, 81; Peckham, 51–52; Phillips, *Damned Yankee*,135–136; Ethan S. Rafuse, "Crittenden Compromise," in *Encyclopedia of the Civil War*, 520–521; Ryle, 204; Snead, *Fight for Missouri*, 44–45; *Union Army*, vol. 4: 232.

28. Winfield Scott was born near Petersburg, Virginia on June 13, 1786, joined the army as a captain in 1808, fought in the War of 1812, rising from the rank of lieutenant colonel to brigadier general by the end of the war. He was promoted to major general in June 1841, and then to Commander-in-Chief of the army on July 5, 1841. Scott successfully led the U.S. Army in the Mexican War. A hero in both the War of 1812 and the Mexican War, Scott was promoted to lieutenant general on

St. Louis, Jan. 12, 1861.—Lieut. Gen. Winfield Scott:
Dear Sir—(after alluding to their personal intercourse the letter proceeds):
I hope that the cloud overhanging our country may pass away and that
we shall have the pleasure of seeing you in St. Louis, as you partially
promised me we should have when on our trip.

Forty men arrived here under the command of Lieut. Robinson, who
will guard the arsenal (which is within the city limits) and protect my office
should there be a necessity for it. It is to be hoped, and is thought, there will
arise no necessity for their services; yet in the present excited condition of
the country no one could tell what a day may bring forth, and it seems to
me better to take time by the forelock than to wait until the danger is so
near at hand that time would not be afforded too avert it. I think it would
be well to have about two hundred men, well officered and armed, kept in
the arsenal until our troubles are passed, should any trouble then occur this
band would furnish a nucleus around which the Union loving, law-abiding
and conservative elements of our city would rally to prevent any unlawful
proceedings. With respect and esteem, your obedient servant,

Isaac H. Sturgeon,
Assistant Treasurer United States, St. Louis, Mo.

From 12th of January, 1861, to 9th of February, 1861, nothing more was done
by Mr. Sturgeon than observe the movements of those whose purpose seem to be
to seize the arsenal if possible.

On 9th of February, 1861,

Maj. David Hunter

afterwards major general of the United States Army, arrived in St. Louis and
stopped at the Planters' house and Mr. Sturgeon called upon him on private business.[29] Maj. Hunter and Mr. Sturgeon had been officially connected for eight

---

March 29, 1847, "for eminent service " for the capture of Vera Cruz and the Battle of San Juan de
Ulloa. Scott remained as Commander-in-Chief of the army until his retirement on November 1,
1861. During the Civil War, Scott was credited for devising the "Anaconda Plan" which called for
control of the Mississippi River and a blockade of the Southern ports. Though initially criticized ,
the plan eventually resulted in the defeat of the Confederacy. Scott was also "the only non-West-
Pointer of Southern origin in the R.A. [Regular Army] to remain loyal to the Union." He died on
May 29, 1866, at West Point. Boatner, 728–729; Faust, 662–663; Heitman, vol. 1: 870; Sifakis,
Who Was Who in the Union, 358–359.

29. David Hunter was born in Washington, District of Columbia on July 21, 1802. He attended West
Point, with an appointment from Illinois, graduating in 1822 (number 25 of 40). Assigned to Fort
Dearborn, Michigan, in Chicago, Hunter served until 1836, when he resigned to pursue a business
in real estate. Hunter returned to the army in 1842, as an army paymaster. At the beginning of
the Civil War, Hunter was named the colonel of the 3rd U.S. Cavalry and on May 17, 1861, was
promoted to brigadier general of volunteers. Hunter was wounded at the Battle of Bull Run, after
which he was promoted to major general on August 13, 1861. He commanded the Department of
Kansas from November 20, 1861 until March 11, 1862, when he was reassigned to command the

years, and had business transactions outside of their official relations. Were personal friends, and both being Union men conversed freely on the troubles of the country, and Mr. Sturgeon expressed to Maj. Hunter his fears that the force at the arsenal was insufficient to hold it and that there was danger of an attempt take it any day. Maj. Hunter was on his way to Washington and was requested by Mr. Sturgeon to represent to the proper authorities there that it was his own opinion that the force at Jefferson barracks should be moved to the arsenal.

In mingling with the people on that day the necessity of speedy action was so forcibly impressed upon his mind that after night he called at the Planters' house again to see Maj. Hunter to deliver to him or leave for him if not in the following note:

St. Louis, Feb. 9, 1861.—Maj. David Hunter:

Dear Sir—I am more than ever impressed with the importance of having all the force that is here placed at the arsenal. In case of trouble (which in God's name I hope will not come) they are useless at the barracks, and why have the forces twelve miles apart?

Let them be together and at the place where the munitions of war are that are to be protected. There is nothing to defend at the barracks.

Before our state convention meets I apprehend we are to have an explosion in the South; and if so, God only knows what is to become of it.[30]

Had I the power I would have all the force at the arsenal, and I would keep up rigid military watchfulness until the crisis is entirely passed. If

---

Department of the South. Hunter continued to serve east of the Mississippi River until the end of the war, retiring from the service on July 31, 1866. He died in Washington on July 2, 1886. *O.R.*, vol. 8: 370, 606, 644; Boatner, 418–419; Sifakis, *Who Was Who in the Union*, 207; Ezra J. Warner, *Generals in Blue: Lives of the Union Commanders* (Baton Rouge, LA, 1964), 243–244, hereafter cited as Warner, *Generals in Blue*.

30. The State Convention met on February 28, 1861, in the Jefferson City County Courthouse to settle the question as to whether Missouri should remain in the Union. A total of 99 delegates were present, 82 of whom were born in slaveholding states. The Convention spent but two days in Jefferson City, where they initially passed a resolution that all delegates take an oath "to support the Constitution of the United States and of the State of Missouri." The measure easily passed, showing strong support for remaining in the Union. The Convention then elected Sterling Price as President on the 29th, after which they adjourned to complete the Convention in St. Louis. On Monday March 4, the day Abraham Lincoln was inaugurated as President, the Convention reconvened, in the Mercantile Library Hall in St. Louis to complete their business. In the end the Convention did not support secession, much to the surprise of Governor Jackson, and totally "demoralizing" Southern rights men, to the point "that they were in no condition to attack the arsenal, as they intended to do if the election had gone in their favor." The Convention adjourned on March 22, to meet again on the third Monday in December to reconsider the "special order of business"– the secession question. For a complete list of convention delegates see Append A. Arthur Roy Kirkpatrick, "Missouri On the Eve of the Civil War," *Missouri Historical Review* 55 (April, 1961), 103–104, 106, hereafter cited as Kirkpatrick, "Missouri On the Eve of the Civil War"; Laughlin, 593, 601; Ryle, 214–215, 232; Snead, *Fight for Missouri*, 78–79, 87–88; Snead "First Year in Missouri," 264.

this is to be done it may save the property and lives of our citizens. Yours
very truly.

Isaac H. Sturgeon.

Upon arriving at the Planters' House Mr. Sturgeon found Maj. Hunter in his
room and handed him the note, saying it was written thinking he might find him
in his room. [31] They again

Talked Over the Situation

when Maj. Hunter inquired of Mr. Sturgeon if he knew Gen. Scott previously. Mr.
Sturgeon explained that he did very well. He then advised Mr. Sturgeon to write
a "private" letter to Gen. Scott, explaining as I had to him. He said all knew that
Gen. Scott was loyal. That the president might be, but if Mr. Sturgeon wrote him,
he was so surrounded by the rebels it might never reach him and in that event
would do harm instead of good. Whilst sitting conversing with Maj. Hunter Capt.
Nathaniel Lyon, afterwards Gen. Lyon came into Maj. Hunter's room and was
introduced to Mr. Sturgeon. [32] A question arose as to who would be in command of
the forces at the arsenal, and it was stated that he was a Virginian and some fears
were entertained of his loyalty. Gen. Lyon remarked that if he were in command
these doubts would be removed, and was bitter in the denunciation of those striv-
ing to disrupt the Union. As Mr. Sturgeon reflects, Maj. Hunter assured Gen. Lyon
that if he could have him placed in command it would be done, and all recollect
he was placed in command. He was mortally wounded in the war that followed,
at the battle of Wilson's Creek.

Mr. Sturgeon, after leaving Major Hunter's room, repaired at once to his

---

31. The Planters' House was a four and one-half story hotel, located on the west side of 4th Street, between Pine and Chestnut Streets. It began construction in 1837, and opened for business on April 3, 1841. Prior to the Civil War it was an important social center and meeting place, charac-terized as "'the epitome of elegance and grandeur, a place of romance and gaiety, a center of lavish entertaining and extravagant spending.'" A fire in 1887, closed the hotel. It was later refurbished, a new hotel opened in 1922, and still later it was converted to an office building. Winter, 67–68.

32. General Nathaniel Lyon was born in Connecticut on July 14, 1818, graduated from West Point in 1841(number 11 of 52). He arrived in St. Louis on February 6, 1861, and served in the U.S. Army until his death at Wilson's Creek, Missouri, on August 10, 1861. His actions in Missouri, during 1861, particularly the Capture of Camp Jackson on May 10, 1861, propelled Missouri into the Civil War. Frank Blair also credited Lyon with the "salvation" of Missouri, which would have joined the Confederacy "if he had not come there." And to many modern-day authors, like Daniel O'Flaherty, "Lyon was one of the ablest soldiers to ever wear and American uniform, and one of the most fearless" as subsequent events would show. See volume IV of this series, *Missouri in 1861* for a complete biography. Banasik, *Missouri in 1861*, 353–355; Daniel O'Flaherty, *General Jo Shelby Undefeated Rebel* (Chapel Hill, NC, 1954; reprint ed., Wilmington, NC, 1987), 80, hereafter cited as O'Flaherty; *The War in the West* (Original title, *Report of the Joint Committee On the Conduct of the War*, Washington, DC, 1863; reprint ed., Millwood, NY, 1977), 157, here-after cited as *War in the West*; Warner, *Generals in Blue*, 286–287.

Brigadier General Nathaniel Lyon

residence, and feeling that no time was to be lost, that night wrote the following letter, which he carried and placed in the post office that night, that it might go by the first mail:

[Private] St. Louis, Saturday night, Feb. 9, 1861
Lieut. Gen. Winfield Scott, Washington D.C.:
Sir—The troops at this point, in my opinion, should all be concentrated inside the walls of the arsenal, and should go on as rapidly as possible to fortify it, and make all the arrangements necessary to protect themselves and defend the arsenal, if needs be. Every precaution should be taken and the strictest vigilance kept up at the arsenal until the crisis in our national affairs has passed and quiet in our country restored.

The troops at Jefferson barracks, which is twelve miles below the arsenal, should not be gotten to the arsenal for several hours, if at all, were an attack made on the arsenal. My opinion is, that if they attempted to come to the arsenal after the attack began, they

Would Be Cut Off

and destroyed before they could reach them. It is clear to my mind that all the force here should be concentrated inside the walls of the arsenal at once, whilst there is little excitement, and if they should not be needed we will thank God for it.

Every preparation and precaution should be made to resist any desperate mobocratic and military attempt that might be made any day to take the arsenal, and the force should be in perfect readiness to meet any such attack at any moment.

Pardon me for suggesting that imperative orders should be given to the proper officers here to place the forces as I have suggested, and every preparation should be made for a desperate defense if the government intends to protect and hold its property against state and all other force that may be brought to take it.

I fear the extreme South are resolved to bring on war to unite the border slave states with them, and that it will begin very soon, and if it does, God only knows what may happen here. If war begins in the South before a letter from you can reach here, then the order for troops to move from Jefferson barracks should be given by telegraph; otherwise it will be best given by the letter, when the troops could be moved up to the arsenal without attracting attention or producing any excitement. All the works here for the defense of the arsenal could go on inside of its walls without attracting special notice, which it seems important to avoid. The troops should not be moved by telegraph unless absolutely essential, as the message might be taken on the wires and precipitate the seizure of the arsenal before the troops at the barracks could be got to the arsenal. Very respectfully,

Isaac H. Sturgeon,
Assistant Treasurer, United States, St. Louis Mo.

As soon as Gen. Scott received the letter above, he

Ordered All the Troops

at Jefferson barracks to be moved to arsenal, and the work of putting it in a state of defense was rapidly pressed. It is not improbable if these precautionary measures had not been taken at the insistence of Mr. Sturgeon the arsenal and treasures in his hands might have been seized and the city involved in a bloody conflict, that might have resulted in great loss of life and destruction of property.

Gov. Jackson seems to have been well aware of the defenseless condition of the arsenal and told Mr. Sturgeon in a personal conversation in St. Louis after the cautionary measures were taken by Mr. Sturgeon (of which Gov. Jackson had then and perhaps never any knowledge) that there was a time when ten armed men could have walked into the arsenal and taken possession of it.[33] Mr. Sturgeon recollection is that he said he had counseled the seizure when it could so easily have been made, but it was not then done and that now to take it would cost much blood and the possible destruction of the city.

Mr. Sturgeon says he counseled with no one as to the steps he was taking except as stated in these papers. The officers of the troops nor anyone was aware except as stated that these movements were at his insistence.

---

33. Claiborne F. Jackson, "a true son of the South," was born on April 4, 1807, in Kentucky, moved to Missouri in 1826, and was independently wealthy by the age of thirty. He was "tall, erect and [a] good-looking" man, according to Thomas Snead, who further noted that Jackson was " kind hearted, brave and courteous; a thoughtful, earnest, upright man, a political leader, but not a soldier." Entering politics, at the age of 29, Jackson was elected to the Missouri Legislature in 1836, and for the next several years maintained a high profile in Missouri politics. "He had a reputation as an astute politician of considerable maneuverability." As a Democrat, Jackson supported slavery and believed in "States Rights." Inaugurated Governor of Missouri on January 3, 1861, Jackson maintained his position throughout the Civil War, even after being driven from the state by Federal forces in late 1861. Jackson did not survive the war, dying on December 7, 1862, at Little Rock, Arkansas. See *Missouri in1861* for a picture and complete biography. Banasik, *Missouri in 1861*, 350–352; Lyon, 423; McElroy, 20, 25, 27; Snead, "First Year in Missouri," 266.

It Is Not Improbable

Claiborne F. Jackson

that the prominent part taken in the capture of Jackson by the German element of St. Lewis partially resulted from Mr. Sturgeon, through Gen. Blair, having placed Lieut. Robinson in communication with the armed political organization known as "Black Jaegers." The Germans of our city were loyal almost to a man, and many experienced soldiers and military man and were an invaluable a too the loyal Americans in organizing the forces that on 10th of May, 1861, captured Camp Jackson.[34] Subsequent events seem to indicate that Maj. Bell, who was in charge of the arsenal at the beginning of our trouble, was relied upon as being loyal to the Southern cause, but when Gen. Lyon was placed in command every loyal man knew that the interest of the government was in safe hands.[35] The letter of a prominent officer of Camp Jackson to Gov. Jackson stated that Maj. Bell was relied upon by the rebel element, and it was, therefore fortunate that he was in time superseded by those who were ready to do and die for the Union.[36]

* * * * * * *

---

34. Details on the capture of Camp Jackson will be covered in a later letter.

35. Lyon was placed in command of the arsenal on March 13. Prior to that date Lyon " had frequent conversations with the Committee of Safety…in regard to the condition of affairs in St. Louis" and offered his advice on the direction the committee should take. NOTE: The "Committee of Safety," or "Safety Committee" or Committee of Public Safety all refereed to the same organization. Members of the Committee of Safety were "O. D. Filley, John How, Samuel T. Glover, James O. Broadhead and J. J. Witzig–all leading men of the community." James O. Broadhead, "Early Events of the War in Missouri," *War Papers and Personal Reminiscences. 1861–1865. Read Before the Commandery of the State of Missouri, Military Order of the Loyal Legion of the United States* (St. Louis, 1892; reprint ed., Wilmington, NC, 1992), vol. 14: 5, hereafter cited as Broadhead, *Missouri MOLLUS*; Brooksher, 33.

36. The letter was written by General D. M. Frost to Governor Jackson on January 24, 1861. See **Appendix A** for a copy of the letter.

Item: Arrival of Nathaniel Lyon in St. Louis, in the Spring of 1861, and comments on Lyon, by General Justus McKinstry.
Published: January 2, 1886.

Gen. Lyon's Arrival in St. Louis

On Monday night at the meeting of the Gen. Lyon Post, G. A. R., they had a portrait of Gen. Lyon presented to the post by Capt. Jas. Eads, who was represented in the presentation by ex-Gov. Thos. C. Fletcher.[37] In his speech, which was reported in full in the REPUBLICAN on Tuesday morning, Gov. Fletcher paid some eloquent compliments to the memory of Gen. Lyon. He also related some interesting incidents, interesting in themselves and appropriate to recall on such an occasion, but which Gen. Justus McKinstry yesterday informed a REPUBLICAN reporter certainly did not occur in the precise manner represented. When Lyon left West Point he was assigned to the regiment in whose ranks McKinstry was serving.[38] He was with Gen. Lyon, or had opportunities for watching his career in the Florida war, the Mexican war, the service of the Pacific Coast and commencement of the late Civil War. Hence he was considered quite well qualified to speak of Gen. Lyon's career.[39]

"What attracted my attention to Gov. Fletcher's eulogy of Gen. Lyon was this:" and then Gen. McKinstry read the following

---

37. James B. Eads was born on May 23, 1820, moved to St. Louis in 1833, and was a self educated individual. He was a civil engineer and played an important role in the Civil War, building the "City Class of Ironclads," which proved "vital to the early victories in the West." The title of "Captain" was an honorary title given to Eads for his extensive knowledge of the Mississippi River; however, he was listed as both a captain or a colonel in the Missouri Militia in the *Supplement to the Official Records*. See **Appendix B** for a complete biography. Janet Hewett, ed., *Supplement to the Official Records of the Union and Confederate Armies*, 100 vol. (Wilmington, NC, 1994–2001), pt. 3, vol. 1: 61, 71–72, 74, 76, hereafter cited as *O.R.S.*; "James Buchanan Eads,"in Wikipedia.org.

   Thomas Clement Fletcher was born on January 22, 1827, in Herculaneum, Missouri, moved to St. Louis in 1856, where he became a lawyer and friend of Frank Blair. During the Civil War Fletcher commanded the 31st Missouri Infantry, until sickness forced him to resign in the Summer of 1864. During Price's 1864 Missouri Raid, Fletcher again led a regiment, fought at Pilot Knob and was elected Governor of Missouri on November 8, 1864. After his term expired he opened a law office in St. Lois, but then moved to Washington, DC, where he died on March 25, 1899. See Appendix B for a complete biography. "Thomas Clement Fletcher," in Wikipedia.org; Gerteis, *St. Louis*, 309, 334; Roger D. Hunt and Jack R. Brown, *Brevet Brigadier Generals in Blue* (Gaitherburg, MD:, 1990), 207, hereafter cited as Hunt & Brown; Winter, 127.

38. Lyon's first assignment was to the 2nd U.S. Infantry. McKinstry had graduated four years prior to Lyon in 1833. Heitman, vol. 1: 650, 674.

39. The Seminole or Florida War that McKinstry was referring too took place from November 1, 1835 to August 14, 1842. A total of 41,122 regulars and volunteers participated in the war, suffering a total of 940 killed and wounded. The Mexican War (April 24, 1845–July 4, 1848) saw 112, 230 regular and volunteers serving, while suffering 16, 988 casualties of all type including those who died of disease. After the Mexican War, Lyon served in California (1849–1853), where he fought the "Clear Lake Indians." Ibid., vol. 2: 281–282; Snead, *Fight for Missouri*, 120.

Extract from Gov. Fletcher's Speech

"I well remember the day on which he landed at the wharf in our city, in the early spring of 1861. He was a captain and had only a small company in his command. [40] I accompanied Frank Blair, William Mckee, Bart Able and some other friends to call on him.[41] I shall never forget the clear, emphatic and wonderful impressiveness of his statement of his purpose to assert and maintain the national authority as supreme. His words were few, but so full of a resolute will but then made our hearts to burn within us, and made us to feel that in him we had a leader who could be trusted and every respect. I will not follow his career; its history will never fade from the memory of any man who is entitled to be enrolled as

40. Lyon departed Ft. Scott, Kansas, on February 1, 1861, and arrived at the St. Louis, by railroad and not by boat, with an 80-man company of the 2ⁿᵈ U.S. Infantry on February 6, 1861. McElroy, 50–51; Peckham, 56; Phillips, *Damned Yankee*, 127–130; Snead, *Fight for Missouri*, 123–124; Ashbel Woodard, *Life of General Nathaniel Lyon* (Hartford, CT, 1862), 236, hereafter cited as Woodard.
41. Barton Able, a man whom Frank Blair "probably loved the best," was born about 1823, and immigrated to St. Louis in 1840, from Illinois. He initially clerked on river boats and within a short time became a river boat captain. Later, he opened a brokerage house, buying and selling goods on a commission. Abel was elected to the Missouri Legislature in 1856, and was a delegate to the Democratic National Convention the same year. By 1860, Able was a Republican, who was described as a "sincere, honest and influential" man, who participated as a delegate to the Republican National Convention. With the outbreak of the Civil War, Able's knowledge of transportation on the local rivers, garnered him an appointment as Superintendent of Western Steamboats to oversee Union requests for the movement of men and supplies on the Missouri and Mississippi Rivers. Later, he became a stockholder in the Union Newspaper Company, in 1862, which published the *St. Louis Union*–an anti *Missouri Democrat* periodical. Following the war Able recommend Frank Blair for President in 1868, as a Democrat. Blair failed to get the nomination, but was unanimously chosen as the vice-Presidential candidate. Final disposition unknown. *O.R.S.*, pt. 3, vol. 1: 61–62; Gerteis, *St. Louis*, 72–73; Parrish, *Frank Blair*, 148, 254; Smith, *Blair Family*, vol. 1: 338 and vol. 2: 211,349, 391.
   William McKee was born in New York and later moved to St. Louis, where he became a prominent newspaperman. A confidant of Frank Blair, McKee was noted as "a Free-Soiler of courage and ability" in 1848. By the 1860 canvas for President, McKee was an Unconditional Unionist, a Republican and principle owner and publisher of the *Missouri Democrat*. By September 1861, McKee broke with Blair over the removal of General John C. Frémont, who advocated emancipation of slaves in Missouri, while Blair was against it. In July 1863, McKee ran afoul of General John M. Schofield after publishing a confidential letter to the general from President Lincoln. Arrested on July 10 for "'anti-Radical acts,'" McKee was immediately paroled for ten days but was later released at the behest of President Lincoln. Following the war McKee was supported by the Missouri Radicals for the St. Louis postmaster, but failed to get the appointment. McKee supported U.S. Grant for President in 1868, and, in 1872, sold the *Democrat*, founded the *St. Louis Globe* and three years later re-acquired the *Democrat*, founding the *St. Louis Globe-Democrat*. During Grant's terms as President, McKee, with the support of Grant's personal secretary, "controlled federal patronage in St. Louis and manipulated the federal whiskey tax," in 1872. Upon investigation of what was called the "Whisky Ring," McKee along with 100 others were convicted in November-December 1875, of stealing from the Government; however, McKee was quickly pardoned and served no time in jail. Donald B. Connelly, *John M. Schofield and the Politics of Generalship* (Chapel Hill, NC, 2006), 67; "From St. Louis," *Chicago Daily Tribune* (Chicago, IL), July 12,1863; Gerteis, *St. Louis*, 195, 320, 336; Hodes, 734, 740; Parrish, *Frank Blair*, 125, 178; Smith, *Blair Family*, vol. 1: 240 and vol. 2: 57.

a comrade and polls of the Grand Army. I have met all the most distinguished officers of the Union Army, and I say this, without intending to disparage any, that, in my opinion, he had a more comprehensive knowledge of the science of government than any one of them, his quickness of perception equal to Sherman and any willpower equal to Grant.[42] As a writer's compositions were faultless in style, logic and vigor."

"In the first place," said Gen. McKinstry as he readjusted his spectacles, "Gen. Lyon (and his company) were ordered here by Gen. Harney, and he arrived here over the Missouri Pacific Railroad.[43] He arrived here after dark at the Seventh

42. Ulysses S. Grant was born on April 22, 1822, in Ohio, graduated from West Point (number 21 of 39) in 1843, and fought in the Mexican War where he was breveted a captain. Resigning on July 31, 1854, Grant tried farming, selling real estate, and clerking in a store. With the coming of the Civil War, Grant was appointed colonel of the 21st Illinois Infantry on June 17, 1861, and was sent briefly to Missouri. He commanded in Jefferson City for a week in August 1861, as a newly appointed brigadier general, after which he was transferred to southeast Missouri. On November 7, 1861, he fought and lost the Battle of Belmont, Missouri, his only engagement in the Trans-Mississippi area. Grant completed his Civil War service in the East, rising to the rank of Commander of the United States Army. Elected President of the United States in 1868, Grant served two terms, after which he traveled and entered into some unfavorable business adventures. Grant died on July 23, 1885, in New York City. Boatner, 352–352; Heitman, vol. 1: 470; Warner, *Generals in Blue*, 183–186.

William T. Sherman was born on February 8, 1820, in Lancaster, Ohio, and was raised by Senator William Ewing, a friend of the family, following the death of his father in 1829. He graduated from West Point (number 6 of 42) in 1840, served in California during the Mexican War, where he received a brevet to captain for "gallant and meritorious service." Sherman resigned from the army in 1853, dabbled in banking, law, real estate and headed the Louisiana State Seminary of Learning and Military Academy. At the beginning of the Civil War Sherman was in St. Louis serving as the President of St. Louis Streetcar Company. Reentering the army, Sherman was given command of the 13th U.S. Infantry and rose quickly through the ranks being promoted to major general of volunteers on August 1, 1862. Sherman served his entire time in the Western Theater, captured Atlanta on September 2, 1864, marched to the sea and accepted the surrender of Joe Johnston on April 17, 1865, in North Carolina. Following the war Sherman remained in the service, being promoted to lieutenant general in 1866, and Commander-in-Chief of the Army on March 8, 1869. Sherman resigned from the army in 1884, and died on February 14, 1891, in New York City. Boatner, 750–751; Faust, 681–683; Heitman, vol. 1: 882.

43. William S. Harney was born in Tennessee, joined the Regular Army in 1818, fought Seminoles in Florida, served in the Mexican War and fought Indians on the frontier. On June 14, 1858, he received a promotion to brigadier general in the regular army. Harney assumed command of the Department of the West, in St. Louis, on November 17, 1860. By the Civil War, Harney was one of only four general officers in the U.S. Army and expected to support the South, but he never did. St. Louis Unionists, led by Frank Blair, did not trust Harney, in part, because of a conversation Harney had with John M. Schofield. Harney stated that he didn't understand "'Why the State had not yet passed an ordinance of secession." Schofield then expressed his concerns "with many others…that General Harney's Union principles were [not] quite up to standard that the situation required"–simply put, Harney was "too conservative to suit Blair's purposes." Further, both Schofield and Frank Blair believed Harney to be loyal to the Union, but believed that "he had friends and connections, who were men that whilst professing to be Union men, sympathized silently with the movement against the government." The Committee of Safety, with the urging of Frank Blair, sent Dr. Charles Bernays, editor of the *Anzeiger des Westens*, and personal friend of President Lincoln to Washington to urge the removal of Harney following the Camp Jackson Affair. Harney was relieved on May 16, though the order was held by Blair "pending the outcome

Street depot. I was chief quartermaster here at the time and I packed him and his company on the street railroad and sent them down to the arsenal. Consequently

No Such Interview

as Gov. Fletcher says he and McKee and Blair and Bart Able had with Gen. Lyon could have taken place on his arrival, for he never arrived at the wharf."

"But what about the assertion of Gen. Lyon that he would maintain the national authority?"

"He certainly never made it in my presence and if he did make it at any time, it was a ground presumption and imprudence, as any soldier will tell you; a captain talking as though he had come here to command."

"And the eulogy in the latter part of the quotation concerning comprehensive knowledge of the science of government, etc."

Gen. McKinstry smiled in a very suggestive way but was silent. Then he said:

"General Lyon made his appearance in my regiment in Florida a rough, uncouth man, without any polish what ever. In my judgment he was tyrannical by nature, and wouldn't admit of opposition to his view in any way or shape. My attention on that point was first drawn to him by a little incident that occurred in the Florida war. He had fallen in command of a company through the sickness of the captain, or something of that kind, stationed on the bank of the St. John's River for sometime. He was picked up by his men one day and was thrown into the river for mismanagement of the men. He was the only officer there at the time. I remember, also, I think it was in 1842, at Madison barracks, Hackett's Harbor, N. Y., Lyon was tried by a general court-martial for

---

of Harney's attempt to restore order and maintain the peace." On May 31, Blair had enough and directed the relief order delivered to Harney. Before departing St. Louis a dejected Harney penned a letter to the Adjutant General of the Army, ending his letter with these words: "'During a long life dedicated to my country, I have seen some service, and more than once I have held her honor in my hands; and during that time my loyalty, I believe, was never questioned; and now, when in the natural course of things, I shall, before the lapse of many years lay aside my sword which has so long served my country, my countrymen will be slow to believe that I have chosen this portion of my career to damn with treason my life, which is soon to become a record of the past, and which I shall most willingly leave to the unbiased judgement of posterity.'" Harney retired from the army on August 1, 1863, and died on May 9, 1889, in Orlando, Florida. See Banasik, *Confederate Tales of the War Part One:1861* for picture and complete biography. *O.R.*, vol 3: 374; Michael E. Banasik, *Confederate "Tales of the War" in the Trans-Mississippi Part One: 1861. Unwritten Chapters of the Civil War West of the River Volume VII* (Iowa City, IA, 2010), 185–186, hereafter cited as Banasik, *Confederate Tales, 1861*; Boatner, 376; Quoted in Wiley Britton, *The Civil War on the Border A Narrative of Military Operations in Missouri, Kansas, Arkansas, and the Indian Territory, During the Years 1861–62, Based Upon Official Reports of the Federal Commanders, etc. Volume 1* (New York, 1899), 18, hereafter cited as Britton; Brooksher, 71, 76–77; Frederick H. Dyer, *A Compendium of the War of the Rebellion* (Des Moines, 1908; reprint ed., Dayton, OH, 1978), 254, hereafter cited as Dyer; Heitman, vol. 1: 502; McElroy, 30–31; Rassieur, 15; John M. Schofield, *Forty-Six Years in the Army*, (New York, 1897), 33, hereafter cited as Schofield; *War in the West*, 158–159; Warner, *Generals in Blue*, 208–209.

Mismanagement of His Men

and was sentenced to be reprimanded in a general order by the General in Chief, Scott.[44] Scott's order was so severe in terms as to engender the most bitter and unrelenting dislike on the part of Lyon which cropped out on all occasions when Scott's name was mentioned. And if anybody will turn to Peckham's life on Lyon he will see where after the commencement of the war, Lyon was constantly giving utterances to reflections upon Scott's loyalty. All this, in the estimation of those who knew Scott in the old Army, was based upon that reprimand."

"I remember also," said Gen. McKinstry after a pause, "he was sent from Bonaci Cal., in pursuit of a band of Indians who have been committing some depredations. He followed the tribe to an island in a lake north of Bonaci which could only be reached by a fording. Lyon got on the island with his company and made quick work of the Indians. He made as an excuse for the massacre that in the underbrush he and his men, couldn't distinguish the squaws from the bucks, and they were all killed. [45]At the time he came here in 1861 he was

Under Charges

preferred by Surgeon Madison Mills, United States Army for causing the death of a soldier by mistreatment.[46] A court-martial had been ordered to assemble at Fort Leavenworth for the trial of the charges, but the attack on Camp Jackson enable

---

44. Hackett's Harbor was located on Lake Ontario. The incident that General McKinstry referred too occurred in December 1842. Lyon was the Officer of the Day at Madison Barracks and had a man "bucked and gagged" for drunkenness and threatening comments to Lyon. On December 28, Lyon was court-Merthiolate for "illegal, arbitrary and unmilitary conduct." Following a ten day hearing Lyon was found guilty and sentenced "'To be suspended from rank and command for five calender months" and restricted to Madison Barracks; however, on March 23, the sentence was commuted, returning Lyon to duty. Phillips, *Damned Yankee*, 32–35; Woodard, 61.
45. On May 6, 1850, Lyon led an expedition against a mixed group of Indians located on an island in Clear Lake, which was about 70 miles from Bonaci. Utilizing a company of dragoons, with a mountain howitzer, to cut off any retreat from the Indian camp, Lyon crossed over to the island with his infantry in a make-shift barge. The Indians found their crude weapon were no match for Lyon's infantry and retreated into the reeds surrounding the island. Lyons' men went in after the Indians and killed about 100 warriors, after which they proceeded to slaughter the women, children and old men who remained in the village. By the time the bloodletting was done between 200–400 Indians had been killed, while Lyon suffered no losses. Ashbel Woodard, gives a good account of the engagement, but failed to address the slaughter of the women, children and old men. Phillips, *Damned Yankee*, 66–69; Woodard, 167–171.
46. Madison Mills was born on October 15, 1810, in New York City. He entered the army as an Assistant Surgeon on April 1, 1834, fought in the Mexican War as a major and surgeon. At the beginning of the Civil War, Mills was stationed at Ft. Leavenworth, Kansas. He was promoted to colonel "for meritorious service during the campaign and siege of Vicksburg." On March 13,1865, Mills was breveted a brigadier general. Mills remained in the army after the war, dying on April 28, 1873, at Ft. Columbus, New York. Heitman, vol. 1: 713; Hunt & Brown, 416.

Blair to get an order in Washington to have the order for the trial countermanded, and the charges were never investigated."[47]

"But here's an amusing part of the matter," said Gen. McKinstry reading from the response of Mr. George D. Reynolds to Gov. Fletcher's speech:[48]

"Lyon's name has been dropped from our muster rolls. The records 'Died in action,' is written against it. Is it too wild a fancy to believe that some day in eternity–if eternity has a day–the 'Old Commander,' in the far off land to which we are all marching now with hastened tread, may cause to be sounded the 'Assembly' for all the host of our Grand Army? If he does, there will be no general commander who can probably pass in review on that great day, nor salute, with more confidence of duty well performed as he goes marching by, than Gen. Nathaniel Lyon."

"That is amusing," said Gen. McKinstry, "from the fact that Lyon was an atheist, opened and avowed.."

"If Gen. Lyon arrived in St. Louis at night and by railroad, general, where did Gov. Fletcher get the foundation for that interview at the wharf?"

"I know Gov. Fletcher to be a have some graceful speaker; a man of capacity and a capable soldier; one who did good service in the war, and one for whom I have high steam but he is decidedly off in his statements about

The Interview on the Landing

"I can't imagine how his mind became impressed with it. I only comment on it, because the motto of my work which will be published next summer, giving both the Union and Confederate sides of the troubles here in Missouri in 1861 is 'History is not the thing done, but thing were recorded.' Lyon was a brave, gallant man, and this thing as a final oration would perhaps be very well, but it gives a

47. While stationed at Ft. Riley, in 1860, a private in Lyons' company died of starvation "under suspicious circumstances." Charges were subsequently preferred against both Dr. Mills and Lyon, and a Court of Inquiry was ordered to assemble at Ft. Leavenworth on April 14, 1861. Lyon appealed to Frank Blair to squash the Inquiry; however, events were changing quickly in Missouri in April 1861, and the Inquiry went away as the Civil War began. Phillips, *Damned Yankee*, 151–153.
48. George Delachaumette Reynolds was born on December 16, 1841, in Gettysburg, Pennsylvania, moved to Springfield, Illinois, at a young age and graduated from Illinois State University in 1861. With the beginning of the Civil War, Reynolds joined an Illinois artillery unit, rising to the rank of sergeant major in the 2nd Illinois Artillery Regiment. He later joined the 6th U.S. Artillery Regiment (colored), being appointed the unit's lieutenant colonel. He was mustered out in March 1866, returned to Quincy, Illinois, where he clerked for a local law firm. Admitted to the bar in Hannibal, Missouri in1867, Reynolds opened a law office in St. Louis, in 1871. Reynolds moved to Colorado in October 1876, married Julia Vogdes, with whom he had three children. Returning to St. Louis in 1877, Reynolds was appointed a U.S. Attorney in 1889, and served until his retirement in 1894. A Republican, Free Mason, an Episcopalian and a member of the Loyal Legion of the United States, Reynolds was noted as "one of the most active and able" lawyers in Missouri in the early 1900's. Final Disposition unknown. Walter B. Stevens, *St. Louis History of the Fourth City 1763–1909 Vol.II* (St. Louis, 1909), 678–691, hereafter cited as Stevens.

wrong impression of facts and of Lyon's traits of character as they were known to the old army."

"What was the general opinion of Gen. Lyon in the old army?"

"In my opinion he was considered a brave man, but a singular compound. As an illustration of his singular composition, he suffered himself to be personally insulted by a Southern officer and declined to appeal to the code on the ground that he didn't approve of it yet he was an atheist."

"Don't ask me further, for in my memoirs I had devoted quite a space to him and his services. He is entitled to the respect of all loyal men, and I can truly say of him:

> 'In men, who men condemn as ill,
> I find so much of goodness still;
> In men, whom men, proclaimed divine,
> I find no such much of sin and blot
> I believe to draw the line from where God has not.'"

* * * * * * *

Item: Governor Claiborne F. Jackson, the Missouri Legislature and the Secession Crisis, by General Justus McKinstry.
Published: September 12, 1885.

Missouri in the Civil War

In his forthcoming book on the part taken by Missouri in the Civil War General Justus McKinstry says:

The governor of Missouri, Claiborne F. Jackson, was a secessionist. He was also a sagacious politician, maintaining harmonious private correspondence with the secession leaders of the Southern states. His belief was that by adroit management he could use the state of Missouri to espouse the secession cause. His conduct was silent and wily. Among secessionists not only in Missouri but if all the border states the phrase, "armed neutrality," first employed by Hon. J. J.. Crittenden, became popular. In the case of the counties absolutely sovereign the phrase has meaning.[49] Where two sovereignties are at war and third sovereign country,

---

49. John J. Crittenden was born on September 10, 1787, in Woodford City, Kentucky, and graduated from William & Mary College with a law degree in 1807. Moving briefly to the Illinois Territory, Crittenden served as the Territory's Attorney General and in 1811, entered politics, being elected to the Kentucky Legislature. He fought in the War of 1812, after which he continued a long political career in Kentucky, spanning over fifty years. He served in the Kentucky House and Senate, U.S. Senate, and one term as Kentucky's Governor. With the secession crisis, Crittenden was the leading component for compromise, crafting the "Crittenden Compromise (see note 27)," which was rejected by all parties in the conflict. Having failed to avert the coming war, Crittenden attempted to keep Kentucy out of the conflict, convincing the State Legislature and Governor to eventually assume the position or armed neutrality. On May 20, 1861, Governor Beriah Magoffin

not interested in the issue may say, I have no concerns in this quarrel, and hence will not at present become a party to it, but my territory may be invaded, or my rights otherwise assailed by one or other of the belligerents, or perhaps the victor in the contest may impose upon the vanquished such terms as will enable it in its increased strength and boldness to menace my peace in the future. I will, therefore, gather an army and put myself in a military attitude, so that I can interfere if my old rights shall be violated or my safety in peril. The military attitude of a third independent sovereignty is called an armed neutrality. In 1812, when Russia and Prussia and Sweden made war upon Napoleon, resulting in his dethronement and banishment to Elba, Austria at first maintained an armed neutrality, though circumstances favoring, she made also an armed mediation.

But in the Case of A State

of the Federal Union, "armed neutrality" is an absurdity. The phrase was applied not to succeeded states, which engaged in out right hostility, but to the border states which proposed to remain in the Union. As to such states, they were undeniably parts of one of the belligerents, and hence neutrality was an impossibility. The Constitution and laws of the United States were, as always, their supreme law. Their citizens held citizenship under and owed allegiance and service to the government of the United States, but the phrase, though absurd, suited the purpose of the border states secessionists. It seemed to justify them in expressions of incivility to the Federal government and of sympathy with the South and, what was of greater account, and making military preparations for a contemplated secession by procuring hostile state legislation, by directing all public funds to military use and by placing all departments of the state government in the hands of Southern sympathizers. But the pretense in Missouri of maintaining armed neutrality was an absurdity. Not less absurd was the profession in Missouri of respect for state rights, state sovereignty. The doctrine in a state sovereignty in its proper, limita-

---

issued a Proclamation declaring Kentucy's neutrality. Seven days later the Border State Convention, headed by Crittenden, met in Frankfurt to discuss the newly initiated war, in an attempt to end the conflict before it escalated out of control. On June 3, the Convention adjourned and issued a statement "To the People of the United States," that was meant to end the conflict. It contained two simple proposals: First–The U.S. Congress to issue a Constitutional Amendment guaranteeing the rights of slave owners and Second–"If this should fail to bring about the results so desired to us and so essential to the best hopes of our country, then let a voluntary convention be called, composed of delegates from the people of the States, in which measures of peaceable adjustment may be devised and adopted, and the nation rescued from the continued horrors of civil war." The convention failed, after which Crittenden spent his remaining days "defining the war goals as a struggle to preserve the Union." Crittenden did not survive the war, dying on July 26, 1863. "Addresses of the Convention of the Border States," Frank Moore, ed., *The Rebellion Record A Diary of American Events*, 12 vols. (New York, 1861–1868; reprint ed., New York, 1977), vol. 1: Doc. 250–253, hereafter cited as *Rebellion Record*; Boatner, 208; Faust, 192; J. Stoddard Johnson, *Kentucky, Confederate Military History*, vol. 9: 21–22; Christopher M. Paine, "Crittenden, John Jordan," in *Encyclopedia of the Civil War*, 522–523; *Rebellion Record*, vol. 1: Diary 3, 74.

tions is undeniably true, and is one of the most precious features in our system of government. The secessionists ended in holding an extreme view of this doctrine, but if we assume, as the secessionists did, that a state may of constitutional right withdraw from the Union, then we must

Locally Conceded

that his sole allegiance after the exercise of this right was to his state and to say any new government with which his state may have formed a connection, and that he could not, in law or in morals, owe allegiance to the United States, which, by hypothesis, had become a foreign government, with which this state was at war.[50] Thus we see that a citizen of Georgia, holding that State sovereignty involves secession as a valid constitutional right, would be logical in transferring his allegiance to the Confederacy, and not granting it to the United States, with which both the Confederacy and his home state were waging war. But with a Missouri secessionist the case was different. He might, at the onset, as an individual citizen, desire of the secession of Missouri, and he might labor to that end. But when the

---

50. The "extreme view" that Southern States had a right to secede, was based upon English law and its evolution from the early Fourteenth Century to 1860, and the eventual secession of South Carolina in December. According to Kent M. Brown, a modern-day Kentucky lawyer, the United States Constitution was a "contract" or "compact" between the thirteen original States to govern their relationship and responsibilities within the Union of States under auspicious of a Federal Government. And upon signing of the document three States, New York, Virginia and Rhode Island, signed the Constitution with the provision that they may rescind or withdraw from the compact "subject to the people's right of recission." This compact or contract was reaffirmed several times prior to the Civil War by the original framers of the document according to Brown, who wrote: "The Framers and Ramifies of the Constitution unquestionably understood it to be a 'compact.' Not only did the document, in form, contain all the elements of a contract, but the prevailing political thought of Revolutionary America understood the fact that written constitutions were 'compacts.'" As a contract between the States and all the States who joined after the original thirteen, if "one of the parties fails to perform a particular task (i.e. or 'breaches the contract') the other party may seek certain remedies." Three remedies are then possible; First–the aggrieved party could take the other to court and receive damages; Second–the courts could force the offender of the contract to comply with the contract or compact; and Third–the contract could be rescinded, thus terminating the relationship between the two parties. In the case of the Southern States, the election of Abraham Lincoln as President was viewed as a"breach of contract" or an "overt act" against the "Souther people" and their rights. Lincoln, who was supported by abolitionists, "did not run in the southern states" and openly caused fear in the South. Given the huge slave population in the South, the recent raid on Harper's Ferry by John Brown, and the fear that Lincoln would free the slaves, depriving the whites of their lively-hood; all of which caused a "'Crisis of fear'" throughout the South. Consequently, South Carolina, followed by the other deep Southern States, seceded or withdraw from their compact with the other states in the Union. Despite it all, "In the end," according to Brown, "one reaches the inescapable conclusion that secession was perfectly constitutional"–but not in Missouri, which failed to get the consent of the people. And when the Confederacy fired on Ft. Sumpter, they essentially had declared war on the United States, allowing President Lincoln to prosecute a war, though not a War of Rebellion, but one of aggression by the Confederacy. Kent Masterson Brown, "Secession A Constitutional Remedy for the Breach of Organic Law," *North & South* 3 (June, 2000), 12, 14, 16–17, 19; Lyon, 432.

State decided, as Missouri did, by an overwhelming vote that it would not secede, his same favorite doctorate of State sovereignty logically required him to abjure secession, and with fervor of national and state patriotism, stand by the union. A Missouri secessionists, by adhering to the rebellion, abjured state sovereignty. The general assembly of 1860—61 was all the Gov. Jackson could desire. It favored secession by an overwhelming majority, and seemed not to doubt that it represented the sentiment of this state.[51] In an exuberance of confidence, it passed an act calling a convention, and vested the convention with the plenary power. It turned out that the governor and the general assembly had mistaken the temper of the people. The convention which met February 28, 1861, was overwhelmingly

For the Union

Sterling Price, a former governor of the state and a strong Union man, was made president of the convention. Union resolutions were adopted by a large majority.[52] Before adjourning the convention created a committee with power to reconvene it whenever the public exigencies should require.[53] As already suggested,

---

51. When the Missouri General Assembly met on December 21, 1860, it consisted of an overwhelming majority of supporters for a possible secession. Of the 33 members of the Missouri Senate 25 were considered either Breckinridge or Douglas Democrats, while the other eight were either Constitutional Unionists or Republicans. The Missouri House seated 132 members, of whom 83 were Democrats and 49 Republican or Constitutional Unionists. And John McAfee, a Breckinridge Democrat, supported slavery, but not Stephen Douglas, was elected Speaker of the House by a vote of 77 to 43 over the Constitutional Union candidate. "This action shows that the Democrats of the House were quite well united on the vital question of the day"–slavery. However, when delegates were selected for the February Convention to consider Missouri's relationship with the Federal Government and possible secession the matter of slavery took a back seat when compared to preserving the Union. Of the 140,000 votes cast, 110,000 for the Unionist candidates while a mere 30,000 supported secessionists. Further, of the 99 delegates elected to the February Convention, none were Breckinridge Democrats, while 88 of the 99 were slave owners, who ultimately wished to preserve the Union. And by the time the Convention had ended on March 22, following a 23 day session, they had voted "to remain in the Union." while the supporters of Governor Jackson "went down to ignominious defeat." Kirkpatrick, "Missouri On the Eve of the Civil War," 100–101, 104; Laughlin, 583, 592; Lyon, 427; Rassieur, 12; Ryle, 210, 212–213, 233.
52. Two reports were given for the Convention's consideration on Missouri's relationship with the Federal Government; the Majority Report, was given by H. R. Gamble and was submitted on March 9, while the Minority Report was authored by John T. Red from Marion County, who represented the Fourth District and Harrison Hough from Mississippi County, who represented the Twenty-Fifth District–Their report was submitted on March 11. Of the two reports Gamble's contained seven resolutions that became the focus of the debate that lasted throughout the Convention. Of the seven resolutions, Nos. 5 and 7 were resubmitted, with amendments, and all were eventually passed with over ninety percent of the vote in favor of passage. See **Appendix A** for a copy of the seven Resolutions that were passed. Laughlin, 594–595, 597, 599; Rassieur, 7–8; Ryle, 220–222, 229–232.
53. On March 21, the last point of business was presented to the convention; a draft reply to a representative of the State of Georgia, who had recently addressed he Convention. The reply "disapproved of the constitutional right of secession and held that it would 'be ruinous to the best interests of Missouri.'" There was staunch opposition to the reply–"It was first tabled, and next made

the decided action of the convention elected to determine this issue of secession ought to have been conclusive to those holding extreme views of state sovereignty, yet to the president's call for Missouri's quota of troops Gov. Jackson returned April 17, 1861, an undignified reply, using such language as the "president war," "inhuman and diabolical," and curtly refusing troops. It turned out that the question of Missouri furnishing troops did not depend on his excellency.[54] Meanwhile public excitement increased every hour. Pursuant to the governor's proclamation the legislature convened in special session on May 2, 1861.[55] Its actions was anger hurried, revolutionary. As an evidence of the frenzy that prevailed, an act was passed referring to the capture of Camp Jackson, which was styled and invasion and rebellion, and authorizing the governor "to take such measures as he might be necessary to repel such invasion or put down such rebellion." By that foolish act the general assembly abdicated its legislative authority invested the governor with the power of a Roman dictator. Though there

was no other act indicating so lamentably the loss of reflection, there were many showing a lack of wisdom. The school fund, always regarded as sacred by men who have children, were diverted to the military fund. By another act, each county was authorized

To Issue Bonds

bearing 10 per cent, to the amount of $30,000, which was to be loaned to the state to be paid out to the militia and volunteers ((   )) respectively. Another authorized ((   )) for the manufacture of arms and purchase real estate on which to erect powder mills. Another authorized him to seize and hold all railroads and telegraphs in this state. The one of the most unique productions of that body was the militia act. It was of interminable length, and but two of its provisions will be here noticed. One section made it unlawful for any number of the inhabitants of the state (not residents, for that would not include, for example, Iowa volunteers, or United States regulars) to unite together in the semblance of an armed orga-

---

the special order of business for the third Monday in December next. And finally, a committee of seven was appointed "to call the convention together, if necessary," though not specifying what the purpose of said convention would take. The Missouri Convention then adjourned on March 22,1861. Laughlin, 601; Ryle, 232.

54. Following Governor Jackson's refusal to provided troops, the St. Louis Committee of Safety, headed by Frank Blair, mustered in four regiments as required by the War Department, plus an additional five regiments of Home Guard. Peckham, 102–103, 113–114, 117–118.

55. On April 22, 1861, Governor Jackson called for an "extraordinary session" of the Missouri Legislature to assemble in Jefferson City on May 2. The Governor also issued an order, at the same time, for the Missouri Militia to assemble in their various districts, on May 6, for their yearly training as "provided by law." When calling for the special secession Governor Jackson stated that it was "'for the purpose of enacting such laws and adopting such measures as may be deemed necessary and proper for the more thorough organization and equipment of the militia of the State, and to raise the money and such other means as may be required to place the State in a proper attitude of defense.'" Quoted in Britton, 6

nization unless they were first mustered in under the militia act, as a part of the Missouri Militia, and actually made it the duty of the district militia commander "to disarm the same."[56] At this distance of time such legislation provoked a smile. The other provision is almost as amusing. The Constitution of the United States requires every state officer to take an oath to support the Federal Constitution. The then Constitution of Missouri required every officer to take an oath to support the Federal and State Constitutions. Yet this Militia Act provided that all persons mustered into the militia should, "with naked right hand uplifted, swear that you will bear true allegiance to the State of Missouri, and that you will serve her honestly and faithfully against all enemies and oppressors whatsoever; that you will support the constitution of the state of Missouri and observe and obey orders of the governor. of Missouri, and the orders of the officers appointed over you."

This from legislators who stickled for the State Constitution, and, this from legislators who vehemently

Asserted State Sovereignty

but months after the people had pronounced with solemnity and with marked unanimity against secession. The capture of Camp Jackson fired the Southern heart

---

56. Prior to the capture of Camp Jackson, the May 2 session of the Legislature accomplished nothing, failing to pass any meaningful legislation. However, upon hearing of the capture of Camp Jackson, from J. W. Tucker, editor of the *St. Louis Journal*, the Legislature passed the Military Bill, "in less than fifteen minuets," with only eight dissenting votes, essentially making the Governor "an autocratic ruler." The bill was to take effect immediately. As passed, the Military Bill placed every "every able-bodied man into the Militia of Missouri" and provided for the organization of what would be called the Missouri State Guard (MSG). The Governor subsequently appointed Sterling Price, a major general commanding the Guard, thus making him a "military dictator." This was immediately followed by a second bill, which authorized "the Governor to take such measures as he might deem necessary or proper to repel invasion or put down rebellion" in Missouri. This second bill also gave Governor Jackson $30,000 to carry out his mandate. Additional acts passed following Camp Jackson giving the Governor the power to seize the railroads and telegraph lines and " buy foundries for casting cannon;" specifically the Ballentine Foundry in Bonneville. Still, another act appropriated $25,000 "for constructing of a State road to the Southern boundary of the State," and yet another for issuing small bonds of $30,000 from each of the State's counties and taking a $1,000,000 loan from the banks to raise $3,000,000 for arming the State. This last act also provided for the seizing of the "school fund" and other funds from various charitable institutions in the State And the last bill to pass, prior to adjournment, appropriated "$10,000 to cultivate friendly relations with the Indian Tribes on the border." Overall, "by this bill a military fund was created for the purpose of arming and equipping the militia; and all the money in the treasury, or to be received during the current year; however it had been previously appropriated , was devoted for this purpose." NOTE: Camp Jackson will be addressed in a following letter. Britton, 7, 14; Brooksher, 64; Alfred H. Guernsey, and Henry M. Alden, *Harper's Pictorial History of the Civil War, etc.*, 2 vols. in 1 (New York, 1866; reprint ed., n. p., N.D.), 107, hereafter cited as Guernsey & Alden; Laughlin, 604–605; McElroy, 88–90; Moore, *Missouri, Confederate Military History*, vol. 9: 35; Peckham, 114, 164, 166–168, 172, 176–177; William Garret Piston and Thomas P. Sweeney, "Don't Yield An Inch: The Missouri State Guard," *North & South* 2 (June, 1999): 14, hereafter cited as Piston & Sweeney, "Missouri State Guard"; Rassieur, 19; Smith, *Blair Family*, vol. 2: 42; Snead, *Fight for Missouri*, 172–173; *Union Army*, vol. 4: 242–243.

of Gov. Price and he accepted from Gov. Jackson the part of major general of the Missouri State Guard under this singular act. The legislature adjourned March [May] 15, and it is safe to say that no body of grown men ever exhibited so much terror and so much folly in so short a time. The convention met again July 22, 1861.[57] It's only act falling within the scope of this narrative was a displacement of Jackson, then in arms against the federal government, and outside the limits of the state, and the election of Hamilton R . Gamble as governor.[58] Gov. Gamble made arrangements with the administration at Washington. In pursuance of which he organized a force of 10,000 men called the Missouri State Militia [MSM], to be paid by the United States and to be under the command of the federal officers commanding the military department, but to render service only in Missouri. The arrangement proved a wise one.[59]

---

57. On July 6, 1861, per the agreement at the February Convention, a majority of the Committee of Seven called for the Convention to reassemble on July 22, in Jefferson City. A total of 97 members were present, who quickly appointed Robert Wilson as the new President, vice Sterling Price, who had joined the rebel cause. The Convention then appointed a Committee of Seven to "consider the present condition of public affairs in Missouri." The Committee quickly reported that the offices of the Governor, Lieutenant Governor and Secretary of State had been vacated and the needed to filled. To further their actions, the Convention then appointed Hamilton R. Gamble, "the leading man in the Convention," and former head of the Missouri Supreme Court as an eighth member of the Committee. And when the Convention adjourned on July 31, H. R. Gamble was elected the Provisional Governor (68–0, with 21 absent and eight not voting), Willard P. Hall became the Provisional Lieutenant Governor and Mordecia Oliver was elected to the Secretary of State position. "All in all" declared the *Chicago Tribune*, "the elections made at Jefferson City are well approved here" in St. Louis. The Convention also passed a requirement that "all citizens, before being allowed to vote," would have to take a loyalty oath as well as "all incumbents of office and all who be qualified for office thereafter." To close out the Convention Governor Gamble issued an extensive address, explaining why the Convention took the actions that they did–See **Appendix A** for a copy of that address. Though not addressed by any future author, the Missouri Supreme Court, according to the *Washington Telegraph*, "unanimously refused to recognize this usurping government." "Address to the People of Missouri," *Rebellion Record*, vol. 2: Doc. 446–450; C., "Affairs In Missouri," *Chicago Tribune*, July 31, 1861; "From St. Louis," *Chicago Tribune*," August 1, 1861; "Gov. Reynolds and Missouri," *Washington Telegraph* (Washington, AR), May 20, 1863; Laughlin, 611–612, 614; McElroy, 136–137.; Rassieur, 21.
58. Hamilton R. Gamble was born in Virginia in 1798, moved to Tennessee and then Missouri. He was a lawyer by profession, opened a law office in St. Louis and was appointed to the Missouri Supreme Court in 1851. In 1858, he moved to Pennsylvania, but returned to Missouri during the secession crisis of 1860–1861. Elected Provisional Governor of Missouri on July 31, 1861, Gamble did not survive the war, dying on January 31, 1864. And according to Margueritt Potter, "Hamilton Rowan Gamble…more than any other man belongs the credit for keeping Missouri in the Union." See **Appendix B** for a complete biography. Faust, 297; Margueritt Potter, "Hamilton R. Gamble. Missouri's War Governor," in *The Civil War in Missouri: Essays from the Missouri Historical Review, 1906–2006* (Columbia, MO, 2006), 65, hereafter cited as Potter, "Hamilton R. Gamble"; Sifakis, *Who Was Who in the Union*, 147; *Rebellion Record*, vol. 2: Diary 50; Winter, 120–121.
59. On August 30, 1861, Governor Gamble departed St. Louis, for Washington DC, to secure funding for the MSM. After arriving in Washington, Gamble negotiated with the Lincoln Administration to fund the proposed militia force for Missouri. The new force "to be armed, equipped, clothed, subsisted, transported and paid by the United States during such time as they shall be actually engaged as an embodied military force in service, in accordance with the regulations of the U.S. Army." And most importantly, "said militia not to be ordered out of the State except for the

Gov. Jackson died December 5, 1862 at a farmhouse in the state of Arkansas, and to this day no stone marks his resting place.[60] His brief gubernatorial career had been stormy. Unwilling to abide by the solemnly expressed voice of the people on the question of secession, his obstinate and persistent effort had been not to lull, but to aggravate the storm. Amid war and its ravages, among strangers and unwept he perished. Had he adhered logically to his doctrine of state sovereignty and accepted as ultimate the voice of the people of Missouri, he might have done immense good and calm the surging elements of discord and saving the state from the deluge of misery that rolled over it and whose waves he helped to swell.

Note: See Appendix A for extended comments on the Secession Crisis by William H. Lyon, who wrote: "Looking specifically at the actual events of the secession crisis, one sees how complex the situation was" and ultimately why the secession faction failed to succeed in removing Missouri from the Union.[61]

* * * * * * *

immediate defense of the State." Gamble returned to Missouri, arriving in St, Louis on the evening of September 10. It was reported on September 12 that the Governor had secured the funding for his proposed MSM; however, the funding was not settled, in part, because of objections by General John C. Frémont, commanding the Department of the West. On November 6, President Lincoln approved Gamble's Militia Plan, adding that the Commander of the Department of the West, must be commissioned a major general commanding the MSM. The following day General Orders No. 96, War Department, Adjutant General's Office approved Gamble's Plan to fund the MSM. *O.R.*, vol. 3: 470, 565–566; *O.R.*, Series 3, vol. 1: 618–620; "Affairs In St. Louis," *Chicago Tribune*, September 12,1861; "From St. Louis," *Chicago Tribune*, August 31, 1861.

60. Most of what General McKinstry has written about the death of Governor Jackson was false. After being driven from Jefferson City, Governor Jackson eventually ended up in Little Rock, Arkansas. Suffering from stomach cancer, tuberculosis and pneumonia, Governor Jackson succumbed "in a laudanum haze," on December 7, 1862; not "at a farm house," but in the Pulaski House in Little Rock. He was buried in the Mount Holly Cemetery, in Little Rock, where he remained until 1871, when he was re-buried, by family members, in the Sappington Cemetery, near Arrow Rock, Saline County, Missouri. Banasik, *Missouri in 1861*, 352; Arthur Roy Kirkpatrick, "Missouri Secessionist Government, 1861–1865," *Missouri Historical Review* 14 (October, 1950), 131, hereafter cited as Kirkpatrick, "Missouri Secessionist Government"; Christopher Phillips, *Missouri's Confederate: Claiborne Fox Jackson and the Creation of the Southern Identity in the Border West* (Columbia, Mo,2000), 273, 294–295, hereafter cited as Phillips, *Missouri's Confederate*.

61. Lyon, 441.

Item: Recruitment for Missouri troops in April 1861, by Colonel David Murphy.[62]
Published: July 4,1885.

The First Federal Company Raised in Missouri

The following sketch of the incidents attending the muster of the first Federal company raised in Missouri outside of St. Louis is from the trenchant pen of Col. David Murphy of this city, whose portrait is here given:

During the first three months of the year 1861 in many portions of the state of Missouri, the popular idea was that whatever fighting might follow the acts of secession of the Southern states would naturally be confined to the extremists, as they were then called, of Massachusetts and New England on one side and South Carolina and her neighboring states on the other side. But, so far as Missouri was concerned, there should be maintained a position of "armed neutrality," and

---

62. David Murphy was born on August 20, 1835 (a biography of Murphy has the date as October 20, 1835, while Murphy, in the Compiled Service Records has the date as August 20), at Woolwich, England. The Murphys moved to the United States in 1842, initially settling in New York City. In 1855, David Murphy relocated to Iowa, where he worked as a carpenter, and then to Franklin County, Missouri, in 1858 where he worked as a carpenter and then a teacher. During the secession crisis, Murphy organized the men from Franklin County to form Company A (Rifle Battalion) of Blair's 1st Missouri Infantry (Three months), on April 25, 1861. Murphy was elected 1st lieutenant and his company was mustered in on May 8, 1861, at the St. Louis Arsenal. Following Camp Jackson Murphy's company fought at Wilson's Creek, where he was wounded, in the knee, after which his command reorganized and Murphy was promoted to captain on October 20, 1861, commanding Company I, 1st Missouri Light Artillery Regiment. His company was disbanded in January 1862, and Murphy was given command of Company F, 1st Missouri Artillery Regiment on February 28, 1862. Murphy's company saw action at Newtonia, Missouri (September 30, 1862) and Prairie Grove, Arkansas, where he was credited by one author for helping to save the Union Army. Promoted to major for his performance at Prairie Grove, on March 19, 1863, Murphy was made chief-of-artillery in Francis Herron's Division during the Siege of Vicksburg. Murphy then resigned from the army July 10, following the surrender of Vicksburg. Returning to St. Louis, Murphy resumed teaching and was married. With the death of his wife in the latter part of 1863, Murphy reentered the army in 1864, at the request of Colonel Thomas Fletcher, to become the Adjutant of the 47th EMM, and at Pilot Knob (September 27, 1864), Murphy assumed the duel role of commander of Ft. Davidson's artillery and Adjutant of his regiment. Following the successful stand at Pilot Knob, Murphy was elected colonel of the 50th EMM. Following Price's Raid, Murphy returned to Franklin County, where he entered into the practice of law, being appointed a circuit attorney for the Ninth Judicial Circuit, even though he had never received a law degree. He married for the second time in 1866, was a newspaper editor, of the *Franklin County Observer* (1867–1870), and finally obtained a law degree from the St. Louis Law School, graduating in 1871. Murphy continued in the practice of the law well into the early 1900's. Final disposition unknown. *O.R.*, vol. 41, pt. 1: 447; *O.R.*, Index, 685; *O.R.S.*, pt. 2, vol. 36: 36–37, 40, 43, 47–48; Michael E. Banasik, *Embattled Arkansas: The Prairie Grove Campaign of 1862* (Wilmington, NC, 1996), 371, hereafter cited as Banasik, *Embattled Arkansas*; *Dyer*, 1313, 1321; Dwight L. Gifford, *Where Valor and Devotion Met: The Battle of Pilot Knob* (Winfield, MO, 2014), 106–107; Stevens, 302–305; *Union Army*, vol. 4: 279–280.

COL. DAVID MURPHY.

Colonel David Murphy

neither section of the country was to be allowed to come in contact with other by the marching over Missouri soil.[63]

It was in this spirit, and acted with this idea, that the young men of Missouri formed military organizations, practiced marching and drilling, and casting aside all political differences continued to in perfect harmony and good friendship. But the echo of the first cannon fired by Gen. [Pierre Gustave Toutant] Beauregard and his forces on the American flag floating over the battlements of Fort Sumter, reverberated and resounded over the land.[64] It awakened in Missouri as in other states a thrill of patriotic impulse which tolerated no further dalliance with treason if any form, however disguised.

On the night of the 14th of April, 1861, in front of the courthouse at Union, Franklin County, Mo., I was contemplating with serious mind, what would be the next step in the angry controversy which had so long been waging, when my name was called; and I was notified by a member of the semi-military company of that place, that I was wanted in the courtroom to take my place as drill officer in a very positive tone of which I informed the messenger that my convictions of

63. Following the firing on Ft. Sumter, the *Missouri Republican*, declared—"Let us take the same position that Kentucky has taken—that of armed neutrality. Let us declare that no military force levied in other States, shall be allowed to pass through our State, or camp upon our soil. Let us demand of the opposing sections to stop further hostile operations until reason can be appealed to in Congress, and before the people; and when that fails it will be time enough for os to take up arms." The concept of "armed neutrality" was further codified in Missouri following the Camp Jackson Affair. Better known as the Price-Harney Agreement, it was signed on May 21 and temporarily staved off further civil war in Missouri. Under the agreement the Missouri Government would maintain order in the state while the Federal Government, represented by General William Harney, would not militarily interfere in Missouri. The agreement lasted three weeks, until General Lyon effectively repudiated the agreement on June 11, at the Planter's House in St. Louis, when he declared that Missouri and the Federal Government were now at war. See *Confederate Tales, 1861* for a copy of the agreement, *O.R.*, vol. 3:374–375; Banasik, *Confederate Tales, 1861*, 181–182; Britton, 18; Robert E. Shalhope, *Sterling Price: Portrait of a Southerner* (Columbia, MO, 197), 160–162, hereafter cited as Shalhope; Snead, *Fight for Missouri*, 161–162, 198–200.

64. P. G. T. Beauregard commanded the Confederate forces at Fort Sumter and the Confederate Army of the Potomac at the Battle of Bull Run, Virginia, on July 21, 1861. He would serve until the end of the war as one the Confederacy's highest ranking generals. Ezra J. Warner, *Generals in Gray: Lives of the Confederate Commanders* (Baton Rouge, LA, 1959), 22–23, hereafter cited as Warner, *Generals in Gray*.

duty did not warrant any further participation in the organization, composed as it was of two elements, Union and the Secession, that the time had come for those who were in favor of defending the flag to take their places under its folds, and for those who rejoiced in the act of war which have been enacted in Charleston harbor, to take their place separate and apart from those who were determined to stand by the Union.

My refusal was communicated to the assembled company, and my information was that, there was a sudden breaking of ranks, and "armed neutrality," from that day was no more thought of by the young men of that part of Missouri.

The next day I closed the public school under my charge, and, without tendering my resignation to the director, I proceeded at once to St. Louis with the intention of enlisting in one of the regiments then in process of organizing under the auspices and direction of Frank P. Blair. Meeting the mature gentlemen on Fourth Street opposite the Planters' hall, I informed him of my purpose, and asked for instructions.

"Why did you come to St. Louis to enlist? Can you not raise a company in your county said Blair."

Hadn't Thought of It.

I told him that I had not thought of as hazardous a step as that. In fact, it never entered my mind to make the attempt.

"Go back to your county, sir, organize a company of men, bring them back to St. Louis, and I will find a place for yourself and company in my regiment."

The next day I return to Franklin County, consulted with some of the prominent Union men there and secured from them promises of support and active aid in my undertaking and they were at once enrolled as an organizing committee. Those Southern sympathizers were not inactive during this time, but were putting forth their best efforts to create a fervor of enthusiasm for the cause of the South. Meetings were being held in many parts of the county, the stars and bars floated from many a tall flag staff, and it was with great difficulty and the exercise of the greatest vigilance that the older heads were able to control the younger ones and avoid violent conflicts on the occasions of those gatherings. But there was one sentiment that met with unanimous approval among all the adherence of the South, and that was that whatever St. Louis might do in the way of contributing men for the United States arsenal, not one man would be allowed to arrive or enlist in Uncle Sam's service from Missouri. Within the week then allowed for the organization of my company an incident occurred which in my judgment, materially aided me in my work. I was standing on the sidewalk in front of one of the stores facing the courthouse square, when the same young man who had before summoned me to take part in the drill approached me and asked me to step over to the fence enclosing the square. I complied with his demands and followed him.

When the fence was reached he turned upon me and said: "I understand that you are raising a company to take down to the United States arsenal. Is that so?"

I replied that it was none of his business; that if I saw fit to undertake such a task that I would do so.

At this moment I turned my eyes in the direction of one of the stores, and then I saw in the open door, a number of the relatives and friends of the young man watching our every move.

In a loud tone of voice I declared myself for the Union and against its enemies; and defied him and his friends to interfere with me then or at any time.

Information was quickly conveyed to my friends, and by the time we returned, to the first place of meeting I was surrounded by a coterie of daring men as the county could produce, and instead of being allowed to be intimidated or deterred from the work in hand, a nucleus for the company was then and there was formed, and each one forming the same started out to bring in one or more recruits to swell the ranks. With fifty or more men enrolled, we met secretly in the basement of Vitts mill, and completed the organization in the presence of the organizing committee before mentioned. I was then ready to start the next day for the United States arsenal and made known to the committee my plan for reaching said rendezvous. It was to march from Union to Pacific, eighteen miles, at night, take the accommodation train which left in the morning and by this means reach the arsenal during the day following our departure from Union. But the committee dissented from my plan, and urged as a ground for dissent the fact that I was taking the flower of the county from their midst; that even if we should succeed in reaching Pacific without meeting with armed opposition, the feeling of resentment would be so strong in the heart of the residence of the "Virginia neighborhood," as it was called, through which we would march, that revenge might be taken on the families and friends of the movement and civil war precipitated upon the then comparatively peaceful community. The plan of the committee was then announced as follows: the committee would see that all the men of the company should be at Washington on the Pacific Railroad on a certain date during the week, and that we should proceed to St. Louis by train from Washington.

On the afternoon of the day designated, about thirty men assemble at the station, awaiting the arrival of the train which was to convey us to St. Louis. There was no gathering of friends and relatives to bid us goodbye. The committee had taken the precaution that nothing of that kind should occur.

The only manifestations made were those of a few Southern sympathizers, who seem to be in possession of some gratifying knowledge. Many were the nods and winks which they exchanged, but their import and significance were for the moment unknown to the boys, who were on their way to don the blue.

But when the train stopped at the water tank above the depot there was a great shouting and hurrahing in the direction of the incoming train. The fact was soon discovered that on the train were two companies of the State Guard, or Minute Men of St. Louis, on their return from Jefferson City, whether they have been as an escort of the steamer *Isabel*, guarding the powder and military stores which Gov. Claiborne F. Jackson and the state officers had purchased from St. Louis parties.[65]

My friends gathered around, and with the organizing committee first mentioned, implored me to dismiss the man, abandoned the enterprise for a more favorable opportunity, and thereby save the danger of the conflict in this peaceable community.

Went Along with 'Em

But to me the voices of my alarm friends were like the buzzing of bees. I disregarded their appeals, and in fact, ignored their presence. I thought only of my men, who stood in the ranks, calmly awaiting my orders. My own feelings at that moment were hard to describe. I had no idea as to what would be the outcome if the state forces were of a hostile disposition. Whether they would scalp us, or mutilate our bodies, or to what excess they would go, I did not know. But, thinking only that I was in the presence of the enemy, I'd put on as bold a front as possible, and in a harsh and positive tone of voice–more like that of a steamboat mate that a new recruit–I commanded the man to enter the first car of the train. The men obeyed without a word of objection, and promptly too, and in a few minutes we were bowling away in the direction of St. Louis.

The two companies of "minute men" under Capt. Joseph Kelly and Martin Burke were in the two rear cars, the intervening cars of the train, occupied by terrified passengers, who imagined that the savage yells of the state soldiery indicated that war was about to begin sure enough.[66] When South Point was reached,

---

65. According to Thomas L. Snead, Joseph Kelly's Company escorted a lot of "several hundred hunting rifles, some camp and garrison equipage, and about seventy tons of gunpowder" to Jefferson City on May 7. The supplies were procured in St. Louis by purchase and "partly by force," with the powder costing $65,000, while the camp and garrison equipment, including "blankets, cloth clothing, etc." costing another $10,000. Of the powder, James Harding recorded that two owners were "compelled to have their magazines broken open" by Martin Burke's and Joseph Kelly's Companies when they refused to sell their powder. The two companies, under Kelly's orders, then boarded a steamboat for Jefferson City. The 100-man escort had nothing to do with the arms from Baton Rouge which arrived after Kelly had left St. Louis for Jefferson City. Louis S. Gerteis, *The Civil War in Missouri: A Military History* (Columbia, MO, 2012), 42, hereafter cited as Gerteis, *Missouri*; James E. McGhee, ed., *Service With the Missouri State Guard: The Memoir of Brigadier General James Harding* (Springfield, MO, 2000), 12–13, hereafter cited as McGhee, *Service With the Guard*; William Garret Piston and Richard W. Hatcher III, *Wilson's Creek: The Second Battle of the Civil War and the Men Who Fought It* (Chapel Hill, NC, 2000), 88, hereafter cited as Piston & Hatcher, *Wilson's Creek*; Snead, *Fight for Missouri*, 162–163.

66. Joseph M. Kelly, an Irishman, was a resident of St. Louis, a Catholic by religion and soldier in the British Army before coming to America. Prior to the Civil War, Kelly commanded the Washington Blues, a St. Louis, Missouri Volunteer Militia Company. At Wilson's Creek (August 10, 1861), Kelly commanded a 142-man MSG regiment, was wounded in the hand "which partially disabled it for life, and he would have lost it if he had not... put his pistol under his pillow and threaten to shoot any doctor who should attempt to amputate it." While still in the Guard, Mosby M. Parsons

as I sat at an open window with my weather eye on those "rear cars," a number of the "boys in gray" came up to where I was and invited me "to come of that there car."

"Why should I come out of this here car?" said I.

"Because," said Lieut. Bob O'Finney, the spokesman, who knew me well, "There is a lot of Dutch volunteers in that car, and we are going to clean them out, so you had better get out, or you might get hurt."[67]

I had barely sufficient time to inform the war-like Bob that I was in that car to stay, and that if he thought the job was going to be a one-sided affair, that he had best dismiss his mind on that accord, when the train started and the belligerent minute men scramble back to the aforesaid rear cars as rapidly as possible. Thereupon Capt. Joe Kelly came forward into our car. We had an explicit understanding that both parties must remain in their respective cars until St. Louis should be reached.

"You may go to the arsenal," said Capt. Kelly, "without interference on my

---

appointed Kelly commander of the 6th Division, MSG on April 9, 1862. Later, Kelly joined the staff of General Parsons, being appointed Adjutant General of a regular CSA brigade and later Parsons' Division. During the war one veteran recalled that Kelly "was a good officer and a man of deep religious sentiment, but he had a habit of swearing with almost every sentence." *O.R.*, vol. 8: 815; Banasik, *Missouri in 1861*, 163 n.12; Michael Flanagan, "The Memoirs of Dr. Robert J. Christie," Internet site flanagan@bcl.net, 58; Joseph A. Mudd, "What I Saw At Wilson's Creek," *Missouri Historical Review* 7 (October, 1912-July, 1913), 98; National Archives, Record Group 109, Confederate Records, Chapter 7, vol. 394, Parsons's staff; Richard C. Peterson, et al., *Sterling Price's Lieutenants: A Guide to the Officers and Organization of the Missouri State Guard* (Jefferson City, MO, 1995), 172, 181, hereafter cited as Peterson, el. al.

Born in Ireland, Martin Burke immigrated to the United States and eventually settled in St. Louis. A merchant by trade, Burke was a devout Catholic, his bother being a priest. Prior to the war he joined the St. Louis Greys Volunteer Militia, being elected 1st lieutenant in 1855. On June 27, 1860, following the election of John Knapp as lieutenant colonel of the 1st Missouri Militia Brigade, Burke was promoted to captain, a position he would hold until his capture at Camp Jackson. After his release Burke joined the Confederate Army, being elected captain of Company D, 1st Missouri Infantry (CSA), effective August 26, 1861. Burke served his entire time east of the Mississippi River, being wounded at Shiloh (April 6–7, 1862) and again at Champion's Hill (May 17, 1863). By war's end he had been promoted to lieutenant colonel commanding his regiment. *O.R.S.*, pt. 2, vol. 38: 382; Missouri Volunteer Militia Scrapbook, pages 5, 7, 11–12, 17 of unnumbered pages, W. R. Babcock Collection, Missouri Historical Society, hereafter cited as Missouri Militia Scrapbook; Phillip Thomas Tucker, *The South's Finest: The First Missouri Confederate Brigade From Pea Ridge to Vicksburg* (Shippensburg, PA, 1993), 87, 173.

67. Robert C. O'Finney or Finney as he was listed in various sources, served as a member of Burke's St. Louis Greys, rising in the ranks from 5th Sergeant to become a 2nd lieutenant by the time of his capture at Camp Jackson. When captured Finney was assigned to the Grimsley Guards, having been recently elected 2nd lieutenant. Following Camp Jackson, Finney joined Guibor's Battery, being elected the third lieutenant. He fought at Wilson's Creek, on August 10, after which his name disappears from all records, though he may have been at Pea Ridge where he was a captain serving as an aid-de-camp to General John B. Clark, Jr. *O.R.*, vol. 8: 320; "Battle of Wilson's Creek, MO.: Secession Narratives–Lieutenant Barlow's Account," *Rebellion Record*, vol. 2: Doc. 519–520; Carolyn Bartels, *Trans-Mississippi Men at War, Volume I: Missouri C.S.A.* (Independence, MO, 1998), 164, hereafter cited as Bartel, *Trans-Mississippi Men*; Missouri Militia Scrapbook, pages 18, 20 of unnumbered pages; Peckham, 133; Peterson, et. al., 109.

part, but," said he, significantly, "I'll not be responsible for your safety after you get there." I assured him that we were amply able to take care of ourselves either there or in the arsenal and with that he returned to his command.

We reached St. Louis at dusk, proceeded to Turner Hall and from there, on the next day, April 28, the men were marched by two at intervals of a block between each couple until the thirty men were within the walls of the United States arsenal. That night another detachment of the company joined us, and when the ranks were filled we were mustered into the service of the United States by Maj. Rufus Paxton [Saxton], U. S. A., for the term of three months, and were designated Co. A, Rifle battalion, First Regiment Missouri volunteers, the first company to enter the service for Missouri outside of St. Louis.[68]

* * * * * *

68. There was no Company A (Rifle Battalion) in the 1st Missouri Infantry (Three months), but there was a Company A (Rifle Battalion) in the 3rd Missouri (Three months) commanded by . When Murphy's men were mustered into Blair's 1st Regiment, they became members of Company A; however, Murphy was not the officer in the command. The unit was led by Captain Joseph Indest. Peckham, 120–121.

Major Rufus Paxton or variation of not found in the *Historical Register*; however, Murphy probably meant Rufus Saxton, the man who commanded Company A. Born in 1824, in Massachusetts, Saxton graduated from West Point in the Class of 1849 (number 18 of 43). At the time of the muster in of Murphy's men, Saxton was a 1st lieutenant serving in the 4th U.S. Artillery. After Camp Jackson, Saxton served on General Lyon's staff, after which he completed his military service east of the Mississippi River. Saxton was promoted to brigadier general in April 1862, a grade he held until the end of the war. He retired in 1888, and died in 1904. Boatner, 722–723; Gerteis, *Missouri*, 15; Heitman, vol. 1: 777, 862.

Item: Camp Jackson, Missouri, May 10, 1861 by Captain Otto C. Lademann, Late Captain Third Missouri Volunteers.[69]
Published: March 19, 1887.

The Capture of Camp Jackson

St. Louis, March 17

[Editor *Republican*]

In the days of my boyhood while attending college in Prussia, I happen to get hold of a German translation of "Uncle Tom's Cabin," and the impression which this remarkable book left in my mind was so decisive that when I afterwards landed on the shores of this republic I found myself a determined abolitionist, although I had never beheld a Negro slave. Accordingly, when the stormy year of 1861 came, my sentiments were naturally with the North and I was one of the first to become a member of the St. Louis "Union Guards," in January of the same year.[70]

We immediately began to drill at the old Washington Hall, on third and Elm streets, our chief instructor being Maj. Larned.[71] As I had originally been educated with a view of entering the Prussian army, and my fondness for the military

69. Otto Lademann joined Company E, 3rd Missouri Volunteers (Three months), on April 27, 1861, being appointed First or Orderly Sergeant on June 1. On July 25, he was transferred to Company B, being made a brevet Second Lieutenant. In addition to Camp Jackson, Lademannn was at Carthage (July 5) and at Wilson's Creek (August 10, 1861) where he was captured. Though captured at Wilson's Creek, Lademann was not properly exchanged until the latter part of 1862. Lademann was mustered out of the Third Missouri (Three months) on September 3, and when the regiment was reorganized as a three year regiment, Lademann joined Company F. Lademann eventually became the captain of Company F and during the Atlanta Campaign he commanded the 4th Ohio Light Battery composed of men from the 3rd, 12th and 17th Missouri Infantries. *O.R.*, vol. 62: 399–400; *O.R.S.*, pt. 2, vol. 36: 415–416; *O.R.S.*, Series 2, vol. 4: 695, 733; Otto C. Lademann, "Wilson's Creek," *Missouri Republican*, April 2, 1887; William Marvel, *Biographical Sketches of the Contributors to the MOLLUS* (Wilmington, NC, 1995), 182–183; Natioal Archives, Record Group M405, roll no. 413, Union Compiled Service Records, Third Missouri Infantry (Three month); Peckham, 121; Piston & Hatcher, *Wilson's Creek*, 77, 190; Winter, 50.
70. The "Union Guards" was one of several companies raised by Frank Blair, beginning on January 11, 1861, to ensure the security of the St. Louis Arsenal. Organized by the Safety Committee, the Union Guards replaced the Wide Awakes to counteract secessionists threats against the arsenal. The various commands were universally referred too as the "Union Guard" or "Union Legion" and included such colorful companies like the Black Jaegers, Lafayette Guards, Union Guards, Mounted Rangers and Mounted Citizen Guards to name but a few. Peckham, 44–45, 433, 438; Ryle, 196, 199–200.
71. Little is known of Major Larned, save he was a regular army officer on furlough in St. Louis in January 1861. A review of the *Historical Register of the United States Army* lists ten "Larneds;" two died before 1861, one was discharged in 1815, one joined after the Civil War, three joined during the Civil War, while only one attained the rank of captain, and Charles T. Larned was noted as a paymaster with no rank listed ;finally Benjamin F. Larned was a colonel and Paymaster of the U.S. Army. Heitman, vol. 1: 616; Steven Rowan, *Memoirs of a Nobody: The Missouri Years of an Austrian Radical, 1849–1866* (St. Louis, 1997), 278, hereafter cited as Rowan.

profession had not diminished, I entered upon my duties with the zealous aim of proving a good and brave soldier. After having become thoroughly acquainted with "Scott's Tactics," I was placed in charge of a squad of old, gray-hair patriots, to whom I was to reveal the mysteries of "Hay-foot, straw-foot, right, left," etc.[72] In February, pending the election of delegates to the famous state convention, we were provided with arms of the very poor quality and informed that we might be called upon by the authority of Mayor [Oliver D.] Filley to act as guardians of peace.[73] The election, however proceeding without any turbulence and resulting in a great Union victory, there was no necessity for our services. Meanwhile the diligence of the Southern sympathizers did some active work forming companies of "minute men."

Thus matters dragged on until the historic events of Fort Sumter, Lincoln's call for 75,000 volunteers, and

Gov. Johnston's [Jackson's] Refusal

to organize Missouri's quota of four infantry regiments [to] put an end to that awful suspense which had delayed the final issues for such a long time.[74] The

---

72. Lademann actually had previous experience as a drill instructor, in 1858–1859, while serving in the Illinois Volunteer Militia. Otto C. Lademann, "The Capture of 'Camp Jackson,' St. Louis, MO., Friday, May 10, 1861," *War Papers Being Papers Read Before the Commandery of the State of Wisconsin MOLLUS*, 4 vols. (Milwaukee, 1914; reprint ed., Wilmington, NC, 1993), vol. 4: 71, hereafter cited as Lademann, "Camp Jackson."

73. Oliver D. Filley was born on May 23, 1806, in Bloomfield, Connecticut, and moved to St. Louis in 1829 (Gerteis and Winter says 1833). A tinner by trade, Filley opened a stove manufacturing plant in 1849, with his brother, Giles (Winter says Chauncey, a New York cousin), who had moved to St. Louis in 1835. Filley married his sweetheart from Connecticut in 1835, and fathered seven children with his wife Chloe. A friend of Thomas H. Benton, Filley was also a director of the Bank of Missouri and a "early supporter of Frank Blair." A successful businessman, slave owner, and founding member of the Missouri Republican Party, Filley ran for St. Louis Mayor in 1858. and won a one year term. In 1859, Filley was re-elected to a two year term. As mayor, Filley "instituted the Fire Alarm Telegraph System, the first paid Fire Department, and horse car railroad lines." During the secession crisis, Filley was one of the founding members of the St. Louis Safety Committee, being elected President or Chairman of the group, which Walter Ryle labeled "the controlling element of the Union cause in St. Louis." During the war the Filley 's stove factory built iron plates for the Ead's ironclads and thirty cannon for the defense of St. Louis. In 1862, Oliver became a stockholder in the *St. Louis Union* which supported his friend Frank Blair. After the war Filley returned to his mercantile roots, dying on August 21, 1881, in Hampton, New Hampshire. Cari Carter, ed., *Troubled State: Civil War Journals of Franklin Archibald Dick* (Kirkville, MO, 2008), 235, hereafter cited as Carter; Gerteis, *Missouri*, 12; Gerteis, *St. Louis*, 41, 74; Parrish, *Frank Blair*, 148; Peckham, 35; Phillips, *Damned Yankee*, 141; Rowan, 279 n.14; Ryle, 191, 198; Smith, *Blair Family*, vol. 1: 211; Winter, 118–119.

74. Fort Sumter, South Carolina was fired on by Confederate troops on April 12, 1861, catapulting the country into the Civil War. The fort surrendered on April 14. The following day President Abraham Lincoln issued a call for 75,000 militia troops, to serve for three months. The troops were to "suppress" the rebellion and "cause the laws to be duly executed." On April 17, Governor Jackson responded to the call for troops refusing to comply. Jackson called the request "illegal, unconstitutional, and revolutionary in its object, inhuman and diabolical,." See **Appendix A** for

patriotic energetic work of Blair and Lyon, as well as the difficulties under which these fearless leaders labored, are well known to the reader, and all that I can add to the history of their success at Camp Jackson is the narrative of some particulars which may be read with interest by those who participated in the affair. It was on Friday, 26th of April that I entered the arsenal as a private of Co. E of Col. Siegel's [Sigel] Regiment, Third Missouri Volunteers [Three Months].[75] One-by-one or very small squads, we had to sneak down to the arsenal, so as to avoid a collision with the Southern sympathizers, but at the gate we assembled, that our company, under command of Capt. John E. Strodtmann [Strodkamp], marched in like true soldier boys, to be sworn in for ninety days' service. The little brick stable inside of the walls, which sheltered us that night, is still there, and reminding those of us who survived the war of the many incidents, serious and humorous, that usually attend the earlier days of recruit life.[76] It was very amusing to witness the above

---

Jackson full reply. *O.R.*, Series 3, vol. 1: 67–68, 82–83; Boatner, 299–300.

75. Franz Sigel, also known as the "Professor" or "Flying Dutchman," was born on November 18, 1824, in the grand duchy of Baden (Germany), graduated from the military academy at Karlsrule in 1843, and fought on the losing side in the German revolution in 1848, which was also known as the Hecker-Struve Insurrection. Immigrating to the United States in 1852, Sigel was living in St. Louis in 1861, when the Civil War began. During the early months of the war, the "Professor" as Sigel was often referred too, proved to be a recruiting magnet for Federal troops, of German ancestry in Missouri as the phrase "I fight mit Sigel" became a rallying cry for the German population. Native American troops had another opinion, with most not liking the man, seeing him as a "weasel." For his performance at Wilson's Creek, one Iowan wrote that Sigel "was no good; he was timid and inefficient." Still, Sigel was made a brigadier general on August 7, 1861, and for gallantry at Pea Ridge, Arkansas (March 6–8, 1862), he was promoted to major general. After Pea Ridge, Sigel was reassigned to the Eastern Theater of operations, where he completed his Civil War service. He died on August 21, 1902, in the state of New York. For a complete biography see *Missouri in 1861* of this series. Banasik, *Missouri in 1861*, 362–364; Jay Monaghan, *Civil War on the Western Border 1854–1865* (New York, 1955), 149, hereafter cited as Monaghan; "Francis Sigel, the Hero of Carthage," *Chicago Tribune*, July 17, 1861; Phillip Rutherford, "The Carthaginian Wars," *Civil War Times Illustrated* 25 (February, 1987), 43, hereafter cited as Rutherford; E. F. Ware, *The Lyon Campaign in Missouri: Being a History of the First Iowa Infantry and of the Causes Which Led up to its Organization, and how it Earned the Thanks of Congress Which it got Together With a Birdseye View of the Conditions in Iowa Preceding the Great Civil War of 1861* (Topeka, KS, 1907; reprint ed., Iowa City, IA, 1991), 336, hereafter cited as Ware.

The 3rd Missouri Infantry (Three months), like all the early Missouri regiments entered into the U.S. Service at the St. Louis Arsenal beginning on April 22, 1861, being issued arms and ammunition through it would not be mustered in until days later. In addition to the capture of Camp Jackson (May 10, 1861), the regiment was also at Carthage (July 5, 1861) and Wilson's Creek (August 10). Following Wilson's Creek the regiment return to St. Louis where it was mustered out on September 4, 1861. Dyer, 1323; Schofield, 34; *Union Army*, vol. 4: 257.

76. The *Official Records* and *Supplement* have the name as Strodtmann, while the muster roll has it as Strodkamp. Regardless, Strodkamp was born about 1827, and a resident of St. Louis, when he joined Company G, Third Missouri Infantry (Three months) on April 27, 1861. He was elected captain of the Company and later transferred to Company E, which he commanded at the Battle of Carthage on July 5, 1861, where he was wounded in the right shoulder. Returning to St. Louis, Strodtmann was mustered out on August 12. He later joined the 2nd Missouri Light Artillery Regiment, commanding Battery A, completing the remainder of his service in garrison duty in Missouri. *O.R.*, vol. 3:19; *O.R.*, vol. 22, pt.2: 765; *O.R.*, vol. 34, pt. 2: 204; *O.R.S.*, pt. 2, vol. 36: 439; Dyer, 1316–1317; David C. Hinze and Karon Farnham, *The Battle of Carthage: Border War in*

perplexity of the boys when they each received a ration of flour, beef, coffee, etc., together with camp-kettles and mess-pans, instead of regular meals. To be sure, many of them, ignorant of the science of cooking, retired to the hay loft that night with empty stomachs: In the course of the war we often would have welcomed such as "meal," as a feast not enjoyed so frequently as to be under estimated. The next morning we were supplied with muskets, and I was promoted to the position of second, or "drill" sergeant. A few days later, when an order from regimental headquarters called on

Brigadier General Franz Sigel

anyone to become a commissioned officer to report in person for special service. I was so fortunate as to be the favorite one. On 8th of May Col. Siegel sent for me and ordered me to go to the levee and ascertain

The Character and Destination

of the cargo of the steamer *J. C. Swan*, which had passed the arsenal on the previous day with a Confederate flag flying. Accompanied by a former steamboat man, I selected from my men, I proceeded on my mission and as we were neither in uniform nor carrying any arms we could easily ascertain of what the cargo of the boat anchored near the foot of Market Street and consisted and how it had been disposed of before our inspection occurred. The captain of the boat evidently cared nothing to hide his sentiments, for the *J. C. Swan* still flaunted its brand-new rebel flag right in the face of good old St. Louis. That day I could inform Col. Sigel the cargo had consisted of very heavy boxes marked marble slab, but containing cannon, as my informant thought, large quantities of shot and shell, and six small brass mortars, all of which had taken from the Baton Rouge arsenal in Louisiana, and had that very morning been loaded on drays and carted to Camp Jackson for the purpose of annihilating Gen. Lyon and the "damn Dutch," according to the informant's narrative.[77]

Southwest Missouri, July 5, 1861 (Campbell, CA, 1997). 197, 202, 277 n. 72, hereafter cited as Hinze & Farnham; National Archives, Record Group M405, roll no. 413, Union Compiled Service Records, 3rd Missouri Infantry (Three months).

77. On January 9, 1860, a 250-man force boarded the steamer *Natchez* at New Orleans, Louisiana, and the following day they captured the Baton Rouge Arsenal. With the bombardment of Ft. Sumter, on April 12, and President Lincoln's call for troops, on April 15, events began to move quickly in Missouri. On April 17, following Governor C. F. Jackson's refusal to supply troops to the Federal Government, Jackson sent Captains Bazil Duke and Colton Greene to Montgomery, Alabama, to request the Confederacy's support in capturing the St. Louis Arsenal. Six days later, President Jefferson Davis agreed to help the Missourians capture the arsenal, by providing two

After staring at me as if absent-minded (a look peculiar to Col. Siegel) he told me that I would have to go to Camp Jackson to find out the number and quantity of the guns as well as the quantity of ammunition.[78] At the same time he cautioned me to carefully observed the arrangement of the camp, its approaches, topographical position, and everything else of military interest. I can't say that I liked the kind of service very much; it looked to me so much like espionage, but

---

12-lb howitzers and two 32-lb siege guns. These supplies, plus 500 muskets, several mortars, with ammunition, were procured from the Baton Rouge Arsenal. Following Davis' approval, Duke and Greene proceeded to New Orleans where Greene contracted the *J. C. Swan* to deliver the goods. From New Orleans the pair boarded the Swan, which was described as a "stern wheel river boat," and moved to Baton Rouge, where they loaded their munitions. Proceeding up river the *Swan* delivered their cargo late on the night of May 8 or early morning on the 9th. Major James R. Shaler loaded the munitions unto numerous conveyances and delivered them to Camp Jackson, where they were stored in a wooded area near General Daniel M. Frost's tent. The *Swan* and many of the munitions were subsequently seized following the capture of Camp Jackson. NOTE: Hans C. Adamson and Louis Gerteis both incorrectly named the boat the "*Swon*." Additionally, James Broadhead wrote that the Chief of Police, who was James McDonough, directed the move of the munitions which was not correct according to Thomas Snead. *O.R.*, vol. 3: 386–387; *O.R.*, Series 2, vol. 1: 107–108; Hans Christian Adamson, *Rebellion in Missouri: 1861 Nathaniel Lyon and His Army of the West* (Rahway, NJ, 1961), 44, hereafter cited as Adamson; Britton, 7; Broadhead, Missouri *MOLLUS*, vol. 14: 20; *Confederate Military History*, vol. 10: *Louisiana* by John Dimitry, 20–21, hereafter cited as Dimitry, *Louisiana, Confederate Military History*; Gerteis, *St. Louis*, 112; McElroy, 63, 69–70; Moore, *Missouri, Confederate Military History*, vol 9: 31; Parrish, *Frank Blair*, 100; Peckham, 96, 136; Phillips, *Damned Yankee*, 181–182; Piston & Hatcher, *Wilson's Creek*, 33; Snead, *Fight for Missouri*, 167–168.

78. Federal spies were coming and going to Camp Jackson from the time that the camp was established on May 6. Nathaniel Lyon, not wanting to leave any thing to chance, made a personal reconnaissance of the camp which he considered a "nest of traitors" on May 9. Borrowing a dress and carriage from Frank Blair's mother-in-law, Mrs. Mira Alexander, Lyon dawned a black veil and bonnet to cover his heavy beard and headed to Camp Jackson. Seated next to Lyon, was J. J. Witzig, a member of the Safety Committee, who frequently took carriage rides with Mrs. Alexander. The pair had no difficulty entering Camp Jackson, allowing Lyon to complete his reconnaissance at a leisurely pace, taking about thirty minuets. Returning to his headquarters Lyon completed his plans for taking the camp the following day. As it turns out General Harney, the Department commander, was due to return to St. Louis on Saturday the 11th and Lyon feared that Harney would not approve his actions. However, when Harney did return to St. Louis, on May 11, he supported Lyon's actions and further issued a Proclamation on May 14 "in which he declared the Military Bill an indirect Secession Ordinance...and pronounced it null and void." See **Appendix A** for a copy of the Proclamation. NOTE: In Covington's and Smith's accounts of the incident, they state that Witzig followed the Lyon barouche in his own buggy. James Covington, William Smith and Christopher Phillips also stated that Mrs. Alexander was the mother-in-law of Frank Blair, while Adamson recorded it was Blair's mother; however, Rowan, quoting from the Charles Drake Papers states that Mrs. Alexander was Dick's mother-in law. Cari Carter, a relative of Franklin Dick, settles the matter recording that Mira Alexander was indeed Frank Blair's mother-in-law and the carriage used in the spying came from her and not from Dick as Adamson, Covington and Peckham recorded. See **Appendix A** for Harney's complete Proclamation. *O.R.* vol. 3: 369; Adamson, 41, 44, 49; Brooksher, 56–58; Carter, xii, xxiv, xviii; James W. Covington, "The Camp Jackson Affair: 1861," *Missouri Historical Review* 55 (May, 1961), 204–205, hereafter cited as Covington; Gurnsey & Alden, 107; Parrish, *Frank Blair*, 100; Peckham, 139–141; Phillips, *Damned Yankee*, 178; Rowan, 293–294 n. 5; Smith, *Blair Family*, vol. 2: 44; Snead, *Fight for Missouri*, 168–170; Snead, "First Year in Missouri," vol. 1: 266; *Union Army*, vol. 4: 242.

compelled to obey orders, and anxious to serve the Col., I was willing to overcome these scruples and wended my way

To the Camp.

No difficulty was experienced in gaining entrance. It was pleasantly situated in "Lindell's pasture," bounded in general on the north by Olive Street, east by Compton Avenue, south by Laclede Avenue., and west by Grand Avenue. The surface presented a green swand [swath] well shaded by handsome forest trees, a little dry creek running from north to south, and dividing the camp into equal parts, the one on the east side being the smaller and gently sloping from Compton avenue toward the creek. There I found the artillery and cavalry. The larger (western) part occupied by the infantry, including the headquarters of

General Daniel M. Frost

Gen. Frost, sloped from Grand avenue toward the creek.[79]

To the best of my recollection the front or "color" line of infantry camp, looked eastward toward, facing the city. A light, wooden bridge south of Olive Street formed the line of communication between the two parts of the camp. West of the bridge in front of the color line I found the ordinance and the ordinance stores brought up by the steamer *J. C. Swan*. These stores I found to consist of boxed up iron guns of antediluvian pattern and some solid shot, unfixed shell and grapeshot, in addition to which I noticed six small brass mortars fixed on oak boards, which only lacked pestals to make the handsomest apothecary signs imaginable. I did not notice any gun carriages. All that I beheld was utterly unfit for troops destined to operate in the field and duty fit for a military museum or junk-shop. The old Wesleyan Cemetery, opposite the southwest corner of the camp, was the most commanding height, topographically, covering the view of the entire camp, and a good position for the artillery. There was another elevation of a similar nature on

---

79. The "Lindell's pasture" was commonly known as "Lindell's Grove." In accordance with Missouri State Law, Governor Claiborne F. Jackson issued General Order No. 7 on April 22, 1861, which ordered the Missouri Volunteer Militia to assembled. Brigade commanders were required to specify the point of assembly by May 3, 1861. In St. Louis, General Daniel M. Frost ordered his brigade to assemble on May 6, 1861 at Lindell Grove on Olive Street Road. "Governor's Proclamation–General Order No. 7," *Missouri Republican*, May 2, 1861,; "Military–General Order No. 23," *Missouri Republican*, May 5, 1861.

the northeast corner of Olive Street and Compton Avenue (on the other side of the) where the natural level of the prairie was some

Eighteen or Twenty Feet Above

that of Olive Street in consequence of its grading, and also affording a sweeping position for artillery. This spot would actually be occupied on the 10th of May, the day of our advanced, by Backhoff's [Backof's] Battery.[80]

With this information I returned to the arsenal, making a written report to Col. Sigel, accompanied by a little map, sketched under my direction, by Private Robert J. Fisher, afterwards captain in the Seventeenth Missouri volunteers.[81] The next day I was again ordered to appear before Col. Siegel, who I met in consultation with some volunteer officers of the artillery, discussing Fisher's sketch which was lying on the table before them. Maj. Backoff interrogated me concerning the practicability of the wooden bridge in Camp Jackson for artillery. After explaining to the gentlemen present why I considered the bridge was out of the question, but that the cemetery on the opposite elevation would offer a dominating position to a battery, I was dismissed for the day. On the morning of the Friday, the 10th, I took

---

80. Backof's Battery was Battery A of Backof's Battalion, Missouri Light Artillery (Three months). Battery A was composed of four 12-pound howitzers and was mustered into service on April 22, 1861. At Camp Jackson, the battery was commanded by Major Franz, Francis or Frank Backof, who was born in the Duchy of Baden (Germany), in about 1822. Conscripted into the military, Backof rose in the ranks to become a sergeant-major of artillery. During the 1948 revolution in Germany, Backof fought on the losing side, serving part of the time with Franz Sigel. Captured during the revolution, Backof was sentenced to prison, but had his sentence computed in 1851, if he immigrated. Moving to St. Louis, Backof was employed as a contractor and served at one time on the City Council. He joined the Missouri Volunteers on April 22 and was promoted to major, commanding at battalion of artillery, on May 18, 1861. Following Camp Jackson, Backof's Battalion or portions thereof served at Carthage and Wilson's Creek, after which it was mustered out of the service. Later, as the war progressed, Backoff re-enlisted in the Missouri Volunteer forces, commanding Battery L, 1st Missouri Artillery Regiment. The battery fought at Prairie Grove (December 7, 1862), its only major engagement. When the regiment was reorganized in February 1864, Backoff was promoted to major. No futher information found on him after that date. NOTE: Some accounts have Backof's Battery with six guns, all 6-pounders. However, Lademann has it as only four guns. *O.R.*, vol. 22, pt. 2: 417; *O.R.S.*, pt. 2, vol 36: 66, 136–138; Banasik, *Embattled Arkansas*, 533; William G. Bek, "The Civil War Diary of John T. Beugel, Union Soldier," *Missouri Historical Review* 40 (April, 1946), 309–310, hereafter cited as Bek, "Beugel Diary"; Covington, 205; Otto C. Lademann,"The Battle of Carthage. Friday, July 5, 1861," 4 vols. *War Papers Being Papers Read Before the Commandery of the State of Wisconsin MOLLUS* (Milwaukee, 1914; reprint ed., Wilmington, NC, 1993), vol. 4: 132, hereafter cited as Lademann, "Battle of Carthage"; Lademann, "Camp Jackson," 72; National Archives, Record Group M405, roll no. 347, Union Compiled Service Records, Backof's Missouri Artillery Battalion (Three months); Piston & Hatcher, *Wilson's Creek*, 34–35, 344.

81. Robert I. or J. or S. Fisher or Fischer, joined Company F, 3rd Missouri Infantry (Three months) on April 27, 1861, fought at Carthage on July 5, and was promoted to corporal on July 24. After Wilson's Creek, he returned to St. Louis where he was mustered out on August 12, 1961. National Archives, Record Group M405, roll no. 412, Union Compiled Service Records, 3rd Missouri Infantry (Three months).

out the company to drill as usual, when at 10 o'clock, we were instructed to return to quarters immediately, where we were ordered to hasten with our dinner. Each man received 10 rounds of ball cartridges, which, for the want of cartridge boxes, we put in the pockets of our coats or pantaloons, the caps in our vest pockets.[82] We were also directed to pick out, each, a white belt and a plate, from a large pile in the main arsenal building. I presume this was for the purpose of adding to our military appearance, for the rotten old things seem to be worth little, and they must have been slumbering in the quiet shades of arsenal since the Mexican War.

Shortly after 12 noon, the company was re-formed in order to "Load at will! Load." With joyous a clarity our boys responded, every man

Fully Understanding

that we were about to move on Camp Jackson. At about 1 o'clock the head of our column marched out of the arsenal, led by our regimental band, playing a gay march, our national colors proudly fluttering in the soft May breeze.[83] If we did present a rather motley appearance in our simple citizen garb, our shiny new muskets and their glittering bayonets, sparkled brightly in the rays of the sun and with proud steps we eagerly marched forward to strike the first offensive blow in St. Louis. On our road, along Carondelet Ave., Elm, Seventh, Walnut, Tenth, Olive, and west to Camp Jackson, our march was filled with signs of positive approval,

---

82. Adamson wrote that the men were issued forty rounds of ammunition, clearly wrong. Adamson, 53–54.

83. A total of seven columns departed various locations; the volunteers comprised three of the columns, while the Home Guard numbered four. Blair's 1st Regiment, initially marched from Jefferson Barracks at 8:00 a.m., then to the arsenal where they arrived between noon and 1:00 p.m. All the commands, including Blair's command next headed for Camp Jackson. Of the volunteers, Blair's 1st Regiment moved from the arsenal, followed by the regulars. Henry Boernstein's 2nd Missouri marched from the Marine Barracks Hospital, while Sigel's 3rd Missouri and Nicholas Schuettner's 4th Missouri Volunteers both came from the arsenal, following Blair;s regiment 1. Blair's 1st Regiment deployed on the north side of Camp Jackson; Boernstein's 2nd Regiment deployed to the west of the camp; Sigel's 3rd took their post east of the camp with Backof's Artillery, while the 4th "stopped along Laclede [Avenue] at the southern side of the camp but near its east end." Per orders, the 1st Reserve Regiment of the Home Guard departed Jaeger's Garden and "occupied the rising ground east of the camp" just to the south of Sigel's regiment. Herman Kallmann's 2nd Reserve Regiment, departed from their headquarters on Chouteau Avenue, sending only John T. Fiala's 1st Battalion. They followed the 1st Reserve to guard the western approaches to the camp from Chestnut Street. John McNeil's 3rd Reserve left from "Turner Hall at Third and Walnut Street" to control the southeastern corner of Camp Jackson, while B. Gratz Brown's 4th Reserve Regiment marched from their headquarters at "Uhrig's Cave" (Peckham says it was Bechner's Garden, on Fifth Street") to block the approaches to the camp from Garrison Avenue. All were schedule to arrive at 2:30 p.m.; however assorted delays, caused by a "severe storm" the night before, held up the various columns, according to Christopher Phillips, but all still managed to arrive at about the same time 3:15 p.m. and surrounded the camp. *O.R.* Series 2, vol. 1: 108; *O.R.S.*, pt. 2, vol. 36: 251, 370, 463–465; Adamson, 53, 56; Broadhead, *Missouri MOLLUS*, vol. 14:22; Covington, 205; Gerteis, *St. Louis*, 103–104; Parrish, *Frank Blair*, 101; Peckham, 118; Phillips, *Damned Yankee*, 187; Winter, 44.

cheering and waving of handkerchiefs, some kind matrons even shedding tears in the expectation of mishaps. At Turner's Hall we exchanged military compliments with Col. [John] McNeil's Third Missouri Reserve Corps, his regiment presenting arms when we passed by.[84] From Olive to Tenth, however, we were greeted with a dead and ominous silence, interrupted occasionally by gestures expressing utmost contempt, a half audible malediction or fervor with that the " Dutch" might get to a very hot place.[85]

It was about 2:30 when we reached our destination. The right of our regiment halted near the corner of Compton Avenue, and Olive Streets. The guns of Maj. Backhoff's battery were placed on our right and rear on the prairie commanding the camp. We could see the First Missouri Infantry (Col. Blair) rapidly advancing up Grand Avenue at a double-quick pace, endeavoring to reach Olive;[86] another column was seen debouching from Market Street and quickly

---

84. John McNeil was born on February 14, 1813, in Halifax, Nova Scotia, Canada, moved to Boston and in 1840, made St. Louis, Missouri, his permanent home. On May 8, 1861, the 3rd Missouri Infantry U.S. Reserve Corps was mustered into service with McNeil appointed colonel the same day. After Camp Jackson the 3rd participated in an expedition to Fulton, Missouri, where they had an engagement with General Thomas A. Harris' 2nd Division, MSG, losing 22 killed and wounded. The regiment then was mustered out of the service on August 18, 1861. McNeil, for his part, was appointed a colonel (to date from December 7, 1861), and assigned to command the 2nd MSM Cavalry Regiment. On June 4, 1862, McNeil was assigned to command the North-east Division of Missouri a position he held during the incident at Palmyra, where several rebel supporters were executed. For his executions at Palmyra and for his earlier elimination of rebel prisoners, during the Summer of 1862, McNeil was branded a "'butcher.'" On November 29, 1862, he was promoted to brigadier general and a brevet major general on April 12, 1865. McNeil spent his entire Civil War career in Missouri, except for a short stint, commanding in Louisiana. The highlight of McNeil's career came during Peice's 1864 Missouri Raid where he commanded a brigade in Alfred Pleasant's Division. See *Confederate Tales, 1862* for a complete biography and photograph. *O.R.*, vol. 3: 1; *O.R.*, vol. 13: 417; *O.R.*, vol. 22, pt. 2: 378–379, 666; *O.R.S.*, pt. 2, vol. 26: 448,-4540; Michael E. Banasik, *Confederate "Tales of the War" In the Trans-Mississippi Part Two: 1862. Unwritten Chapters of the Civil War West of the River Volume VII* (Iowa City, IA, 2011), 176–177, hereafter cited as Banasik, *Confederate Tales, 1862*; Dyer, 1323, C. M. Farthing, *Monroe County Missouri: "Chronicles of the Civil War in Monroe County"* (Independence, MO, 1997), 69; General Orders of Missouri (1862), General Orders No. 12 (April 9, 1862), Missouri Historical Society; Heitman, vol. 1: 679; Joseph A. Mudd, *With Porter in North Missouri: A Chapter in the History of the War Between the States* (Washington, 1909), 308–309; Sifakis, *Who Was Who in the Union*, 259–260; Warner, *Generals in Blue*, 306; Winter, 114.

85. Of the 1850 population of St. Louis about 15,000 were Irish immigrants, who settled along the rivers of Missouri and disliked Germans, or Dutch as they called them. The antipathy for Germans dated back to the days of William the Orange and his persecutions against Ireland in 1689. Beginning in the late 1840's Missouri received 150,000 German immigrants who had fled their homes following the 1848 Revolution. St. Louis received about one half the number. The Germans brought with them their many customs, but more importantly, their dislike of slavery and Irish-men. The Southerners, Irish, and old resident French were supporters of the "Sacred Institution of Slavery," thus ensuring unending conflict with the Germans of Missouri, who were frequently referred too as the "Damn Dutch." McElroy, 14–17, 38.

86. The 1st Missouri Infantry (Three months) entered Federal Service on April 27, 1861, electing Frank Blair as their colonel and were probably mustered into the army on April 30 or May 1. Following Camp Jackson the 1st was reorganized as a three year command on June 11 (Dyer says June 10). and proceeded by river boat to Jefferson City. They fought at Boonville (June 17), Dug

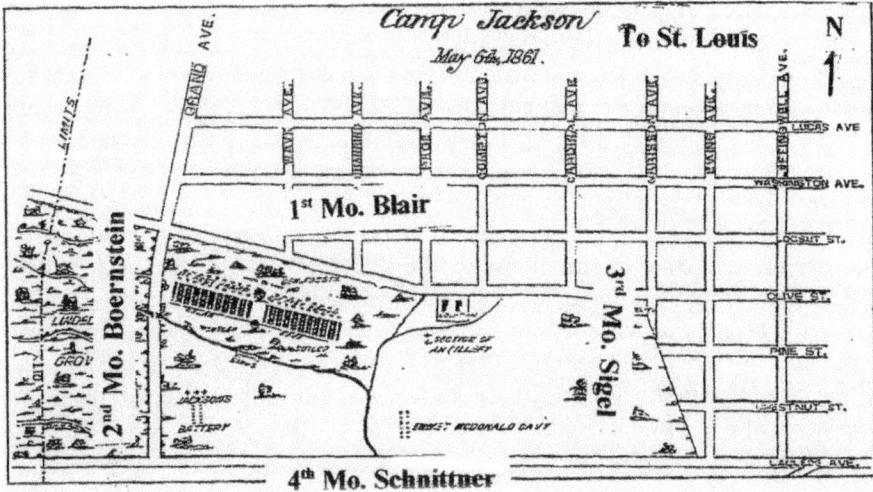

Moving Westward

to reach Grand Avenue, whilst a battalion of regulars, under Capt. [Thomas W.] Sweeney and Lieut, [William L.] Lathrop, moved from Olive southward to form a junction with the Market Street column, breaking down all fences while advancing to admit the uninterrupted maneuvering of troops.[87] The "state troops" being

Springs (August 2) and Wilson's Creek, after which the regiment returned to St. Louis. Reorganized a second time, the regiment was designated the 1st Missouri Light Artillery Regiment on September 1, 1861, and was mustered in on September 18, 1861. The command then served until the end of the war with the last units being mustering out on August 23, 1865. *O.R.S.*, pt. 2, vol. 36: 7, 15–16, 19, 23, 26; Dyer, 1321; Phillips, *Damned Yankee*, 165; Rassieur, 38; Snead, *Fight for Missouri*, 164; *Union Army*, vol. 4: 257, 280.

87. Thomas W. Sweeny was born in Ireland in 1820, immigrated to the United States at the age of twelve, settled in New York, and served in the 2nd New York Infantry as a 2nd lieutenant, during the Mexican War. At the Battle of Churubusco, Sweeny lost his right arm, but remained in the army until the beginning of the Civil War. A Regular Army captain (January 19, 1861), Sweeny was at the capture of Camp Jackson in 1861, and later at Sigel's defeat at Wilson's Creek. Sweeny was promoted to a Missouri brigadier general on May 20,1861, commanding the five-regiment United States Reserve Corps, but resigned on August 14, following the Battle of Wilson's Creek. "Although Sweeny was a regular army man, West Pointers looked on him with condescension, because he had risen from the ranks." Appointed the colonel of the 52nd Illinois Infantry on January 20, 1862, Sweeny completed his Civil War service on the east side of the Mississippi River. On March 16, 1863, Sweeny was promoted to brigadier general. In December 1865, Sweeny was dismissed from the army, and the following year he participated in the "Fenian Raid" into Canada which attempted to claim the country for Ireland. Even though the operation ended "ignominiously," he was reinstated into the U.S. Army in the Fall 1866. Sweeny retired from the army in 1870, and died on April 10, 1892. Boatner, 823; Broadhead, *Missouri MOLLUS*, vol. 14: 19; Heitman, vol. 2: 939; R. I. Holcombe and W. S. Adams, *An Account of the Battle of Wilson's Creek or Oak Hills* (Springfield, MO, 1883; reprint ed., Springfield, MO, 1961), 7, hereafter cited as Holcombe & Adams; Monaghan, 149; Warner, *Generals in Blue*, 491–491.

Warren L. Lothrop was a resident of Leeds, Maine, and a Mexican War veteran. He entered hemmed in on all sides by a largely superior force, outnumbering them several times, were asked to surrender.[88] The surrender does not reflect in the slightest degree on the military honor of Gen. D. M. Frost and the troops under his command; they simply submitted to the inevitable.[89] Shortly after 3 o'clock our regiment was ordered to shoulder arms and march into the camp, and the column moved into the camp grounds from the northeast corner, passing the "state troops," who were formed on our right without arms or accouterments, officers retaining their horses and side arms. While we marched in and the "state troops" out we passed very close to each other. The behavior of both parties was decorous and gentlemanly. Some slight bantering jokes were exchanged, the rank and file of the "state troops," assuring us that they would see us again under more advantageous circumstances (which they certainly did), and we answering that we would try and take care of them in the same manner as to-day. Some of the officers of the state troops, however, looked exceedingly disheartened.[90] But the attitude, of the mob

---

the U.S. Army on June 23, 1846, as a private in the Engineer Corps, rising through the ranks Lothrop was promoted to a 2nd lieutenant of the 4th U.S. Artillery on February 21, 1857. Being stationed in St. Louis during the secession crisis, Lothrop joined Blair's 1st Missouri Infantry (Three months), being mustered in as the captain of Company B on April 22. Lothrop remained with the 1st Missouri as the war progressed, becoming the major of the reorganized 1st Missouri Light Artillery Regiment. Later he was promoted to lieutenant colonel of the command and then colonel on October 21, 1862. Lothrop remained in the army after the war ended, being promoted to lieutenant colonel in the Regular Army "for gallant and meritorious service during the war." He died on October 31, 1866. Heitman, vol. 2: 642; McElroy, 53; Peckham, 120.

88. The force surrounding Camp Jackson were estimated at between 6–7,000, while the State Militia, when they surrendered, numbered 79 officers and 590 men for a total of 669. Of the offers and men taken at Camp Jackson, only 489 were "found desirous of joining their fortunes with secession and General Price," according to Charles Howland, Commissioner of Exchanges. This would suggest that 180 supported the Union or wanted to remain completely neutral. Further, there were some among the exchanged who never joined the Confederacy like Captain James George and Lieutenant Colonel John Knapp; George returned to St. Louis and apparently never reentered either of the armies, while Knapp joined the Union Army commanding 8th EMM in September 1863, and later served as aid to the Governor Hall during Price's 1964 Raid. O.R., vol. 34, pt. 4: 87; O.R., vol. 41, pt. 1: 464; O.R., Series 2, vol. 1: 116, 123; "The Riot In St. Louis, MO, May 10, 1861," Rebellion Record, vol. 1: Doc. 234; Phillips, Damned Yankee, 187; Snead, Fight for Missouri, 171.

89. According to John Q. Burbridge, who was present at Camp Jackson, General Frost was given ample warning of the approaching Union troops and could have easily ordered his camp disbanded before Lyon's command arrived. Instead, Frost intended to remain in place and resist any attack that occurred at night; however, Frost told a group of officers "from different parts of the state." that "if Captain Lyon marches out in the day, surrounds my camp and demands a surrender in the name and by the authority of the United States Government, I shall not resist but shall surrender to the United States flag." "Acts and Deeds of Col. Burbridge's Regiment," 6–7, Thomas L. Snead Papers, Missouri Historical Society, hereafter cited as , "Col. Burbridge's Regiment"; Banasik, Missouri Brothers in Gray, 11.

90. Of the 79 state officers captured at Camp Jackson many went on to join the MSG and later the Confederate Army. The most prominent among the captives was Captain Emmett MacDonald, who was elected by the other officers to challenge their capture and designation as "Prisoners of War." Urial Wright, a prominent lawyer and secessionist, sued in the Samuel Treat's Federal District Court of Eastern Missouri, on behalf of Captain MacDonald, claiming "that a Federal force

city roughs, pressing close to our lines, was execrable. Frenzied with rage at the success of the Unionists, they menaced our troops with

Bludgeons and Drawn Revolvers

employing at the same time the vilest epithets in the slang dictionary. Occasionally I would see one of our men leave the ranks to apply the but of his musket to some young rough who been conspicuous in venting his spiteful salutes.

Our regiment, in marching west, south of Olive, reached the little bridge connecting the camp, after crossing which we filed to the left, and, coming to a front, faced the city in the rear of the creek, right toward Market Street, the left near Olive. The state troops had left the camp, and being placed between the ranks of Col. Blair's First Missouri were being conducted to arsenal. As Blair's Regiment moved eastward its place was taken by Col. [Henry] Boernstein's Second Missouri, the rear of which extended back to Grand Avenue.[91] Two of our companies

had no right to capture a State force" that was legally assembled under the laws os the State of Missouri. Furthermore, the parole offered him "implied that the Camp Jackson muster had been an act of rebellion." MacDonald eventually won the case and his unconditional release in Springfield, Illinois. In early November 1861, the St. Louis law firm of Decker & Voorhis as a continued response to the Camp Jackson seizure, initiated a law suit against Frank Blair and some twenty other Unionist officers who participated in the capture of Camp Jackson. The suit sought damages of $10,000 each as "they were greatly damaged in reputation, in their business relations and in other respects…in consequence of this imprisonment and illegal and wilful and malicious and wrongful detention." The results of the suit are unknown, though I suspect that nothing became of it. Banasik, *Missouri Brothers in Gray*, 13; William Bell [Bull], "Camp Jackson Prisoners," Confederate Veteran 31 (July, 1923): 261; "The Camp Jackson Affair to Be Tried In Court," *Chicago Tribune*, November 7, 1861; "Colonel Emmett McDonald," *The Daily Southern Crisis* (Jackson, MS), February 13, 1863; Gerteis, *St. Louis*, 128; Gurnsey & Alden, 107; "The Riot In St. Louis, MO, May 10, 1861," *Rebellion Record*, vol. 1: Doc. 235; W. J. Tenney, *The Military and Naval History of the Rebellion in the United States* (New York, 1866; reprint ed., Mechanicsburg, PA, 2003), 51, hereafter cited as Tenney.

91. After President Lincoln's call for four Missouri volunteer regiments, Frank Blair had no trouble securing the men necessary to man the various commands. The 2nd Missouri Infantry (Three months) was one of those regiments. Mustered in on April 26, 1861, the regiment elected the fifty-six year old Henry Boernstein the colonel of the command. In addition to Camp Jackson, the 2nd, or portions thereof, were also at the Battles of the First Boonville, Dug Springs and Wilson's Creek or performed garrison duty at Boonville and Jefferson City. Toward the end of July 1861, the regiment returned to St. Louis where it was mustered out; however most of the command reorganized and on September 10, 1861, became the 2nd Missouri Volunteer Infantry (Three years). The new command served briefly in the Trans-Mississippi, fighting at Pea Ridge, Arkansas (March 6–8, 1862), before completing their service in the Western Theater of operations. Boernstein, for his part, returned to civilian life, following the demise of the three month command, leaving the fighting "to younger more capable" men; however, the Chicago Tribune recorded that Boernstein left because of ill health. Born in Hamburg, Germany in 1805, Boernstein tried a number of profession, including a five year stint in the Austrian Army, before journalism caught his attention while studying at the University of Vienna. Following the 1848 Revolution in Germany, he moved briefly to Illinois in 1849, before settling in St. Louis in 1850, where he became the editor, and, later owner, of "the most important German-language newspaper in Missouri," the *Anzeiger des Westerns*. "Boernstein also owned a hotel and a brewery and operated the city's largest

had been left at entrances of the camp, surrounded by the aforementioned mob, and it was here where, at nearly half passed 3 or 4 o'clock, the firing commenced. After a few scattering shots the fire assumed the form of "fire by file." It never grew into a full round volley. I could see it creep rapidly along the front of the Second Missouri, their fire completely enfilading the position of our regiment. But the height of the Olive Street elevation caused their balls to pass harmlessly over our heads. When the fire reached our left wing (standing near the south of Olive) it was taken up by our men and quickly crept along our front which was directed as described toward the city. The whole commons were covered with a mass of fleeing men, women, horses and vehicles of all kinds, all:

Running Pell-Mell,

down the line of our regiment for the shelter of the city.

Col. Siegel came rushing down the line of our regiment, and ordered us to "cease firing; lie down," and the firing ceased as rapidly as it had commenced, the whole episode lasting but a couple of minutes. Yet it threw a gloom over the whole day, the killed and wounded being, with very few exceptions, noncombatants and including some ladies, for whom everyone felt the deepest sorrow. The firing was one of those unavoidable accidents that frequently happened to new and undisciplined troops, and the parties to be blamed for it are those desperate roughs, with their ready revolvers, who undoubtedly commenced the fray. It had the affect of clearing the environs of the camp of all sightseeing people, men and women, who ought to have remained home, for it is the greatest folly for noncombatants to force their presence on the scene of armed conflicts unless their occupation or duty compels them to be present.[92]

---

theater as an opera house." Following his brief wartime service Boernstein took a diplomatic post in Bremen, in September 1861, where he remained until 1866. Boernstein next moved to Vienna, where he died in September 1892. NOTE: According to Frederick Dyer the regiment organized on April 22 and was mustered out on August 31; however, Boernstein's memoirs clearly have the date as April 26, while the muster out occurred at the end of July or early August 1861. *O.R.*, vol. 3: 13, 48; Banasik, *Confederate Tales, 1861*, 107–108 n. 134; C., "Affairs In Missouri," *Chicago Tribune*, July 10, 1861; Dyer, 1322; Gerteis, *Missouri*,18; Rowan, 4–6, 283–284, 290–292, 318–319, 335–337, 355; *Union Army*, vol. 4: 257; Winter, 43.

92. The incident that Lademann described was variously known as the "Camp Jackson provocation," the "St. Louis Massacre" or the "Camp Jackson Massacre," depending on wether you supported the North or the South. Following the capture of Frost's Missouri Militia Brigade, the prisoners were marched off to the St. Louis Arsenal, being met by an angry, rock-throwing, epithet mocking crowd and curious onlookers. In the rear of the column, according to Lademann in another article, "some rebel scoundrel, perched in a tree, fired his pistol on our troops and wounded Capt. [Constantin] Blandowski of the 3rd Missouri." However, it appears that the initial fire began at the front of the escorting column, manned by regular troops. One mob member, "as the crowd cheered around him," fired three shots at Lieutenant Rufus Saxton, missing him. A few shots were fired over the heads of the crowd and the bayoneting of the belligerent, and drunk pistoleer, dispersed the crowd with no further incident at the front of the column. Shortly thereafter, Captain Blandowski was shot in the leg, and as he fell, according to John McElroy and James Covington,

The Fourth Regiment (Col. [Nicholas] Schuettner [or Schittner]) was added to the garrison of the camp, Col. Siegel was placed in command and at 5:00 p.m. all other troops had left the camp and marched back to the arsenal.[93] While the Fourth Regiment occupied the tents our regiment was kept on duty. We were ordered to stack our arms and bivouac near the color line, to be ready during the whole night in case any attack should be attempted. As soon as the arms were stacked and rank broken, I went out on

A Little Foraging Expedition.

Wending my way to the pavilion tent of the former commander of the camp, taking advantage of my reconnaissance two days previously, I secured a nice mattress, which I consider much preferable to the swarthy bed of mother earth. The discovery of a suspicious box standing nearby induced me to have this strange article temporarily examined. We did not feel distressed at all when we detected a few bottles of wine carlet, and we signified our appreciation of the welcome gift by drinking heartily to the health and prosperity of the absent donor ("A la guerre! Comme a la guerre"). I then selected from a large pile of partly ruined accouterments (boys had kept bad faith with us) a nice belt, a bayonet scabbard

he ordered his troops to fire, the crowd scattering in panic. In the end 25 civilian men, women, children and a baby, along with 3 unarmed prisoners from Camp Jackson were killed with between 40–75 wounded. "Lyon and his officers stopped the firing as quickly as it began, but the civil war had come to" Missouri. Boernstein's Regiment lost two killed and six wounded, Sigel's 3rd Regiment lost two killed and four wounded, including Captain Blandowsky. The captain's leg was amputated on May 23, and he died three days later. Adamson, 62–64; Banasik, *Missouri Brothers in Gray*, 12; William Bell [Bull], "Camp Jackson Prisoners," 260–261; R. S. Bevier, *History of the First and Second Missouri Confederate Brigades 1861–1865. And From Wakarusa to Appomattox, A Military Anagraph* (St. Louis, 1879; reprint ed., Florissant, MO, 1985) 25, hereafter cited as Bevier; Brooksher, 62–63; Covington, 209; "Col. Burbridge's Regiment," 4; Gerteis, *St. Louis*, 108–109; Guernsey & Alden, 107; Heitman, vol. 1: 862; Lademann, "Camp Jackson," 73; McElroy, 78; Peckham, 154–156; Phillips, *Damned Yankee*, 157, 191–192; Piston & Hatcher, *Wilson's Creek*, 36; Piston & Sweeny, "Missouri State Guard," 14; "The Riot In St. Louis, MO, May 10, 1861," *Rebellion Record*, vol. 1: Doc. 235–236; Rowan, 298, 309; Tenney, 52; Winter, 51–53, 66; Woodard, 252.

93. The 4th Missouri Volunteer Regiment (Three months) was originally raised in January 1861, by Nicholas Schittner, and was part of the Union Legion, being further known as the Black Jaegers. With the President's call for troops, the 4th was organized as a ten company command under Schittner and mustered into the service on April 22–23, 1861. Camp Jackson was it only operation of note, after which they performed garrison duty at assorted posts. The regiment was mustered out on July 30, 1861. Prior to the Civil War Schuettner or Schittner (O.R. has the spelling both ways) was a common carpenter, living in an alley in St. Louis. With the coming of the secession crisis, he "led the Schwarze Jaeger, a German hunting club that took to the streets of St. Louis to counter the influence of the pro-Southern Minuet Men." Basically Schuettner was a "thuggish street-gang leader...devoted to terrifying secessionists in south St. Louis." And by 1860, Schittner was a "manufacturer of brick molds." Elected colonel of the 4th Regiment, Schittner's name disappears from the Official Records following his three months of service. After the war he became the superintendent of the St. Louis Engineer Office, and died between 1866 to 1869. O.R., Index, 1103; Gerteis, *Missouri*, 18; Rowan, 23, 282; Peckham, 433, 444; *Union Army*, vol. 4: 258

and a cartridge box. Having thus completed my military outfit I stretched my weary limbs on my captured mattress and indulged in a smoke in the absence of any kind of a supper what ever.[94] As the shades of night approached we commenced to build fires with the very limited supply of wood on hand. The rumor spread through the camp at that time that a big riot was in town and that innocent Germans had been shot.[95]

With us everything had quieted down after the sun had set. I was glad to have captured the mattress, for blankets, overcoats and other comfortable things were not in our possession. Went shortly after sundown a fine drizzling rain surprised us, I utilized my mattress still more by dividing it and covering my body with one part. I don't know how long I had rested in the arm of Morpheus when I was

Suddenly Awakened

Henry Benecke [Bencke], one of Sigel's orderlies, demanded my immediate appearance at headquarters.[96] I found Col. Sigel stretched out on a camp cot, suf-

---

94. As part of the agreed terms of surrender, according to William C. Streeter, a member of the State Militia, "our private property was not supposed to be molested or taken from us." However, as the Militia awaited their fate in the arsenal, Streeter noticed through a window that the German troops "had with them not only all our camp equipment and arms, but also all of the private baggage of the men…This private baggage was broken open and stolen right there in our sight." William C. Streeter, "'Volunteer' Reviews History of First Missouri Regiment," Missouri Historical Society, Camp Jackson Papers.

95. In addition to the documented clashes between the St. Louis civilians and the Federal troops it appears that the enraged secessionists also took out their ire on the local German populace. "Most of Lyon's men were Germans…[and] many of them were Catholics." As such they "gave the impression that Missouri's traditional social and political structure was under attack from fanatical outsiders." In response, according to Colonel Boernstein, "Germans were mistreated on the street and a few murdered in a cowardly fashion." Overall, the night of May 10, "was given up during the early part… to a howling, frenzied crowd of infuriated people." And the following morning James Peckham noted that German dead were found scattered throughout the city; one on Market street near 15th ; another on 10th and Clark; still two more near Franklin and 7th and Franklin and Morgan. James Broadhead, a member of the Safety Committee, simply recorded "'The night after the Camp Jackson affair was a bad night for mobs.'" Quoted in Gerteis, St. Louis, 114; McElroy, 80; Peckham, 158; Piston & Sweeney, "Missouri State Guard," 14; Rowan, 301; William H. Wherry, "General Nathaniel Lyon and His Campaign In Missouri In 1861," Sketches of War History 1861–1865 Papers Prepared for the Commandery of the State of Ohio, MOLLUS (Cincinnati, 1896; 70 vols., reprint ed, Wilmington, NC, 1991), vol. 4: 75, hereafter cited as Wherry, "General Lyon."

96. Henry Bencke, an aid to Franz Sigel, was born about 1835, and a resident of St. Louis when he joined Company K, 3rd Missouri Infantry (Three months) on May 5, 1861, though he was not mustered in until May 19. A sergeant, Beneke volunteered his services to Colonel Sigel as a mounted orderly, providing his own horse, without compensation. He mustered out of the 3rd Missouri on August 30, but later joined Sigel's staff as a lieutenant and upon the resignation of several lieutenants in Martin Welfley's Missouri Battery, Sigel assigned Bencke to the battery, commanding the third section of artillery. In addition to being at Camp Jackson he was also present at Pea Ridge, Arkansas. After Pea Ridge Bencke disappeared from the Official Records. NOTE: There was no record found on Bencke in the Compiled Service Records of Welfley's Missouri Battery. O.R., vol. 8: 236–237; O.R.S., pt. 2, vol. 36: 159; Britton, 247; National Archives, Record Group M405,

fering severely from the kick of a horse received early in the afternoon. What a strange coincidence, Gen. Lyon met with a similar accident.[97] I was directed to go to Gen. Lyon and inform him that everything was quiet in camp, and ask his instructions for the next day. I was to go in a closed carriage, and when I remarked that my only weapon was a big .69 caliber blunderbuss not very well suited for use in such close quarters, the colonel gave me his revolver to use in case of need. Taking with me the tallest corporal in my company, I started immediately.

As it was raining pitchforks, I got to the arsenal unmolested, where I found Gen. Lyon surrounded by Col. Blair and the officers of his regiment. The captured state troops were encamped in front of his quarters and the main arsenal, along the wooden fence near the track of the Iron Mountain Railroad, Gen. Frost occupying the officers quarters south of the main arsenal building. After delivering my verbal message, Gen. Lyon consulted with Col. Blair for a few minutes, and thereupon instructed me to convey to Col. Sigel the order that all arms, accouterment, ordnance stores, camp and garrison equipage should be conveyed to the arsenal as early as possible the next morning.[98]

It was after midnight before I had carried out this new order, and at last I was permitted to retire to my cold quarters, the rain continuing to pour down in torrents. After expelling an intruder with some difficulty for my snug little bed, I crawled back into the folded mattress. But I had hardly enjoyed my repose for half an hour when Orderly Benecke again made his appearance desiring once more my presence at headquarters. The colonel was certainly piling duty on me at a rapid rate, yet I was animated by the desire of securing my shoulder straps, I did not hesitate to respond with alacrity. This time I had a more difficult task to fulfill and it seemed doubtful whether I could return with equal success as before. I was to drive to the city once more, engaged all the vehicles I could get hold of, and order them to be ready in the morning for the purpose of executing Gen. Lyon's order. Once more I repaired to the city. Under difficulties which were, however, offset

---

roll no. 343, Union Compiled Service Records, Welfley's Missouri Battery; National Archives, Record Group M405, roll no. 412, Union Compiled Service Records, 3rd Missouri Infantry (Three months).

97. Even as Lyon was pondering how to move the Camp Jackson prisoners to the arsenal, he dismounted from his horse to better consider the situation. Pacing the area Lyon came to close the hind quarter of Major Horace Conant's horse, which lashed out, kicking Lyon in the stomach. Thrown to the ground and unconscious, the doctor of Blair's regiment, who was near by, came to Lyon's aid and after thirty minuets was able to revive him. While unconscious, Captain Thomas Sweeny, of the regulars, completed the negotiations of the surrender. Adamson, 61; McElroy, 77; Phillips, *Damned Yankee,* 189–190.

98. As enumerated by Captain Sweeny the principle military stores consisted of the following: three 32-lb smoothbores; 1,200 rifles; six brass field pieces; six 6-inch brass mortars ; one 10-iron mortar; and three 6-inch iron cannon, 25 kegs of powder, with an assortment of shot and shell. Additionally, the camp equipment included 240 tents of various types, 227 spades, 38 hatchets and 191 axes. From the Baton Rouge Arsenal there was also a box of musket parts, bayonets and scabbards. Covington, 201; Peckham, 160.

somewhat, my good luck I was able to secure the assistance of teamsters and of draymen, by the authorized offer of

Liberal Rewards.[99]

In a happy frame of mind I returned to the camp once more, at 4 a.m. reported to the colonel and at last had the benefit of enjoying my soaked couch for a few hours at least.

On the following day the plan mapped out by Gen. Lyon was executed with the best possible exactness, and we returned to the arsenal at noon, being greeted on our march through "Frenchtown" with indiscernible outbursts of patriotic enthusiasm, cheers upon cheers accompanying us all along the route. We reached the gate of the arsenal at 12 m.[meridian or noon], tired, hungry and most of us drenched to the skin; but we marched with a feeling of natural pride, at the same time returning to its legitimate owner the embryo museum of antiquated "materials of war" originating from the Baton Rouge arsenal. Although later military events far surpassed the capture of Camp Jackson in magnitude, yet this little affair exerted a most important influence in maintaining the ascendancy of the Union cause in St. Louis and Missouri.[100]

Otto C. Lademann
Late Captain Third Missouri Volunteers.

---

99. To solve his problem, Lademann went to Frenchtown, which was populated almost entirely by Germans. Arriving at a local saloon, at 2:00 a.m., where the inhabitants were loudly celebrating the capture of Camp Jackson, Lademann laid his proposal before the gathered crowd. "They assured me," Lademann recalled that "they would attend to the matter." The first wagons began arriving at Camp Jackson shortly after daylight and by 10:00 a.m "the whole camp was on wheels, lock stock and barrel, horse, foot, and dragoons, each wagon loaded with a few tents or guns or muskets or some of that old junk from Baton Rouge Arsenal." Lademann, "Camp Jackson," 74.

100. The capture of Camp Jackson fermented additional riots in St. Louis. On May 11, while a battalion of the newly formed 5th U.S. Reserve Corps (Boernstein says it was the 6th) was "passing Fifth and Walnut Sts....A boy about fourteen years old" fired a shot into the troops from the steps of the Presbyterian Church. The troops responded, killing another seven or eight citizens with "a large number wounded." The 5th lost an additional four killed (Broadhead has only three killed) and several wounded (Britton put the total losses at four military and two civilians killed with ten wounded; Brooksher has two soldiers and four civilians killed).This incident, according to Colonel Boernstein was"hushed up," probably because some of the soldiers, who were killed and wounded were shot by their own men. And on June 17, a similar incident occurred on Seventh Street as the troops neared the intersection of Olive and Pine. The startled troops of the 2nd Reserve Corps "fired in all directions, at the windows of houses, upon the by-standers, –anywhere!" And when the smoke had cleared five innocent civilians attending the Recorders Court Room were killed, with "several wounded." NOTE: The *Missouri, Confederate Military History* also mentions this second riot but says it happened on May 12, a day that Boernstein recorded as "a general flight of the 'upper ten,' the rich, proud slaveholders," who fled the city for Illinois, fearing attacks from the German population that never materialized. Britton, 12; Broadhead, *Missouri MOLLUS*, vol. 14: 19; Brooksher, 67; Coleman, 6–7; Diary of Events (May 11, 1861), *Rebellion Record*, vol. 1: Diary 67; Guernsey & Alden, 107; Moore, *Missouri, Confederate Military History*, vol. 9: 34–35; Rowan, 303; Tenney, 52; Winter, 63–64.

* * * * * * *

Item: Operations against General Thomas Harris, near Florida, Missouri on July 17, 1861, by General U. S. Grant and Mark Twain or Samuel Clemens.
Published: December 26, 1885.

Two Accounts of One Campaign

The Washington *National Tribune* compiles the following two accounts of a celebrated campaign in Missouri.[101]

I (U.S. Grant, then a colonel of volunteers) took my regiment to Palmyra and remained there for a few days, until relieved by the Nineteenth Illinois. From Palmyra I proceeded to Salt River, the railroad bridge over which had been destroyed by the enemy.[102] Col. John M. Palmer at that time commanded the Thirteenth Illinois, which was acting as a guard to the workmen who were engaged in rebuilding the bridge.[103] Palmer was my senior and command the two regiments as long as we remained to gather. The bridge was finished in about two weeks, and I received

---

101. The *National Tribune* began publishing in October 1877, and eventually became the *Stars and Stripes*. It is still being published today. Library of Congress, *Newspapers in Microform*, vol. 1: 155.

102. Grant's regiment, the 21st Illinois Infantry, was mustered into the service on June 28, 1861, crossing the Mississippi River on July 11, into Missouri, and on July 14 arrived at Palmyra. The following day the regiment moved to the Salt River bridge, joining John Palmer's command. Following its operations in northeast Missouri the 21st Illinois moved to southeast Missouri where they participated in the Battle of Fredericktown on October 21, 1861. The regiment then moved to the east side of the Mississippi River where they completed their military service, being transferred to Texas at the close of the war. They were mustered out on December16, 1865. *O.R.S.*, pt. 2, vol. 9:422, 452; *Union Army*, vol. 3: 262–263.

The 19th Illinois Infantry, commanded by Colonel John B. Turchin, was mustered into U.S. Service on June 17,1861, served briefly at Cairo, Illinois before relieving the 21st Illinois on July 15, 1861. After spending but a brief time in the Trans-Mississippi the 19th Illinois, was transferred to Fort Holt, Kentucky. They then completed their military service east of the Mississippi River, being mustered out on July 9, 1864, in Chicago, with only 350 men on their rolls. *O.R.*, vol. 3: 480; Dyer, 1052–1053; *Union Army*, vol. 3: 259–261.

103. John M. Palmer was born in Scott City, Kentucky, on September 13, 1817, and moved to Illinois at the age of fourteen. He graduated from college in 1836, and became a lawyer in 1839. .A Free Soil Democrat, Palmer served as a judge and a Illinois State Senator and in 1839 ran as a Republican for U.S. Congress but lost. With the beginning of the Civil War, Palmer was elected colonel of the 14th Illinois Infantry (not the 13th) on May 25, 1861, the day the 14th was mustered into U.S. Service. The regiment, with Palmer served briefly in the Trans-Mississippi. Palmer was promoted to brigadier general on December 20, 1861, after which he was transferred, with his command to the Island No. 10 Campaign. Palmer and the 14th then completed their military service east of the Mississippi River. The regiment was mustered out on September 22, 1865. Palmer was promoted to major general on November 29, 1862, and resigned from the army on September 1, 1866. Following the war Palmer was elected Governor of Illinois (1868) and U.S. Senator (1891). Palmer also ran for President, in 1896, as a Gold Democrat, but lost. He died in Springfield, Illinois, on September 25, 1900. Faust, 554–555; Heitman, vol. 1: 767; *Union Army*, vol. 3: 253–256.

orders to move against Col. Thos. Harris, who was said to be encamped at the little town of Florida, some twenty-five miles south of where we then were. . . .[104]

As we approach the brow of the hill from which it was expected we could see Harris' camp, and possibly find his men ready formed to meet us, my heart kept getting higher and higher until it so the as though it was in my throat. I would have given anything then to have been back in Illinois, but I had not the usual courage to halt and consider what to do; I kept right on. When we reached a point from which the valley below was in full view, I halted. The place where Harris was encamped a few days before was still there, and the marks of a recent engagement were plainly visible, but the troops were gone. My heart resume its place. It occurred to me at once that Harris had been as much afraid of me as I had been of him. This was a view of the question I had never taken before; but it was one I never forgot afterwards. From that event to the close of the war I never experienced trepidation upon confronting enemy, though I always felt more or less anxiety.

Inquiries at the village of Florida divulged the fact that Col. Harris, learning of my intended movements, while my transportation was being collected, took time by the forelock and left Florida before I had started from Salt River. He had increased the distance between us by forty miles. The next day I started back to my old camp at Salt River.[105]

(From a war paper by Mark Twain in the December *Century*.)

---

104. General Thomas Harris was born in Warren County, Virginia, in 1826, and immigrated to Hannibal, Missouri, at an early age. Prior to the Civil War, Harris fought in the Mormon War, served in the Missouri Militia being elected lieutenant colonel of his regiment at the age of 17. He became a soldier of fortune, fighting first in Cuba and then Venezuela, finally returning to Hannibal in the 1850's, where he became involved in politics. Harris was elected to the Missouri House and ran unsuccessfully for the Missouri Secretary of State in 1856. With the beginning of the Civil War, Harris was appointed a brigadier general commanding the 2nd Division, MSG. Harris raised some 2,000 troops for the MSG and led them at the Siege of Lexington in September 1861, after which he was appointed to the Confederate Congress. Following the war Harris eventually settled in Kentucky, where an old friend appointed him Secretary of State and in 1885, Harris was elected to the Kentucky Legislature. He died on April 9, 1895, near Louisville, where he was buried. Banasik, *Missouri in 1861*, 349–350.

105. On July 10, 1861, Tom Harris' command attacked Monroe Station, burning "the station house and cars." A total of six passenger cars and eighteen freight cars were destroyed. The following morning five Federal companies under Colonel Robert Smith were placed under siege. And while Smith was held in place at Monroe Station, Harris' men captured Hunnewell Station and sent four captured box cars, which they had fired, down the railroad to burn the Salt River bridge, located eleven miles from Smith's command. Monroe Station was relieved on the 11th at 4:30 p.m., but it was already too late–the Salt River bridge had been destroyed. On July 15, Grant relocated to the Salt River bridge to guard the workers, taking six of his companies. Three more companies were located at Hunnewell with Grant's headquarters, which was four miles from the bridge, while Company B guarded a different bridge on the Hannibal & St. Joseph Railroad. On July 16, Grant took six companies and marched about 17 miles to engage Harris' command at Florida, only to find that the rebels had left the area the day before. The destroyed bridge was valued at $6,000 with repairs expected to be completed by July 20. *O.R.*, vol. 3: 40–41; *O.R.S.*, pt. 2, vol. 9: 444, 452,460, 477, 494; O. P. H., "North Missouri," *Chicago Tribune*," July 22, 1861; Tenney, 81.

The rest of my war experience was of a piece with what I have already told of it. [106]We kept monotonously falling back upon one camp or another, and eating up the country. . . . The last camp with which we fell back upon what is a hollow near the village of Florida, where I was born–in Monroe County. Here we were warned one day that a Union colonel was sweeping down on us with a whole regiments on his heels. This looked decidedly serious. Our boys went apart and consulted; then we went back and told the other companies present that the war was a disappoint-ment to us and we were going to disband. They were getting ready themselves to fall back on someplace or other and were only waiting for Gen. Tom Harris, who was expected to arrive at any moment; so they tried to persuade us to wait a little while, but the majority of us said no, we were accustomed to falling back, didn't need any of Tom Harris' help; we should get along perfectly well without him, and save time too. So about half of our fifteen, including myself, mounted and left on the instant. An hour later we met Gen. Harris on the road. *** Harris ordered us back, but we told him there was a Union colonel coming with a whole regiment in his wake, and it looked as if there was going to be a disturbance, so we had con-cluded to go home *** In time I came to know that Union colonel whose coming frightened us out of the war and cripple the Southern cause to that extant–Gen. Grant. I came within a few hours of seeing him when he was as unknown as I was myself.—(*National Tribune*)

* * * * * *

---

106. Samuel L. Clemens, better known as Mark Twain, enlisted in the Ralls County Rangers, 2nd Divi-sion, MSG, in the first part of July 1861, being elected a lieutenant in the command; two weeks later he departed the army, worked on a river boat for a short time. Later he headed to Carson City, Nevada, with his brother, "who had just been appointed the territorial secretary for Nevada." Clemens had enough of army life having recovered from an ankle injury he had suffered shortly after joining the MSG. Dino A. Brugioni, *The Civil War in Missouri As Seen From the Capital City* (Jefferson city, MO, 1987), 33; Monaghan, 137–138; Peterson, et. al., 106; Quoted in Nathaniel Cheairs Hughes, Jr., *The Battle of Belmont: Grant Strikes South* (Chapel Hill, NC, 1991), 256 n. 9, hereafter cited as Hughes.

Chapter 2

Battles of Carthage
and
Wilson's Creek

Item: Battle of Carthage, Missouri (July 5, 1861), by Otto C. Lademann, late captain 3rd Missouri Volunteers.
Published: March 26, 1887.

[Editor Note: There were various times presented by the participants for the assorted actions which took place at Carthage on July 5. The times listed below mainly follow those presented and explained by David Hinze and Karen Farnham in their book on Carthage.][1]

Carthage

St. Louis, March 24
[Editor *Republican*]

In my little sketch of the capture of Camp Jackson your printer made a "Gov. Johnston" out of Gov. Jackson. I presume that this was one of those unavoidable typographical errors which are the terror of all writers, both amateur or professional. With this slight digression let me come to the theme in hand. After the capture of Camp Jackson our regiment (Third Missouri Volunteer Infantry, Col. F. Sigel) remained at the arsenal until about the middle of May, when a general distribution of the volunteer troops was determined upon and the regiment was ordered to Rock Springs, remaining there a couple of weeks and drilling diligently. We returned to the arsenal about the last of May, the regimental headquarters being established in Concordia Park. It was here that an attempt was made to organize the regiment for three years service, under the proclamation of President Lincoln calling out troops for three years or during the war.[2] The captain and first lieutenants were appointed. Capt. Anslem Albert was designated a Lt. Col., then serving in place of Lt. Col. Hassendeubel, then serving in that capacity.[3] The sec-

---

1. Hinze & Farnham, 265–266 n. 19.
2. On May 3,1861, a call for 500,000 volunteers was made to the various states. Missouri's quota, under this call, was 31,544 of which 25,238 were furnished; 22,324 were furnished for three years, while the remaining 2,914 were for one year or less. Frederick Phisterer, *Statistical Record of the Armies of the United States* (New York, 1907), 4.
3. Anslem or Anselme Albert was born in Hungary, received a military education and severed in the Austrian Army, as an officer, until 1845, when he resigned. He participated in the Hungarian

ond lieutenants were not appointed, but their positions left open for meritorious noncommissioned officers.[4]

On June 13 we were ordered to prepare to march, our field equipments being in wretched beyond description. [5] We had been provided with a very indifferent

---

Revolution in 1848, on the losing side. Fleeing initially to Syria, Albert immigrated to the United States, settling in New Orleans and later moved to St. Louis, where he was a newspaper reporter for the German language *Handels Zeitung*. With the coming of the Civil War, Albert joined Sigel's 3rd Missouri Infantry (Three months), being elected captain of Company A on May 10 and then appointed adjutant to Colonel Sigel on June 17, at Waynesville, Missouri. On July 24, Albert was appointed lieutenant colonel of the 3rd following the resignation of Francis Hassendeubel. Albert fought at Carthage on July 5, 1861, and at Wilson's Creek on August 10, where he commanded the regiment, but was wounded and captured. Before Albert was mustered out of the service on August 30, he was appointed a colonel on August 23 and served on General Frémont's staff as an aid-de-camp, beginning on September 20, 1861. Though never officially mustered as a colonel, Albert was appointed as an acting brigadier general, commanding a brigade in Frémont's "Army of the West" on October 10, 1961. Departing Frémont's army on November 19, following Frémont's relief, Albert remained with the Army of the West. He later left the army sometime after February 6, 1862, and joined Frémont on March 31, 1862, in the East. He served with Frémont until June 8, 1864, when he resigned from the service. Final disposition unknown. *O.R.*, vol. 3: 19, 502, 508; *O.R.*, vol. 8: 545; *O.R.*,vol. 53: 503; *O.R.S.*, pt. 2, vol. 36: 437; Dyer, 1751; Gerteis, *Missouri*, 52, 220 n. 48; Heitman, vol. 1: 155; Piston & Hatcher, *Wilson's Creek*, 189, 261; *War in the West*, 265–266.

4. Francis Hassendeubel was born about 1818, and a veteran of the Mexican War. He served as a second lieutenant in Meriwether Lewis Clark's Battalion of Missouri Volunteers during Doniphan Expedition to California and later commanded a battery in the Santa Fe Battalion, under Sterling Price. At the beginning of the Civil War, Hassendeubel was a resident of St. Louis and at one time served as the St. Louis City Engineer. He joined the 3rd Missouri Infantry (Three months) on April 22, 1861, being elected lieutenant colonel on May 4. Hassendeubel fought with distinction at Carthage on July 5, 1861, resigning on July 24, 1861, to accept the colonelcy of the 17th Missouri Infantry. The 17th Missouri Infantry, completed its organization on October 12, when the last two companies were organized. His command fought at Pea Ridge (March 6–8, 1862), but Hassendeubel was not present, after which he was transferred to the east side of the Mississippi River, with his command, where Hassendeubel completed his service. During the Vicksburg Campaign, Hassendeubel received a mortal wound from a shell fragment on June 28 and died near Vicksburg, at the divisional hospital on July 17, 1863. He was returned to St. Louis, where he was buried on July 30, 1863. *O.R.*, vol. 8: 280–281; *O.R.S.*, pt. 2, vol. 36: 437; *O.R.S.*, pt. 2, vol. 37: 116, 119; Dyer, 1323; Heitman, vol. 2: 54, 109; Lademann, "Battle of Carthage," 135; National Archives, Record Group M405, roll nos. 412 & 511, Union Compiled Service Records, 3rd Missouri Infantry (Three months) and 17th Missouri Infantry; William Garrett Piston and Thomas P. Sweeney, *Portraits of Conflict: A Photographic History of Missouri in the Civil War* (Carl Moneyhon and Bobby Roberts, gen. eds., *Portraits of Conflict Series*, Fayetteville, AR, 2009), 268, hereafter cited as Piston & Sweeney, *Portraits of Conflict, Missouri*.

5. General Lyon assumed commanded of the Department of the West on May 31, 1861, and moved quickly to consolidate his hold on Missouri. Following the Planter's House meeting, on June 11, Lyon moved his command to Jefferson City, capturing the city on the 15th. However, before departing St. Louis, for Jefferson City, Lyon ordered Colonels Sigel and Salomon to "move down to Springfield and Neosho, and operate in the rear of Jackson and Price," while at the same time "oppose the threatened invasion" of rebel troops from Arkansas (William Wherry, a member of Lyon's staff, says that Lyon issued the order on the night of June 12). General Tom Sweeney was given overall command of what was known as the "Southwest Column," including Sigel's command, and was directed to proceed to Springfield, with "as many troops as he possibly could," there to await the arrival of Lyon with the main body of the army. Lyon's plan was meant to trap Governor

uniform consisting of a gray flannel blouse, gray jeans pantaloons with a red belt and a gray wool hat, all very cheep and of an exceedingly poor quality. The rotten white belts, which I mentioned in my previous article, had been supplemented with a cartridge box without tin cases, and we found after a week's march, all the powder in our box, nothing fixed to the paper of our cartridge but the ball. We possessed neither blankets nor overcoats, but each man was provided with the flimsy haversack and a tin canteen without cover.

Equipped in this manner we embark on the cars at the Fourteenth Street Depot and proceeded

By Rail to Rolla,

Mo., where we were joined by the Fifth Missouri volunteer infantry, Col. C. E. Solomon [Salomon], and the artillery battalion of Maj. Backhoff [or Backhof], consisting of Essig's and Wilkin's batteries of four pieces each, mostly 12-pound howitzers.[6] Leaving Rolla June 17 we marched to Springfield, Mo., where we arrived Sunday, June 23, 1861.[7] Our detachment was designated as Sigel's Brigade

---

Jackson's fledgling MSG between his command and that of Sweeney and Sigel. As Lademann indicated, Sigel's command departed St. Louis on the 14th, arriving in Rolla at 1:00 p.m. the same day. Sigel then waited in Rolla for the balance of his regiment, while he equipped his command with transportation for the movement to the southwest. Additionally, Sigel was further delayed, awaiting the arrival of Major David Bayles and his 300-man command of the 4th U.S. Reserve Corps (Companies D, G, and H), Missouri Infantry (Three months), who were to garrison the city, while Sigel headed to Springfield. On June 16, not 17, Sigel departed for Springfield. O.R., vol. 3: 381; O.R.S., pt. 2, vol. 36: 466–467; Adamson, 115; Britton, 38–39; Brooksher, 82–93; William O. Coleman Letters (October 27, 1909), W. L. Skaggs Collection, Arkansas History Commission; Hinze & Farnham, 61–62; Peckham, 292; W. L. Webb, *Battles and Biographies of Missourians or the Civil War Period of Our State* (Kansas City, MO, 1900; reprint ed., Springfield, MO, 1999), 63, hereafter cited as Webb; Wherry, "General Lyon," 78.

6. Essig's Battery (Three months) was commanded by Christian Essig and was Battery A of Backoff's Battalion. It consisted of four 12-pound brass howitzers, the same guns that were at Camp Jackson. Wilkins' Battery was commanded by Theodore Wilkins and contained two 12-pound howitzers and two 6-pound smoothbores. Wilkins' command was Battery B (Three months) of Backoff's Battalion. Lademann, "Battle of Carthage," 132; United States Record and Pension Office, *Organization and Status of Missouri Troops, Union and Confederate, In the Service During the Civil War* (Washington, 1902; reprint ed., Lexington, KY, 2013), 217–219, hereafter cited as United States Pension Office, *Organization of Missouri Troops*. See **Appendix B** for a biography on Frederick Salomon.

7. There was a great deal of confusion as to when the 3rd Missouri arrived at Springfield. In a previous article, Lademann had his command arriving on Friday, June 27; however, Friday was actually June 21 or June 28. David Hinze and Karen Farnham have Sigel's command arriving "on the edge of Springfield " on June 23, a Sunday. John Buegel of the 3rd Missouri has the command arriving on the 25th, while the *Supplement to the Official Records* has the date as either June 23 or 24, which suggests that the command arrived at Springfield on the 23rd but did not enter Springfield until June 24. And yet others have the date as June 24, but stated that it was Sunday when Sigel entered, his band striking "up a spirit stirring air." O.R.S., pt. 2, vol. 36: 437, 439–442; "Battle of Carthage–New York 'World's' Narrative," *Rebellion Record*, vol. 2: Doc. 347, hereafter cited as "New York 'World's' Narrative"; Bek, "Buegel Diary," 311; Guernsey & Alden, 139; Hinze &

but Col. Sigel, while practically acting as the brigade commander, retained command of our regiment at the same time.[8] The Third Missouri Infantry had twelve companies, instead of ten, having Cos. A and B rifles, commanded by Capts. Anselm Albert and Joseph Conrad, respectively, besides having ten companies of infantry.[9] The aggregate strength present for duty at the departure from St. Louis was about 2000 combatants. I don't think that Col. Salomon's regiment had over 800 present for duty, and each battery may be put down at 100 men, making the total force of Sigel's Brigade 1800 infantry 200 artillery and eight guns. We had no cavalry except a few mounted orderlies employed on the staff of Col. Siegel.[10]

In leaving Springfield Col. Sigel made one of its inexplicable maneuvers; we left Springfield on the evening of June 27, marching in the direction of Mount Vernon, nearly due west of Springfield. Night marches are very destructive of men as well as materials, and no good officer will order them except in a case of necessity, generally in front of the enemy to cover the retrograde or flank movement, but such was not the case here; we marched all night in the rain; going to camp exhausted near daybreak, where we remained all day till 4:00 p.m. when we resumed our march and reached Mount Vernon late at night.[11] Here Col. Sigel in-

---

Farnham, 63; Holcombe & Adams, 6; Elmo Engenthron, *Borderland Rebellion: A History of the Civil War On the Missouri–Arkansas Border* (Branson, MO, 1980), 42, hereafter cited as Engenthron; Lademann, "Battle of Carthage," 130.

8. Not true. The commander of the 3rd Missouri, at Carthage, was Lieutenant Colonel Francis Hassendeubel, who led the regiment from June 2 to July 15, 1861. "The Battle of Carthage–New York 'Times' Narrative," *Rebellion Record*, vol. 2: Doc. 249, hereafter cited as "New York 'Times' Narrative"; National Archives, Record Group M405, roll no. 412, Union Compiled Service Records, 3rd Missouri Infantry (Three months).

9. Joseph Conrad was born on May 17, 1828, in Wide-Shelters, Nassau, Germany, and educated at the Hesse-Darmstadt State Military School, graduating in 1848. He was thirty-two when he joined the 3rd Missouri (Three months) on April 22, 1861, being elected captain of Company B on May 27, 1861. After mustering out of the 3rd, Conrad became the lieutenant colonel of the 15th Missouri Infantry on May 24, 1862; and the colonel on November 29, 1862. By war's end he had received a brevet to brigadier general "for gallant and meritorious service in the Atlanta Campaign" in 1864. Following the war Conrad remained in the army, rising to the rank of colonel and retiring on October 23, 1888. He died on July 16, 1897 at Atlantic City, New Jersey. *O.R.*, vol. 3: 38; Boatner, 172; Heitman, vol. 1: 322. Hunt & Brown, 127; National Archives, Record Group M405, roll no. 412, Union Compiled Service Records, 3rd Missouri Infantry (Three months).

10. For the up coming battle on July 5, Sigel reported that he had 950 men "engaged" with two batteries of artillery; 550 men for the 3rd Missouri and 400 for the 5th Misosuri. Additionally, 125–150 men manned the eight pieces of artillery that Sigel possessed, giving his command at least 1,075–1,100 men. Not mentioned by Sigel were the 400 reserves that he had in Carthage before the battle began, who were never "engaged." See **Appendix C** for the **Union and MSG Orders of Battle,** with losses. *O.R.*, vol. 3: 17; Stephen D. Engle, *Yankee Dutchman: The Life of Franz Sigel* (Baton Rouge, LA, 1993), 63–64, hereafter cited as Engle; "Great Battle In Southwestern Missouri," *Waukegan Weekly Gazette* (Waukegan, IL), July 17, 1861; Peckham, 294; Snead, *Fight for Missouri*, 225; Snead, "First Year In the War," 259–260.

11. After Sigel arrived in Springfield, he rested but a short time, departing in the late evening of June 25, or early morning hours of June 26, with his command–Companies C, D and F, of Salomon's 5th Missouri, with Backhof's Artillery Battalion were to follow after they reached Springfield the following day. In addition to Sigel's infantry, his column also include a couple of squads of Home Guards, Voerester's Pioneer Company, a "small body of regulars" and 54 wagons, 32 of which

dulged his favorite practice of detaching troops. He left Capt. August Hackmann with his Co. F, as a garrison in Mount Vernon and marched to Sarcoxie the next day, reaching Neosho, Mo., two days later.[12] Here he again detached a company under command of Capt. Jos. Conrad as a garrison, when we left for Carthage, Mo. While Col. Sigel had thus succeeded in scattering one fourth of his available from Springfield to Neosho, when his Springfield garrison only was of any military value, he had maneuvered himself into

An Exceedingly Dangerous Position.

On his left flank he found Gen. Ben McCulloch with a force of from 4000 to

---

were impressed from Springfield and dubbed "Sigel's beer wagons" by the locals. Sigel, for his part, was acting on his own initiative, responding to erroneous intelligence which placed General Price with 700 men in the vicinity of Neosho. With limited cavalry, no supply line and unsure of the enemy's strength or the local terrain "the move" according to David Hinze and Karen Farnham "was certainly a bold one, although time would tell whether it was wise or foolhardy." Thomas L. Snead, simply recorded that the move was made "with more boldness than discretion." Sigel's plan was to place his troops between Governor Jackson's retreating forces from Boonville and the rebel forces coming from the south–a move of a "confident and aggressive commander," considering the MSG to Sigel's north numbered about 6,000 men and Ben McCulloch's command of Arkansas and Texas troops to the south numbered roughly 5,000, with another 1,700 MSG under General Price. See **Appendix C, Union Order of Battle** for additional details on Voerester's Pioneers, which Lademann misidentifies as Foerester's Pioneer Company as well as the Home Guard troops. NOTE: Brooksher, Hinze and Farnham have Sigel with only 32 wagons; however, both Lademann and a period newspaper put the number at 54 and 50 respectfully. Adamson, 136–137; "Battle of Carthage," *Rebellion Record*, Doc. 247; Brooksher, 121; Engle, 62–63; Hinze & Farnham, 95–98, 101; Holcombe & Adams, 7; Ingenthron, 43–45; Lademann, "Battle of Carthage," 132, 138; "New York 'World's' Narrative," Doc. 248; Rutherford, 46; Snead "First Year In the War," 268.

12. Sigel's column reached Sarcoxie on June 28 at 5:00 p.m., and headed to Neosho on the morning of June 29, arriving later in the day. Meanwhile, Salomon's column pushed on to Sarcoxie, where they arrived on the evening of the 29th; there, Salomon received orders from General Sweeny to immediately return to Springfield while also receiving Sigel's orders to join the main column at Neosho. Salomon disregarded Sweeny's order and headed to Neosho the following day. Meanwhile, back at Springfield, Lieutenant Colonel Christian D. Wolf departed the city on June 28, with Companies A, E, G and I, 5th Missouri (Three months) and headed to Neosho where they were to link up with Sigel's main column. Salomon's column reached Neocho on July 1, while Wolf's joined Sigel's force on July 2. NOTE: Hinze and Farnham have Sigel arriving at Neosho on July 1; however the *Supplement to the Official Records* clearly has the date as June 30. *O.R.*, vol. 3: 16; *O.R.S.*, pt. 2, vol. 36: 440–441, 492–494; Hinze & Farnham, 92, 99; "New York 'World's' Narrative," Doc. 248; Peckham, 294.

August Hackmann commanded Company D not F, at Carthage as indicated by Lademann. Initially, Hackman joined Company F on April 25, 1861, being elected captain on May 9. He was later noted, in the Compiled Service Records, as commanding Company D, being mustered out on August 12, 1861; after which his name disappears from the Official Records–Hackman's command did not remain in Mt. Vernon, but was ordered to Sarcoxie on June 30, and then on to Neosho, where they arrived on July 2. *O.R.*, vol. 3: 15–17; *O.R.*, Index, 384; "Battle of Carthage," *Rebellion Record*, vol. 2: Doc. 247; Hinze & Farnham, 221; National Archives Record Group M405, roll no. 412, Union Compiled Service Records, 3rd Missouri Infantry (Three months); Peckham, 121.

5000 Louisiana, Arkansas and Texas troops, a large number of them mounted, while on his right flank was gathered to Missouri State Guard, Maj. Gen. Sterling Price commanding, some 6000 strong, but only two thirds armed.[13] The position would have been an admirable one for an enterprising officer with a sufficient force of the three arms combined to attack and beat on the right or left before the two armies had a chance to unite their forces, but Col. Sigel with his remaining 1200 muskets and eight guns was no match for either of them.[14] However, he determined to attack the force on his right flank, the Missouri State Guard, commanded by Gens. [James S.] Rains and [Mosby M.] Parsons owing to the absence of Gen. Sterling Price.[15]

---

13. Born in Tennessee in 1811, Ben McCulloch fought at the Battle of San Jacinto, searched for gold in California in 1849, and was a U. S. Marshall in Texas. He received the surrender of the Federal forces in San Antonio in February 1861, and was commissioned a brigadier general on May 11, 1861. McCulloch commanded the District of the Indian Territory, which embraced the territory south of Kansas and west of Arkansas in the early part of the war and was killed at the Battle of Pea Ridge on March 7, 1862. See *Missouri in 1861* of this series for a complete biography. *O.R.*, vol. 3: 575; Banasik, *Missouri in 1861*, 356–357; Warner, *Generals in Gray*, 200–202.

    At the end of June 1861, McCulloch's command–to the left flank" of Sigel–was located near Maysville, Arkansas–to the southwest of Sigel, and seven miles from the Missouri line. McCulloch's command consisted of about 2,700 Confederate troops , with another 2,000 Arkansas State Troops. Sterling Price with his command of MSG numbered about 1,700 men and was located at Cowskin Prairie, in the southwest corner of Missouri. The MSG troops on Sigel's "right flank" were to the north of Sigel and were commanded by Governor Jackson, Price having been sent to Arkansas in mid-June to seek assistance from Arkansas and the Confederate Government to combat the Federal forces in Missouri. *O.R.*, vol. 3: 606; Adamson, 129, 136.

14. See **Appendix C** for the **Union Order of Battle at Carthage**.

15. James Spencer Rains was born on October 2, 1817, in Tennessee, later moved to southwest Missouri, settling near Sarcoxie. He served in the Missouri Militia in pre-Civil War days, and was a state senator (1854–1861) when the war began in April 1861. Appointed a brigadier general in the MSG, commanding the 2nd Division at the Battle of Carthage. Rains served throughout the war. After the war Rains settled in Texas, where he died on May 19, 1880. See Banasik, *Confederate Tales, 1861* for a picture and complete biography. Banasik, *Confederate Tales, 1861*, 190–191; Bruce S. Allardice, *More Generals in Gray* (Baton Rouge, LA, 1995), 190–192, hereafter cited as Allardice, *More Generals in Gray*.

    Mosby M. Parsons, a resident of Jefferson City, Missouri, was born in Virginia in 1822, moved to Missouri at age thirteen, and was a veteran of the Mexican War. During the secession crisis Parsons ran for Lieutenant Governor in 1860, as a Breckinridge Democrat, with Hancock Lee Jackson, in opposition to Claiborne Jackson and Thomas Reynolds, but lost handily. On May 17, 1861, Parsons was appointed a brigadier general, commanding the 6th Division, MSG. Parsons led his command in all the 1861 battles that his division participated in, but was not present at the Battle of Pea Ridge, being absent at the time in Richmond, Virginia. On April 8, 1862, Parsons succeeded Price as commander of the MSG, and on November 5, 1862, he was commissioned a brigadier general in the Confederate Army. At the Battle of Prairie Grove (December 7, 1862), Parsons commanded a brigade and later a division during the Red River and Camden Campaigns. Parsons spent his Civil War years, except for three months, in the Trans-Mississippi Department. At war's end he went to Mexico, where he was killed on August 16, 1865. See *Missouri Brothers in Gray* for biography and photo. See also Banasik, *Confederate Tales, 1864–1865*, for further details on Parsons' death. Michael E. Banasik, *"Confederate Tales of the War" In the Trans-Mississippi Part 5: 1864–1865. Unwritten Chapters of the Civil War West of the River* (Iowa City, IA, 2019), 63–82, hereafter cited as Banasik, Confederate Tales, 1864–1865; Banasik, *Missouri*

On Thursday, July 4, 1861, after parading and firing a national salute, we left Neosho and its beautiful spring to march to Carthage, Jasper County, Mo. The march was hot and dusty, and it was late in the evening when we reached Carthage, encamping in the bottom of a creek southeast and outside of town.[16] At daybreak next morning we resumed our march in a northerly direction, until we reached and crossed Coon Creek [Dry Fork Creek or Bear Creek], some eight or nine miles from town, where we encountered the Missouri State Guard drawn up in line of battle on a slight swell or rise of the apparently endless green prairie, the troops forming a dark line against an azure skies of the horizon and the three banners gayly floating over the line.[17]

General James S. Rains

Brothers in Gray, 146–148; Banasik, Missouri in 1861, 380–381; Lyon, 430; Peterson, et. al., 34; Snead, Fight for Missouri, 313.

16. With his command concentrated on July 3, Sigel broke camp at Neosho on the early morning of July 4, leaving Conrad's Company A (Rifle Battalion), 3rd Missouri Infantry (Three months) to garrison Neosho, and headed north toward Carthage. And following a twenty-two mile march the Federals arrived at modern-day Carter Springs one mile east of Carthage and south of the Spring River–there they rested for the night, throwing out pickets in all directions. To the north, the MSG were camped at Lamar, having no idea that a Federal force was located in Carthage. As the MSG rested, General M. M. Parsons sent out a 95-man forage team, under command of his Quartermaster, Lieutenant Colonel Thomas Monroe, to work the mills near Carthage. Loading his wagons in Carthage, in the late afternoon, Monroe was informed that Federals were approaching the area. Monroe quickly finished his loading of supplies and sent his teams galloping back to Lamar, while he remained to survey the arrival of Sigel's column. Informed of Sigel's presence, at 6:00 p.m., Parsons ordered his command to break camp and prepare for a night march to Carthage. Upon hearing the intelligence from Carthage, Governor Jackson canceled Parsons orders and directed his whole command to march at dawn the next morning, thus setting the stage for the battle on the 5th. O.R., vol. 3: 35; O.R.S., pt. 2, vol. 36: 437–438, 440–441; Adamson, 144–146; Britton, 53; Brooksher, 116–117; Monaghan, 151; Moore, Missouri, Confederate Military History, vol. 9: 48; Ward L. Schrantz, Jasper County, Missouri in the Civil War (Carthage, MO, 1992 ed.), 32–33, hereafter cited as Schrantz; Snead, Fight for Missouri, 223–224.

17. On July 5, "the morning was clear and sunny, warm even at sunrise" and within a short time "as the sun crested the surrounding hills…[it] became intensely hot." With the coming of dawn both armies were on the move–the MSG heading south to Carthage, the cavalry moving at a "lope," from Lamar at 4:00 a.m., led by Joe Shelby's Ranger Company. To the south Sigel's command, led by some of his mounted Home Guard troops, passed through Carthage a little after 3:00 a.m., heading north toward Lamar, having learned the night before that the rebels were less than a dozen miles north of Carthage. At 5:00 a.m., Siegel's advance captured a three-man picket of the State Guard posted two miles north of Carthage. Two hours later, near Breir Forks, Shelby spotted the Federal troops approaching from Carthage and promptly informed General Rains, who,

Col. Siegel made the following judicious disposition of his troops; on the right he placed the first battalion of the Third Missouri Infantry, Lt. Col. Francis Hassendeubel; the center was formed by the Fifth Missouri Infantry, Col. C. E.. Salomon; on the left was place the second battalion of the Third Missouri Infantry, Maj. Henry Bishoff [Bischof] commanding; on the right and left of the Fifth Missouri in the intervals between it and the second wing out stations, were placed the two batteries of four guns each.[18]

upon surveying the situation, ordered Shelby to "check" the enemy's advance. Thirty minutes later Shelby made contact with Sigel's mounted Home Guard, killing one while having one man slightly wounded. With Shelby holding the enemy in check, Rains began to deploy his command on a "gentle southerly slope" north of Double Trouble Creek. Meanwhile, Sigel, having been halted by Shelby, just north of Dry Fork Creek, reenforced his Home Guard with two companies from the 3rd Missouri, and two pieces of Essig's artillery, forcing Shelby back to Rains' main line three miles away. It was about 9:30 a.m. and the stage was set for the real battle to begin. NOTE: Several authors have misidentified Double Trouble Creek as Coon Creek or Elk Creek. Further, David Hinze and Karen Farnham, with Donald Gilmore, have incorrectly identified where Shelby initially engaged Sigel's command as north of Buck Branch Creek–or three miles south from Dry Fork Creek and six miles from Rains. Further, Rains implies, and Ingenthron confirmed, that Shelby made contact at Dry Fork Creek, not the Buck Branch. Additionally, Dry Fork Creek was also referred too as Coon or Bear Creek. *O.R.*, vol. 3: 17, 20; Adamson, 146–147; Banasik, *Missouri in 1861*, 202; "Battle of Carthage," *Rebellion Record*, vol. 2: Doc. 246; Britton, 55; Brooksher, 120 George B. Davis, et. al., *Atlas to Accompany the Official Records of the Union and Confederate Armies* (Washington, DC, 1891–1895), plt. 33, no. 6 hereafter cited as Davis, *Civil War Atlas*; Charles V. Duncan, *John T. Hughes: From His Pen* (Medesto, CA , 1991), 79, hereafter cited as Duncan; Virginia Easley, "Journal of the Civil War In Missouri: 1861, Henry Martyn Cheavens;" *Missouri Historical Review* 56 (October,1961), 17, hereafter cited as Easley, "Cheavens Journal"; John N. Edwards, *Shelby and His Men or the War in the West* (Cincinnati, OH, 1867; reprint ed., Waverly, MO, 1993), 31, hereafter cited as Edwards; Engle, 64; Gerteis, *Missouri*, 45; Hinze & Farnham, 111–112, 116, 265 n.16; Donald L. Gilmore, *Civil War on the Missouri-Kansas Border* (Gretna, LA, 2006), 119, hereafter cited as Gilmore; Ingenthron, 46; McElroy,139; Monaghan, 152; O'Flaherty, 67–69; Peckham, 294; *Rebellion Record*, vol. 2: Diary 19; Rutherford, 43–44; Schrantz, 34–35; *Union Army*, vol. 5: 228.

18. "Both sides formed in silence and stood looking at each other," according to William Barlow of Henry Guibor's Battery, even as the Union forces made their dispositions. Salem Ford of Richard Weightman's Brigade, recalled that he "had never seen so many men in one body, they being well drilled and armed...[while] our side was quite the reverse." Sigel's command had crossed Double Trouble Creek facing the MSG, who were aligned on the northern slope of the creek and about 800 yards from the Unionists as follows: MSG cavalry from the 4th and 6th Divisions, under Ben Rives, William Brown, Charles B. Alexander and Charles L. Crews held the far left of the Guard line. The far right contained Robert Peyton's 2nd Division cavalry led personally by General Rains. Clark's Infantry with his dismounted cavalry, were deployed next to the cavalry on the left of the line. Next to Rains's cavalry, Richard Weightman's Brigade of Rains' Division was deployed, while Parson's infantry under Joseph Kelly and George Dills was positioned adjacent to Weightman. Between Parson's infantry and Clark's infantry, Slack's Infantry under John T. Hughes and John C. C. Thornton took their post. And to the rear of the main line Governor Jackson, who commanded the MSG at Carthage, established his "toothless reserve line," including his baggage wagons and unarmed horsemen. John Edwards labeled this reserve simply a "the line of spectators." The State troops thus deployed maintained their position hoping to lure their foe into an attack. Adamson, 147; Bevier, 37; Edwards, 31; S. H. Ford, "Reminiscences of Capt. S. H. Ford," Missouri Historical Society; Hinze & Farnham, 125, 139; Jeffery Patrick, ed., "Remembering the Missouri Campaign of 1861: The Memoirs of Lieutenant William P. Barlow, Guibor's Battery,

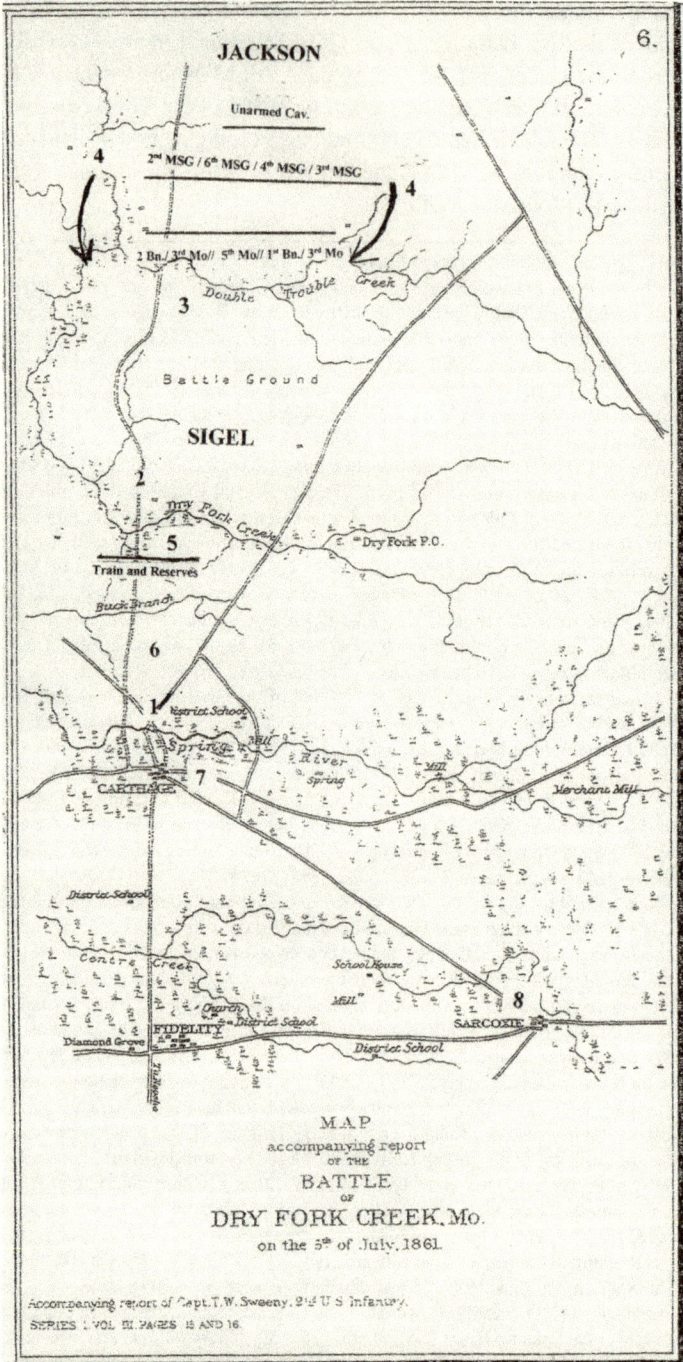

MAP
accompanying report
OF THE
BATTLE
OF
DRY FORK CREEK, Mo.
on the 5th of July, 1861.

Accompanying report of Capt. T.W. Sweeny, 2nd U.S. Infantry.
SERIES 1. VOL. III. PAGES 15 AND 16.

KEY TO THE BATTLE OF DRY FORK CREEK OR CARTHAGE
(JULY 5, 1861)

1. MSG Picket captured two miles north of Carthage at 5:00 a.m.

2. Joe Shelby makes contact with Sigel's advance just north of Dry Fork Creek at 7:30 a.m.

3. By 9:30 a.m. both sides have deployed on the north side of Double Trouble Creek. Artillery duel begins at 9:50 and lasts till about 11:00 a.m.

4. During the artillery duel MSG cavalry begins to flank federal line, causing Sigel to order a retreat

5. Sigel delays MSG advance at Dry Fork Creek from noon to 2 p.m. and then orders a retreat to Carthage.

6. In flanking Sigel's lines MSG arrive at the Buck Branch to block the Federal retreat and are easily dispersed after ten minute engagement—the time is between 3:00 and 3:30 p.m.

7. Sigel makes final stand at Carthage at 6:00 p.m, then withdraws to Sarcoxie.

8. Sigel's command staggered into Sarcoxie between 3:00 and 3:30 am on July 6.

Our train, consisting of some fifty four-horse teams, hired for the occasion in St. Louis, was parked on the prairie two and a half miles in our rear.[19] The infantry was formed

In a Column of Companies,

closed in mass, interval between the three different infantry columns and the intervening two batteries being still large enough to allow a rapid deployment of the columns. In this formation we advanced to within 1000 yards of the enemy's line, halted and our two batteries commenced the action by throwing shells and spherical case shots at the enemy at between 1 and 2 o'clock p.m..[20] The Missouri State

Missouri State Guard," *Civil War Regiments: A Journal of the American Civil War* 5 (No. 4, 1997), 31, hereafter cited as Patrick, "Guibor's Battery"; Rutherford, 44; Schrantz, 35.

Henry Bischof or Bishoff organized Company A (Rifle Battalion), 3rd Missouri Infantry (Three months), which was mustered in on April 22, 1861. Elected major of the regiment, on May 4, 1861, Bischof commanded the 2nd Battalion at Carthage, after which he led a detachment of the regiment to St. Louis on July 25, where they were mustered out of the service on August 14. Bischof then joined the 3rd Missouri Infantry (Three years) which was organized in St. Louis in the Fall of 1861. Elected lieutenant colonel of the regiment, effective November 28, 1861, Bischof commanded the garrison in Rolla with a portion of the 3rd Missouri, while the rest of his regiment participated in the Battle of Pea Ridge in March 1862. Bischof later rejoined his regiment, marched to Helena in the Summer of 1862, during which time he was plagued by a "congestive fever." Recommended for a thirty day certificate to recover his health, Bischof never had an opportunity to take the leave, dying in Helena on August 20, 1861. *O.R.*, Index, 1109; *O.R.S.*, pt. 2, vol. 36: 381–382, 437, 439; Dyer, 1323; National Archives, Record Group M405, roll no. 403, Union Compiled Service Records, 3rd Missouri Infantry (Three years); National Archives, Record Group M405, roll no. 412, Union Compiled Service Records, 3rd Missouri Infantry (Three months).

19. The train was placed south of Dry Fork Creek and was protected by Voerester's Pioneer Company, while a short distance to their front, immediately behind Dry Fork Creek, Sigel had placed a company of infantry with one artillery piece from Essig's Battery to protect the command "against movements of the [enemies'] cavalry towards our rear and our baggage." *O.R.*, vol, 3: 17; Lademann, "Battle of Carthage," 133.

20. Sigel's command pushed passed Double Trouble Creek to the north side of the stream and aligned themselves for battle. Finally, and almost simultaneously, both sides opened fire with their artillery. Wilkin's Battery on the Union left appears to have fired the first shot at 9:50 a.m., not 1:00 p.m., according to George W. Taylor, Rains' Medical Director. Wilkin's shot was immediately answered by Hirman Bledsoe's MSG Battery. Toward the center of the MSG line, Henry Guibor's Battery followed suit and opened the fight against the Union center, closer to 10:00 a.m., which Essig's Battery answered at the same time. And so the artillery duel continued for the next hour with little damage done to either side. On the MSG side the initial Union shots unnerved many of the men and livestock, this being their first time under artillery fire. In John T. Hughe's Extra Battalion, Alonso Shelton recalled of the duel: "Our boys gave as good as they sent us, then I had the 'buck ague' but I soon got over it after I found they did not hit anything but the ground." And any skittishness that the Guard felt soon disappeared as recorded by J. B. Clark who noted that his men "received the fire with the coolness and composure of veterans." On the Union side, the men "cheered and rejoiced at seeing so many enemies fall at each explosion of a shell, but they never stayed down, they always got up again," and, according to Otto Lademann, "we soon found that we were doing little execution." Overall the artillery fire, on both sides, proved to be nothing more than "ineffective artillery practice." *O.R.*, vol. 3: 17, 21, 23, 30, 35–34; Adamson, 150; Banasik, *Missouri in 1861*, 203; Bevier, 37; Duncan, 79; Edwards, 31; Hinze & Farnham,

Guard instantly replied, their fire consisting of solid shot alone; and thus occurred an artillery duel of about an hour's duration that made a great deal of noise but finally did very little harm.[21]

At about 2:30 o'clock p.m. large bodies of mounted men were detached from both flanks of the enemy's position, and avoiding our position by a wide circuit united in our rear, taking a good position in the dry bed of some creek or branch, where nothing but their heads remained visible. This movement effectively cut us off from our train.[22] To counter it Lt. Col. Hassendeubel was sent to the rear with his battalion of infantry and a section of howitzers. When [he] arrived within

---

131–132, 265–266 n. 19; Lademann, "Battle of Carthage," 134; Patrick, "Guibor's Battery," 31; Peckham, 295; Alonzo H. Shelton Reminiscence, Missouri State Historical Society, Western Historical Manuscript Collection (KC166), 7, hereafter cited as Shelton Reminiscence; Snead, *Fight for Missouri*, 225; Webb, 67.

21. According to several sources the MSG had limited ammunition of poor quality for their artillery. Of the Guard ammunition E. A. Pollard wrote: "They had...no shells, and very few solid shot or rounds of grape and cannister. Rude and almost incredible devices were made to supply these wants: trace chains, iron-rods, hard pebbles and smooth stones were substituted for shot." Sigel was likewise amazed at the resilience of the MSG, in the face of the artillery duel commenting: "'Great God' was the like ever seen! Raw recruits, unacquainted with war, standing their ground like veterans, hurling defiance at every discharge of batteries against them, and cheering their own batteries whenever discharged." Bevier, 39; "Col. Burbridge's Regiment," 21; McElroy, 139; Piston & Hatcher, *Wilson's Creek*, 103; O'Flaherty, 69; E. A. Pollard, *The Lost Cause: A New Southern History of the War of the Confederates, etc.* (New York, 1867; reprint ed., New York, 1970), 157, hereafter cited as Pollard.; Snead, "First Year in Missouri," vol. 1: 269; Webb, 66–68; W. N. M., "Battle of Wilson's Creek," in *Southern Bivouac* (Reprint ed., Wilmington, NC, 1993), vol. 3: 50, hereafter cited as W. N. M., "Battle of Wilson's Creek."

22. Lademann has lumped together the withdrawal of Sigel's command from the Double Trouble Creek area at 11:00 a.m., and the action at the Buck Branch in the early afternoon, totally skipping the engagement at Dry Fork Creek, where the most severe fighting took place during July 5. See **Appendix C for Extended Comments on the Engagement at Dry Fork Creek.**

As to Sigel's retreat from Double Trouble Creek–Near 11:00 a.m. the MSG artillery being low on ammunition slackened their rate of fire, giving the impression to the Unionists that they had "silenced" the Guard artillery. About this time Sigel also noticed a "great horde of [Jackson's unarmed] horsemen vanish into the woods," on his left while other cavalry moved around his position on his right. To counter the MSG movement, Sigel directed his artillery, with some skirmishers, to engage the flanking cavalry, while his remaining infantry prepared to assault the enemy's right and center. However, even as the Federals prepared to advance Captain Theodore Wilkin, commanding a battery, notified Sigel that he was low on ammunition and could not advance. It was now shortly after 11:00 a.m., and Sigel, not wanting to assault the Guards line without artillery support, canceled the attack. Weighing heavily on Sigel's decision was his added belief that he faced overwhelming odds, with the possibility of being surrounded and cut off from his train. Sigel then ordered a retreat, "by successive stages," to the south side of Dry Fork Creek, where his reserve and his train were positioned, three miles to his rear. Moving first was Hassendeubel's detachment, followed by Salomon's troops who would cover the retreat from the south side of Dry Fork Creek. The retreat, according to one Guardsman, was made in a "double-quick time and in good order." *O.R.*, vol. 3: 17–18; Adamson, 150–151; Banasik, *Missouri in 1861*, 203; Duncan, 79–80; Engle, 64; Gerteis, *Missouri*, 47; Hinze & Farnham, 138,140–142; Ingenthron, 46; Lademann, "Battle of Carthage," 134–135; "New York 'Times' Narrative," Doc. 249; "New York 'World's' Narrative," Doc. 248; Peckham, 295; Schrantz, 36; Snead, *Fight for Missouri*, 226; *Union Army*, vol. 4: 228.

about 1000 yards of the enemy's cavalry the two howitzers commenced throwing shells, and Lt. Col. Hassendeubel deployed his battalion in line (( )) charging the cavalry with his infantry at double-click and to develop his ((( )).[23] While this movement was being executed Col. Siegel came up with his staff and, addressing Lieut. Col. Hassendeubel, said: "For God's sake, Col. Hassendeubel, don't deploy your column, you will be cut to pieces." When Lieut. Col. Hassendeubel replied: "Never mind, Col. Siegel, those fellows have no sabers," and, turning his horse to his battalion, shouted at the top of his voice: "Battalion, forward! double-quick, march!" With a joyous yell we bounded over the prairie as long as our breath lasted and when we got a good distance off fired a volley at the State Guard cavalry. They scattered over the prairie like chaff, but our whole trophies consisted in a single prisoner, a captain, I believe, who had the misfortune to have his horse riddle and was stunned by the fall. Several riderless horses were galloping over the prairie, but their dismounted, nimble riders scampered off so lively that we could not catch any of them.[24] When the battalion had been reformed we marched on until we

---

23. While the engagement at Dry Fork Creek was taking place Hassendeubel hurried off to supplement the train guard with his detachment of Sigel's command, consisting of his 1st Battalion, 3rd Missouri, with Wilkin's Artillery and the 1st Battalion, 5th Missouri, under Lieutenant Colonel Christian D. Wolff. At the same time Sigel sent orders to the train to reverse their direction, pending a retreat. Following the three mile march at the double-quick, Hassendeubel arrived at the train and organized his detachment for the defense of the train–the time was near 2:00 p.m., even as the Guard had turned Sigel's flank at Dry Fork Creek. The train, under Lieutenant Sebastian Engert, was organized into columns facing south, even while Hassendeubel's artillery fended off Guard cavalry. About 3:00 p.m., the train headed south, under Hassendeubel's guard even as Salomon's detachment hurried to the train, led by Colonel Sigel. When fully protected Sigel placed artillery and infantry on both flanks, and in the front and rear of the "solid square" column that had to cross Buck Branch Creek en route to Carthage. Meanwhile, the Guard cavalry, under Colonels Ben Rives and William Brown, were successful in reaching the rear of the Federal line, taking a position south of Buck Branch Creek, a marshy, narrow creek and bottom, about five miles from Carthage, thus setting the stage for probably the most critical moment of July 5. To Rive's and Brown's north they spied the approaching Federal train; if they could hold their line, even for a short time, they would prevent the Federal retreat long enough for the State Guard infantry to catch the fleeing Federals. NOTE: In their account of the engagement at Buck Branch, Hinze and Farnham have the time as 2:00 p.m. citing Colonel Weightman's account of the battle; however, Weightman's account is one hour behind all the other times cited by other participants, making the actual time about 3:00 p.m. *O.R.*, vol. 3: 18, 24, 34; Hinze & Farnham, 163–166; Rutherford, 46.

24. Approaching the Buck Branch ford, Colonel Hassendeubel led the retreating Union column with three companies of his regiment, even as Col. Sigel, with Salmon's detachment was closing on the retreating train. Seeing the rebel cavalry covering the ford, Hassendeubel ordered his two pieces artillery to fire at the Guard cavalry, who were barely visible behind the banks of the creek. With the artillery firing Hassendeubel ordered a bayonet attack on the defending horsemen. With a "loud hurrah" the Federals took after the Guard cavalry, running 500 yards, "when the want of breath stopped someone, and he fired his gun," about 400 yards from the enemy which prompted the others in the command to also halt and let loose. For Rives' and Brown's men it was a critical moment; unfortunately, the lack of experience, poor weapons and untrained horses produced a stampede of the rebel cavalry, with riderless horses running amok and men running in every direction. Hassendeubel's attack lasted about ten minuets, and when the smoke had cleared the Buck Branch ford was secured and one lone Guard captain was taken prisoner (another source

Formed a Junction

with our unprotected train to the great relief of our quartermaster, Lieut. Sebastian Engert.[25]

The retrograde movement of the right wing had been followed by the rest of the command. To cover our retrograde and check enemy a strong rearguard was left at Coon Creek [Dry Fork Creek], whose passage was guarded by Essig's battery.[26] Here a very lively skirmish was engaged in between the contending forces; while the head of our column leisurely continued its march towards Carthage, which later place we reached at about sundown.[27]

Passing through and beyond the town and our camping ground of the previous

---

says two or three prisoners were taken), along with 35–85 horses and mules, with 65 shotguns and "some revolvers." It was between 3:30 and 4:00 p.m. when Salomon's detachment joined the train and took the lead of Sigel's retreating command, escorting it across Buck Branch, unmolested by any Guard unit. Meanwhile, Hassendeubel rejoined the column, protecting the rear as Sigel's command moved on to Carthage. "Battle of Carthage," Rebellion Record, vol. 2: Doc. 246; Hinze & Farnham, 165–166, 168–170; Lademann, "Battle of Carthage," 135–136; "New York 'Times' Narrative," Doc. 249–250; "New York 'World's' Narrative," Doc. 248; Peckham, 296; Schrantz, 38.

25. Sebastian Engert was appointed the Quartermaster of the 3rd Missouri (Three months), when the unit was organized on April 22, 1861. Later, when the unit re-organized, as the 3rd Missouri Infantry (Three years), Engert was appointed Quartermaster of the unit on February 8, 1862, severing with the 3rd through the Atlanta Campaign of 1864. Final disposition unknown. Dyer, 1323; John B. Gray, *Annual Report of the Adjutant General of Missouri for 1864* (Jefferson City, MO, 1865), 65, hereafter cited as Gray, *Missouri Adjutant General Report*; Union Army, vol. 4: 257.

26. See **Appendix C** for **Extended Comments on The Engagement at Dry Fork Creek.**

27. After crossing Buck Branch, Sigel's command "made good time across the flat land" toward the Spring River, which was five and a half miles from Carthage. "Each one of the horses," according to George Taylor, "attached to the gun carriages was mounted by a rider, as were the horses attached to the baggage-wagons, and with whip in hand they put it at a gallop and kept this rapid rate of travel until they crossed a level prairie, five miles in width." The Spring River marked the last obstacle where the MSG would have any chance to cut off the retreating Unionists before nightfall. Rive's and Brown's Regiments, were scattered and of little use in the pursuit. Weightman's Brigade of the MSG led the rebel infantry pursuit, but was held at bey, by Sigel's artillery "in a sort of leapfrog movement" on their way to Carthage, discharging an occasional round to discourage infantry pursuit. To Hans Christian Adamson, this made Christian Essig the "outstanding hero of the Battle of Carthage." To the west Rains' 2nd Division cavalry moved to flank Sigel's column, but they never managed to get in front of the retreating Federals before they successfully navigated the Spring River ford. It seems that Rains' famished troopers stopped to gobble down some huckleberries, delaying their march, which in turn garnered them the title of "'Huckleberry Cavalry.'" When Sigel finally reached the Spring River, he occupied the hills north of the river to cover the train as they crossed the ford in relative safety and "unmolested" by the State troops. And to protect his command on the south side of the Spring River, from flanking rebel cavalry, Sigel dispatched Lieutenant Colonel Wolf, with his battalion and two pieces of artillery of Wilkin's Battery, to cover the eastern approaches to Carthage, while two more companies from the 3rd Missouri covered the approaches from the west. It was about 6:00 p.m. when Sigel's command entered Carthage. O.R., vol. 3: 18; Adamson, 151; Banasik, *Missouri in 1861*, 202; "Battle of Carthage," *Rebellion Record*, vol. 2: Doc. 247; Brooksher, 124; Hinze & Farnham, 172–175; Lademann, "Battle of Carthage," 136; "New York 'World's' Narrative," Doc. 248; Rutherford, 46; Schrantz, 38; Snead, *Fight for Missouri*, 227.

night, our retreat continued on the Sarcoxie road, still pursued by the mounted State Guard, which however, was careful to keep out of musket range; when about two and a half miles from Carthage the prairie terminated and we struck a belt of timber. It was about 9 p.m. and of course pretty dark, when Col. Siegel halted the command to fire a volley, our rear artillery participating with one shot for each gun, into the dark and silent prairie, for what purpose I never could tell, after which waste of our ammunition we again took up our line of march, rapidly and silently moving into the timber.[28]

It was a weary night march; we had been in motion all day, eating nothing since breakfast. I had the misfortune of scalding my right foot with hot water the evening before, but had reported to my company, and limped along ever since the first shot was fired. During the night my friend Henry Bencke permitted me

To Ride His Horse

(he being the attached Sigel's staff) for several miles. The rest of the night I spent perched on a caisson of my friend, Lieut [August] Krumsleck of Wilken's battery. The distance to Sarcoxie was about 15 miles, and it was near daybreak when we got there.[29]

---

28. At Carthage, Sigel again made a stand–his last of the grueling day–while his train continued their retreat toward Sarcoxie. Weightman's Guard brigade followed closely behind Sigel, crossing the Spring River first, after which they engaged Sigel's troops west of town and pushing them into Carthage. Slack's infantry followed Weightman, rushing into Carthage from the west while Weightman came in from the south. In Carthage, Sigel's troops fortified the courthouse, and sheltered "themselves behind houses, walls and fences," while placing artillery to cover all the roads into the town square. For forty minutes to an hour the engagement continued in Carthage, before the Unionist were forced out of the town, as Parsons' infantry with Guibor's and Bledsoe's artillery joined in he late afternoon fighting from the north side of Carthage. Meanwhile, Sigel had established a defensive position east of Carthage, where they had camped on the night of July 4, on a commanding height. Sigel further directed Company E, 3rd Missouri to "hold the enemy in check until further orders," covering the retreat of the army. With the sun setting, Sigel pulled back his remaining troops, from east of Carthage leaving Company E to their own devices. Between 7:00–8:00 p.m., in the fading light, Slack and Parsons' infantry made their last assault on Sigel's line, being met by a couple of infantry volleys and a few rounds of cannon shot. And then it was over–Sigel abandoned his last position, his command having successfully withdrawn toward Sarcoxie; the final retreat covered by Company E, 3rd Missouri, which eventually rejoined their brigade. The Guard continued their pursuit for the next two miles and finally surrendered to the darkness–it was 9:00 p.m. and the guns were finally silent and the battle over. "The Missouri Mob," according to Alonzo Shelton, of Slack's Division, "had licked the trained [D]utch in their first fight." Banasik, *Missouri in 1861*, 203–204; Bevier, 38; Hinze & Farnham, 181–182, 185, 187–191. 195–198; 136–137; Lademann, "Battle of Carthage," 136–137; Schrantz, 39; Shelton Reminiscence, 8; Snead, *Fight for Missouri*, 227.

29. According to most sources Sigel's command reached Sarcoxie, after a 12 mile march (others say it was 18 miles), arriving between 3:00–3:30 a.m. on July 6. They then rested for a short time before resuming their retreat, first to Mt. Vernon, where they staggered in between late afternoon and 11:00 p.m. They rested the following day and were joined by General Sweeny from Springfield with reenforcements on July 7. Two days later, with Sweeny in command, the brigade returned to Springfield, at a"leisurely" pace, where they arrived on July 9 or 10. It appears that the

Neosho, Carthage and Sarcoxie form merely a triangle, the former two being the base in the latter apex. General McCulloch with his mounted Texas and Arkansas troops, had taken Neosho and captured Capt. Jos. Conrad and his company of rifleman, detached there by Col. Siegel on July 5, could have easily captured Sarcoxie long before our arrival, in which case Col. Sigel and his command would have been caught like rats in a trap.[30]

---

command camped south of Springfield on July 9 and re-entered the town on July 10. *O.R.S.*, pt. 2, vol. 36: 440–442, 491, 493, 495; Bek, "Beugel Diary," 312; Bevier, 38; Gerteis, *Missouri*, 48; Hinze & Farnham, 209–210; McElroy, 141; Monaghan, 155; Peckham, 296–297; Snead, *Fight for Missouri*, 227.

August George Krumsleck or Krummsick or Krumsick was born about 1836, and initially joined Wilken's Battery as a private, being mustered in on May 8, 1861. He was later made the Quartermaster Sergeant of Backof's Artillery Battalion. On June 13, 1861, he was promoted to lieutenant in Wilken's Battery B, Backof's Battalion, fought at Carthage and was mustered out of the service on August 22, 1861. Krumsick then joined the 3rd Missouri (Three years), as an assistant surgeon and was captured while attending wounded at Searcy Landing, Arkansas, on May 19, 1862. Released unconditionally, by General Thomas C. Hindman, on July 14, Krummsick later left the 3rd Missouri, to become the colonel of the 55th EMM in 1864. Final disposition unknown. *O. R.*, vol. 13: 71–72; *O.R.*, vol. 34, pt.3: 655; *O.R.*, Series 2, vol. 3: 594; *O.R.*, Series 2, vol. 4: 221; Scott H. Akridge and Emmett E. Powers, *A Severe and Bloody Fight: The Battle of Whitney's Lane & Military Occupation of White County, Arkansas, May & June, 1862* (Searcy, 1996), 82–83, 135; National Archives, Record Group M405, roll no. 347, Union Compiled Service Records, Backof's Artillery Battalion.

30. Having received information that Federal troops were closing in on Governor Jackson's MSG "of disorganized, undisciplined men," General Ben McCulloch ordered his Arkansas command northward, "without authority,"to save the Missourians. Departing his Maysville, Arkansas camp on July 4, McCulloch entered Missouri the same day with about 2,300 men, being joined by General Price, who added another 1,700 men to the force marching against Sigel's Unionists. On July 5, McCulloch, having learned "from authentic information that if the governor was to be rescued....it was necessary to move with more celerity." Dividing his command, McCulloch sent his cavalry forward to assist Jackson's MSG. At 11:00 a.m., the same day, McCulloch ordered eleven companies of his force to proceed to Neosho, where he learned that a Federal force was encamped. Thomas Churchill led six companies to attack Neosho from the west, while James McIntosh with another five companies were to attack from the south. The time set for the attack was for 2:30 p.m. Arriving near Neosho at 2:00 p.m., Churchill dismounted his command, awaiting the appointed time to attack. Meanwhile, McIntosh arrived in the area about 1:45 p.m., and, "fearing that information would be carried into the town to the enemy," McIntosh dismounted his command, ordering them to double-quick into the town. Even as McIntosh rushed into Neosho, Churchill received word to "press forward with his command." However, by the time Churchill had reached the town courthouse, he found that Captain Joseph Conrad had already surrendered his command. In all Conrad surrendered 94 men according to Sigel; however, rebel sources put the number at 137, in addition to seven wagons, and 150 stand of arms. Additionally Henry Cheavens, from Ben Rive's Regiment noted that when his command passed through Neosho on July 6, the courthouse contained 125 prisoners. Further, Elmo Engenthron, in his book *Borderland Rebellion*, noted that 125 men accepted parole while 12 did not, giving further credence to 137 as the correct Federal loss at Neosho. NOTE: In his initial reports of the capture of Neosho, Ben McCulloch under reported the captures, writing on July 9–"In the hurry of reporting of this affair I made the amount of property and prisoners less than it actually was." The numbers presented above were McCulloch's revised numbers. Union sources generally reported the losses as between 80–94 captured. The difference probably reflects the captured teamsters and Home Guard that were with Conrad but never counted in the command strength. *O.R.*, vol. 3: 38–30, 606–607; *O.R.S.*, pt. 1, vol. 1:

Fortunately for us Gen. McCulloch contented himself with his Neosho success, and left Sarcoxie occupied where we, on the morning of Saturday, July 6, commenced to prepare a much needed breakfast. We had barely started when the cry arose, "They're coming," and, hastily emptying our half-cooked victuals on the ground and reloading our train, we marched off with alacrity, continuing our retreat to Mt. Vernon. All day we tramped along, weary and exhausted, reaching Mt. Vernon late at night. Although half starved, we were too much worn out to think of eating, but fell down and went to sleep where we had stacked our arms. At 3 o'clock on Sunday morning we were alarmed, placed in position outside the town, where we remained until 7 a.m., when we were dismissed and permitted to cook some food, the first since Friday morning. About noon Gen. Sweeney arrived with reinforcements, consisting of B. Gratz Brown's Fourth Reserve Corps, two companies of our own regiment and the Zouave Company of the Third Reserve Corps, Col. Wm. [John] McNeil.[31] On Monday, the 8th at 6 a.m. the whole force, now commanded by Gen. Sweeney, started back to Springfield, Mo., camping that night at Little York and reaching Springfield about noon the next day, which place we ought never to have left.

Otto C. Lademann

Editor Note–Aftermath of the Battle of Carthage: Losses and comments on the effect of the battle.

In July 1861 the Civil War was still in its infancy and the Battle of Carthage made headlines from San Francisco to New York City, and throughout the South, being the "first major conflict of the Civil War west of the Mississippi

---

223–224; Edwin C. Bearss, "Fort Smith Serves General McCulloch As A Supply Depot," *Arkansas Historical Quarterly* 24 (Winter, 1965), 329, hereafter cited as Bearss, "Fort Smith"; Britton, 63–66; Duncan, 82; Easley, "Cheavens Journal," 19; Hinze & Farnham, 199–200; Ingenthron, 49; O'Flaherty, 73; Moore, *Missouri, Confederate Military History*, vol. 9: 52; Piston & Sweeney, "Missouri State Guard," 22; Snead, *Fight for Missouri,*, 236–237; *Union Army*, vol. 6: 635.

31. Lademann was mistaken–The two companies of "his own regiment" were actually Companies B and H of he 5th Missouri (Three months). Additionally John McNeil commanded the 3rd Regiment U.S. Reserve Corps, not William McNeil. *O.R.S.*, pt. 2, vol. 36: 490, 494; Peckham, 126.

Benjamin Gratz Brown was born on May 28, 1826, in Lexington, Kentucky, to a slave owning family. He was educated at Transylvania University and Yale, graduating from the latter place in 1847. Admitted to the Kentucky bar, Brown moved to of St. Louis, where he joined his first cousin Frank Blair in the practice of the law. An Unconditional Unionist, Brown was a member of the first Republican Convention in Missouri and co-editor of the *Missouri Democrat*. In 1856, following a series of insulting exchanges between Thomas C. Reynolds (Missouri lieutenant governor in 1860) and Brown, a duel was held in which Brown was shot, but later recovered. At the beginning of the Civil War, Brown was an anti-slavery man and commanded the 4th U.S. Reserve Regiment from Missouri. In 1863, Brown was appointed to the U.S. Senate (1863–1866), in a large part because of his stand against slavery, to serve out the remainder of the term of Waldo Johnson, who had been expelled from the senate. Brown was elected to a two year term as Missouri Governor in 1870, and served as the vice-presidential nominee of the Liberal Republican-Democratic Party, with Horace Greely, in 1872. Returning to the law, Brown remained an active lawyer in St., Louis until his death in St. Louis on December 13, 1885. Gerteis, *St. Louis*, 69–71; *History of Audrain County*, 38, 40; McElroy, 65; Ryle, 73, 135, 196; "Senator Brown of Missouri," *Chicago Tribune*, November 19, 1863; Winter, 142.

River;" However, to William Barlow of Guibor's MSG Battery "The affair at Carthage hardly rose to the dignity of a respectable skirmish but was impressive and grand to us then." [32]

Of the engagement Wiley Britton wrote that the battle "created intense excitement throughout Western Missouri." Praise was heaped upon Sigel, with one New York newspaper declaring that Sigel was "perhaps, the best educated tactician, we have in Missouri." The Chicago Tribune labeled Carthage "Col. Sigel's splendid victory." And despite the fact that Sigel had retreated from the State Guard, the *Waukegan Weekly Gazette* recorded that "The victory was really with Sigel."

Most secondary authors, and period commentator, John M. Schofield labeled Sigel's retrograde movement a "masterly retreat," while John McElroy wrote that "Sigel received unstinted praise for his skillful retreat and the masterly handling of his artillery." Elmo Ingenthron called the retreat "militarily sound." The men of Sigel's command were praised as "veteran troops" for the way they conducted their retreat, while an Eastern newspaper declared that European troops "could not excel the coolness and intrepidity of our volunteers." Further, Sigel's men "commended their commander highly for his actions" as the phrase "'I fight mits Sigel'" echoed through the German-American community. And the *Union Army* series noted that the engagement on July 5, "brought Sigel into notice as a master in conducting a running fight against almost overwhelming odds."[33]

In analyzing Colonel Sigel's performance at Carthage, David Hinze and Karen Farnham provided the following sketch on Sigel:

> For his part, Sigel displayed a wholesale lack of caution by marching his small force, sans cavalry, directly against what he knew as a superior enemy army. When the gravity of his mistake sunk in, he still remained on the field until Southern cavalry began to move around his flank and infantry pressed his attenuated front. His strategy and field tactics suggest an arrogance born of overconfidence. But for the ill-equipped and indifferently led enemy, Sigel and his men would have suffered a resounding defeat.[34]

Despite all the period bravado surrounding Colonel Sigel and the engagement at Carthage, most contemporary and secondary authors acknowledge the importance of the battle to the fledgling MSG. To E. A. Pollard, "the results of the day were greatly encouraging to the Missourians. These raw and poorly

---

32. Ingenthron, 51; Monaghan, 156; Patrick, "Guibor's Battery," 31.
33. Britton, 63; C., "Affairs In Missouri," *Chicago Tribune*," July 18,1861; Engle, 65; "Great Battle In South-Western Missouri," *Waukegan Weekly Gazette*, July 13, 1861; Ingenthron, 47, 51; McElroy, 141; Monaghan, 155–156; "New York 'Times' Narrative," Doc. 250; "New York 'World's' Narrative," Doc. 249.
34. Hinze & Farnham, 203.

armed men had driven a well-disciplined enemy from the field." To W. L. Webb, Carthage was simply "a great day." R. S. Bevier wrote that July 5 had an "inspiring effect" on the State troops. William Piston and Thomas Sweeney wrote that the affair "provided a badly needed psychological boost for the Missouri State Guard." Daniel O'Flaherty went even further, writing that Carthage was a "decisive engagement" for the MSG, ranking "with some of the important engagements of the war" which allowed Jackson's MSG to link up with the Confederate forces in northwest Arkansas and eventually win the Battle of Wilson's Creek. And John Edwards wrote of the Battle of Carthage:[35]

> "The advantages to the Confederate were great, because they preserved their organization, got acquainted with artillery, felt confidence in themselves and their leaders, and were within hail almost of succor and supplies."[36]

As to losses, both sides experienced rather low casualties, considering the fight lasted for close to twelve hours and was conducted over ten miles. Sigel's losses are variously reported by several different sources; however, most period and modern-day authors used Sigel's Official Report, which listed 13 killed and 31 wounded.. That said, Nicholas Fuester, commanding Company G, 5th Missouri recorded that Sigel lost 13 killed and 150 wounded, while a Union surgeon from Hannibal, according to George Taylor, told him that Sigel's loss "was not less than two hundred"–the difference between Sigel's account and Fuester's & Taylor's probably reflect the slightly wounded. And Colonel John Dubois, who arrived at Springfield shortly after Sigel's return reported that Sigel had lost 30 killed with 100 prisoners, while Frank Backhof in the Compiled Service Records, noted that his command suffered a "severe loss in the Battle of Carthage," but giving no numbers, leading one to believe that Sigel's Official Report was leaving out some of his losses, like the slightly wounded or those of the Home Guard units that took part in the engagement but were never reported. Period newspapers listed the losses as 8 or 24 killed and 45 wounded ("Battle of Carthage," *Rebellion Record*, vol. 2: Doc. 247); 20 or 21 killed and 40 wounded ("New York 'Times' Narrative," 249; C, "Affairs In Missouri," *Chicago Tribune*, July 24,1861); and 8 killed and 45 wounded ("Great Battle in South-Western Missouri," *Waukegan Weekly Gazette*, July 11, 1861). Elmo Ingenthron and Virginia Easley put Sigel's losses at 18 killed and 53 wounded (Ingenthron, 49; Easley, Cheavens Journal, 19 n. 29). Given the varied accounts of the engagement, the one I've selected comes from Dyer's *Compendium* (same as Easley and Ingenthron), which listed 18 killed, 53 wounded and 5 missing or captured.

---

35. Bevier, 39; O'Flaherty, 71–72; Piston & Sweeney, "Missouri State Guard," 22; Pollard, 168; Webb, 67
36. Edwards, 31.

The captured were wounded who were abandoned by Sigel when he gave up Carthage during his retreat to the State forces.[37] The MSG losses were fairly well reported in the *Official Records*, though it appears that the slightly wounded were generally left out; however, where known, I've included them in the final totals, which I place at 24 killed or mortally wounded, 62 wounded with one man missing for a total of 87 (See Appendix D for details). That said, various sources have the MSG losses ranging from 74 killed and wounded (Adamson, Britton, McElroy and Snead); 77, killed, wounded and missing (Hinze & Farnham), 80 killed and wounded (Rutherford); to 170 killed and wounded (*Union Army* series), while Union newspaper accounts placed MSG losses from "not less than 200 killed" to 500 killed and wounded, with 45–50 prisoners. And General Sigel put the Guards losses at not "less than 350 to 400," while the officers of the 1st Iowa, upon arrival in Springfield, reported that it was "generally believed...that Jackson lost 1,181men killed." As too the accuracy of the Federal accounts of MSG losses Rains' Medical director recorded–"This statement is made [regarding MSG losses] with a view to correct those falsehoods which the enemy is industriously circulating in the vain hope of propping up their failing cause, or to keep down our Southern friends in maintaining sovereignty of the State." Taylor then listed the losses in Rains' Division as "seven killed and thirty six wounded,"–total 43; while Rains listed 44 officers and men as casualties. Additionally, Taylor was further supported by yet another Guard doctor, who also questioned the reported Guard losses of 500, labeling those published in the *Missouri Republican* as "falsehoods"–This unnamed doctor put the overall MSG losses at 10 killed and 36 wounded, for total of 46.[38]

In addition to the casualties listed above, the Federals, according to Sigel lost"one baggage wagon; however Guard sources indicate that they captured more wagons than Sigel reported. One rebel "eyewitness" stated that Sigel left "eighteen wagons of provisions, camp equipage, mules and one wagon load of cakes, pies, etc." in the area following the battle. Further, Colonel Ben Rives,

---

37. *O.R.*, vol. 3: 19; *O.R.S.*, pt. 2, vol. 36: 493; Adamson, 151; Banasik, *Missouri in 1861*, 204; Britton, 63; Dyer, 797; Easley, "Cheavens Journal," 19 n. 29; Engle, 65; Hinze & Farnham, 202; Ingenthron, 49; McElroy, 141; Monaghan, 155; National Archives, Record Group M405, roll no. 347, Backhof's Missouri Artillery Battalion (Three months); Rutherford, 47; Schrantz, 40; Snead, *Fight for Missouri*, 227.

38. The losses reported by the "unknown doctor" seem to be indicative of only Rains' Division, but does show that they were light. *O.R.*, vol. 3: 10; Adamson, 151; Banasik, *Missouri in 1861*, 204; "Battle of Carthage," *Rebellion Record*, vol. 2: Doc. 247; Britton, 63; Hinze & Farnham, 205; "Great Battle in South-Western Missouri," *Waukegan Weekly Gazette*, July 13, 1861; Charles F. Larimer, ed., *Love and Valor: Intimate Civil War Letters Between Captain Jacob and Emeline Ritner* (Western Spring, IL, 2000), 39–42, hereafter cited as Larimer; McElroy, 141; "New York 'World's' Narrative," Doc. 248; "New York 'Times' Narrative," Doc. 250; *Rebellion Record*, vol. 2: Diary 20; Rutherford, 47; Schrantz, 40; Snead, *Fight for Missouri*, 227; *Union Army*, vol. 5: 228; VEMAX, "Reliable News From Missouri," *The New Orleans Bee* (New Orleans, LA), July 23, 1861.

of the Fourth Division, MSG stated in his official report that Captain John H. McNeil "succeeded in capturing a portion of the transportation and baggage of the enemy," clearly indicating that the rebels captured more than "one" wagon as reported by Sigel.

Other losses in the Guard, according to Union newspaper accounts, amounted too 45–50 rebel prisoners, about 85 horse, 65 double-barreled shot guns and some pistols, none of which Sigel mentioned in his official account, leading one to question either the press accounts or Sigel's incomplete report. Another possibility was that Sigel let the animals go, didn't parole the prisoners, and never secured the weapons he captured, all of which seems unlikely.[39]

* * * * * * *

Item: The Battle of Wilson's Creek (August 10, 1861), by Otto C. Lademann, late captain 3rd Missouri Volunteers.
Published: April 2, 1887.

Wilson's Creek

St. Louis, March 24
[Editor *Republican*]

Permit me to open my third article with another correction. Passing over the idea that your printer made a red, "belt" out of the "welt" on my gray jeans pantaloons, he introduced a military novelty by placing my two batteries of four guns each "on the right and left of the Fifth Missouri, in the interval between it and the second wing out stations," in place of "between it and the wing battalions."

After our return to Springfield, on Tuesday, July 9, we went into camp south of town on the right of the Forsyth road. Gen. Lyon and his troops joined us about July 13, the general establishing his headquarters in Springfield, but his troops encamped several miles west of the town, on the Little York prairie.[40]

Nothing of much military importance occurred with our command during the month of July, but after July 23 the term of enlistment of many of the men of our

---

39. *O.R.*, vol. 3: 19, 34; Col. B. A. Rives Papers, "Sketch of Colonel B. A. Rives of Ray County, Missouri," Missouri Historical Society, 1; "New York 'Times' Narrative," Doc. 249–250; "New York 'World's' Narrative," Doc. 248; Peterson, et. al., 139; VEMAX, "Reliable News From Missouri," *New Orleans Bee*, July 23, 1861.

40. According to the *Supplement to the Official Records*, Sweeney arrived back in Springfield on July 10 (See note no. 29 above), while Lademann in his second article on Carthage has the command arriving in Springfield at 10:00 a.m. on the 9th, camping "south of the city, on the Forsyth road." It appears that the various commands did not enter Springfield until July 10. See **Appendix C** for **Extended Comments on Lyon's march to Springfield, July 3–13, 1861.** *O.R.S.*, pt. 2, vol. 36: 440–442, 491, 493, 495; Lademann, "Battle of Carthage," 139; Peckham, 297.

regiment expired and they were sent to Rolla and St. Louis as rapidly as possible.[41] This greatly reduced our effective force, in fact our regiment became a skeleton.[42] Col. Hassendeubel and Maj. Bischoff left, and Capt. Abselom [Anselm] Albert took command as lieutenant colonel; having reenlisted for three years, or during the war, before leaving St. Louis. I was detached from my company, E, and assigned to duty with Co. B as acting second lieutenant.[43]

On Thursday, August 1, active

---

41. On July 20, General Thomas Sweeney led an expedition to Forsyth, Missouri, to break up a rebel encampment which was reported in the area. The expedition consisted of a 500-man battalion of the 1st Iowa Infantry, the 2nd Kansas Infantry, Companies C and D, 1st U.S. Cavalry and a section of Totten's Company F, 2nd U.S. Artillery; in all about 1,200 troops. Sweeney entered Forsyth on the early afternoon of the 22nd, easily capturing the town, while suffering the loss of three men wounded (Sweeney says only two). Additionally, Sweeney reported the capture of three prisoners, seven horses, while killing 8–10 and wounding several. The Expedition left Forsyth at noon on the 23rd and returned to Springfield on the afternoon of July 25. For a complete look at the Forsyth Expedition see *Missouri in 1861*. *O.R.*, vol. 3: 44–45, 399; Banasik, *Missouri in 1861*, 119 n. 207, 120–126; Edwin C. Bearss, *The Battle of Wilson's Creek* (Boseman, MT, 1988), 9–11, hereafter cited as Bearss, *Wilson's Creek* ; Britton, 73–75; Dyer, 797; Holcombe & Adams, 8.

The first unit to depart Springfield, for muster out, was the 4th U.S. Reserve Corps, which departed for St. Louis between July 17–20, arriving in St. Louis on the 26th. On July 25, Lieutenant Colonel Christian D. Wolff led a detachment of roughly 400 troops composed of men from the 1st, 3rd, 4th and 5th Missouri Infantries (Three months) back to St. Louis for mustering out. Accompanying Wolff was Major Bischof, who commanded the 3rd Missouri detachment, including Joseph Conrad's company, which was captured at Neosho on July 5. In all those being mustered out numbered about 2,000 officers and men. Other commands due for muster out included the remainder of the 3rd Missouri (Three months), a couple of companies from the 2nd Missouri (Three months), the last troops of the 5th Missouri (Three months), the 1st and 2nd Kansas and the 1st Iowa–substantially Lyon's entire command. All agreed to remain beyond their term of service to fight at Wilson's Creek on August 10. *O.R.S.*, pt. 2, vol. 36: 436, 439, 465–469,489; Adamson, 172; Brooksher, 146; Ingenthron, 51; Piston & Hatcher, *Wilson's Creek*, 189; *War in the West*, 87.

42. On August 4, 1861, Lyon recorded that the strength of his command was 5,868, with only sight difference from what the various brigades carried into the Battle of Wilson's Creek; However, Sigel's Brigade has 220 more men than is commonly accepted as at the battle. On August 4, the 3rd Missouri had 700 officers and men while the 5th Missouri fielded 600 for a total of 1,300–392 more than Sigel recorded as at Wilson's Creek (Sigel says they totaled 912 "men."). However Sigel also noted that he left two companies in Springfield as a garrison and if one assumes that Sigel's supposed strength at Wilson's Creek was 1,200, this would suggest that the men he left behind totaled about 200. Further, though not stated, I suspect these 200 men were those whose term had expired and were unwilling to participate in the upcoming battle. With the confusion surrounding Sigel's strength at Wilson's Creek , this gives rise to the question as to what was Sigel's actual strength. Using available information, it is estimated that Sigel's Brigade numbered 1,156 officers and men at the battle on August 10. See **Appendix D, Union Revised Order of Battle, Introduction to Sigel's Command** for details on Sigel's Brigade at Wilson's Creek. *O.R.*, vol. 3: 48; Banasik, *Missouri in 1861*, 378; Bearss, *Wilson's Creek*, 163; Britton, 107; Piston & Hatcher, *Wilson's Creek*, 337; F. Sigel, Letter (July 30,1895), "Battle of Wilson's Creek," *Missouri Historical Review* 1 (October, 1906 -July, 1907), 148, hereafter cited as Sigel's Letter; Snead, *Fight for Missouri*, 310.

43. Albert became the lieutenant colonel of the 3rd Missouri (Three months) on July 24, following the resignation Francis Hassendeubel, and was never the lieutenant colonel of the 3rd Missouri (Three years). See note. no. 3 above for details.

Operations Were Resumed.

Sigel's Brigade marching to Wilson's Creek on the Cassville or Telegraph road, camping at night on the future battlefield and resuming the march next day. The day was intensely hot, our movement very slow, but soon accelerated by hearing the booming of cannon in front, caused by the insignificant skirmish at Dug Springs.[44] Another slow and laborious advance was made next day, but on Sunday, August 4, we bent our steps homeward to Springfield, which place we reached on Monday, the 5th, re-occupying our old encampment.[45]

Before proceeding to the narrative of the events in which the Third Missouri Infantry participated it is imperative that I should give a sketch of the military situation in the state of Missouri at the commencement of August, 1861.

The city of St. Louis occupying the most prominent position, geographically as well as strategically, in the Mississippi Valley, it was of vital importance to the Union as well as to the Confederate Army. It certainly constituted one of the greatest military errors of the Confederate government that it neglected to strain every nerve to obtain possession of it.

It is a well-known fact that the determined Union feeling of the German citizens of St. Louis enable to Frank P. Blair and Gen. Lyon to organize a sufficient federal force to hold the key of the Mississippi Valley and move forward from it in

A Determined Offensive.

After various military makeshifts the state of Missouri was finally assigned to the "Western department," commanded by Maj. Gen. John C. Frémont, headquarters at St. Louis, Mo., where he arrived, July 25, 1861.[46]

---

44. See **Appendix C** for **Extended Comments of the Skirmish of Dug Springs, August 2, 1861**.

45. The day following the engagement at Dug Springs Lyon moved forward, having received reports of 10–15,000 rebels in his front. Contacting only rebel scouts on August 3, Lyon camped for the night at Alexander McCulla's Store, which was located near the county line between Christian and Stone Counties on the Wire or Telegraph road, which led to Fayetteville, Arkansas–It was about twenty-four miles from Springfield. While encamped on August 3, Lyon, upon consultation, ordered a retreat to Springfield, believing the city was in imminent danger of falling; he reached the city near sundown on August 5. In ordering the retreat, Lyon feared that he could not hold Springfield, because of the large number of mounted rebels and fully expected to have to abandon the city, but not before he gave some type of resistance. The forthcoming engagement at Wilson's Creek was Lyon's attempt to halt the rebel advance and save Springfield. When the Unionists failed to win the battle on August 10, they abandoned the city. *O.R.*, vol. 3: 47; Bearss, *Wilson's Creek*, 27–29; Brooksher, 172–173; Samuel J. Crawford, *Kansas in the Sixties* (Chicago, 1911), 29, hereafter cited as Crawford; Snead, *Fight for Missouri*, 254; Ingenthron,, 78, 317; Moore, *Missouri, Confederate Military History*, vol. 9: 55; Piston & Hatcher, *Wilson Creek*, 142–145; Ware, 285, 293.

46. The Department of the West was in existence at the beginning of the Civil War, but was discontinued on July 3, 1861. The newly created Western Department embraced the state of Illinois and all states and territories west of the Mississippi River and east of the Rocky Mountains. Dyer, 254–255.

In all professions, success constitutes the supreme test of merit, but especially so in the military profession, and no matter what personal necessity or scientific attainments a general officer may possess, if he is not successful in his campaign he is rated at incompetent general.

When Gen. Frémont arrived in St. Louis he was well aware of the position of Gen. Lyon and his troops. One week after Frémont's arrival in St. Louis, Lyon commenced his unsuccessful advance upon Dug Springs,. While Gen. Frémont's name was a tower of strength on the unsettled condition of affairs at that time, he did not evidence much military skill in his operations.

Being fully cognizant of Gen. Lyon's perilous position and inadequate means at his command, Gen. Frémont ought to have made superhuman efforts to reinforce Lyon and provided him with a sufficiency of troops, ordnance and commissary stores.[47] The fate of the state of Missouri and the important city of St. Louis depended upon the issue of the battle then eminent between his army and the combined forces of Gens. McCulloch and Price, for no mortal man could anticipate the absolute nonsense which those gentlemen made of their victory after they gained it. Gen. Frémont utterly

Ignored the Necessities

of Lyon, but permitted himself to be imposed upon by some vapury [vaporing] demonstrations of the Confederate general, Hardee, in Northeast Arkansas and some equally vague maneuvers of Gen. Pillow, C. S. A. and Jeff Thompson, M. S. G., in Southeast Missouri.[48] Gathering all troops at his disposal, he embark them

John C. Frémont was a famous explorer, scout, Mexican War veteran, and the first Republican candidate for President in 1856. He was assigned to the command on July 3,1861, and assumed command of the Western Department, on July 25, 1861, being delayed in New York City for "several weeks," procuring arms and equipment for 23,000 men. Many of those who served under Frémont in Missouri had little respect for him as one veteran recalled: "If there ever was an empty, spread-eagle, show-off, horn-tooting general, it was Frémont....He had no ability of any kind." And author Hans Christian Adamson wrote of Frémont: "It has been said of Frémont–whatever greatness he may have had, and he had much–the Great Pathfinder was neither a good executive nor a competent soldier." William Brooksher simply called Frémont A "naive, flamboyant General." See *Missouri Brothers in Gray* for biography. *O.R.*, 3: 390, 406; Adamson, 176; Banasik, *Missouri Brothers in Gray*, 135, 137; Brooksher, 140; John C. Frémont, "In Command In Missouri," *Battles and Leaders of the Civil War*. 4 vols. (New York, 1887–1888), vol. 1: 278–279, hereafter cited as Frémont; Ware, 248.

47. A short time of after the arrival of General Frémont, in St. Louis, a correspondent for the *Chicago Tribune* expressed a different opinion of the situation, writing on August 5: "Gen. Lyon sadly needs reinforcements, and probably considers himself badly treated because none are sent him. It is evident, however, that the management of the military department is in competent hands, and that General Frémont will do all that any man can do to facilitate operations." Continuing his comments the *Tribune* correspondent summed up to current situation in Missouri writing–"There are not troops enough in this state to proceed with aggressive operations as vigorously desired." C., "Affairs In Missouri," *Chicago Tribune*, August 7, 1861.

48. William J. Hardee was born in 1815, graduated from West Point in 1842 (number 26 of 45), fought in the Seminole War and the Mexican War, where he was captured and later exchanged.

on a magnificent fleet of ante bellum steamers and brought them down to Cairo where they encountered a good, long rest but no enemy.[49]

By the incompetent generalship of the department commander Gen. Lyon found himself in a more than perilous position when he returned to Springfield from Dug Springs on Monday, August 5, slowly followed by the combined forces of Gen. McCulloch, C. S. A., whose effective strength was about 5,000 of all arms, with eight guns, and the Missouri State Guard about 6,000 men and seven guns, under the command of Maj. Gen. Sterling Price, thus forming a total strength of 11,000 men and fifteen guns.[50]

This [rebel] army advanced to Wilson's Creek, about 12 miles southwest of Springfield, on Tuesday, August 6, and went into camp, where the great

---

When Georgia seceded from the Union, Hardee resigned from the U.S. Army and was appointed a colonel in the Confederacy. Made a brigadier general in June 1861, Hardee was assigned to Arkansas for duty, where he organized his command at Pitman's Ferry in the summer of 1861. By the end of 1861, Hardee had transferred to the east side of the Mississippi River, where he completed his military service, rising to the rank of lieutenant general by the close of the war. He died on November 6, 1873 in Selma, Alabama. Boatner, 374; Faust, 338.

Gideon J. Pillow, was born on June 6, 1806, in Williamson City, Tennessee, was a Mexican War veteran, and a lawyer by profession. At the beginning of the Civil War, he fought at Belmont, Missouri (November 7, 1861) and Fort Donelson, Tennessee (February 15, 1862). After he passed the command of Fort Donelson to General Simon B. Buckner, and fled, Pillow was later reprimanded for his actions. He never commanded again in the Confederate Army. After the war he practiced law in Memphis and died near Helena, Arkansas, on October 8, 1878. Boatner, 653–654; Faust, 585; Warner, *Generals in Gray*, 241.

Meriwether Jeff Thompson was born on January 22, 1826, in Harpers Ferry, Virginia, moved to Missouri in 1847, and settled near St. Joseph. At the beginning of the Civil War, he was elected brigadier general of the 1st Division MSG and commanded the Missouri troops in southeast Missouri. Known as the Missouri "Swamp Fox," Thompson served almost exclusively in the Trans-Mississippi. He was captured on August 22, 1863, near Pocahontas, Arkansas, and was exchanged on August 3, 1864. During Price's 1864, Missouri Raid, Thompson assumed command of Shelby's Iron Brigade when its commander was wounded. At war's end, Thompson moved to Memphis, Tennessee, and later to New Orleans. Toward the end of his life Thompson returned to St. Joseph, Missouri, where he died on September 5, 1876. Allardice, *More Generals in Gray*, 219–220.

49. Frémont was appointed commander of the Western Department on July 3, but then lingered in Washington, New York and Philadelphia, while seeking guidance for his department and obtaining weapons for his new command. However, "his critics…claimed that he was frittering away valuable time," when he should have been in Missouri. Finally on July 18, Frémont was directed to proceed to his command. And, upon his arrival in St. Louis on July 25, Frémont found his department in a chaotic state–the city was threatened from the south and southeast by rebels under Gideon Pillow and M. Jeff Thompson, and, General Lyon with a large portion of the combat ready troops was in southwestern Missouri. Further, Frémont believed that the safety of St. Louis and Missouri depended on securing Cairo, Illinois and Bird's Point, Missouri. See **Appendix C** for **Extended Comments** on **The problems that Frémont faced upon his arrival in St. Louis.** Adamson, 172–173, 177; Frémont, 279–289; Snead, *Fight for Missouri*, 252; *War in the West*, 161.

50. For the upcoming Battle of Wilson's Creek the rebel army numbered 5,024 effectives in McCulloch's command, while Price's MSG fielded 5,298 effective officers and men for a grand total of 10,342. The combined rebel artillery numbered 15 pieces; 7 for Price and 8 for McCulloch. Banasik, *Missouri in 1861*, 381.

Telegraph–Fayetteville or the Cassville Road crosses Wilson's Creek.[51] McCulloch and his Confederate forces on the right i.e.: south and back of the Fayetteville Road, and Gen. Prices 'troops on the left i.e.: north and west of the road, their encampment extending along the valley of Wilson's Creek about five miles. The effective force of Gen. Lyon, by reason of the casualties of the service

And Expiration of Terms

all the ninety days' men to have dwindled down to about 6000 men, with eighteen guns.[52]

Close proximity of enemy made it impossible for him to retreat unmolested, being encumbered with large masses of political fugitives, and cumbersome trains, which would have enabled the enemy to force an engagement upon him at any time under the most disadvantageous circumstances.

On the other hand, the disparity of numbers made an attack very hazardous, for there naturally was little or no difference in the material, composing the two armies or their war experience; yet a bold and fierce attack was the only possible means of saving his men and materials, a sharp and stinging offensive blow, which would so stop the enemy as to secure him an unmolested retreat to Rolla. Under the circumstances this was undoubtedly the proper military course to pursue and quite in accordance with the character of this heroic, gallant officer commanding the federal forces.[53] In his disposition of the troops designated for that attack he

---

51. The Telegraph or Wire Road was also known as the Cassville or Fayetteville Road, which ultimately led to Fayetteville, Arkansas. William H. Wherry, "Wilson's Creek and the Death of Lyon," in *Battles and Leaders of the Civil War* 4vols. (New York, 1887–1888) vol. 1: 289, hereafter cited as. Wherry, "Wilson's Creek."

52. For Wilson's Creek, Lyon divided his command into two parts. The main body was led by General Lyon, while Colonel Sigel led the second part. Lyon's column was composed of three brigades numbering 4,305 officers and men, while Sigel's command fielded 1,156 officers and men. These numbers differ from those that I put forth in 2001, in my book *Missouri in 1861*, due to new information discovered since that time. These new numbers reflect the addition of a 13th Illinois Infantry Detachment, a Pioneer Company and Lyon's bodyguard not previously known. See **Appendix D** for the **Union Revised Order of Battle for the Wilson's Creek.** Banasik, *Missouri in 1861*, 377–378; "Battle of Wilson's Creek, MO.: Missouri 'Democrat' Narrative," *Rebellion Record*, vol. 2: Doc. 511; Dyer, 1341; Piston & Hatcher, *Wilson's Creek*, 80, 337.

53. Various participants gave an assortment of reasons for Lyon attacking the Confederates at Wilson's Creek, even though they initially supported a retreat to either Rolla or Ft. Scott, Kansas. Frank Blair said Lyon feared the massive rebel cavalry that would attack his retreating column—besides Lyon "had a great reluctance to do any retreating at all," believing that "he could vanquish them" on their chosen field. Anselm Albert recorded that "It was thought that it might be more dangerous to retreat without fighting them than to fight them." Still another member of Lyon's staff simply recorded that they were "in no condition to retreat,...could not withstand an attack...,and, in the judgement of the officers the only course left was to attack the enemy." Tom Sweeney was the only one of Lyon's command to argue against a retreat, believing that the loyal citizens of the southwest must not be abandoned as it would "overwhelm the Union cause in that part of the State." In the end, Sweeney "pleaded eloquently against" a retreat, according to the *Missouri Democrat*, declaring, "it would be the ruin of the Union cause in that quarter of the

committed serious error in dividing his little army into two columns, the larger one of about 4500 men and ten guns under his personal command, advancing west to Little York P. O., and thus turning south, thus attacking the left and rear of the Confederate and Missouri State Guard combined, while the smaller column of about 1,000 infantry and six guns, marched south from Springfield, on the Forsyth Road, whence turning to the right and changing the direction of the march to the west, they encountered the right flank of the enemy at the confluence of Wilson's and Tyrel's [Terrell] creeks.[54]

State, and urged a battle as soon as the enemy were within striking distance." Sweeney "his face flushed livid red," closed his argument stating "Let us eat the last bit of mule flesh and fire our last cartridge before we think of retreating." Eventually Sweeney convinced Lyon not to retreat, but to attack. Lyon agreed stating that he would not retreat "'before we are whipped.'" And, according to the *New York Tribune*, Lyon agreed with Sweeney's recommendation to "save his own reputation and that of his officers under him." Overall Lyon acknowledge the need to retreat, but deemed it necessary to attack the rebels at Wilson's Creek "to hurt him such that he cannot follow" our retreat from the area. To author James Peckham, "Springfield was the place to defend St. Louis" and any threat coming from southeast Missouri or Columbus, Kentucky was nothing more than "balderdash." With all the arguments as to why Lyon decided to fight at Wilson's Creek, Daniel O'Flaherty put it simply–Lyon "had determined to fight, on the theory that an offense was the best defense." See **Appendix C** for **Extended Comments on Lyon's decision to attack.** "Battle of Wilson's Creek, MO.: Missouri 'Democrat' Narrative," *Rebellion Record*, vol. 2: Doc. 513; "Battle of Wilson's Creek, MO.: New York 'Tribune' Narrative," *Rebellion Record*, vol. 2: Doc. 515; Bearss, *Wilson's Creek*, 46–47; Brooksher, 172–173; Frémont, 282; Alice L. Fry, *Kansas and Kansans in the Civil War: First Through the Thirteenth Volunteer Regiment* (Kansas City, KS, 1996), 20, hereafter cited as Fry; Gerteis, *Missouri*, 57; O'Flaherty, 80–81; Jeffery Patrick, ed., *Nine Months in the Infantry Service: The Civil War Journal of R. P. Matthews. And Roster the Phelps Regiment Missouri Volunteers* (Springfield, MO, 1999), 25, hereafter cited as Patrick, *Nine Months in the Infantry*; Phillips, *Damned Yankee*, 247–248; *War in the West*, 165–166, 233–234, 264; Ware, 303–304; Woodard, 303–304.

54. As initially planned, on August 8, Lyon proposed "to march with all our available force," attack the enemy, "and endeavor to rout him before he recovers from his surprise"–essentially making a "spoiling attack." However, on the morning on August 9, Colonel Sigel came to Lyon, and again, proposed "a different and peculiar strategy, which contradicted the most fundamental military principle," according to Stephen Engle. Sigel again proposed splitting Lyon's force–something one never does with an inferior force in the face of a superior enemy, especially "with inexperienced officers and troops." Further, according to Albert Castel, Lyon would be performing "one of the most difficult maneuvers in warfare–a coordinate attack from two widely separated directions." Lyon had previously rejected "Sigel's Plan" of a "concentric surprise," on August 8, which was also universally condemned by all of the officers, who had attended the meeting. Sigel had proposed leading an independent brigade, which would attack the enemy's rear while Lyon with the bulk of the army attacked the front. At first Lyon rejected the proposal, but on August 9, following his meeting with Sigel, that concluded in the early afternoon, he gave in, with "no hesitation." However, John Schofield, Lyon's Adjutant, believed the plan to be of "an extreme of rashness." Lyon reasoned that the importance of the German troops in the command and Sigel's influence over them, might cause Lyon's original plan to fail, if not wholeheartedly supported by Sigel. "Sigel's Plan" was adopted, despite objections from virtually all of his subordinates, and the movement was set to begin at 6:00 p.m. on the night of August 9. Bearss, *Wilson's Creek* 47, 49; Albert Castel, *General Sterling Price and the Civil War in the West* (Baton Rouge, LA, 1968), 40, 46 hereafter cited as Castel; Engle, 70–72; Monaghan, 164;-165; Phillips, *Damned Yankee*, 249–250; Piston & Hatcher, *Wilson's Creek*, 177–178; Schofield, 43; Ware, 303–304; Wherry, "General Lyon," 83.

Whatever of the strategical advantages

A Combined Attack

on both wings of the enemy offered, they were largely outbalanced by the tactical disadvantage of a divided force, the great difficulty of effectively executing combined maneuvers, with green troops, and the inadequate strength of the Sigel column, which barely permitted it to make a respectable demonstration, let alone a real attack, except under the combined command of officer of superior skill, courage and resources.

This was the situation of affairs on Friday, August 9, when towards sundown the two column of Gen. Lyon's Army started on their eventful march, both well knowing that the next morning's sun would shed its golden rays on a bloody field of carnage, where their devotion to the union of our states would be put to the severe test of a death struggle on a field of battle.

Confining my narrative from this point to the movement of Col. Sigel's column, in which I participated, I want to say right here that in the relation of military events there does not exist a more important factor than time; the correct time, as far as possible, of all the events related, although this task is extremely difficult, because a battle presented over shifting scenes of the highest mental and physical activity of all its participants, and its complete description is beyond the pen of mortal man, but a truthful description of the tactical formation of the troops engaged, and their movements, with the correct time when the movements were made, gives to the military student a reliable general picture of the whole action.[55]

The Column of Col. Sigel consisted of his old brigade greatly reduced in strength by discharges and detaching of four companies of the Fifth Missouri Infantry and two guns under Maj. [F. W.] Cronenbold, our ex-county judge, as commandant of Springfield., thus reducing our actual strength to 1000 muskets and six guns, besides two companies of regular cavalry, under the command of Capt. Eugene Carr, attached to Sigel's Brigade for the occasion, counting about 125 Sabres.[56]

---

55. See **Appendix C** for **Extended Comments on Lyon's Column at the Battle of Wilson's Creek**.

56. According to Colonel Sigel he detached two companies as a garrison in Springfield, which was not acknowledged by any other source. Further, a review of the *Supplement to the Official Records* has all the companies for the 3rd and 5th Missouri (Three months) at the Battle of Wilson's Creek, except for Company D, 3rd Missouri and Company A, 5th Missouri, neither of which have any comments or notations on the unit. *O.R.S.*, pt. 2, vol. 36: 439, 496; Sigel's Letter, 148.

Major F. W. Cronenbold was the major of the 5th Missouri Infantry (Three months), serving until the unit mustered out on August 26, 1861. No further record found on Cronenbold. Peckham, 123; *Union Army*, vol. 4: 258.

Eugene A. Carr was born on March 20, 1830, in Concord, New York, graduated from West Point (number 19 of 44) in 1850, and served on the frontier fighting Indians until the beginning of the Civil War. A captain (June 11, 1858) of cavalry, Carr commanded Company I, 1st U.S. Cavalry which he gallantly led at the Battle of Wilson's Creek and on August 16, 1861, Carr was commissioned the colonel of the 3rd Illinois Cavalry. At the Battle of Pea Ridge (March 6–8, 1862),

The cavalry leading the advance, Third Regiment following, left in front, the six pieces of artillery, under command of Lieut. Gustavus Adolphus Schaefer and the Fifth Missouri Infantry, Col. C. E. Salomon in the rear, was the order of march of Col. Sigel's column.[57]

After following the Forsyth Road for several miles we struck off to the right, marching through field and forest, on lanes and byways, always in a westerly direction. The loyal population of Green County, had provided us with excellent guides, and with unerring exactness we were striking for the enemy right flank.

The night was dark and cloudy, occasionally we had light showers of rain, some thunder and lightning intermixed. The only interruption of the hushed nightly stillness was the occasional barking of watchdogs guarding the slumbers of some peaceful husband and his family resting from their daily toil. On we marched in dead silence, smoking was prohibited, no commands were given aloud, a subtle, undeniable clanking of our arms and rumbling of artillery carriages being the only sounds emanating from our column. At about midnight

The Column was Halted

and word passed along the line that we would have a couple of hours' rests. We went to sleep where we stood, my bad luck deposited me in a bed of Spanish needles–no bed of roses by any means. At 2 a.m. we resumed our march and just as the gray dawn day faintly streaked the eastern horizon we arrived in the neighborhood of Wilson's Creek. On its eastern bluff, opposite the mouth of Tyrel's [Terrell's] Creek.[58]

---

he was wounded three times and received the Congressional Medal of Honor for his service. Carr was promoted to brigadier general, effective March 7, 1862, and by war's end he was breveted a major general effective March 11, 1865. Remaining in the army following the war, Carr served primarily in the west. Overall, Carr's "military reputation rests mostly on his exploits as an Indian fighter." To his Indian opponents he was known as "'War Eagle.'" He retired from the Army, as a brigadier general on February 15, 1893, and died on December 2, 1910, in Washington DC and was buried at West Point. *O.R.*, vol. 3: 56, 89; Boatner, 127–128; Faust, 115; Heitman, vol. 1: 285; Warner, *Generals in Blue*, 70–71.

    See **Appendix D** for a breakdown of Sigel's Brigade at Wilson's Creek.

57. Gustavus Adolphus Schaefer or Schaerff originally joined Company E, 3rd Missouri Infantry (Three months), being elected a lieutenant in the command. Latter he was detailed, with a number of "infantry recruits," to man a battery of artillery at Wilson's Creek. Holcombe & Adams, 28; Peckham, 122.

58. With the appointed hour for departure approaching Sigel addressed his command, rather simply, urging them to be "brave in the face of the enemy." Niceties aside, Sigel's command departed Springfield at 6:30 p.m., on August 9, heading south out of town, down the Forsyth or Yokermill Road, to attack the rebel force in the rear at Wilson's Creek. The column was led by five local guides: C. B. Owens, John Steele, Andrew Adams, Sam Carthal and L. E. D. Crenshaw (Adams and Steele were members of the Phelps Regiment of Home Guard.–an additional 20 guides assisted Lyon's column the same day.). About 11:00 p.m. Sigel's column halted for a three hour rest before continuing on to Wilson's Creek, where they arrived near 4:30 a.m. on August 10, halting near the confluence of Terrell's and Wilson's Creeks. By the time that Sigel had halted his command, it was positioned about a mile from the rebel encampment. Meanwhile, his advance guard,

Wilson's Creek here runs in here in a genera north and south course, the valley through which it meanders about half a mile wide, skirted by bluffs on the east and west, the creek hugging the eastern bluff, which is the more abrupt of the two, the western elevation, being less prominent and more gently sloping towards the creek. The great Fayetteville, Cassville or Telegraph Road constituting the center of the enemy's position and his principal line of communication, runs about one mile west and nearly parallel with Wilson's Creek, at the mouth of Terell's Creek, from south to north, from where it strikes the bold bluff of Skegg's Branch a few hundred yards from Sharp's house.[59] It turns abruptly there running parallel to Skegg's Branch until 100 yards east of Sharp's house it turns north again and descends the bold bluff of Skegg's branch, crossing said watercourse and running alongside of Wilson's Creek for three fourths of a mile. It crosses said creek at a ford, ascends the eastern bluff and leads off in a northwesterly direction to Springfield, distance about ten miles. Skegg's Branch runs parallel to Terell's Creek and about one and a half miles north of it, both running from west to east.

It Was on the Eastern Bluff

of Wilson's Creek, nearly opposite to the mouth of Terrell's Creek, where Col. Sigel's column halted at daybreak on Saturday, August 10, 1861; from 50 to 100 stragglers being captured by us, who were going out into the country of private foraging expeditions, and were greatly surprised when informed that they were in the hands of United Sates troops. At our feet in the misty valley of Wilson's Creek was a large encampment of Confederate cavalry still enjoying their sweet morning slumbers, with the exception of some enterprising cooks hovering over the camp fires preparing breakfast.[60] Just as the sun had risen over the eastern

---

under Captain Eugene Carr, had captured 40 rebels, who were found "in the vicinity of the [rebel] camp digging potatoes, picking and roasting corn, gathering tomatoes and other vegetables for the rebel commissary department." Carr, in turn, turned his captives over to Company K, 5th Missouri, who were tasked to guard the prisoners, thus preventing them from alerting the rebel camp of their presence. Of the prisoners, according to the New York Tribune, "ten or fifteen " were Negroes," who were "simply acting as servants." *O.R.*, vol. 3: 86, 89, 91; "Battle of Wilson's Creek, MO.: New York 'Tribune' Narrative," *Rebellion Record*, vol. 2: Doc. 517–518; Bearss, *Wilson's Creek*, 51, 54–55; Brooksher, 176–177; Engel, 72–73; Holcombe & Adams, 29–30; Otto C. B. Lademann, "The Battle of Wilson's Creek, August 10, 1861," *War Papers Being Papers Read Before the Commandery of the State of Wisconsin MOLLUS*, 4 vols. (Milwaukee, 1914; reprint ed., Wilmington, NC, 1993) vol. 4: 433, hereafter cited as Lademann, "Wilson's Creek"; Patrick, *Nine Months in the Infantry*, 36, 117, Roster, 2, 34, 42; Piston & Hatcher, *Wilson's Creek*, 190; Franz Sigel, "The Flanking Column At Wilson's Creek," *Battles and Leaders of the Civil War*, 4 vols (New York, 1887–1888), vol. 1: 304–306, hereafter cited as Sigel, "Flanking Column."

59. Joseph D Sharp's farm was a prominent feature on the Wilson's Creek Battlefield. The farm comprised a total of 1,272 acres of largely unimproved land with a barn and assorted pens, while the house was a large two-story building. Sharp's farm typically produced corn, wheat and oats with some potatoes, butter, cheese and other lesser items. In 1860 the farm was valued at $11,000. Piston & Hatcher, *Wilson's Creek*, 152.

60. From Sigel's position he could see about twenty-five percent of the rebel army. To his front were

horizon, and was dispelling the morning mist in the valley below us, the loud boom of a cannon came rolling down the valley of the creek, and informed us that Gen. Lyon had commenced the action. Our guns having been in position for some time, we presented our morning compliments to the Confederate cavalry below us, in the shape of half dozen shells. Gracious, how all the boys lumbered out of their blankets and struck behind for the nearest wood.[61]

The troops we attacked were the mounted regiments of Cols. Greer and Churchill, Texas and Arkansas men and mounted Missourians under Col. Brown [and] Ltc. Col. Major[.][62] [A]fter some little cannonading and the disappearance of all

rebel cavalry from McCulloch's command (E. Greer's 800-man Texas Cavalry; T. J. Churchill's Arkansas Cavalry–600 men; and J. McIntosh's Arkansas Mounted Rifles–400 men) and some MSG cavalry (J. P. Major's Battalion and W. B. Brown's Regiment–679 men total). To the north of the cavalry encampment, and out of view, were camped N. B. Pearce's Arkansas Brigade (2,324 men), and the infantry of McCulloch's Brigade (920 men)–all camped east of Wilson's Creek. West of Wilson's Creek the bulk of Price's MSG was camped. NOTE: William R. Brooksher presents a detailed map (pages 184–185) of the locations of the Confederate units on the morning of August 10. Adamson, 209; Banasik, *Confederate Tales, 1861*, 65; Banasik, *Missouri in 1861*, 378–380; Brooksher, 182, 184–185; Ingenthron, 84; Piston & Hatcher, *Wilson's Creek*, 221–223; Snead, *Fight for Missouri*, 259; Wherry, "Wilson's Creek," 291.

61. After arriving in the vicinity of Wilson's Creek, Sigel deployed his command–Charles Farrand's Company C, 2nd U.S. Dragoons deployed to the front of the main column, which moved into a ravine on the main road. Next came Sigel's infantry, led by the 3rd Missouri, who deployed, in column. The remaining two artillery pieces under Lieutenant Edward Schuetzecbach fell in with the infantry. On a knoll to the right of Sigel's main force and about 500 yards from the rebel camp, Sigel placed four of his artillery pieces, supported by Company K, 5th Missouri Infantry and Eugene Carr's Company I, 1st U.S. Cavalry which covered the artillery's right flank. And to disguise the approach of his artillery to the knoll, Sigel had the wheels of the artillery "muffled" as they moved into position undetected. When the battle opened the main body was to cross to the west side of Wilson's Creek, near the Dixon house, advancing to the Fayetteville Road, there to block any rebel retreat. At 5:30, according to Sigel, firing was heard from the direction of General Lyon's column, indicating that the battle had been joined. Sigel's four guns on the knoll then let loose with their rounds, "striking the loosely organized troops like a thunderbolt." "Confusion" followed in the rebel camp as the men made a "headlong exodus from the camp," scattering into the woods to the northeast and northwest, as the shelling created the "greatest of excitement and consternation." However, according to Dr. Samuel Melcher of the 5th Missouri, even though the firing created a "stampede…the shots passed over their heads…doing little, if any, damage to life or limb." It seems that the green gunners of the battery thought "it only necessary to load and fire [so] they kept banging away till the whole camp was deserted" without adjusting the elevation of the guns. "It was bang–bang–bang! Great fun and to hell where the shots went." NOTE: Adamson, McElroy and Snead have Sigel crossing Wilson's Creek, near the Dixon house, before the battle began, while most others, and Colonel Sigel, have the column east of Wilson's Creek until the firing began. *O.R.*, vol. 3: 86–87, 89, 91; Adamson, 212, 216, 229; Bearss, *Wilson's Creek*, 66–69; Bek, "Beugel Diary," 312; Britton, 87, 93; Brooksher, 196, 198; Gerteis, *Missouri*, 67; Holcombe & Adams, 40; McElroy, 172; Moore, *Missouri, Confederate Military History*, vol. 9: 56; Piston & Hatcher, *Wilson's Creek*, 221–222, 228; Pollard, 161; Sigel, "Flanking Column," 304; Snead, *Fight for Missouri*, 270–271; Wherry, "Wilson's Creek," 294.

62. See **Appendix C, Extended Comments on Selected Officers and Captains of the 3rd Texas Cavalry** for the biography of Elkanah B. Greer.

Thomas J. Churchill was born on March 10, 1824, near Louisville, Kentucky, educated at St. Mary's College and studied law at Transylvania College. He served in the Mexican War as a lieutenant of mounted rifles in Marshall's Kentucky Regiment, was captured, and exchanged troops in the valley we descended from the eastern bluff and crossed Wilson's Creek near the mouth of Tyrell's Creek, where we encountered a herd of cattle and some men driving them, upon whom some of our advanced men opened a lively fuselage, greatly scaring both cattle and drivers.

Crossing the Valley

of Wilson's Creek and reconnoitering the woods on the west side of it, we changed our direction, and turn northward toward the Fayetteville, Cassville or Telegraph Road, which we reached in the neighborhood of Mr. Sharp's house without meeting any further resistance. [63] We struck this road at about 8 a.m., preserving and

during the latter part of the war. Moving to Little Rock, Arkansas, in 1848, Churchill married and became a local plantation owner. In 1859–1860, Churchill organized a militia cavalry company, armed with lances and sabers. At the beginning of the Civil War he organized the 1st Arkansas Mounted Rifles and fought at Wilson's Creek and Pea Ridge. Transferring to the east side of the Mississippi River, as a brigadier general (March 4,1862), Churchill served under Kirby Smith in Kentucky. In the latter part of 1862, Churchill was given command of Arkansas Post, which he surrendered in January 1863. After his exchange, Churchill commanded a division and a corps in the Trans-Mississippi Department, participating in the Red River and Camden Campaigns. He was promoted to major general on March 18, 1865. After the war, Churchill returned to Arkansas where he was elected governor in 1880. He died on May 14, 1905. *Confederate Military History,* vol. 10: *Arkansas by John M. Harrell,* 395–396 hereafter cited as Harrell, *Arkansas, Confederate Military History*; Stewart Sifakis, *Who Was Who in the Confederacy, etc.* (New York, 1988), 53, hereafter cited as Sifakis, *Who Was Who in the Confederacy*; Warner, *Generals in Gray,* 49–50; W. E. Woodruff, *With the Light Guns in '61-'65 Reminiscences of Eleven Arkansas, Missouri and Texas Light Batteries, in the Civil War* (Little Rock, AR, 1903), 7, hereafter cited as Woodruff.

Colonel William B. Brown was a resident of Saline County, Missouri, and a Kentuckian by birth. Prior to the Civil War Brown was known as a "reckless and perilous adventurer," who accompanied John C. Frémont on his expedition to the Pacific Ocean. In May 1861, he organized the "Saline Cavalry Company," being elected the unit's captain. On June 28, 1861, Brown was appointed the colonel of the 1st Cavalry Regiment, 6th Division, MSG. When leading his troops into battle, Brown used an old hunting horn that he blew when his command was charging the enemy. He died at the Second Battle of Boonville (September 13, 1861) while leading his command. Richard H. Musser, "The War in Missouri," *Southern Bivouac,* 6 vols. (reprint ed., Wilmington, NC, 1993), vol. 4: 750–752; Peterson, et. al., 30, 174, 176.

James Patrick Major was born on May 14, 1836, in Fayette, Missouri. He attended West Point, Class of 1852, where he graduated number 23 of 49, in 1856. After serving on the Texas frontier, fighting Kiowas and Comanches Indians, Major resigned from the army on March 21, 1861, and joined Earl Van Dorn's staff. At Wilson's Creek, Major commanded the 1st Cavalry Battalion, 3rd Division, MSG. Major later transferred to the east side of the Mississippi River, where he served for a time as Van Dorn's Chief of Artillery. On July 21, 1863, he was promoted to brigadier general. Returning to the Trans-Mississippi Department, Major commanded a Texas cavalry brigade and a division during the Red River Campaign, where he received high praise for his actions at Pleasant Hill and Mansfield, Louisiana. After the war, Major, lived in France, but returned to Louisiana, then Texas where he became a planter. He died in Austin, on May 7, 1877 (Heitman and Roberts say May 8). Boatner, 503; Heitman, vol. 1:685; *Confederate Military History,* vol. 11: *Texas* by O. M. Roberts, 245–246, hereafter cited as *Texas, Confederate Military History*; Warner, *Generals in Gray,* 209–210.

63. Even as Sigel's guns fired into the rebel camp, his infantry column crossed over Wilson's Creek, moving at a "leisurely" pace, and headed to the Fayetteville or Wire Road. Meeting little resistance

BATTLE OF
WILSON'S CREEK
OR
OAK HILLS,
AUGUST 10TH 1861.

UNION   CONFEDERATE

general order of march as we had left Springfield, our cavalry advanced having
been reinforced by Co. A rifles of the Third Missouri infantry,Capt. S. Judest [Jo-
seph Indest], deployed as skirmishers.[64] Here we had arrived at the rear of the enemy's center. Mr. Sharp's house had been converted into a Confederate hospital,
filled with surgeons and wounded soldiers. At the time I thought it was an error
of Col. Sigel to abandon the eastern bluff of Wilson's Creek, for there you had
a splendid chance of developing a bold, effective offensive to compel the enemy
to largely detach against him, and consequently to create a powerful diversion in
favor of Gen. Lyon, but after having crossed Wilson's Creek and struck the Telegraph Road it was imperative upon Col. Sigel to continue his march until he could
form a junction with Lyon's troops. A slight detour to the left would have accomplished this object in spite of the enemy. But Col. Sigel determined differently. He
formed his two infantry battalions in column closed in mass across the Telegraph
Road in front of Sharp's house sandwiching his six guns between the two infantry
columns fronting toward Springfield his bare left flank resting on the edge of the
bluff descending Skegg's Branch. Here a mortal hour was spent by Col. Siegel

from the disorganized rebel command, Sigel's men came to a halt, in column, on the east side
of Sharp's field, near the center of the rebel cavalry camp; there they waited the arrival of the
artillery from the eastern knoll–the time was about 6:30 a.m. Thirty minutes later the remaining
troops from the east side of Wilson's Creek rejoined Sigel's column. To the right of Sigel's resting
column, the rebels were in the process of rallying so Sigel deployed his artillery which fired into
the Confederates–it was 7:15. The rebels quickly scattered and by 7:45 the Federals moved forward, passing through a cattle herd and an area described as a "slaughtering place," reaching their
target road at 8:00, thus blocking the rebel retreat route. "Judged strictly as a maneuver, Sigel's
march from Springfield....was a magnificent accomplishment," according to Piston and Hatcher.
"He had moved a great distance in almost complete secrecy, opening his surprise attack at exactly
the right moment. The effect on the enemy was devastating." If this had been the end of the story
all would have hailed Sigel's accomplishment; however the sequel would prove his undoing and
a disaster. There the command would sit, all was quiet, and by 8:30, straggling had begun as
men from the two infantry regiments retired to the rebel camp, looting the tents and securing for
themselves a hearty breakfast of "coffee, biscuit and fried green corn." And W. L. Webb, in his
book *Battles and Biographies of Missourians* alleged that Sigel, himself, also "plundered" the
rebel camp, while Sigel denied that neither he nor his men had plundered the enemy camp *O.R.*,
vol. 3: 87; Adamson, 243, 245; Britton, 93–94; Castel, 42–43; Duncan, 89; Holcombe & Adams,
41, 46; Piston & Hatcher, *Wilson's Creek*, 227–231; Shalhope, 177; Sigel, "Flanking Column,"
305–306; Webb, 84–85.

64. Joseph Indest originally organized Company H of Sigel's command, then transferred to Company
A (Rifle Battalion), 3rd Missouri Infantry (Three months), following the promotion of Henry Bis-
coff to major in mid-June 1861. Wounded in the leg at Wilson's Creek, Indest recovered and later
joined the 3rd Missouri Infantry (Three year), being made the captain of Company A, on February
8, 1862, to rank from January 18, 1862. On the march to Helena, Arkansas, in 1862, Indest was
captured on May 12, near Searcy Landing and sent to St. Louis to await exchange, for 1st Lieutenant Joseph Fry of the Confederate States Navy. Following his exchange he later participated
in the Battle of Arkansas Post (January 11, 1863) and the Vicksburg Campaign. Court martialed
in September 28, 1863, Indest was later released, transferring to the Invalid Corps, in St. Louis,
where he briefly became a mamber of the 22nd Veteran Reserve Corps. On March 6, 1864, Indest
assumed command of Company G; however he was relieved a week later, reason not given. Final
disposition unknown. *O.R*, Series 2, vol. 4: 222, 316;.*O.R.S.*, pt. 2, vol. 36: 375, 382–386, 437–
438, 441; *O.R.S.*, pt.2, vol. 80: 181; Gray, *Missouri Adjutant General Report*, 54; Peckham, 121;

In Absolute Idleness.

To judge from the position Col. Sigel occupied it must have been his idea to hold the enemy in check until Gen. Lyon succeeded in beating and capturing them, for what other object could he have in view, placing his troops on the Cassville Road?[65]

The confederates soon discovered our position and the Arkansas battery of Capt. Reid posted on the eastern bluff of Wilson's Creek about opposite the mouth of Skegg's Branch, soon opened fire upon us, and after getting the proper range, became exceedingly uncomfortable for the clumsy, tactical formation employed by Col. Sigel made our column a very good artillery target.[66]

---

65. After reaching the Fayetteville Road Sigel deployed his command, intending to advance into the rear of the rebels, who were confronting General Lyon. Even while positioning his troops, for the continued advance, a number of rebel stragglers approached his command and the firing to his northwest had ceased. This led Sigel to believe "that the attack of General Lyon had been successful, and that his troops were in pursuit of the enemy." Sigel in turn erroneously assumed he was about to confront a defeated and retreating enemy and deployed his command accordingly. Sigel placed Carr's Cavalry to his far left and rear, while Farrand's troopers held the far right. To the front a battalion of the 3d Missouri took their position, in line of battle, to the right and supporting the artillery; and to the rear Sigel placed the remainder of his infantry–the 5th Missouri was to the left of the Wire Road while the 3rd Missouri was to the right. With no exception the deployment was terrible–The upcoming rebel attack would show, according to Hans Christian Adamson, that "The cavalry and the Dragoons had been so far off on the flanks to be out of sight and the encounter terminated so swiftly that there was no time to call them into action." William Piston and Richard Hatcher agreed with Adamson, noting that Carr's command was "so deeply in the foliage that his men were beyond effective supporting distance," and was virtually unusable for the coming rebel attack, while Farrand's Cavalry "were not in the best position to respond quickly," being positioned in the Texans' old camp where they had "great difficulty in exiting the camp." One battalion of the 3rd Missouri and the artillery were positioned upon a bluff, about a hundred yards distance from the Skegg's Branch and behind the military crest of the hill–thus allowing an enemy to advance upon them, unseen, from a ravine to their front. And the remaining troops were deployed in "columns of companies," to the rear–a fine Napoleonic tactic, if they were attacking, not defending. And so Sigel's command sat awaiting the next move. "No orders came to advance," recalled John Bugel of the 3rd Missouri. "It was maddening and at the same time ridiculous." The time was 8:30 a.m. *O.R.*,vol. 3: 87; Adamson, 248; Bearss, *Wilson's Creek*, 71–72; Bek, "Beugel Diary," 312–313; Brooksher, 199–200; Gerteis, *Missouri*, 69; Lademann, "Wilson's Creek," 434; Piston & Hatcher, *Wilson's Creek*, 246–247, 250.; Sigel, "Flanking Column," 305.

66. John G. Reid, a resident of Ft. Smith, Arkansas, commanded the Ft. Smith Battery of four guns, being organized as a Arkansas State Battery in June 1861 (W. E. Woodruff says it was a Confederate Battery). The men, according to one observer, were of "excellent material," who were well drilled in the operation of the battery. The unit fought at Wilson's Creek, after which the battery was disbanded, in late August or early September 1861, and Reid left the army. Reid returned to the army on July 17, 1862, being appointed a captain and ordered to raise an artillery company at Fort Smith, which he commanded at the Battle of Prairie Grove, Arkansas, on December 7, 1862. The battery and Reid disappeared from all known records sometime after the Battle of Prairie Grove. Final disposition unknown. Banasik, *Embattled Arkansas*, 516, 526; Bearss, "Fort Smith," 338; Bearss, *Wilson's Creek*, 75; Letter (July 17, 1862), Newton to Carroll, Copy Letter Book, Hindman's Command (June 1-December 18, 1862), 90–91, Peter W. Alexander Collection, Columbia University; Charles Edward Nash, *Biographical Sketches of Gen. Pat Cleburne and Gen. T. C. Hindman, etc.* (Little Rock, AR, 1895; reprint ed., Dayton, OH, 1977), 124–125; Stewart

When the fire of Capt. Reid's Battery became very uncomfortable, Col. Sigel directed Lieut. Schaefer (his chief of artillery officer), to take two guns and place them in a cornfield on our right, where he could get a good view of the enemy artillery, for the purpose of drawing its fire upon himself and away from our infantry.

Lieut. Schaefer instantly complied with the order, and just as he returned to report to Col. Sigel that he had executed the order, the Col. angrily accused him "Who has ordered that fire over on the right?" Lieut. Schaefer, with a very perplexed look, replied, "This was by your orders, Col. Sigel," when the Col. with his usual absent-minded dear, replied "So sir! I ordered it? Well, bring the guns right back where they were."

Lieut. Schaefer, saluting, wheeled his horse and soon returned with two guns, placing them where they had been before.

This Little Incident

coming under my personal observation as one of the closers of the rear company of a column of Third Missouri Infantry, immediately in front of the artillery, and having personally overheard the order given to Lieut. Schaefer, struck me as a very peculiar from officer disposing of one third of his artillery force and forgetting all about it in fifteen minutes. Barely fifteen minutes had elapsed after this little episode when he discovered a line of infantry advancing upon our bare and exposed left flank from the direction of Skegg's Branch. Those of us who wanted to opened fire upon the line were forbidden to do so, our commanding officer having determined that the advancing line was a part of Gen. Lyon's troops–the First Iowa infantry.[67]

Sifakis, *Compendium of the Confederate Armies Florida and Arkansas* (New York, 1992), 40; Special Orders No. 29 (July 17, 1862), Special Order Letter Book (June 1-December 18, 1862), Hindman's Command, 40–41, Peter W. Alexander Collection, Columbia University, hereafter cited as Special Order Book No. 1; Telegram (July 19, 1862), Hindman to Carroll, Copy Book of Telegrams, Telegram file, Peter W. Alexander Collection, Columbia University; Woodruff, 24–25.

67. The 1st Iowa Infantry went "into quarters" on April 18, 1861, at Keokuk, Iowa, and elected John F. Bates, colonel of the regiment on May 11, 1861. The unit and was mustered into U.S. Service on May 14, 1861, and headed for Missouri on June 13,where they joined Lyon's column at Boonville on June 21. As part of Lyon's column, the 1st Iowa arrived in the Springfield vicinity on July 13. On August 10, the 1st Iowa participated in the Battle of Wilson's Creek, after which they returned to Iowa, having been mustered out of the service on August 21. Ware, 92, 96, 98, 105,127, 345–346.

Following the initial shook, caused by Sigel's surprise attack upon the rebel rear, General McCulloch organized for defense. He quickly ordered the various elements of his command to attack Joseph Plummer coming down the east side of Wilson's Creek–the threat of Sigel's column would be dealt with after Plummer's had been neutralized (See **Appendix C, Extended Comments on Lyon's Column at the Battle of Wilson's Creek** for details). Meanwhile, Sterling Price handled Lyon's main attack at Bloody Hill, which rose 100 feet above Wilson's Creek to their east. After crushing Plummer's attack, in a "relatively brief" period of time, McCulloch, mounted on his unsaddled horse, grabbed a portion of the 3rd Louisiana, enticing them to follow him with

At or about 9 o'clock a.m. while Col. Sigel was wasting his precious time on the bluff south of Skegg's Branch, and in front of Sharp's house, the battle has been raging with intense fury between Lyon's and Price's troops, on the eminence called "Bloody Hill" afterwards, hardly one mile due north of the position occupied by him. When the supposed First Iowa Infantry had crawled up steep slope of Skegg's Branch to with an ten yards of the summit, where our naked left flank was exposed to them, Dr. Todd, a private of Company K, Capt. Theo Mesermann [Meumann], skipped out from the ranks, and walked down the bluff a few steps and asked in a loud voice: "Who are you?" The answer he got was a rifle shot, which pierced his forehead and killed him instantly.[68]

"Come my brave lads, I have a battery for you to charge, and the day is ours!" McCulloch then led two companies of the 3rd Louisiana toward Sigel's position, directing the remaining units of the 3rd Louisiana to follow. Moving across Wilson's Creek, to the west side, McCulloch moved down the Wire Road to Skegg's Branch where Sigel's skirmishers fell back from the advancing rebels, reporting them to be men from Lyon's column. You see, the 1st Iowa Infantry wore "steel gray uniforms" similar to those of the 3rd Louisiana, who also exhibited the same marching style as the Iowans. Dr. Melcher, from the 5th Missouri, also noted the approaching troops, remarking that they looked like men from Lyon's column. However, no one confirmed the identity of the approaching troops as they disappeared under the military crest of Sharp's hill or bluff that was occupied by Sigel's command. After entering the intervening, tree-covered ravine, between Skegg's Branch and Sharp's house, McCulloch deployed his command into line, having been joined by another detachment from the 3rd Louisiana under Colonel James McIntosh–in all about 400 men were present, including a portion of the 3rd Louisiana and some reorganized MSG under Captain Thomas Staples. Meanwhile, to McCulloch's right and just north of the Skegg's Branch, MSG troops under Lieutenant Colonels Thomas H. Rosser and Walter O'Kane deployed their commands, and moved forward supported by Hirman Bledsoe's Battery positioned near the Wire Road. And farther to the east side of Wilson's Creek, and on Siegel's right flank, Captain John G. Reid's Battery was located. Sigel saw the approaching men, unsure as to who they were, but believing that they may be Lyon's men. Earring on the side of caution, Sigel took "great pains to avoid friendly fire casualties" and directed that his men "not to engage the troops that would soon appear in their front," thus setting the stage for the disaster that followed–the time was about 8:30 a.m. *O.R.*, vol. 3: 100, 105, 120; Adamson, 245–247; Bearss, *Wilson's Creek*, 86–87; Britton,95; Brooksher, 200–201; Duncan, 86; Holcombe & Adams, 43, 46–47; Moore, *Missouri, Confederate Military History*, vol. 9: 56–57, 59; Phillips, *Damned Yankee*, 253–254; Piston & Hatcher, *Wilson's Creek*, 213, 220, 250–253; D.J. Smith, "From the Springfield Battle," *Rome Tri-Weekly Courier* (Rome, GA), September 5, 1861; Shalhope, 177; Snead, *Fight for Missouri*, 272–273, 276–280; Sigel, "Flanking Column," 305; W. H. Tunnard, *A Southern History. The History of the Third Regiment Louisiana Infantry* (Baton Rouge, LA, 1866; reprint ed., Dayton, OH,1988), 52, hereafter cited as Tunnard.

68. As McCulloch's troops worked their way up the slope to Sigel's position, Dr. Melcher suggested that the Union flag bearer wave his flag three times, indicting that they were Union troops. When no response from the advancing troops was received, Sigel sent Private Charles Todt [not Todd], from Company K, 3rd Missouri, to check on the identity of the advancing column. Led by General McCulloch, the rebels were a scant forty yards from the top of the bluff when Todt appeared. After an exchange of words, Todt realized that the advancing troops were rebels, raised his weapon to fire, but Henry H. Gentles, 3rd Louisiana, emptied his piece first, killing Todt. General McCulloch turned to Gentles, who had just saved his life, remarking, "That was a good shot." Immediately after which McCulloch turned to Captain John P. Vigilini, of the 3rd Louisiana, and said "'Captain, take your company up and give them hell." This was followed by a barrage of artillery fire from Bledsoe's and Reid's guns as they peppered the Federal line. *O.R.*, vol. 3: 117; Brooksher,

The shot was followed by a volley of the whole line, composed of parts of the Third Louisiana Infantry and some Missouri troops under the direct command of Gen. McCulloch.[69] The effects of this volley were singular. The bullets passing harmlessly over the heads of infantry, knocked the greater number of

The Drivers

of the artillery out of the saddle, and the fright produce on the horses by the rattle of the musketry, added to the discomfiture of the drivers; made them plunge, as with one accord, into the infantry columns of Third Missouri volunteers, owing to the great tactical skill displayed by Col. Sigel in the disposition of his troops on the Telegraph Road. While our battalion presented an indescribable mixture of men, horses, guns and caissons, the enemy, now only fifteen feet away from our naked left flank, gave one tremendous cheer, and rushed in. Col. Siegel's tactical skill having deprived us of every opportunity of employing our arms, there was nothing left for us but to run, and run we did like good fellows.[70]

200–202; Holcomber & Adams, 47; Piston & Hatcher, *Wilson's Creek*, 253; Sigel, "Flanking Column," 305; Tunnard, 52–53.

Captain Theodore Meumann commanded company K, 3rd Missouri Infantry (Three months), and upon reorganization commanded Company E, 3rd Missouri (Three years). He was later promoted to major, then lieutenant colonel and completed his military service as the colonel October 15, 1863) of the 3rd or 15th Missouri Infantry. During the Atlanta Campaign (May–September, 1864) Meumann commanded the 3rd Missouri, which fielded but 218 officers and men and by the end of the campaign the 3rd was down to barely 135 effective officers and men. Following the campaign General C. R. Woods noted that Meumann performed his "duty nobly and deserves the highest of praise." The non-veterans of the 3rd Missouri were mustered out in September 1864, and the remainder, with Meumann, were consolidated with the 12th and 17th Missouri infantries. Meumann completed his service commanding the 15th Missouri in the 4th Corps at Nashville, Tennessee. Final disposition unknown. *O.R.*, vol. 38, pt. 1: 103; *O.R.*, vol. 38, pt. 3: 124, 144, 166; *O.R.*, vol. 39, pt. 2: 554; *O.R.*, vol. 49, pt. 2: *535; O.R.S.*, pt. 2, vol. 36: 403–404; Gray, *Missouri Adjutant General Report*, 65; Peckham, 122; *Union Army*, vol. 4: 257–258.

69. The Third Louisiana Infantry (also known as the Pelican Rifles) was organized in April and May 1861, and entered Confederate Service on May 17, with 1085 officers and men, largely from northern Louisiana. The unit fought at Wilson's Creek, Missouri, and Pea Ridge, Arkansas, before moving to the east side of the Mississippi River. Again bloodied at Corinth and Iuka, Mississippi in 1862, the Third was captured at Vicksburg, Mississippi on July 4, 1863. The 3rd Louisiana was paroled and returned to Louisiana where it awaited exchanged. On July 21, 1864, the 3rd Louisiana was officially exchanged, while stationed in Shreveport, Louisiana, but it never participated in another battle. Louis Hebert, a Louisiana native, commanded the unit until his promotion to brigadier general on May 26, 1862. Boatner, 391; Dimitry, *Louisiana, Confederate Military History,* vol. 10: 305–307; Ingenthron, 145; Tunnard, 26–29, 319.

70. Rushing up the hill, Viligini's Company stopped about fifteen feet from the top, where they were fired on by Sigel's artillery, which blasted their shells over the rebel heads, due to their poor positioning. In response the Louisianans sent a volley into the Unionists, then charged over the crest of the ridge into the defending artillery. Confusion reined in the Federal lines, as many thought that Lyon's men were firing into their commands, supported by Totten's Battery. Cries of "'It is Totten's Battery! It is Totten's Battery!'" rang out among the Unionists, while others, in German shouted "'They are firing at us! They make a mistake!'" Sigel's defending Germans "simply could not understand that it was the Confederates who were charging and firing" into their ranks. With

Gaining the Telegraph Road by cutting diagonally across the timber in the rear of Sharp's house where the roads runs nearly do south, I was requested by Capt. Meumann and Lieut. George Schuster to aid them in gathering some men and turned back to attack enemy in order to save our regimental colors, the color bearer being wounded and unable to get along. I complied with pleasure, and confronting the enemy with such man as we could gather, we advance until we had secured the color bearer with his colors and taking him to our midst, continued the retreat.

At a big spring running across the road, about one mile from Sharp's house , Col. Sigel halted and tried to reform his scattered command.[71]

---

the rebels attacking, Sigel realized his error and ordered his men to fire. "Some Federal soldiers returned fire, but others refused, continuing to believe that they faced friends." An exasperated Colonel Salomon, cursed at his men in three different languages trying to get his men to respond, but to no avail, and when the battle was over, Salomon acknowledged "that his men had acted badly." Nothing seemed to work, and when the MSG support units crested the hill, to the Louisiana's right they slammed into Sigel's left flank (Bearss and Brooksher have McRae's men arriving before the MSG troops). "In a twinkling, men, horses, wagons, guns, all enveloped in a cloud of dust" headed down the Fayetteville Road." "Sigel's whole command took to instant flight" as he lost control–it was "every man for himself" wrote Stephen Engle. And Sigel recorded it was like trying "to stop a herd of stampeded buffaloes." Overall the Louisianans suffered no losses from Sigel's command, but sustained the loss of two killed when Reid's Arkansas Battery mistakenly fired into them. *O.R.*, vol. 3: 117; "Battle of Wilson's Creek, MO.: New York 'Tribune' Narrative," *Rebellion Record*, vol. 2: Doc. 518; Bearss, *Wilson's Creek*, 88–90; Brooksher, 202–203; Engle, 77; Holcombe & Adams, 42, 47; Piston & Hatcher, *Wilson's Creek*, 253–255; Snead, *Fight for Missouri*, 289–281; T.D.L., "Letter From a Member of the Little Rck Artillery," *The Van Buren Press* (Van Buren, AR), August 28, 1861; W.H.T., "The Third Louisiana," *The New Orleans Bee*, August 31, 1861.

71. Within 30 minutes Sigel's column had been shattered and four pieces of artillery captured, while the other two were to the rear "in reserve" and at first escaped capture. One portion of Sigel's column, under Colonel Charles Salomon, numbering about 450 men, headed southwest down the Wire Road to the Gwinn house, where they turned west to the Little York Road, taking one artillery piece with them. Eventually Salomon liked up with Lyon's retreating column and they made it to Springfield without further difficulty (Snead says that Salomon went with Sigel). The other half, of about 250 men, with another piece of artillery headed back to Springfield, via the Dixon house under Colonel Sigel. Sigel followed the route that they had originally taken to Wilson's Creek, halting at Moody's Springs, where Sigel reorganized his shattered command for the continued retreat. Having routed Sigel's column, McCulloch sent two companies from Greer's Texans, with Lieutenant Colonel Major's MSG Battalion, in pursuit of Sigel fleeing troops, while the infantry, after securing the Sharp's farm, were sent back to Bloody Hill to defeat General Lyon's column. NOTE: Sigel's retreat will be covered in the following letter. *O.R.*, vol. 3: 105; Brooksher, 204–206; Holcombe & Adams, 44, 49; Piston & Hatcher, *Wilson's Creek*, 256–257, 260; Sigel, "Flanking Column," 305; Snead, *Fight for Missouri*, 281; Wherry, "Wilson's Creek," 294; Woodward, 324.

George Schuster was the first Lieutenant of Company K, 3rd Missouri Infantry (Three months). He was captured at Wilson's Creek and believed later exchanged; however, as of November 1862, the Assistant to the Commissary of Exchange noted that Schuster had not been properly exchanged and his name was resubmitted for exchanged on November 22, 1862. Schuster became the captain of Company E, 3rd Missouri (Three years), on June 23, 1862, to rank from January 17, following the promotion of Theodore Meumann to major of the regiment. *O.R.*, Series 2. Vol. 4: 694–695, 733; *O.R.S.*, pt. 2, vol. 36: 408–409; Gray, *Missouri Adjutant General Report*, 65; Peckham, 122.

He did not succeed in gathering many of his artillery.

Five Guns

had remained on the spot where they stood when the Confederates attacked, owing to the killing and disabling of nearly all the drivers; one gun, that had come off the field, went with a column composed of the Fifth Missouri Infantry and a large portion of the Third Missouri under Capt. Cramer, who did not follow the Telegraph Road, but striking north and gaining the Little York Prairie, for a junction with Lyon's troops, in the afternoon, finding the Gen. Lyon was dead and Maj. Sturgis commanding the combined troops, reached Springfield without molestation.[72]

Those of our men who, like myself, considered it their duty to stay near the person of their commander feared their differently.

After having rallied as many men at the large springs as possible, Col. Sigel continued his retreat; the only organized troops he had with him now were the two companies of United States cavalry, under Capt. Eugene Carr. (I don't know where Capt. Carr and his cavalry were stationed while we spent our time in idleness in front of Sharp's house)..

Of his whole infantry I don't think he gathered 250 men; of the artillery only

---

72. When the Federals routed from Sharp's farm they abandoned four pieces of artillery. Of the two remaining pieces, one retreated with Colonel Sigel toward the Dixon house, then eastward toward Springfield, while the other retreated with Salomon's force to the west. After crossing Wilson's Creek, Sigel's portion of the retreating column, led by Carr's cavalry, continued eastward. Approaching the James River Branch of the White River, Carr easily crossed, while the infantry, one artillery piece and some wagons lagged behind at the river crossing. About a quarter of Sigel's following troops had crossed the river when the remaining troops were greeted by rebel gunfire even as the lone artillery piece was in mid-stream. Confederate cavalry under Lieutenant Colonel James Major and Captain Tom Staples had beaten the bulk of Sigel's men to the ford, fired a volley and charged the demoralized troops. The Federals scattered, losing their gun. The other gun followed the route taken by the bulk of Sigel's men under Colonel Salomon. Initially escorted by Eugene Carr's cavalry, this artillery piece was abandoned, by Carr, after the wheel horse was killed and Carr proceeded after Sigel's column. This abandoned piece was later found by Company K, 5th Missouri, under Captain Samuel Flagg, who was part of Salomon's column. Flagg "took ropes, fastened them to one cannon, and placed them into the hands of his prisoners, compelling them to draw the cannon off the field." However, Flagg soon gave up his effort and left the gun which was subsequently found by Lieutenant Charles Farrand, commanding the U.S. Dragoons–the last Federal unit to depart the battlefield. Farrand managed to save the gun, without further incident, escorting it safely to Springfield. *O.R.*, vol. 3: 91–92; "Battle of Wilson's Creek, MO.: New York 'Tribune' Narrative," *Rebellion Record*, vol. 2: Doc. 518; Bearss, *Wilson's Creek*, 93–97; Brooksher, 205, 208–209; "Great Battle At Springfield," *Chicago Tribune*, August 16, 1861; Holcombe & Adams, 44–48; Piston & Hatcher, *Wilson's Creek*, 257–261.

John F. Cramer commanded Company A, 3rd Missouri Infantry (Three months). After he was mustered out, he joined the 17th Missouri Infantry, becoming the unit's lieutenant colonel. He was at Seary Landing, Arkansas on May 19, 1862 and on September 25, 1863, he was promoted to colonel to rank from July 18. Cramer did not survive the war, dying at Bellefonte, Alabama, on May 2, 1864, even as his unit began the Atlanta Campaign. *O.R.*, vol. 3: 72, 78; Gray, *Missouri Adjutant General Report*, 93–94; Peckham, 121.

one solitary caisson, upon which was strapped our regimental colors, owing to the wounding and disability of our color-sergeant. to carry them.[73]

I don't believe that the Third Louisiana Infantry and the Missourians constituting the line of troops attacking Sigel's Brigade at the Sharp's house lost a single man owing to the impossibility of Sigel's troops with the exception of a few flank files to fire upon them, and even this slight fire was prevented by positive orders.[74]

If ever the Third Louisiana had a regimental reunion they ought to pass a resolution of thanks to Col. Sigel for making their victory so very easy.

Otto C. Lademann

* * * * * * *

Item: Sigel's retreat from Wilson's Creek., by Otto C. Lademann, late captain 3rd Missouri Volunteers.
Published: April 9, 1887.

Sigel at Wilson's Creek

St. Louis, April 6
[Editor *Republican*]

At the big spring Col. Sigel strenuously exerted himself to restore something like order. This, however, was exceedingly difficult with the green troops of his command which he had succeeded in gathering.

Yet three or four temporary companies were formed, and with the two companies of cavalry under Capt. Carr and the caisson saved out of our artillery work, the little column continued to retreat on the Telegraph Road for about three miles.

At that point Col. Sigel, with singular perverseness, turned to the left (i. e. south), in place of turning to the right, or north, ignore, where he was sure to meet Lyon's column, and marching on a by-road, leading south for about one mile, he again turned to the left then marched to the east in such a manner that about noon we found ourselves happily crossing Wilson's Creek to the east bank, at the north

---

73. After reaching Moody's Spring, Sigel reorganized his command into four companies and continued his retreat to Springfield. Sigel's column now consisted of Carr's Calvary (about 50 men), with 150 "badly disorganized infantry," according to Carr, while Sigel put the force at 250 men. Farrand's Cavalry moved in the same direction of Salomon's column and wasn't with Sigel during the retreat, as implied by Lademann. Leading Sigel's column was Carr's cavalry, while a reorganized company of the 3rd Missouri led the rest of the column. *O.R.*, vol. 3: 90; Sigel "Flanking Column," 305.

74. True. According to a member of Woodruff's Arkansas Battery, the 3rd Louisiana lost no men from enemy fire but did lose two men killed from friendly fire, when Reid's Arkansas Battery hit the unit following the capture of Sigel's guns near the Sharp house. T.D.L., "Letter From a Member of the Little Rck Artillery," *Van Buren Press*, August 28, 1861; W.H.T., "The Third Louisiana," *New Orleans Bee*, August 31, 1861.

of Tyrell's Creek, where, six hours previously, we had crossed to the west bank, at the opening on the engagement.

It did not take the Confederate cavalry long to detect our presences, The memorable place where we had made the cattle attack in the morning was plainly visible from all eastern buffs of the creek as far north as the Telegraph Road. From this point our retreat, which have been unmolested thus far, became a perfect fox chase. On the right, on the left and in the rear the Confederate cavalry were blazing away at us to their hearts' content, and I must admit that

Their Triumphant Shouts

or yells created as much consternation as their fire did. In a situation of this kind it is very delectable to play hunter, but the reverse entirely to play fox. On the chase went, the shouts of our foes replacing the music of the hounds, for two or three miles (I am unable to give the correct distance owing to our extreme celerity), where, and at a little log house, Capt. Carr and his two companies of cavalry separated themselves from us, still continuing to march in an easterly direction, while the few remaining infantry and the caisson, under the leadership of Col. Sigel again faced to the left, thus taking a northerly direction towards Springfield.

A mile or so through open timber brought us to the verge of a bluff, at the foot of which ran a beautiful stream of clear water, limpid water, over a heavily pebbly bottom, and on the other side of the creek, running passed the abandoned dilapidated old mill, flanked by luxuriant cornfields on the right and on the left, there was a broad, open lane, apparently leading direct to Springfield, which look to our distressed column like a harbor or refuge. We rushed down this steep cleverly of the bluff on a narrow, wagon track, wading the creek, about forty yards wide and two feet deep. When in front of the old dilapidated mill Col. Sigel ordered a halt to gather the handful of men remaining about him. The great majority of our little column

Had Been Captured

by this time; only the mounted and strong young soldiers had been able to undergo the chase successfully.

As previously stated, our regimental colors had been strapped to one remaining caisson, owing to wounding of our color sergeant.[75] While getting down that steep and wretched bluff road leading to the creek the cannoneers had lock both hind wheels but when half way down the spokes of both of them gave way at once, leaving the caisson on perch halfway up with our colors still strapped on the top; and this is the identical place where our colors were found by Gen. [M.

---

75. Under normal circumstances the substitute color-bearer would have taken up the flag, but he was killed earlier in the action. Holcombe & Adams, 43.

M.] Parsons mounted men, abandon, but not taken in action.[76] The drivers of the caisson quickly unhitched their horses and joined us at the front of the mill. Upon their arrival Col. Sigel ordered the advance but we had not advanced in the lane ten yards with a tremendous volley of musketry from the cornfield on our immediate left knocked down all the horses and riders at the head of the column. Being so utterly unexpected and surprising utterly scattered our little column into the cornfield on the right, leading to the capture of all except Col. Sigel, Capt. Meumann and Lieut. Schutzenbach [Schuetzenbach]of the artillery, for after passing through the cornfield we found ourselves again confronted by Confederate cavalry, and a gentleman advancing upon us, waving his hat as a token of amity, announced to us from a distance that we were surrounded on all sides, and if we do not surrender it would be his painful duty

To Have Us Shot.

After a hurried consultation we concluded that discretion was the better part of valor and laid down our arms.[77] From front, from rear and from both flanks the

---

76. Lademann was referring to William Brown's MSG cavalry, from Parson's 6th Division, MSG, which included Tom Staples's cavalry company. Staples's company, with several companies from Brown's Regiment, had arrived at the crossing of the James River Branch after Carr's Federals had vacated the area. Carr feared being cut off by approaching rebel cavalry–besides, according to William Piston and Richard Hatcher, Carr, "apparently concluded that the column was doomed and it would be better to save part of it than see it die altogether." Staple's then setup an ambush for the remainder of Sigel's column. With one company of the 3rd Missouri barely across the James River Branch, Staples sprung his ambush. And even as Staple's opened fire James Major arrived with his MSG Battalion, completing the route of the demoralized Unionists, who, however, "fought with desperation." "That fight that ensued was brief but decisive...The outcome was never in doubt, however, and the Federals who escaped did so individually." The 3rd Missouri colors were subsequently captured by Staples, given to General Price and eventually sent to Richmond, Virginia, where they remained until the end of the war. The colors were then returned to Jefferson City. Missouri, where they still can be found. O.R., vol. 3: 90; O.R., vol. 53: 425, 432–433; Banasik, Missouri in 1861, 380–381; Bearss, Wilson's Creek, 97; Brooksher, 208–209; Lademann, " Wilson's Creek," 437; Piston & Hatcher, Wilson's Creek, 259–261; Sigel, "Flanking Column," 305.

77. Following the initial fight at the James River Branch about 100 Federals were captured, in addition to a 6-lb brass smoothbore cannon, several wagons and General Sigel's personal carriage. Those few men remaining were rallied yet again, by Colonel Sigel, near an "old sawmill and started on the road apparently leading to Springfield." Proceeding but 18 yards the Unionists were hit again by another rebel volley from a cornfield to their left. "An orderly of Colonel Sigel... instantly jumped from his horse...pulled down sufficient rails so that" those remaining men could escape into a cornfield to their right. Proceeding through the cornfield, the Federals came upon an open field and continued forward. About half way through the fallow field, Colonel Sigel with Lieutenant Schuetzenbach moved off to the left; the remaining men did not follow but continued on forward about another 300 feet when they encountered "a gentleman" who announced to the hapless Yankees that they were surrounded and demanded their immediate surrender. Completely demoralized, surrounded, and, with no hope of escape the remainder of Sigel's column surrendered, while Sigel with Schuetzenbach escaped. In all, during the ensuing chase of Sigel's command. Colonel Major reported killing 64, and capturing 147 prisoners; however, in his report

boys of the Confederate cavalry sound of the "Tally ho!" The hunt was over.[78] Officers together when this surrender took place were Lieuts. Schaeffer and Chas. Mann of [Theodore] Wilkin's Battalion, Lieut. Col. Anselm Albert, Lieut. George Schuster and the writer.[79] Of the enlisted men there were about thirty left at the finale. Being re-conducted to that fateful lane leading north from the mill, we still found it strewn with the corpses of the men and horses killed only fifteen minutes ago. And retracing our steps across the creek and from which the colors of the Third Missouri had been removed, we gained the top of the bluff and marched back to Wilson's Creek, the number of prisoners be augmented at every step by little squads brought forward from the right and left, and at about 6 p.m. we again reached the fatal crossing, of Wilson's Creek, near the mouth of Tyrell's Creek, where we had crossed and re-crossed to attack and to retreat, at 6 a.m. and at 12 n.[noon]. Here we were permitted to wade into the creek deep enough to enable us to reach the water with our lips for the purpose of quenching our parching thirst,

---

following the battle Sigel acknowledge the loss of only 34 killed, with 130 missing. NOTE: In another article on the battle Lademann makes no mention of Meumann escaping, noting that when Sigel departed the column only Schuetzenbach followed his commander; however, this could simply mean that Meumann had been previously separated and escape via another route. *O.R.* vol. 3: 88; Banasik, *Missouri in 1861*, 378; Lademann, "Wilson's Creek," 437.

78. But what of Colonel Sigel? After Sigel and Schuetzenbach moved off to the left they escaped into a cornfield, where they waited while rebel horsemen rounded up the remnants of his command, and, unknown to Sigel, the Texans were searching feverishly for him. You see, upon his capture, Lieutenant Otto Lademann was questioned by his Texas captors, who wanted to know what Sigel looked like–"He was a small reddish looking man," Lademann replied, "with gold spectacles, a slouch grey felt hat, and a blue blanket worn poncho style." The astonished Texan responded, "'Why that man passed right close to us, and the manner he wore his blanket made us believe he was our man and we let him and the man with him pass without hindrance.'" Meanwhile, back in the cornfield, Sigel spied his chance and he and Schuetzenbach, sprung onto their horses and escape, being pursued by rebel outriders. The chase continued for close to six miles when the rebs finally gave up, not realizing that the man in front of them was Colonel Sigel. Having evaded his pursuers, Sigel made it back to Springfield with his one-man command, and, according to some accounts, went to bed, at 4:30 p.m. In a "wicked stanza" sung in Confederate camps following the battle, Colonel Sigel was mocked:

> Old Sigel fought some on that day,
> But lost his army in the fray;
> Then off to Springfield he did run,
> With two Dutch guards, and nary a gun.

Adamson, 250; Holcombe & Adams, 44; Lademann, "Wilson's Creek," 438; Monaghan, 177–178; Sigel, "Flanking Column," 305–306.

79. All the officers mentioned have been previously covered except for Charles Mann of Theodore Wilkin's Battalion (Apparently Wilkin's took command of Backof's Battalion sometime after the Battle of Carthage). Following his capture at Wilson's Creek, Mann was not exchanged until November 10, 1862; however he subsequently formed an independent artillery company in late 1861. His command fought at Shiloh in April, 1862, while Mann, according to his division commander "was unable to be in the action"–it seems that Mann was honoring his parole, by not fighting. Mann's command subsequently became Company C, 1st Missouri Light Artillery Regiment on July 2, 1862. Mann continued his service east of the Mississippi River, eventually being promoted to major and Chief of Artillery in the 16th U.S. Army Corps. Final disposition unknown. *O.R.*, vol. 10, pt. 1: 207; *O.R.*, vol. 41, pt. 4: 219; *O.R.*, Series 2, vol. 4: 695; *O.R.S.*, pt. 2, vol. 36: 23, 147.

our number being from 150 to 200. And being conducted back to the eastern bluff and up the creek some distance we were lodged for the night on an old field of wheat stubble, guarded by our captors,

The Confederate Cavalry.

The morning of Sunday, the 11th, passed without incident of note. About noon our cavalry guards were relieved by the Third Louisiana Infantry, and we were conducted farther up the valley of Wilson's Creek, near to the headquarters of Gen. [N. B.] Pearce, commanding the Arkansas brigade.[80] Except water we had been without food since Friday noon, and when Gen. Pearce discovered shoulder straps (warned by our two artillery officers) he asked if there were any more commissioned officers. Col. Albert, Lieut. Schuster and myself being pointed out to him, he invited us to his headquarters, and he entertained us royally with fried bacon, biscuits and black coffee. Here we were joined by Lieut. G. N. Finkelnburg, First Missouri Infantry; Lieut. John Kalser, Second Missouri Infantry, another officer of that regiment whose name I don't recollect, and two officers from the Second Kansas, all the latter gentlemen having been captured from Gen. Lyon's column.[81] A singular incident occurred while we were all eating supper.

In short, heavy set, round faced gentlemen approached, and, being introduced to us by Gen. Pearce as Col. [James] McIntosh, Assistant Adjutant General of

---

80. Nicholas Bartlett Pearce was born on July 20, 1828, in Kentucky, educated at Cumberland College and appointed to West Point in 1846. Graduating in 1850 (26 of 44), Pearce served in the Indian Territory and in Western Arkansas until he resigned on April 20, 1858. Entering the business world with his father-in-law, in Osage Mills, Arkansas, Pearce was elected a colonel in the Arkansas Militia. At the beginning of the Civil War, Pearce, "'a very strong Union'" man was appointed a brigadier general of Arkansas troops and given command of Northwestern Military District of Arkansas. Wilson's Creek was his only battle, after which he sent his men home, much to the displeasure of Arkansas State officials. In December 1861, Pearce was appointed a Confederate major in the Commissary Department and served in that capacity for the remainder of the war. Following the war, Pearce obtained a pardon from President Andrew Johnson, and returned to Osage Spring to rebuild his business empire. He became a teacher in 1872, later employed in a wholesale house in Kansas City and moved to Texas after the death of his wife where he worked as a land examiner. He died in Dallas, Texas, on March 8, 1894, at the house of a daughter-in-law. Allerdice, *More Generals in Gray*, 179–180; Michael B. Dougan, *Confederate Arkansas: The People and Politics of a Frontier State in Wartime* (University, AL, 1976), 65; Heitman, vol. 1: 778; Woodruff, 17.

81. Gustavus N. Finkelnburg or Finklenburg or Finkleberg was a lawyer, from St. Louis, when he joined the 1st Missouri Infantry (Three months). Finkelnburg survived the war, and was later appointed as a U.S. District Judge for the First District of Missouri. He later resigned his position, moved to Colorado, where he died in about 1912. Otto Lademann, "A Prisoner of War," 4 vols., *War Papers Being Papers Read Before the Commandery of the State of Wisconsin MOLLUS* (Milwaukee: 1914; reprint ed., Wilmington, NC, 1993), vol. 4: 439, 443, hereafter cited as Lademann, "Prisoner of War"; Piston & Hatcher, *Wilson's Creek*, 310.

Little was known of John Kalser save he was a member of the 2nd Missouri (Osterhaus' Battalion). No further record found in the *Official Records* or the *Supplement*.

Gen. McCulloch, he said:[82] "You German gentlemen are acquainted with military customs, and if you will give your word of honor not to attempt to escape you can have the liberty of our camp, but you two gentlemen from Kansas get up and I will swear you." The two gentlemen had to stand up solemnly swear while we eight Missourian's remained seated discussing the merits of biscuit and bacon, after an enforced fast of fifty-four hours simply by the nod of the head indicating that our word of honor was pledged.[83]

Meeting Gen. Mcculloch.

On Monday, the 12th, at about 10:0 a.m., Col. McIntosh called again and requesting the Missourians to follow him led us to the headquarters of Gen. Ben McCulloch. The general was the stately looking gentlemen, above medium heigh, high forehead, kindly expression of face, wearing whiskers but no mustache, whose long hair, curling up around his ears and all around the back of his head, gave him a decidedly unmilitary appearance, although the general enjoyed a splendid reputation as a leader of Texas rangers, dating from the infant days of the Texas Republic.

He was dressed in a black velvet tunic, braided in front with a black silk braid, in a somewhat English fashion. He received us in front of his tent, bareheaded, and, upon each of us being presented individually, shook our hands is a very cordial manner. He stated to us, that he was very sorry that it was beyond his power to make our sojourn with them pleasant and comfortable, that he was on the point of withdrawing his troops from Missouri, the state not belonging to the Confederacy, and that he would have to turn us over to Maj. Gen. Sterling Price.

Upon the request of Lieut. Col. Albert, who suffered from a concussion on the right hip, Gen. McCulloch placed his private ambulance at our disposal. Even after the lapse of a quarter of a century I think with gratitude of Gen. Pearce, Gen. McCulloch and Col. McIntosh, for the

---

82. James M. McIntosh was born at Fort Brooke (modern-day Tampa), Florida in 1828, graduated from West Point, last in his class, in 1849. Initially serving in the infantry, McIntosh transferred to the cavalry in 1855. At the beginning of the Civil War, McIntosh was a captain in the 1st U.S. Cavalry, from which he resigned on May 7, 1861. McIntosh was promoted to brigadier general on January 24, 1862, and commanded a brigade in Ben McCulloch's Division at the Battle of Pea Ridge, Arkansas in March 1862. He was killed on March 7, 1862. See *Duty, Honor and Country* of this series for a complete biography. Michael E. Banasik, *Unwritten Chapters of the Civil War West of the River Volume VI: Duty, Honor and Country: The Civil War Experiences of Captain William P. Black, Thirty-seventh Illinois Infantry* (Iowa City, IA, 2006), 447–448; Boatner, 533; Heitman, vol. 1: 669.

83. In another article on the same subject Lademann had Colonel McIntosh entering well after the meal had begun, at which time he took the word of the group not to escape, making no mention of the Kansans being sworn to abide by their word of honor. Lademann, "Prisoner of War," 440.

Great and Gentlemanly Kindness

they showed to us when we were there prisoners, and it still makes me feel sad to say that the latter two gentlemen, both officers of great merit and undoubted skill and bravery, were killed by the brigade in which I served at the very next hostile meeting the at Leetown, Ark., in the Battle of Pea Ridge, March 6, in 1862.[84]

Arriving in Springfield at 2 p.m. we found Maj. Gen. Sterling Price established at the old "Chamber's hotel" at the north side of the public square of the small town of Springfield, Mo.; said square being near center of the county jail.

The general occupied the right hand parlor on the ground floor as his quarters and received us with stately courtesy.

Gen. Price was a very handsome man, of a fine, commanding figure, with a very erect military bearing, his silver hair closely cropped and contrasting elegantly with his ruddy complexion. He was dressed in a gray uniform of the Missouri State Guard, collar and cuffs black, his buttons embellished with the ursine coat of arms of arms of our state.–After having saluted each individual name with a slight inclination of the head, he addressed us as follows: "Gentlemen, I suppose you don't want to be placed under guard. If you would give your word of honor that you will make no attempt to escape, you can select any vacant house in town, occupied it, and report personally at my headquarters every morning at 9 o'clock."

With a jester of the hand the general dismissed us, and stalking out single file just as we had entered general's apartment, we soon

Found a Vacant House

suitable for our purpose.

I, being the youngest of the party, was designated by Lieut. Col. Albert to act as

General Sterling Price

---

84. The Battle of Pea Ridge was fought on March 6–8, 1862. Earl Van Dorn commanded the Confederate forces while Samuel R. Curtis led the Federals. After a three day battle a disorganized Confederate Army fled the battle area, having suffered as few as 1,000 casualties or as many as 2,000. Curtis reported 203 killed, 980 wounded and 201 captured or missing. McCulloch was killed on March 7 and McIntosh died a short time later, dooming the Confederate Army to defeat. At the time of the battle, Lademann's company was part of the 3rd Missouri (Three years), the regiment being unassigned, serving as an unattached unit under the army command. *O.R.*, vol. 8: 206, 282; Banasik, *Missouri Brothers in Gray*, 148–150; Boatner, 669.

the commissary, and soon returned to Gen. Price's headquarters with a request for some rations. Pleasantly smiling, Gen. Price turned round to Col. Thomas L Snead, his A. A. G., and directed him to give me a written order on the Commissary Department.[85]

Armed with this precious document I crossed the public square to the southeast corner, where Col. John Reid, Chief Commissary of the Missouri State Guard, had established his headquarters.[86]

---

85. Thomas Lowndes Snead was born on January 10, 1828, in Henrico County, Virginia. Educated at Richmond College, Snead received a law degree from the University of Virginia in 1850, and moved to St. Louis the same year. In 1860, Snead bought the *St. Louis Bulletin*, a decided "states rights" newspaper. At the beginning of the Civil War, he was an aide to Governor Jackson, then Sterling Price's Adjutant and finally became a Missouri Congressmen, in 1864, for the Second Secession of the Confederate Congress. While in the military service, Snead took part in the Missouri engagements of Wilson's Creek and Lexington. After the war, Snead moved to New York City, where he worked for the *New York Daily News* and authored several pieces on the war including *The Fight for Missouri* (1866). He died on October 17, 1890, in New York and was returned to St. Louis for burial. Joanne C. Eakin, *Confederate Records From the United Daughters of the Confederacy Files*, 8 vols. (Independence, MO, 1995–2001), vol. 7: 59; Clement A. Evans and Robert S. Bridgers, gen. eds., *Confederate Military History Extended Edition*, 19 vols. (Atlanta, 1899; reprint ed., Wilmington, NC, 1987), vol. 12: *Missouri* by John C. Moore, 407; Peterson, et. al., 28; Winter, 128.

86. John W. Reid (not Reed; not to be confused with John Reid, commanding an Arkansas battery) was born on June 21, 1821, in Lynchburg, Virginia, and by the beginning of the Civil War was a lawyer and a resident of Lexington, Lafayette County, Missouri. A veteran of the Mexican War, Reid served in the Doniphan Expedition after which he returned to Missouri, and was elected to the Missouri House (1854–1856). During the Kansas border wars in 1856, Reid served as a "general," commanding a body of Missouri "ruffians." With the coming of the secession crisis of 1860, Reid, a leading secessionist in Missouri, was elected to the U.S. House in 1860, but vacated his seat, effective August 22, 1861, having joined the MSG. On May 21, 1861, Reid was appointed to General Price's staff. Following his term of service in the Guard, Reid moved briefly to Jackson County, Missouri, where he spent December 1861, visiting a friend, before he returned to the army, rejoining the Guard in January 1862 in Springfield, Missouri. He joined the Confederate Service on March 22, 1862, and during the Summer of 1862, returned to Missouri on recruiting service where he was captured near Lone Jack in July 1862. Sent to Gratiot Street Prison, in St. Louis, Reid was then forwarded to Alton, Illinois Prison. He was later released or escaped and rejoined Price for the Battle of Helena in July 1863. Surviving the war Reid was paroled in Shreveport, Louisiana, in June 1865. Reid was pardoned following the war, returned to Missouri, where he settle on some land he had bought prior to the war near Kansas City, Missouri. Reid died on November 22, 1881, and was buried in Kansas City. See **Appendix B** for a picture and a complete biography. *O.R.*, vol. 22, pt. 1: 416; *O.R.*, vol. 22, pt. 2: 811; Carolyn Bartels, *Missouri Confederate Surrender New Orleans & Shreveport May-June 1865* (Independence, MO, 1991), "Reed, J" entry, hereafter cited as Bartels, *Confederate Surrender*; Bartel, *Trans-Mississippi Men*, 3; Joseph H. Crute, *Confederate Staff Officers 1861–1865* (Powhatan, VA, 1982), 158, hereafter cited a Crute, *Confederate Staff*; Joanne C. Eakin, *Missouri Prisoners of War From Gratiot Prison & Myrtle Street Prison, St. Louis, Mo. and Alton Prison, Alton Illinois Including Citizens, Confederates, Bushwhackers and Guerrillas* (Independence, 1995), "Reid, John W." entry, hereafter cited as Eakin, *Missouri Prisoners of War*; Edwards, 449; Etcheson, 55, 122, 364; Thomas Goodrich, *War To the Knife: Bleeding Kansas, 1854–1861* (Mechanicsburg, PA, 1998), 158–161, hereafter cited as Goodrich; Donald R. Hale, *Branded as Rebels Volume 2* (Independence, MO, 2003), 270, hereafter cited as Hale, *Branded as Rebels*; *History of Audrain County*, 40; Lademann, "Prisoner of War," 441; James E. McGhee, *Letter and Order Book Missouri State Guard 1861–1862*

Col. Reid was a regular trump; one of the best fellows I ever met. He fairly loaded me down with edibles, adding a valuable gift a couple of pounds of good smoking tobacco, only stipulating that if ever the Yankees caught him, we would treat him with the same liberality.[87]

We were so fixed very comfortably, receiving daily numerous visits of the officers and men of McCulloch's and Price's armies.

The Federal hospital in charge of Drs. [E. C.]Franklin and [S. H.] Melcher (of the Fifth Missouri Infantry) was established in the unfinished courthouse at Springfield and filled to overflowing by the wounded of the late action.[88] Mrs. John S. Phelps, was the Guardian Angel of our sick and wounded in Springfield, and she never will be forgotten by those brave men, maimed and bleeding for their devotion to the Union, to whose wants she and other patriotic ladies ministered with untiring energy day and night.[89]

(Independence, MO, 2001), B, 11–12, 82, 168, Index "Reid, John W." entry, hereafter cited as McGhee, *Letter and Order Book* ; McGhee, *Service With the Guard*, 20; Monaghan, 80–81; Alice Nichols, *Bleeding Kansas*, (New York, 1954), 157, hereafter cited as Nichols; Peterson, et.al., 15, 34; Rassieur, 7; "John William Reid," in Wikipedia.org; Ryle, 73; G. Murlin Welch, *Border Warfare in Southeastern Kansas 1856–1859* (Pleasanton, KS, 1977), 5–7, hereafter cited as Welch.

87. In providing tobacco to Lademann, Colonel Reid was indeed quite generous, giving the captive Yankee a six month supply. "Prisoner of War,"441.

88. Samuel H. Melcher was born on October 30, 1828, in Gilmanton, New Hampshire, received his primary education in New Hampshire and "graduated from the medical department of Dartmouth College, in 1851." At the beginning of the Civil War he resided in St. Louis and on May 7, 1861, was appointed the Assistant Surgeon of the 5th Missouri Infantry (Three months), being mustered into the service on May 11, 1861. Following the rout of Sigel's command, at Wilson's Creek, Melcher stayed behind to tend the wounded and later accompanied General Lyon's body to Springfield. Melcher remained in Springfield, departing the city on November 11, 1861, with the remaining Federal casualties. Returning to St. Louis, Melcher was appointed a brigade surgeon on December 4, 1861, but shortly thereafter organized the 32nd Regiment of EMM and was subsequently appointed colonel. Melcher left his regiment, in the Fall of October 1862, being appointed the Medical Director of the District of South Western Missouri, and the Army of the Frontier on October 26, 1862. In 1864, Melcher served as an aid-de-camp for General Pleasanton, during Price's 1864 Missouri Raid. After the war Melcher moved to Chicago, Illinois in 1897, where he spent his remaining years. He died on August 1, 1915. *O.R.S.*, pt. 1, 1: 236; Charles S. Bently, Edward D. Redington, and Jared W. Young, "Samuel Henry Melcher," *Memorial of Deceased Companions of the Commandery of the State of Illinois, MOLLUS,* (Chicago, 1923; 70 vols., reprint ed., Wilmington, NC, 1993} vol. 13D: 255–257; National Archives, Record Group M393, General Order Book (October 14, 1862-April 10, 1863), Army of the Frontier, General Orders No. 8 (October 26, 1862), 4; Peckham, 118, 123.

Edward C. Franklin was born in New York and the regimental surgeon of the 5th Missouri Infantry (Three months), being mustered into the service on May 18, 1861. After his command arrived in Springfield, in June 1861, Franklin was placed in charge of the General Hospital and remained in the city after its capture, tending the wounded from the Battle of Wilson's Creek. Franklin left Springfield on September 7, 1861, and returned to St. Louis. On September 30, 1861, he became a surgeon of volunteers, later brigade surgeon in General Grant's army, and Medical Director of the Mound City General Hospital. Franklin resigned from the army on August 5, 1862, and returned to St. Louis, where he died on December 10, 1885. *O.R.*, Series 2, vol. 3: 451; *O.R.S.*, pt. 1, vol. 1:236, 268; *O.R.S.*, pt. 2, vol. 9:387; Peckham, 118, 123; Heitman, vol. 1: 434.

89. Mary Whitney (Phelps) was born in Portland, Maine in 1813. She married John Phelps, a future Governor Missouri in 1837, and moved with her new husband to Springfield, Missouri. Like her

Every Morning

at 9 o'clock we had what we designated, our daily nose count.

Filing into Gen. Price's apartment in Indian file and ranging ourselves on the west wall, the general would gravely salute us with: "Good morning, gentlemen." Then with his finger he would count us from right to left, from one to eight upon which he would dismiss us with the courteous wave of the hand and the words: "Call again, tomorrow morning, gentlemen." On Sunday, the 15th of August, Gen. Price informed us that he had received favorable news from Capt. Emmett McDonald [MacDonald], whom he had dispatched Rolla, under a flag of truce, to arrange an exchange of prisoners of war, with Gen. Frémont, and if we would give a written parole he would release us the next day, on condition that we would leave his lines in twenty-four hours after signing a parole in duplicate.[90] We joyfully agreed to accept the general's term, and on Monday, the 19th of August (the very day that I attained the age of 20 years) the following parole written on dark blue paper, in the handwriting of Col. Thomas L. Snead, was signed by me in duplicate, and similar ones by the other seven officers:

---

husband, Mary was staunchly pro-Union and is credited by most sources as saving General Lyon's body after it was left behind in Springfield, following the Battle of Wilson's Creek. Following the Battle of Pea Ridge (March 6–8, 1862) Mary Phelps, left Springfield, with a load of medical supplies, to join her husband's regiment then located in northwest Arkansas. There, as a member of the Western Sanitary Commission, she served as a nurse. After the war Mary established a home for the children of Union men who had died during the war. She died in Springfield on January 25, 1878. Gerteis, *St. Louis*, 210; Monaghan, 249; Patrick, *Nine Months in the Infantry*, 94–95 n. 60.

90. Emmett MacDonald arrived in Rolla on August 16, and proposed an exchange of prisoners by "mutual liberation." Major Sturgis, commanding the Federal forces at Rolla, waited until August 18, before forwarding the information on the requested exchange to Frémont's headquarters in St. Louis. It appears that the rebel prisoners were finally released "without parole," according to Sturgis, while the Federal prisoners (at least the officers) had to sign a written parole. *O.R.*, Series 2, vol. 1: 128–129; "From St. Louis," *Chicago Tribune*, August 19, 1861.

Emmett MacDonald (not McDonald) was born in 1837, in Steubenville, Ohio, and moved with his parents to St. Louis in the 1850's. A lawyer by profession and resident of St. Louis, at the beginning of the Civil War, MacDonald commanded a squadron of cavalry during the Camp Jackson affair. After his capture, MacDonald refused parole and subsequently obtained his unconditional release from Illinois judge, Samuel Treat, who ruled that MacDonald could not be a prisoner of war since he was legally assembled at Camp Jackson. Following his release, Emmett served as an aide-de-camp to Colonel Richard Weightman at the Battles of Carthage and Wilson's Creek, then joined Brigadier General James S. Rains' MSG Division, commanding a light battery of artillery. MacDonald participated in the Siege of Lexington, Missouri, the Battle of Pea Ridge and numerous skirmishes in northwest Arkansas and southwest Missouri. Joining the Confederate Army, MacDonald was appointed the Provost Marshal General of Missouri, on August 5, 1862, by General T. C. Hindman. By the Battle of Prairie Grove (December 7, 1862) MacDonald had risen to the rank of colonel, commanding a brigade of cavalry. At Hartville, Missouri (January 11, 1863) MacDonald received a fatal wound and died a short time later. *O.R.*, vol. 3: 25, 186, 189; *O.R.*, vol. 8: 310, 319, 324; *O.R.*, vol. 22, pt. 1: 208–210; Allardice, *Confederate Colonels*, 263; Lademann, "Prisoner of War," 443; Special Order No. 45 (August 5, 1862), Special Orders Book No. 1; Winter, 119.

The Parole

"I, Otto C. Lademann, second lieutenant, Third Regiment, Infantry Missouri Volunteers, being a prisoner of war to the State of Missouri, do pledge my sacred word of honor that I will not again, during the present war; against either the Confederate States of America or the Missouri State Guard, unless regularly released or exchanged. I reserve to myself, however, the right to give this, my parole, at any time and surrender myself to the Missouri State Guard as a prisoner of war to the State of Missouri.

Given at Springfield, Missouri, this 19th day of August, 1861

Signed, O. C. Lademann
Second Lieutenant, Third Missouri infantry."

Being thus at liberty to return home, we made a bargain with Mr. Fraser for two teams take us to Rolla. [91]

Mr. Fraser two sons were in the ranks of the Missouri State Guard, but the old gentleman had been with Sigel's Brigade to Carthage and back as an assistant wagon master, and to comply with our order to leave Gen. Price's lines in twenty-four hours, we left Springfield that day and spent the night at Frazier's house, some three miles from town.

On our journey to Rolla, only one incident of note occurred, which I am about to relate. On the evening of the second day, while a two miles Southwest of Lebanon, Mo., we were stopped on the road by a party of recruits going to Springfield to join Price's army. We gave all the information about ourselves the gentleman required, and produce our written paroles. But those embryo Confederate soldiers were full of patriotic ardor and very bad whiskey, and after showering on our heads unlimited number of d—s always imparting to us, at the same time, a canine descent of the maternal side, they ordered us out all the wagons and ranging us all in a row along the side of the road told was we would have to

"Hurrah" for Jefferson Davis

or die right there and then.[92] Our party consisted of Lieut. Col. Albert, Lieut.

---

91. Fraser agreed to transport the paroled officers for sixty dollars. The party consisted of eight officers, one enlisted man and Fraser. Lademann, "Prisoner of War," 442.

92. Jefferson F. Davis was born on June 3, 1808, in Christian City, Kentucky. He attended West Pont, Class of 1828, graduating number 23 of 33, and then served for seven years before resigning. During the Mexican War, Davis commanded the 1st Mississippi Rifles Regiment and was wounded at the Battle of Buena Vista. Following the war, Davis was appointed a senator from Mississippi, ran for governor (1851) but lost and was then appointed Secretary of War (1853) under Franklin Pierce. Following Pierce's term, Davis re-entered the U.S. Senate and served until January 21, 1861, when he left the senate. Elected President of the Confederacy on February 22, 1861, Davis fled Richmond, Virginia in April 1865, and was captured on May 10, 1865, in Georgia. Imprisoned at Ft. Monroe, Virginia, he was released two years later, without trial. Traveling abroad for several

Schuster and the writer, of the Third Missouri, Lieut. Kaiser and another lieutenant off the Second Missouri, Lieut. G. A. Finkelnburg of the First Missouri,
Lieuts. Schaeffer and Mann of the artillery and Mr. Panze a former merchant of
St. Louis but now a private of Co. K, Capt. Theo Meunmann. Lieut. Finkelnburg,
the pastor of our party, pleaded with eloquence. Mr. Framer supporting him with
all the persuasion in his power but our tormentors were inexorable. It was death
or "hurrah" for Jeff Davis. The feelings we had for Mr. Davis were very reverse
of admiration, and we concluded that we would not cheer for Mr. Davis. Things
were rapidly coming to a crisis, the bad whiskey in our Confederate friends was
bent upon mischief, and the boys were getting their shooting irons ready to execute their threats. At this critical juncture a buggy hitched to a pair of mules and
driven by a mulatto boy turned round the next corner of the road toward Lebanon,
some 200 yards away, and approaching rapidly was found to contain our savior,

Capt. Emmett M'donald

the 'Baynard' of Missouri (sans peur et sans reproche [withot fear and without
reproach]) who, upon recognizing Lieut. Finkelnburg, as an acquaintance from
St. Louis, inquired what was the matter.

Being informed of our dilemma Capt. MacDonald quietly placed his hands
under the buggy seat, and, pulling out a couple of fine looking Colt navy revolvers, cocked his pistols, and pointing them at the leader of the villainous band informed him of his name and rank and told him that he would fill his carcass with
lead if any more indignities were offered to the parole officers.[93] Those drunken
recruits walk away like whipped curs. Capt. MacDonald remained with us until
they were out of sight and apologized to us very finally in the name of the Missouri State Guard. He died for the same cause he loved so much the very next year
at Hartsville, Mo. still wearing his long hair, coming down over his shoulder. He
was a brave and noble enemy, and six survivors whose life he saved that day still
bear him

A Grateful Remembrance.

On the afternoon of the fourth day, Friday, August 23, we came upon our cavalry picketers several miles out from Rolla. I cannot describe the feeling of relief
and joy we all experience when once more we met our boys in blue and found

---

years, Davis finally settled in Biloxi, Mississippi, where he died on December 9, 1889, eight years
after he had penned *The Rise and Fall of the Confederate Government* (1881). Boatner, 225–226;
Faust, 208–209.
93. In rebuking the rebel soldiers MacDonald said: "'Boys I am Capt. Emmett MacDonald of General Price's staff. The first one of you who touches a hair on the head of any of these gentlemen,
I will kill him like a dog. Now go to Springfield and get away from here!'" Lademann, "Prisoner
of War," 443.

herself inside of our own lines, although everybody in the enemy's ranks had treated us with the greatest kindness and consideration.

In a few days we took the train to St. Louis, where we arrived late at night. Lieut. Col. Albert ordered me to proceed to the residence of Col. Sigel on Gratiot Street, between Fifth and Sixth, and their report are safe arrival.

Col. Sigel was overjoyed when I made my report to him. I found that President Lincoln had appointed him a brigadier general of volunteers for gallantry and meritorious conduct, during my captivity.[94] If by my slight sketches of the events of the first 90 days of the war I have succeeded in recalling to the memory of the surviving Missouri soldiers of 1861, no matter on which side they fought, the romantic charm of clustering round our early military service I feel compensated for my labor.

Those charms were produced principally by the novelty of our situation and our inexperienced in military affairs. Charms rapidly obliterated in the latter days of our struggle by by the fiercely passions engendered by the repeated conflicts

Otto C. Lademann
Late Captain Co. F, Third Rgt. In., Mo. Vols.

* * * * * * *

Item: The aftermath of the Battle of Wilson's Creek and the retreat to Rolla, by Michael E. Banasik

The first of the defeated Unionists to return to Springfield was believed to be Colonel Sigel, who arrived back in town about 4:30 p.m., and, according to many accounts, went to bed–though Sigel would later deny the accusation. The remainder of the army began to staggered in thirty minuets later, with the last unit, Frederick Steele's Battalion, arriving sometime after 6:00 p.m. With the army back in Springfield, pickets were quickly stationed outside city while the surviving officers decided on their next move. Colonel Sigel met Major Schofield of Lyon's column, shortly after he reached Springfield, directing Schofield to gather "all the chief officers who were available" to meet at Lyon's old headquarters. In the discussions, held between 7–8:00 p.m., Colonel Sigel assumed command of the army, from Major Sturgis, and ordered an immediate retreat to Rolla, reasoning that the Confederates would attack the city on the morn.

And even as preparations were underway to evacuate the city, a truce was arranged to remove the wounded from the battlefield, effective 11:30 a.m. to midnight on August 10. Various conveyances headed back to the battlefield to remove the wounded and recover General Lyon's body which had been left behind. You see, previous to the engagement only two ambulances accompanied Lyon's

---

94. Sigel was promoted to brigadier general effective May 17, 1861, but only learned of his promotion when he returned to St. Louis on August 19, 1861. Engle, 86; G.C.C., "From Rolla," *Chicago Tribune*, August 23, 1861; Heitman, vol. 1: 886.

column to the battlefield, while none went with Sigel, necessitating a hodge-podge recovery effort. "The wounded were brought from the field," according to Dr. Philip C. Davis "in wagons, carriages, ambulances, litters and, in fact, every kind of conveyances which could be brought into requisition." In the end, it took "five or six days" before all the Union wounded were recovered, while the Guard wounded were all housed by August 12, according to MSG Doctor John Wiatt.

As the wounded were brought into Springfield, the unfinished courthouse served as the General Hospital for the Union Army and was quickly overflowing with wounded. Virtually all the buildings in the town, including churches, the Bailey House Hotel, with "nearly all the private dwellings" being occupied with wounded as still others lay in the streets waiting a place to recover or be treated. Springfield would eventually house all the Federal and Confederate wounded from the battle and would remain open for the Federal troops until November 11, when the last of the Unionist wounded left for St. Louis.

Meanwhile, back at the battlefield the wounded sought protection from the elements the best they could as they awaited recovery. In one case "'One party of four built a shelter of branches of trees as a protection against the sun,'" while others sought shelter where they could find it, dragging "themselves from the places where they fell to the shade afforded, by the few scrubby oak bushes in the field, and there...they laid down to die." Still others gathered around the body of General Lyon to protect their dead commander while awaiting recovery or their own death.[95]

In all, according to Thomas L. Snead, the Union Army lost 258 killed, 873 wounded, with 186 missing or captured for a total of 1,317, which amounted to about 24.5 percent of the force engaged–the largest percentage of any Civil War battle. These numbers were also accepted by most authors including, Hans Christian Adamson, Edwin Bearss, William Brooksher, William Piston and Richard Hatcher; however these numbers differ from what were reported in the *Official Records* or by Ashbel Woodard, Lyon's biographer, which totaled 1,235–or 223 killed, 721 wounded with 291 captured or missing. Further, depending on other primary and secondary sources, these numbers differ from what Snead listed above–Wiley Britton and John McElroy listed 228 killed, 782 wounded with 292 missing or captured; total 1,302. R. I. Holcombe and W. S. Adams listed Union losses as 1,091, with 235 killed, 754 wounded and 102 missing or captured.

On the Confederate side the reporting, from various authors and sources, seems to be much less uniform. General McCulloch reported the official Confederate loss as 265 killed, 800 wounded with 30 missing or captured–total 1,095;

95. *O.R.*, vol. 3: 63; *O.R.S.*, pt. 1, vol. 1: 236–238, 240–241; Adamson, 272–273; "Battle of Wilson's Creek, MO.: New York 'Tribune' Narrative," *Rebellion Record*, vol. 2: Doc. 519; Bearss, *Wilson's Creek*, 134; Britton, 108; Brooksher, 225–228; Crawford, 36; Joanne Chiles Eakin, *Missouri State Guard Doctor Leaves A Diary in 1861* (Independence, MO, 1999), 9–10, 14, hereafter cited as Eakin, Diary of a Doctor; Gerteis, *Missouri*, 71; "Interesting from Springfield," *Rock Island Register* (Rock Island, IL), September 11, 1861; Peckham, 337, 339; Peterson, et. al., 203; Piston & Hatcher, *Wilson's Creek*, 289–290, 295; Sigel's Letter, 148.

however Thomas L. Snead, Price's Adjutant, seems to be author of the generally accepted "official loss" which he listed as 263 killed, 915 wounded with 64 missing or captured; total 1,242, or about 12 percent of those engaged. John C. Moore, in the *Confederate Military History,* put the losses at 1,218, with no details, while R. I. Holcombe and W. S. Adam, in the first book on the battle, recorded the loss of 265 dead, 900 wounded and 80 missing or captured; total 1,245. Three years after Holcombe and Adams' account, Snead recorded the losses at Wilson's Creek which was subsequently accepted by Wiley Britton in 1899, and John McElroy in 1909, as the Confederates loss at Wilson's Creek. However, my research, as detailed in *Missouri in 1861,* puts the losses at 266 killed, 922 wounded and 112 missing or captured; total 1,300. Other secondary authors writing on the subject of rebel losses put forth their own totals. Hans Christian Adamson put the rebel losses at 282 killed, 1,055 wounded with no missing–total 1,336. Edwin Bearss, William Piston and Richard Hatcher said the rebels lost 277 killed and 945 wounded, while not listing missing or captured–total 1,222. Elmo Ingenthron accepted Holcombe and Adams figures, while Stephen Engel, Sigel's biographer, put the Confederate losses at 257 killed, 900 wounded with 27 missing or captured–1,184 total. And William Brooksher put the Confederate losses at 279 dead with 951 wounded and no missing listed–total 1,230.[96]

Whatever one accepts as the losses at Wilson's Creek, it was clear from the aftermath of the battle that neither side was prepared for the losses they suffered, as the medical staffs were overwhelmed in their efforts to care for the wounded or bury the dead. This was manifestly supported in the various medical accounts by Federal doctors, one who recorded "The attention shown the wounded was good, but not specially praiseworthy" as wounded were left on the field of battle for days after the engagement. In summing up his report of the lack of proper medical care for the Union troops, Dr. H. M. Sprague puts the onus on General Lyon's failure to consider the casualties he was to suffer in the battle. In his official report Sprague wrote: "There was no Medical Director. The regiments had no community of action of feeling. Had the commanding General designated an officer of rank as his Medical Director, there could have been no reason why nine-tenths of the wounded could not have been cared for and sent to [a] general hospital by the time our forces retreated," which occurred the day following the battle.[97]

---

96. There are several reasons for the difference in the various numbers that were reported lost, which have been detailed in my account in Missouri In 1861, which still remain valid today. I refer the reader to those pages for details on the difference. Also, in reviewing the losses put forth by Adamson, it appears that he failed to properly add the losses that he details in his Appendix for the Confederate forces which total 1,236 not 1,336 as he records on page 265 of his book. *O.R.,* vol. 3: 71–72, 106–107; Banasik, *Missouri in 1861,* 377–381; Adamson, 265; Bearss, *Wilson's Creek,* 161–164; Brooksher, 225, 236; Britton, 106–107; Dyer, 798; Engel, 78; Holombe & Adams, iii; Ingenthron, 88; McElroy, 176–177; Monaghan, 181; Moore, *Missouri, Confederate Military History,* vol. 9: 61; Piston & Hatcher, *Wilson's Creek,* 287;"Report of the National Casualties," Rebellion Record, vol. 2: Doc. 506; Snead, *Fight for Missouri,* 310, 312; Woodard, 328.

97. *O.R.S.,* pt. 1, vol. 1: 237–239; Piston & Hatcher, *Wilson's Creek,* 288–289.

Three days after the battle John Wiatt, a MSG doctor, recorded that the battle-field was a "horrible sight...Many of the wounded are lying where they fell in the blazing sun, unable to get water and aid of any kind. Blow flies swarm over the living and the dead alike. I saw men not yet dead, their eyes, nose & mouth full of maggots. And this is the end of the third day after the battle."[98]

The dead were also poorly handled as the Confederates were left with the task to intern those who were killed. "Those affiliated with the Confederate cause, no doubt, received better care than those of the Union," with the rebel dead being buried within days, while the Union dead lay uncovered for weeks. The summer heat necessitated that the bodies be buried quickly "with little or no ceremonies." An old well was the final resting point for fourteen men; a sinkhole took another 34, while in most cases, the remaining dead were buried in sallow graves, where they lay; unfortunately many of these shallow graves were later unearthed by wild dogs or wolves. The Confederates did the best they could; however, the stench of the dead lingered for days. Two weeks after the battle a Mr. Quinllian, of the *Cincinnati Gazette*, visited the battlefield and recorded the following:

> There still remain about seventy-five or one hundred uncovered bodies upon the field of battle, besides a large number of horses. The bodies are in every instance those of Federal soldiers. And are generally lying on hard gravelly ridges. Those who fell in the hollows, or where the ground was soft have been hidden from view. The stench arising from the field was not as overpowering as might be supposed. With a single exception, every face has turned as black as an Ethiopian.
>
> Further still, six months later the bones of hastily buried were still visible in February 1862, when General Samuel Curtis arrived in the area en route for Pea Ridge.[99]

Back at the Union Army's headquarters, in Springfield, an early evening meet-ing, on August 10, scheduled the evacuation to begin at 2:00 a.m. the next morn-ing; however, due to Sigel's command being unprepared to march at the appointed hour, the command was delayed until four when the Unionists abandoned Spring-field. Sigel's Brigade, with the 1st Iowa, led the army followed by 370 wagons, loaded with all the sick and wounded who could travel (about 200), and whatever supplies (valued at from $1,500,00 to $1,750,000) they could carry, including about $250,000 in gold; "no doubt the property of local Southern farmers and businessmen." The train occupied about five miles, when it stretched out, fol-lowed by the rest of the troops, with civilians mixed in among the column–hardly an organized retreat. Sturgis 's Brigade, the rear guard, cleared the city about 9:00 a.m. (Most sources, including Eugene Ware, have the last units departing at 6:00

---

98. Eakin, Diary of a Doctor, 10.

99. Ibid.; Ingenthron, 87–88; Michael A. Mullins, The Frémont Rifles: A History of the 37th Illinois Veteran Volunteer Infantry (Wilmington, NC, 1990), 53.

a.m.; however, William Wherry of Lyon's staff definitively has the time as 9:00 a.m.).[100]

The head of retreating Federal column (Sigel's Brigade) made 27 miles before they stopped on the first day, while the rest of the command camped at Sand Springs, having taken what was known as the "Mountain Road," which was a wise choice. Prior to then the "Valley Road" was the path of choice for Union supply line between Rolla and Springfield, and rebel sympathizers had blocked the road with fallen trees to slow their retreat on the Valley Road. The rapid retreat from Springfield angered the Union troops, who viewed the speed as an admission that they had been defeated and were fleeing for their lives; as such they demanded a change of leadership. During the next two days the rate of travel diminished, as the retreating Unionists, from the rear of the column, finally caught up with Sigel's Brigade about 34 miles from Springfield. A serious discussion then ensued as to whether Colonel Sigel should command the column. On the morning of August 14, with an almost unanimous insistence of the "officers of the command, Major Sturgis resumed command" reasoning that Sigel "had no appointment from any competent command." The command situation resolved, to the satisfaction of the men, the army continued on to Rolla where the head of the column arrived , within eight miles of the city on August 17, camping near water "and other facilities for camp life," with the rest of the army making the city over the next few days.[101]

Meanwhile, back at Springfield, scouts from the rebel army entered the city shortly after the Federals had departed the area, finding the town virtually deserted by the pro-Union population. And by early afternoon (Brooksher, Holcombe and Adams say 11:00 a.m.; Bearss says noon) the victorious rebel army entered the city and promptly confiscated all the medical supplies left behind by the Federal command, forcing Union surgeons to purchase supplies locally, with $5,000 in gold (Holcombe & Adams put the amount at $2,500) that was left behind by the retreating command. Also gone was the Greene and Christian County Home Guard Regiment, which was disbanded, rather than accompanying the defeated Union Army back to Rolla–"every man was to look out for himself." No ordnance stores were found by the victorious rebels as all remaining stocks were destroyed by the retreating column, nor were many supplies found as they too had been destroyed or removed–even the pro-Union local merchants had given away their

100. *O.R.*, vol. 3: 63–64; "Interesting from Springfield," *Rock Island Register*, September 11, 1861; *O.R.S.*, pt. 1, vol. 1: 238; Adamson, 273; "Battle of Wilson's Creek, MO.: Missouri 'Democrat' Narrative," *Rebellion Record*, vol. 2: Doc. 514; Britton, 108–109; Brooksher, 226–227; Crawford, 36–37; Gilmore, 122; Holcombe & Adams, 69; Moore, *Missouri, Confederate Military History*, vol. 9: 63; Peckham, 339; Piston & Hatcher, *Wilson's Creek*, 305; Ware, 342, 344; Woodard, 326.
101. *O.R.*, vol. 3: 64; Adamson, 274–275; "The Battle in Missouri–The Retreat From Springfield," *Daily Chronicle and Sentinel* (Augusta , GA), August 25, 1861; Britton, 108–109; Brooksher, 227; Engel, 81; Holcombe & Adams, 70; McElroy, 185; Patrick, *Nine Months in the Infantry*, 28, 31; Peckham, 339–340; Noble L. Prentis, *Kansas Miscellanies* (Topeka, KS, 1889), 86, hereafter cited as Prentis; Ware, 343- 344.

goods to prevent their use by the occupying army. Further, when the main body of the rebels entered Springfield, between 1:00–2:00 p.m., they also found the body of General Lyon, at his old headquarters, where the retreating Unionists had yet again left it behind.[102]

Following the battle, both sides would claim the victory–the Federals mainly because they had withdrawn from the field and were not immediately pursued. And only when Sigel ordered a retreat to Rolla did the battle become a Confederate victory, according to the same soldiers. Still others felt they had won the battle when the rebels failed to pursue or attack them on the retreat to Rolla. To the individual Union soldier "no man felt that they were whipped." To John McElroy every Union soldier "felt himself a victor." Still another recorded that all "the boys were angry and swearing at the officers" for retreating as "we were better drilled, more hardy, tough and experienced than our opponents. They [the rebels] were a heterogeneous mass of good, bad and indifferent." Sigel, himself, according to Stephen Engel "supposedly" tried to make out the battle as a victory by spreading the rumor that he had caused "'slaughter and dismay into the ranks of the enemy.'" This in turn, Engel continued, "often misled" supporters to the idea of a Union victory; and with "Sigel's victory" his fame was spread by his German troops, who immortalized their commander in Prose and Song (See The Prose and Songs from Wilson's Creek in Appendix A). Besides, many felt as did Wiley Britton, that the "the combined Southern forces were really defeated" despite the fact that the Unionist had abandoned the field of battle.[103]

"Most Union newspapers proclaimed Wilson's Creek to be a Union victory," according to William Piston and Richard Hatcher, with the Missouri Democrat writing–"The Union troops who fought and won the battle...need no higher mark, no brighter name, than the laurels earned justly entitled to them." The Chicago Tribune wrote that General Lyon "by his deeds of valor...had gained one of the proudest victories that ever fell to the lot of a soldier." And even when the particulars of the battle and the subsequent loss of Springfield were known, Union newspapers still continued to proclaim Wilson's Creek to be a Union victory. However, when the correspondent from the *Cincinnati Gazette* confronted a Guard captain during the retrieval of General Lyon's body, on the subject, the correspondent reluctantly replied, "'That it was a drawn battle.'" That said, most supportive Northern newspapers still called the battle a Union victory, concentrating their comments on the odds that Lyon faced, or that Sigel had "'withdrawn of his own free will,'" while others wrote that myth of one Southerner being able to best two

102. NOTE: The death of Lyon and the disposition of his remains will be dealt with in the following letters. *O.R.S.*, pt. 1, vol. 1: 240–241; "Battle of Wilson's Creek, MO.: New York 'Tribune' Narrative," *Rebellion Record*, vol. 2: Doc. 519; Bearss, "Fort Smith," 333; Britton, 109; Brooksher, 232–233; Holcombe & Adams, 68,71;

103. "Battle of Springfield," *Chicago Tribune*, August 21, 1861; W.S. Burke, *Official Military History of Kansas Regiments During the War For the Suppression of the Great Rebellion* (Leavenworth, KS, 1870; reprint ed., Ottawa, KS, n.d.), 10, hereafter cited as Burke; Engel, 82; Britton, 109; McElroy, 180; Prentis, 85, 87.

or more Northern men had been debunked. Southerners disagreed, as one might expect, believing they had won a "decisive victory," while holding firm to their belief of their superior manhood.[104]

Other comments focused on who was responsible for the outcome of the battle, particularly for the death of General Lyon. A correspondent for the *Chicago Tribune* put the blame for the death of Lyon on Secretary of War Simon Cameron for failing to heed General Frémont's request for reinforcements on August 3 or 4. "C" wrote–"The sacrifice of Gen. Lyon and the hundreds of his little band, was *needless and could have been prevented.* Ten days ago [August 3 or 4], having received a request from Lyon for reinforcements, Gen. Frémont telegraphed the same to Secretary Cameron. He was answered by a dispatch asking if the reinforcements were absolutely necessary, which was replied in the affirmative by Frémont. Since that time not a word of answer had been received and [the] Government seemed to have forgotten either its duty, or the imminent peril of a portion of its army."[105]

Overall, who won the Battle of Wilson's Creek continued even after the war had ended and still continues until today. Immediately following the war, James Peckham was even more distinct and fanciful than any other author, on who won the battle, writing in 1866–"The Battle of Wilson's Creek was more than a [Union] victory; it was a complete success in every point. The enemy was driven from the field [not true]; was forced to burn a large amount of his camp and garrison equipment [not true]; was forced to destroy and burn the larger portion of his train [not true], and did not pause in his flight until he ascertained he was no longer in danger of being pursued [not true]." Many years later, William Brooksher, a modern-day author, would put forth his own twist in proclaiming Wilson's Creek a Union victory, writing in 1995–Wilson Creek "was a victory...if one looks at the larger picture–Missouri certainly would not leave the Union in the near term nor, in all likelihood, would it ever secede;" besides, the Union force "was clearly not defeated" when it left the field of battle. That said, overall William Brooksher put little importance in the Battle of Wilson's Creek writing further–"Worst of all, the battle just ended had really not finally settled anything nor, for that matter, probably [had not] been necessary. There was no compelling reason for Lyon to have engaged in it. Springfield had so special strategic value and, although the loss of southwestern Missouri was not particularly desirable to the Union, neither was it particularly important."[106]

As to the consequences of the battle and Lyon's operations in Missouri, beginning with Camp Jackson, there were many. For the Union, the death of Lyon was

104. "Battle of Wilson's Creek, MO.: Missouri 'Democrat' Narrative," *Rebellion Record*, vol. 2: Doc. 511; C., "Affairs In St. Louis," *Chicago Tribune*, August 16, 1861; "Interesting from Springfield," *Rock Island Register*, September 11, 1861; Monaghan, 181; Quoted in Piston & Hatcher, *Wilson's Creek*, 318–319.

105. C., Affairs In St. Louis," *Chicago Tribune*, August 16, 1861.

106. Brooksher, 227, 235; Peckham, 340–341; Piston & Hatcher, *Wilson's Creek*, 319.

viewed as a severe blow, as he had been "the most able and dynamic leader in the West," according to Albert Castel. Further, according to Castel, "Union prestige suffered a damaging blow" while "all of western Missouri now lay open" to the victorious rebel troops, reversing "the tide of war in the West." However, the most significant impact of General Lyon's actions, according to Christopher Phillips was felt "upon the people of Missouri," where Lyon's actions polarized the state, giving rise to the guerrilla bands that would infest the state for the remaining days of the Civil War.[107]

The impact on the Southern side was more so as they could rightly claim a victory, though not a decisive one. Proclaiming victory at "Oak Hills" as they so named the battle, "Southern newspapers celebrated with gusto." "Throughout the Southern Confederacy," according to R.I. Holcombe and W. S. Adams, "and everywhere that the Confederate cause had sympathizers...the event did much for the cause in Missouri, by stimulating recruiting and causing many an undecided individual to come on down off the fence and stand on the southern side."[108]

For the Confederate Army, there was more to the victory than a simple statement that they had won. The fighting ability of the MSG had been vindicated despite General McCulloch's distrust of them. However, there was the question that seems to have been ignored by most period accounts–Why, when victorious, did the Confederates not pursue the defeated Unionists? To Generals McCulloch and Price, and even some junior officers, the answer was simple–they were out of ammunition and none was available for over a hundred miles; however, the rebels were hopeful in securing the necessary ordnance by searching the dead and wounded on the battlefield, but this was stymied by the camp followers who flooded the battlefield, removing guns and ammunition, before the Ordnance Department could secure the area. To MSG Lieutenant William Barlow it was also simple–Following the battle Barlow recalled "I also realized that a beaten army is only a little worse off physically than the victorious one, for we were too badly cut up and too thoroughly exhausted to think of pursuing." Further, even as McCulloch was contemplating pursuit he was informed, erroneously, that Union reenforcements were approaching the battlefield causing him to further hesitate in ordering a pursuit.[109]

The Battle of Wilson's Creek was the second major battle of the American Civil War and to Elmo Ingenthron, the engagement could easily have been named "The Battle That Made the Generals," having produced 64 Union and Confederate general officers, according to researcher Louis W. Reps, during the war with three making the rank during the Spanish-American War. The Union side, according to

---

107. Castel, 46–47; Pollard, 162; Phillips, *Damned Yankee*, 263.
108. Holcombe & Adams, 74; Piston & Hatcher, *Wilson's Creek*, 319.
109. Bearss, *Wilson's Creek*, 135–136; Brooksher, 231–232; "Interesting from Springfield," *Rock Island Register*, September 11, 1861; Patrick, "Guibor's Battery," 38; Peckham, 341–342; William G. Piston and Richard W. Hatcher, *Kansans At Wilson's Creek: Soldiers' Letters from the Campaign For Southwest Missouri* (Springfield, MO. 1993), 77 n. 100, hereafter cited as Piston & Hatcher, *Soldiers' Letters.*

Thomas Snead, would count seven major generals–Gordon Granger (September 1862), Francis J. Herron (November 1862), Peter J. Osterhaus (July 1864), John M. .Schofield (May 1863), and Frederick Steele (November 1862). Of those who were promoted to brigadier general there were twenty-three, among them were– Eugene Carr (March 1861), Powell Clayton (August 1864), Charles C. Gilbert (September 1862), Robert B. Mitchell (April 1862), Joseph B. Plummer (October 1861), Samuel D. Sturgis (August 1861), Thomas W. Sweeney (November 1862), and James Totten (February 1862).[110]

On the Confederate side, Thomas Snead listed the following men who became general officers by the end of the war–Thomas Churchill (March 1862), John B. Clark, Jr. (March 1864), Francis Cockrell (July 1863), Thomas Dockery (August 1863), Colton Greene (no date), Elkanah Greer (October 1862), Louis Hebert (May 1962), Dandridge McRae (November 1862), James McIntosh (January 1862); Mosby M. Parsons (November 1862), Sterling Price (March 1862). Joseph O. Shelby (July 1863), and William Slack (April 1862).[111]

* * * * * * *

Item: Incident from the Battle of Wilson's Creek–The death of General Lyon at Wilson's Creek, by Alexander Becher.
Published: January 15,1887.

Note: See **Appendix C, Extended Comments, Lyon's Column at the Battle of Wilson's Creek**, the paragraph associated with note no. 25 for details on Lyon's death at Wilson's Creek.

Gen. Lyon's Death

Alexander Becher of Allentown, Mo., writes to the *National Tribune* as follows: Gen. Lyon appeared at the head Second Kansas on horseback, and although I was in the second company in front very near the general at the battle, I failed to see him "swinging his hat in the air," neither did I hear him call, "Follow me."[112] Gen. Lyon did, however, very distinctively and emphatically give the command:

---

110. Boatner, 158, 342, 351, 398, 557, 613, 656, 727, 794, 823,843; Heitman, vol. 1: 285; Ingenthron, 92, 318 n. 26; Monaghan, 181; Snead, *Fight for Missouri*, 300–301.

111. Boatner, 155–156, 161, 242, 391, 355–357, 533, 622, 669, 737, 763; Heitman, vol. 2:177; Snead, *Fight for Missouri*, 301; Marcus J. Wright, *General Officers of the Confederate Army* (New York, 1911), 149.

112. The 2nd Kansas Infantry was recruited in May 1861, and was mustered into the U.S. Service on June 20, 1861, at Kansas City, Missouri. The unit then marched to Springfield, Missouri, being commanded by Colonel Robert Mitchell. Joining Nathaniel Lyon's command, the unit took part in the engagements at Dug Springs and the Battle of Wilson's Creek, where the unit lost 5 killed, 59 wounded, including Colonel Mitchell with 6 missing or captured. Retreating to Rolla, with the rest of the army, the Second was ordered back to Kansas where they were mustered out on October 31, 1861. Burke, 16–22; *Missouri in 1861*, 377; *Union Army*, vol. 4: 203–204

"Open column, company distance–Forward, right wheel, double quick–March." When we passed the extreme right, then occupied by the First Iowa, the command came from Gen. Lyon in person; "Left wheel into line." While we're executing this movement–i.e.: When the regiment was in the position of about have wheel into the line–we were fired upon, and our whole line broke somewhat and retired a few paces, but reformed at once in line of battle on the right of the First Iowa.

The Second Kansas had been in line about ten minutes when Gen. Lyon received the fatal shot. Near him at the time were Col. Mitchell, Maj. Cloud and the adjutant of our regiment.[113] Being at eyewitness I am confident that Gen, Lyon did not fall into Lieut. [Gustavus] Shryer's [or Schroyer's] arms, as stated by Capt. Joseph Cracklin.[114] Lieut. Shryer was not less than twenty-five or thirty feet

---

113. Robert Byington Mitchell was born on April 4, 1823, in Mansfield, Ohio. He attended college in Ohio and Pennsylvania and later practiced law in his home town. During the Mexican War, he served as a lieutenant in the 2nd Ohio Infantry. Returning home, Mitchell was elected mayor of Gilead, Ohio, in 1855, but left Ohio in 1856, for Linn County, Kansas. A Democrat, politically, Mitchell espoused the Free Soiler cause, and served in the Kansas Territorial Legislature prior to the Civil War. Mitchell raised the 2nd Kansas Infantry, being appointed colonel on May 23, 1861, and a brigadier general on April 8, 1862. Following his promotion to general officer, Mitchell served on the east side of the Mississippi River, and in 1864, returned to the Trans-Mississippi to command Nebraska Territory (January 1-April 11, 1865) then Kansas (April 11-June 28, 1865). Following the war, Mitchell served as Governor of New Mexico (1865–1867), after which he moved to Washington, D.C., where he died on January 26, 1882. Boatner, 557–558; Sifakis, *Who Was Who in the Union*, 276–277; Warner, *Generals in Blue*, 328–329; *Union Army*, vol. 8: 178.

William F. Cloud was born in 1825, educated in Ohio, a veteran of the Mexican War and a resident of Emporia, Kansas, at the beginning of the Civil War. He organized Company H, 2nd Kansas Infantry and was made the regimental major on June 11, 1861. On April 3, 1862, Cloud became the colonel of the 10th Kansas Infantry and on June 1, he was given command of the 2nd Kansas Cavalry. During the course of the war Cloud often times served as a brigade commander, commanding brigades during the 1862 Indian Expedition and the Prairie Grove Campaign. In early 1865, Cloud was made the major general and commander of the Kansas Militia. After the war, Cloud resigned from his Kansas Militia post, moved to Carthage, Missouri, and entered into private business. By the turn of the Twentieth Century Cloud was a published author, concentrating his writing on Mexico. Final disposition unknown. *O.R.*, vol. 3: 56, 70; Burke, 31–32;. Crawford, 207, 246; Fry, 22, 53; Webb, 351–353.

The adjutant of the 2nd Kansas was Edward Thompson, a resident of Lawrence , Kansas, at the beginning of he war. Fry, 22.

114. Joseph Cracklin was a resident of Lawrence, Kansas, and supporter of a free-state Kansas during the 1856 border war with Missouri. Cracklin commanded the 81-man company from Lawrence dubbed the "Lawrence Stubby." The company, under Cracklin, fought at Black Jack, Kansas, on June 3, 1856, at Franklin, Kansas on August 12, 1856, and defended Lawrence in September. At the beginning of the Civil War, he joined the 2nd Kansas Infantry, being elected captain of Company D and mustered in on June 11, 1861. Following the Battle of Wilson's Creek, Cracklin returned to Kansas where he was mustered out of the service on October 31, 1861. Final disposition unknown. William Connelley, *Life of Preston B. Plumb* (Chicago, 1913), 39–40; Fry, 22; Goodrich, 146, 179–181; Nichols, 123; Piston & Hatcher, *Wilson's Creek*, 68.

Little was found on 1st Lieutenant Gustavus Shryer's or Schroyer save he was a member of Company K, 2nd Kansas Infantry, which was raised in Leavenworth, Kansas. Like other members of the Second, Schroyer was mustered into the service on June 11, 1861, he fought at Wilson's Creek and was mustered out on October 31. Final disposition unknown. Fry, 22; Piston & Hatcher, *Soldiers' Letters*, 73 n. 93.

in front of Gen. Lyon and the regimental staff at that time. On the contrary, Gen. Lyon, leaning from his horse upon Maj. Cloud, was supported in his posture by the major for a moment, when a second lieutenant with a detail of four men bore the body to the rear.[115] About the same time Col. Mitchell of the Second Kansas was carried from the front mortally wounded.

* * * * * * *

Item: Incident from the Battle of Wilson's Creek–The Union rebuttal to the final actions at Wilson's Creek by the 3rd Texas Cavalry, by R. I. Holcombe.
Published: January 9,1886.

The Third Texas at Wilson's Creek

Chillicothe, Mo., Jan.3
[Editor *Republican*]
My attention has been called to the communication which appeared in your "Tales of the War" some weeks since, written by an ex-member of the Third Texas Cavalry, and purporting to describe the part taken by that regiment in the Battle of Wilson's Creek.[116] While I was not a member of the Third Texas, and the writer referred to was, I do not hesitate to say that he has given us a very inaccurate and in many instances an all together preposterous account of the part born by his Regiment.

I am warranted in this statement by the official report of Col. E. Greer, who commanded the regiment, and by other reports of Confederate officers (See Rebellion Record [*O.R.*], vol. 3). The part taken by the regiment, while honorable enough, was not very conspicuous. It numbered about 1,000 men, and its loss was only four killed and twenty-one wounded.[117] The regiment became separated

---

115. In addition to Lieutenant Schroyer, Lyon's body was taken to the rear by Private Albert Lehman, Lyon's orderly, and two members of the 2ⁿᵈ Kansas Infantry–Andrew Keplar (Company G) and Corporal Marsh E. Spurloch (Company G). Piston & Hatcher, *Soldiers' Letters*, 73 n. 93.

116. The article that the author was referring too, was written by Henry L. Lewis, 3ʳᵈ Texas Cavalry, and appeared in *Confederate Tales of the War Part One: 1861* (pgs 93–98).

The 3ʳᵈ Texas Cavalry was also known as the "South Kansas-Texas Regiment" or Greer's Texas Cavalry Regiment. The unit was organized at Dallas, Texas, on June 13, 1861, and moved to Missouri, where it participated in the Battle of Wilson's Creek. Later, 350 men of the unit participated in the Battle of Chustenahlah, Indian Territory, on December 26, 1861, where they routed their foe. In March 1862, Greer's Regiment was at Pea Ridge, Arkansas, after which it was transferred to the east side of the Mississippi River. Arriving in Memphis, Tennessee in April 1862, the regiment completed its military service as part of Ross' Texas Cavalry Brigade, surrendering in May 1865. *O.R.*, vol. 8: 28–29; Harold B. Simpson, *Texas in the War 1861–1865* (Hillsboro, TX, 1965), 112, hereafter cited as Simpson;; Banasik, *Embattled Arkansas*, 8–10.

117. Colonel Greer reported the loss of 4 killed, 22 wounded with 6 missing. Thomas Snead, in his book, *The Fight for Missouri*, recorded that the 3ʳᵈ Texas numbered 800 officers and men, while

early in the engagement, however, and Col. Greer succeeded in keeping only five companies with him, those of Capts. [T.W.] Winston, [R.H.] Cumby, F.M.] Taylor, [D.M.] Short and [S.M.] HaLe. With these he moved to the Federal right flank, and after a little successful fight returned to the Springfield and Cassville road, where it was joined by the rest of the regiment, and where it remained some time.[118] Two companies, [Hinche P.] Mabry's and [Jonathan] Russell's, participated with Lieut. Col. [James] Major's Missourians in the defeat and pursuit of Sigel's division, which occurred rather early in the morning.[119] Soon after the remainder of the Third Texas started in pursuit of that portion of Sigel's column which had retreated to the eastward, and did not return until "about sundown," Col. Greer says, six hours after the battle was over.

The regiment therefore, could not have taken any part in the closing fight against Lyon's men on "Bloody Hill," and the "battery of four guns which the gunners were moving forward with their hands in front of the Third Texas," and the "desperate and bloody" flight which resulted must have existed in the gentleman's imagination only. He says:

> In this last struggle (referring to the fight against Lyon) the Third Texas charged over the battery in front of them and through the infantry that supported it, and about faced and charged back through the Southern lines, while the Federal gunners ran under their gun carriages to get out of the way.

The writer evidently confounds the conduct of his regiment at Wilson's Creek with that of the famous Light Brigade at Balaclava. If any cavalry charge was made on either Totton's or Dubois' batteries, the only two Lyon had, which resulted in the ride through it and "back through the battery smoke," besides "sabering the gunner there," except those who scampered "under their guns carriages"–If this

---

losing 4 killed and 23 wounded, with none missing. I suspect that the missing were finally accounted for with one of the previous missing being subsequently listed as wounded. *O.R.*, vol. 3: 120; Banasik, *Missouri in 1861*, 378; Snead, *Fight for Missouri*, 312.

118. Most authors and period participants agree that Greer's assault on the Federal right flank occurred about 10:00 a.m. toward the end of the battle. For a description of Greer's assault see **Appendix C, Extended Comments, Lyon's Column at the Battle of Wilson's Creek**, the paragraph associated with note. no. 29. *O.R.*, 3: 74, 118–120, 126, 390; Bearss, *Wilson's Creek*, 103–104; Britton, 103–104; Crawford, 34; Fry, 22; Gerteis, *Missouri*, 72; Piston & Hatcher, *Wilson's Creek*, 270–271; Prentis, 80–82; Ware, 322; Woddward, 315–316.

For Captains T. W. Winston (Company A), R. H. Cumby (Company B), F. M. Taylor (Company C), S. M. Hale (Company D) D. M. Short (Company E) see **Appendix C, Extended Comments, Captains of the 3rd Texas Cavalry**. Douglas Hale, *The Third Texas Cavalry in the Civil War* (Norman, OK, 1993), 29, hereafter cited as Hale, *Third Texas Cavalry*.

119. Lieutenant Colonel Major took up the pursuit of Sigel's column a short time after 9:30 a.m., his force consisting of about 300 men, including the "Dead Shot Rangers," commanded by Captain Mabry and the "Cypress Guards" led by Captain Russell. For brief biographies of Captains Mabry and Russell see **Appendix C. Extended Comments, Captains of the 3rd Texas Cavalry**. *O.R.*, vol. 53: 425.

happened at Wilson's Creek, I say, who else saw it besides the gentleman from Grapevine, Tex.?[120]

R. I. Holcombe

* * * * * * *

Item: Incident from the Battle of Wilson's Creek–General N. Lyon's Burial, by J. Coleman Gardner.
Published: August 29, 1885.

Under the caption of "Tales of the War" in your issue of yesterday [August 22, 1885] Capt. [William] Barlow gives several accounts of the arrival and disposition of the body of Gen. Lyons, on the evening of August 10, 1861.[121] The facts are these, so far as my observation extended: About 7 P.M. that evening, I was on the public square when someone remarked that Gen. Lyon's body had just been brought in and was in the yard at his former headquarters and no one to care for

---

120. Grapevine, Texas was located in the northeast corner of Tarrant County, between Dallas and Fort Worth.

As to "who saw it"–several Union participants commented on the attack, including Captain James Totton and others; all who have the attack coming toward the end of the engagement. The more likely explanation for the results of the attack, as reported by Colonel Greer, was a combination of confusion as to when the incident happened and some embellishment in his report. In his Official Report, Greer implies that the attack occurred early in the battle, which simply was not true. Douglas Hale, in the *Third Texas Cavalry* clarifies the situation, noting that Greer arrived at Bloody Hill, in the early part of the engagement then sat for five hours–Hale wrote: "Greer and the first five companies of his regiment clattered along the stony bottom of Skeggs Branch and out unto the western slopes of Oak Hill. Held in reserve for five hours, the Texans skulked through the brush-chocked ravine, just beyond the Yankee flank." There the Texas waited and cheered on the Missourians as they time and time again assaulted Bloody Hill. Finally, after Sigel had been dispatched, General McCulloch returned to Price's boys. "At this point he ordered Colonel Greer forward from the flank against a battery of guns commanded by Captain Totten." See note.118 above for reference on the attack and the attack itself as recalled by the various participants as related in **Appendix C, Extended Comments Lyon's Column at Wilson's Creek** .Hale, *Third Texas Cavalry*, 62, 65–66.

121. William Barlow's account of Lyon's burial first appeared in the *Missouri Republican* on August 22, 1885. It was subsequently re-printed, with annotations, in *Civil War Regiments: The Early Battles* 5 (No. 4, 1997), 28–50, and will not be presented here, except as comments to Gardner's article. Patrick, "Guibor's Battery," 28–50.

William P. Barlow was born in New York City on June 17, 1838 (Ankesheiln says he was born in Michigan), relocated to St. Louis, Missouri, with his parents, in 1852. A printer by trade, Barlow joined the St. Louis Missouri State Militia and was part of the Southwest Expedition to the Missouri-Kansas border, in 1860. At the beginning of the Civil War he was captured at Camp Jackson, paroled; however, Barlow did not honor his parole, and joined the MSG; later he was officially paroled in October 1861. Barlow was the first lieutenant of Guibor's Battery and served throughout the war, surrendering in Alabama. He remained for a time in Alabama, married and resumed his printing occupation. Returning to St. Louis in 1880, Barlow "became one of the founding members of the Ex-Confederate Association" the following year. In 1891, he became the secretary of the Confederate Veteran Home Association in Higginsville, Missouri, and served until his death in 1896, at the age of 58. Wade Ankesheiln, *The Last Guardsmen* (Independence, MO, 2008), 24–25; Hale, *Branded as Rebels*, 16; Patrick, "Guibor's Battery," 27–28.

the remains. James Vaughn, now at Corpus Christie, Tex., John H. Cayner and myself went down College Street to his headquarters and found his body lying just inside the gate, which was open, with his head to the west.[122] We took the body into the house. Gen. Schofield nor anyone else was there at that time. Dr. E. C. Franklin did not stay to see what disposition was made of the body–that he paid Mr. Beal, the undertaker, to take care for the body I no doubt. I do not know that Mr. Phelps did have a tin coffin or casket made in which to place the remains, and Jas. Vaughn made it on Sunday, the 11th, and that on August 12, the remains were buried on Mrs. Phelps farm. Long afterwards they were disinterred and sent east.[123]

I don't think there was a Federal soldier at the grave when Gen. Lyon was buried, unless it was Dr. Melcher. They did not have time to go, and were then well on their way towards Rolla.[124]

J. Coleman Gardner

* * * * * * *

122. James Vaughn "owned a tin-shop in Springfield" and would later make a "zinc" case for Lyon's wooden coffin that would hold the body until it was transported back to St. Louis. Nothing found on Cayner. Holcombe & Adams, *Wilson's Creek*, 103.

123. Dr. Franklin arrived at Lyon's old headquarters at 10:00 p.m., on August 10, to embalm Lyon's body using arsenic; however the solution leaked out of the body, causing him to give up the process of preserving the body for transport to St. Louis. The local undertaker, Presley Beal, was then directed to "make a good, substantial coffin" to transport the body back to St. Louis. Early the next morning the army departed Springfield, leaving Lyon's bloody body still lying where Dr. Franklin had left it the night before. By early the next morning, August 11, several local women, including Mary Phelps, held vigilance over the body, while Dr. Franklin sprinkled the fast decomposing body with "bay rum and alcohol" to help contain the smell. The zinc lined "black walnut" coffin soon arrived and the body was hauled to Mrs. Phelps' farm, where it was initially placed in a cellar on the afternoon of August 11. There it remained until about August 14 (William Barlow says the 12th and Christopher Phillips says it was the 13th), when it was buried, in the Phelps' garden, to prevent any possible "mutilation" of the corpse. On August 22, a party, including John B. Hassler and Danford Knowlton (relatives of General Lyon), arrived from St. Louis, with a 300-pound iron coffin, to transport the body back to St. Louis. The escort party retrieved the body from the Phelps' farm and headed back to St. Louis, where they arrived on August 26. Lyon's body remained in St. Louis where a "suitable demonstration," in Frémont's headquarters, was made the day after its arrival. On August 28, Lyon's remains were sent East, escorted by seventeen individuals, including two reporters, Lyon's two relatives and 13 members of the Union army. On his journey back to Connecticut, Lyon's body was greeted with tearful crowds, which placed wreaths upon the coffin. Military escorts greeted the coffin in Cincinnati and other major cities as the funeral party passed through, and when the body arrived in Hartford (Piston & Hatcher say New Haven), it lay in state for three days. Finally, on September 5, Lyon's was buried, at Eastford, the place of his birth, following an elaborate five hour ceremony. Holcombe & Adams, *Wilson's Creek*, 101–104; McElroy, 186–187; Patrick, "Guibor's Battery," 41–42; Phillips, *Damned Yankee*, 259–261; Piston & Hatcher, *Wilson's Creek*, 302–30r; Woodard, 328–329, 332, 334, 336–339.

124. True. Lyon was buried well after the Union Army had departed the area, his burial being made by members of the MSG–Henry Guibor's Battery. Patrick, "Guibor's Battery," 42.

Chapter 3

Fall Campaign
(September–November 1861)

Item: Use of hemp bales at the siege of Lexington, Missouri, September 13–20, 1861, by unknown, though a Union supporter labeled "Chicago Comrade."
Published: September 25, 1886.

Editor Note: The Siege and Capture of Lexington, Missouri (September 12–20, 1861)–Following the Battle of Wilson's Creek, General Sterling Price remained in the vicinity of Springfield refitting his command and receiving new recruits, which poured into his command. Price also used the time in a vain attempt to garner General Ben McCulloch's support for an expedition to the Missouri River, hoping to control the river and cut off Kansas from the rest of the Union. In the end McCulloch declined and returned to northwest Arkansas, with his regular Confederate troops, while the Arkansas State Troops were mustered out. Undaunted, with McCulloch's response, Price departed Springfield on August 25 and headed north to Fort Scott, Kansas. On September 2, the MSG engaged a Kansas force under Jim Lane at Dry Wood Creek, where Lane was defeated and beat a hasty retreat to Fort Scott. Having neutralized the immediate threat from Fort Scott, Price continued north to the Missouri River, setting his sights on Lexington.[1]

Lexington at that time was the county seat of Lafayette County. It was located about 300 miles from St. Louis by the Missouri River, and at the beginning of the war amassed a population of 5,000, who participated primarily in the hemp growing industry. The city consisted of some manufacturing (hemp) with two colleges. The Masonic College, which embraced some fifteen acres, served as the Federal defensive point during the siege in September 1861.[2]

On September 12, 1861, General Price's army was within two miles of Lexington and halted for the night, having pushed back the enemy's outlying forces. Reinforced the next morning, Price closed in on Lexington, investing the city on all sides, with the exception of the river which was still open to the Federal command. September 14–17 saw little action, save sniping that was meant to cut off the water access to the Federals. During this time the rebel forces continued to increase to about 18,000 men by the siege's end. The common soldier saw no reason for the delay, leading one to record--"Hell is full of better Generals...God give us success, we have no leaders." This delay, according to another soldier, was necessary because: "We had to mold our bullets and make our cartridges

---

1. *O.R.*, vol. 53: 752; Gerteis, *Missouri*, 75, 99–100; McElroy, 191–194.
2. *O.R.*, vol. 3:171; McElroy, 206–207.

and when sufficient ammunition was prepared we were ready." Those in the artillery had similar problems, having to "manufacture ammunition" before an attack could begin.

At 6 a.m., on the morning of the 18th, the attack began in earnest, with the Guard attacking along the river bank from two points, successfully cutting the Federals' water supply and capturing a steamboat that was laden with supplies. Finally, after fifty-two hours of continuous combat, Colonel James Mulligan surrender the city, at 2:00 p.m. on September 20. The critical soldier, who previously despaired at his general's tactics now recorded--"Gen. Price's tactics proved to be the best. If we had charged them our losses would have been heavy." At Lexington the Federals surrendered 3,500 men, 5 pieces of artillery, 2 mortars, 3,000 stands of small arms, 750 horses, $100,000 worth of commissary supplies, and the Great Seal of Missouri. Price put the rebel losses at 25 killed and 72 wounded. [3]

The success of the Battle of Lexington and the small losses that the Guard suffered, was due largely to the use of the hemp bales, that allowed the rebel forces to close the gap between the Union defenders and the Guard, with minimum loss. The article that follows deals with those HEMP BALES.

* * * * * * *

Hemp Bales At Lexington, Mo.

We are all acquainted with the use which Gen. [Andrew] Jackson made of bags of cotton for fortifications at "Chalmette," or New Orleans, where, with less than half the number of the British, he gained the splendid victory over Sir Edward Pakenham.[4]

Those bags of cotton were undoubtedly the best temporary fortification he could have had, unless he would have had baled cotton instead; but that took place before cotton was pressed into bales. Of the advantages of the latter I have

---

3. *O.R.*, vol. 3:185–188; Banasik, *Missouri in 1861*, 182 n. 79; Eakin, *Diary of a Doctor*, 23–28; J. W. (Watt) Gibson, *Recollections of a Pioneer* (St. Joseph, MO, n.d.; reprint ed., Independence, MO, 1999), 114–117; McGhee, *Service With the Guard*, 45; Patrick, "Guibor's Battery," 45.

4. Andrew Jackson, the seventh President of the United States (1829–1837), was born in 1767, in South Carolina, and had settled in Nashville, Tennessee. by the beginning of the War of 1812. Arriving in New Orleans on December 1, 1814, Jackson began preparations to defend the city from an expected British attack. The British fleet arrived in the area a few weeks after Jackson, landing troops on Pea Island, east of New Orleans in Lake Borgne, which became their base of operations.

Sir Edward M. Pakenham, commander of the British forces, was born about 1777, and a veteran soldier. On January 8, 1815, he led a 6,000-man force in the Battle of New Orleans. Opposed to Pakenham, Jackson fielded about 4,700, militia, regulars, citizens, pirates and a battalion of free men of color. The fateful battle lasted but 30 minuets, resulting in the death of Pakenham and the loss of 291 killed, 1,262 wounded, with 484 captured–total, 2,037. For the battle Jackson recorded the loss of but seven killed and six wounded. Donald R. Hickey, *The War of 1812: A Forgotten Conflict* (Chicago, IL, 1989), 206–212; Robert V. Remini, *The Battle of New Orleans: Andrew Jackson and America's First Military Victory* (New York, 1999), xiv, 11–12, 24, 42, 52, 167–168.

had experience in shooting from behind cotton bales, while the rebs were issuing liberal rations of lead on the opposite side of the bales.

It remained for the rebel Gen. Sterling Price, and the siege and Battle of Lexington, Mo. in September, 1861, to use the splendid strategy that was used so long before by Malcom, King Duncan's son, and general, when that commander ordered that each of his soldiers should cut branches from the trees and bear them before them on approaching Macbeth's castle, saying: "Thereby shall we shadow the numbers of our host, and make discovery err in report of us."

Gen. Price discovered that in the vicinity there were large numbers of bales of hemp. Oh, fatal oversight in Gen. [James] Mulligan not to have made the discovery first and used them for his own safety instead of their being used for his destruction.[5]

Gen. Price understood their value at once; a long line of these hemp-bales was established, behind which the rebel sharpshooters were placed. Gen. Price needed not to conceal his approach, like the Indian, nor his strength like Malcom; for he out numbered the Union forces five or six to one; but as a good general, he looked for the maximum of both safety and success. These bales were thoroughly saturated with water, to prevent them taking fire from red-hot shot or the explosion of shells against them; and then commenced the remarkable strategy of the sharpshooters safely delivering their fire, then, at the signal of command, each bale was rolled over toward the enemy, all along the line; in one sense, producing what might be called the long roll, but instead of being a command to fall in it was more properly a command to roll in. Now, this was ever so much better than regular approaches by ditches. A man can roll over into a ditch, but he can't roll the ditch, and as for "dying in the last ditch" no more credit can be accumulated by it than by pegging out decently on top of the ground.[6]

---

5. James Mulligan, an Irishman, was born in Utica, New York in 1829, and moved to Chicago, Illinois, at a young age, following the death of his father. "A strict Catholic," Mulligan graduated from the Catholic College of North Chicago, after which he studied the law and was admitted to the bar in 1854. Prior to the Civil War he served as a militia lieutenant in Chicago Shield Guards. On June 18, 1861, Mulligan was mustered in as the colonel of the 23rd Illinois Infantry Regiment. He reached Lexington, Missouri on September 9, and by virtue of seniority assumed command of the garrison. Mulligan was wounded on the last day of the battle, surrendering the city at 2:00 p.m. on September 20. Captured at Lexington, Mulligan was exchanged in October 1861, for General Daniel M. Frost after which he served the rest of the Civil War years on the east side of the Mississippi River. On July 24, 1864, Mulligan was wounded at Kernstown, Virginia, and captured; he died shortly thereafter. *O.R.*, vol. 37, 2:601; *O.R.*, Series 2, vol. 1:554; *O.R.S.*, pt. 2, vol. 9: 561; "Colonel James A. Mulligan," in *The Battle of Lexington, etc.* (E. N. Hopkins, gen. ed.;,Lexington, MO, 1903; reprint ed., Middletown, DE, 2015), 17, hereafter cited as *Battle of Lexington*; McElroy, 206; "Siege of Lexington," *Chicago Tribune*, September 25, 1861.

6. The individual who was generally credited for the use of the hemp bales was General Tom Harris; however "several others claimed it," including General Price and Colonel Tom Hinkle. Price recorded that he "caused" the hemp bales to be transported to the forward lines, while Hinkle transported and dumped the bales along the streets, having obtained the bales from Wellington, Missouri. Harris for his part recorded that he "request[ed]…132 bales of hemp," which were obtained from the warehouse of "McGrew, Anderson, and Sedwick." Initially the bales were dipped

To the besieged the spectacle of this cordon of approaching and tightening hemp must have seemed to be bales full of baleful and grim suggestiveness of something more inglorious than a soldier's death.

'Tis hardly necessary to add that Gen. Mulligan surrendered.--(Chicago Comrade.)

* * * * * * *

Item: Battle of Belmont (November 7, 1861), by Charles M. Scott, Pilot of the *Belle Memphis*.[7]
Published: January 16, 1886.

Belmont from a Federal View.

St. Louis, Jan. 6
[Editor *Republican*]

An article in your issue of January 2 claims the Belmont was a Federal blunder, yet if all the facts were known it might seem one of the best planned and best executed pieces of strategy of the war, and certainly of the war in the West.[8]

Having been an actor in it, and in a position to see as much of any one man, be that man who he may, I propose to throw some light on the subject, and it will appeal to officers on both sides as to what you know themselves if it does not corroborate my statements.

In the first place let us consider the why attack on Belmont was made. A few days before the movement of Belmont an imperative order from the department commander to Grant ordering him to send out a detachment to Bloomfield, Mo., to break up a force that it was reported Jeff Thompson was organizing there.[9]

---

in the river to wet them and transported o the lines, but after several were lost in the river they were subsequently transported to the front where they were wetted. The hemp bale barricade then was slowly pushed forward, while men sniped at the Federals in relative safety. Dubbed "portable breastworks" by the men of the Guard, the unusual tactic proved to be highly successful for the sieging State troops, eventually resulting in the surrender of the Lexington garrison. McElroy, 213; Patrick, "Guibor's Battery," 48; J. F. Snyder, "The Capture of Lexington," *Missouri Historical Review* 7 (October, 1912), 4; Joseph A. Wilson, "Recollections of the Battle," in *Battle of Lexington, etc.*, 12.

7. Charles M. Scott, an Irishman by birth, was an experienced "First-Class " pilot on the Mississippi River. Following Belmont he would transfer to the *U.S.S. Choctaw* where he would serve in the Mississippi Squadron until the end of the war. By war's end he was a trusted advisor on river matters to Admiral S. P. Lee, commanding the Mississippi River Squadron. United States War Department, *The War of the Rebellion: Official Records of the Union and Confederate Navies* (31 viols., Washington, D. C., 1894–1922), vol. 27: 26, 33, 180 (all citations of refer to Series 1 unless indicated otherwise), hereafter cited as *ONR*; Hughes, 232 n. 12.

8. The January 2, 1886, issue of the Republican contained an article on Belmont written by a member of the 4th Tennessee Regiment. It was covered in the Confederate Tales, Volume 7, Part 1. Banasik, *Confederate Tales, 1861*: 142–158.

9. The Battle of Belmont was fought on November 7, 1861, and was the only battle that Grant

Grant immediately detached Col. Dick Oglesby of the Eighth Illinois, and now governor of Illinois, with his regiment, a couple pieces of artillery and a squad of horse and sent them by boat to Commerce, Mo. to take the road from there to Bloomfield, some forty miles southeast of there.[10]

On the return of the boats to Cairo the rebel spies at that place–the town was full of them–sent [General Leonidas] Polk at Columbus a full account of what was done.[11]

There were several methods of conveying information from Cairo to Columbus, twenty miles below. The most common, was by putting a letter in a bottle,

---

fought west of the Mississippi River. On November 1, John Frémont ordered Grant to make a demonstration toward Charleston and Norfolk, in Missouri, and Blandville, Kentucky, in support of operations against Columbus, Kentucky. The following day while Grant was making preparations, Frémont relinquished his command in Missouri, and sent Grant orders to carry out his demonstration. Grant was also notified the same day that M. Jeff Thompson's rebels were twenty-five miles below Greenville, Missouri, and so ordered an expedition to drive him back into Arkansas. However, Thompson was in Bloomfield, Missouri, and no where near Greenville as previously reported. Still, Grant was to support the move against Thompson, by sending troops from Cape Girardeau and Bird's Point. On November 3, the two columns left their bases in pursuit of Thompson. Two days later Grant received notice that the rebels were reinforcing General Price, and Grant was directed to begin his move against Columbus, as previously ordered. *O.R.* vol. 3: 267–269; Boatner, 57–58; Hughes, 2, 45.

10. Richard James Oglesby was born to a slave holding Kentucky family on July 25, 1824. Orphaned at age nine Oglesby moved to Decatur, Illinois, to live with an uncle. With only a basic education, he eventually studied the law, became a lawyer, and then fought in the Mexican War as a lieutenant. After the war he practiced law, searched for gold in California and returned to Illinois, where he became a founding member of the Illinois Republican Party. Oglesby ran for U.S. Congress in 1858 (lost), but was elected to the Illinois Senate in 1860. At the beginning of the Civil War he was appointed the colonel of the 8th Illinois Infantry (Three months) on April 25, 1861, and yet again when the command reorganized as a Three Year Regiment on July25, 1861. With the exception of a short stint in the Trans-Mississippi, the 8th Illinois and Oglesby spent their entire career east of the Mississippi River. Oglesby was promoted to brigadier general on March 21, 1862, and major general on November 29, 1862. In 1864, Oglesby resigned from the army and ran for Illinois Governor, won, and was inaugurated on January16, 1865. Following Lincoln's assassination, Oglesby denounced President Andrew Johnson and demanded that he be impeached. Other post war activities included a second term as Governor in 1872, then the U.S. Senate in 1873, and a third term as Governor in 1885. He retired from public office in 1889 and died on April 24, 1899, at his home in Elkhart, Illinois. Known as "Uncle Dick," Oglesby was "characterized as having a bluff, friendly manner with wit and good humor." Boatner, 604–605; Sifakis, *Who Was Who in the Union*, 292; Warner, *Generals in Blue*, 346–347.

11. Leonidas Polk was born on April 10, 1806, in Raleigh, North Carolina, graduated from West Point in the Class of 1827 (No. 8 of 38), served in the artillery, but resigned six months after graduation to become an Episcopal minister in 1838. In 1841, he was made the bishop of Louisiana a position he held until the beginning of the Civil War. A close friend of President Jefferson Davis, Polk left the ministry, at Davis' request, to accept a commission to major general on June 25, 1861, to command the Department No. 2 in Tennessee. Polk invaded Kentucky, in September 4, 1861, occupying Columbus, which he fortified. Promoted to lieutenant general on October 10, 1862, Polk served his entire career east of the Mississippi River. He was killed on June 14, at Pine Mountain, Georgia during the Atlanta Campaign. Upon his death a fellow officer noted that Polk "died a gentleman and a high church dignitary;" however "As a soldier, he was more theoretical than practical." Boatner, 657–658; Hughes, 5; Sifakis, *Who Was Who in the Confederacy*, 228; Warner, *Generals in Gray*, 242–243.

corking it tight and fastening to the underside of the board; thrusting it to the current which would soon carry it

Past Our Lines

and below them. There were several parties, ostensibly farmers and fishermen, whose sole business was to watch for and examine everything afloat.

On the second morning, after our return from Commerce, Capt. Curry, the federal scout, reported that there was one regiment on the Belmont side of the river and two or three others were under orders to cross the river next day and take the Cape Girardeau road, to where it crossed the road from Commerce to Bloomfield, and there take that road and take Oglesby in the rear and capture his entire command. Under these circumstances prompt action was required, Grant was equal to the occasion.[12]

He immediately telegraphed Gen. [C. F.] Smith at Paducah and he, Smith promptly ordered out all the force that could be spared and took the road toward Columbus ostensibly to assist in its capture. At the same time he, by drawing in his pickets, gave the rebel spies–Paducah, too, was full of them–every opportunity to carry the news to Columbus.[13]

As soon as the dispatch was sent to Paducah orders were issued to get ready

12. Prior to the battle, Blemont was occupied by Colonel James Tappan as a "camp of observation," and labeled "Camp Johnson." His force consisted of the 13th Arkansas Infantry, two companies of the 1st Mississippi Cavalry Battalion and Watson's Louisiana Battery of six guns. See **Appendix D, Various Order of Battles** for the Confederate forces at Belmont. *O.R.*, vol. 3:355; William K. Polk,"General Polk and the Battle of Belmont" in *Battles and Leaders of the Civil War.*(4 vols. New York, 1887–1888), vol. 1:348, hereafter cited as Polk, "Belmont."

On November 5, Grant received notice from St. Louis that the rebels were reinforcing General Price, and further directed him to begin his move against Columbus, as previously ordered. On November 6, Grant left Cairo to make his demonstration against Belmont and Columbus. Lying up on the Kentucky side of the river, Grant received a message at 2:00 A.M. on November 7, that the Confederates had been crossing troops during the day for the purpose of cutting off his two columns that were supporting the operations against Thompson. To prevent the possible loss of his two columns Grant decided to change the demonstration and attack Belmont to prevent Olglesby's command from being taken in the rear. That said, Oglesby's operations against Thompson was based on faulty intelligence, which, in the end, led Grant to unwisely attack Belmont. See **Appendix D, Various Order of Battles** for the Union command at Belmont *O.R.*. 3:268–270; Hughes, 45–47.

13. Born on April 24, 1807, in Philadelphia, Charles Ferguson Smith graduated from West Point in 1825 (no. 18 of 37) as an artillery lieutenant. He initially served in garrison duty, then 13 years at the Point. During the Mexican War, Smith received three brevets being cited several times for "gallant and meritorious conduct." With the beginning of the Civil War, Smith was commanding the Department of Utah as a lieutenant colonel. Smith was appointed a brigadier general on August 31, 1861, and commanded the District of Western Kentucky effective September8, 1861. He was promoted to major general on March 21, 1862, for his performance at Forts Henry and Donelson in February 1862. A short time after his promotion he injured his leg while boarding one boat from another, dying from infection on April 25, 1862. Both Grant and Sherman "revered Smith" with Grant calling him the "ideal of a soldier," while Sherman noted had it not been for Smith's untimely death "neither Grant nor he would have ever been heard of" during the war.

five of the largest steamers in port, on which were sent four regiments, a section of artillery and a few horse, and it was publicly announced, from what source was unknown, that our destination was Columbus. At the same time every facility was given the Confederate spies to send the news to Columbus.[14] About 10 a.m. of the 6th I was sitting on the outside of the *Belle Memphis* and saw a man apparently fishing, and saw him put into the river, with great care a float and leave it.[15] At first I suppose the float was a buoy to a fish line, and paid no attention to it; but in a few minutes after he had left I saw his buoy was floating off. Curiosity prompted me to examine it, and

Getting into a Skiff,

I pulled out to it, and taking it up I found on the underside a bottle with a written paper corked in it closely. I took the float and bottle to Grant's headquarters onshore and he and [John A.] Rawlings examined it, breaking the bottle found a full description of our force and supposed object.[16] On the evening of the 6th we

Boatner, 769; Heitman, vol. 1: 895; Sifakis, *Who Was Who in the Union*, 375; Warner, *Generals in Blue*, 455–456.

As part of the overall plan for operations against Columbus, C. F. Smith, commanding Paducah, Kentucky, was directed by General Frémont to make a demonstration toward the Mississippi River town. Smith was directed to keep "columns moving to and fro on the road to Melvin and also to make minor demonstrations in the same manner on the roads to Lovelaceville and Mayfield." According to plan, on November 6, at 2:00 a.m., Smith dispatched General Eleazer A. Paine with 2,000 men and four pieces of artillery to carry out the demonstration toward Columbus, via Melvin. An hour later another column of about 800 men, comprised of infantry, artillery and cavalry, started on the road to Mayfield. The purpose of this demonstration was the same as Grant's--"to occupy the enemy in the Mississippi Valley and prevent his throwing part of his forces into Northwestern Arkansas." *O.R.*, vol. 3:299–301.

14. Grant's fleet consisted of the steamers: *Aleck Scott* (carried the 30th and 31st Illinois Infantry; *James Montgomery* (carried the 27th Illinois and 7th Iowa Infantries); *Chancellor* (carried Dollin's Cavalry); *Keystone* (Carried the wagons); *Belle Memphis* (carried 22nd Illinois Infantry plus Grant's HQ and the artillery). Escorting the fleet were the gunboats the *Tyler* and *Lexington*. Hughes, 48–49, 209.
    Note: Hughes has the *Keystone State* as part of the expedition, however, the *Keystone State* was a side wheel steamer purchased in Philadelphia in early 1861, and operated in the costal areas of the United States, not on the western waters. The Naval Records make clear that there were two vessels named the *Keystone*, one being the *Keystone State*, while the other was simply the *Keystone*. *O.N.R.* Index, 218; *O.N.R.*, Series 2, vol. 1:120–121.

15. *Belle Memphis*, also known as the *Memphis Belle*, and *Belle of Memphis* was Grant's headquarters during the expedition. It was described as a "nobel steamer" that was both "large and luxurious." C., "The Battle of Belmont," *Chicago Tribune*, November 11, 1861; Hughes, 49, 232 n.18.

16. John A. Rawlings was a man who, Grant, characterized as more nearly indispensable to me than any other officer in the service." Born on February 13,1831 in Galena, Illinois, John Aaron Rawlins passed the Illinois Bar in 1854, and served as Galena's attorney until the beginning of the war. A Douglas Democrat, Rawlins joined Grant's staff, as a captain and its youngest member effective August 31, 1861. He served with Grant throughout the war, as Grant's "principle staff officer and most intimate and influential advisor," being promoted to brigadier general on August 11, 1863. As the war was coming to a close Rawlins was breveted a major general and Grant's Chief of Staff on March 3, 1865. Following the war Rawlins remained in the army, resigning in 1869 to accept

BATTLE OF BELMONT
November 7, 1862

To Charleston

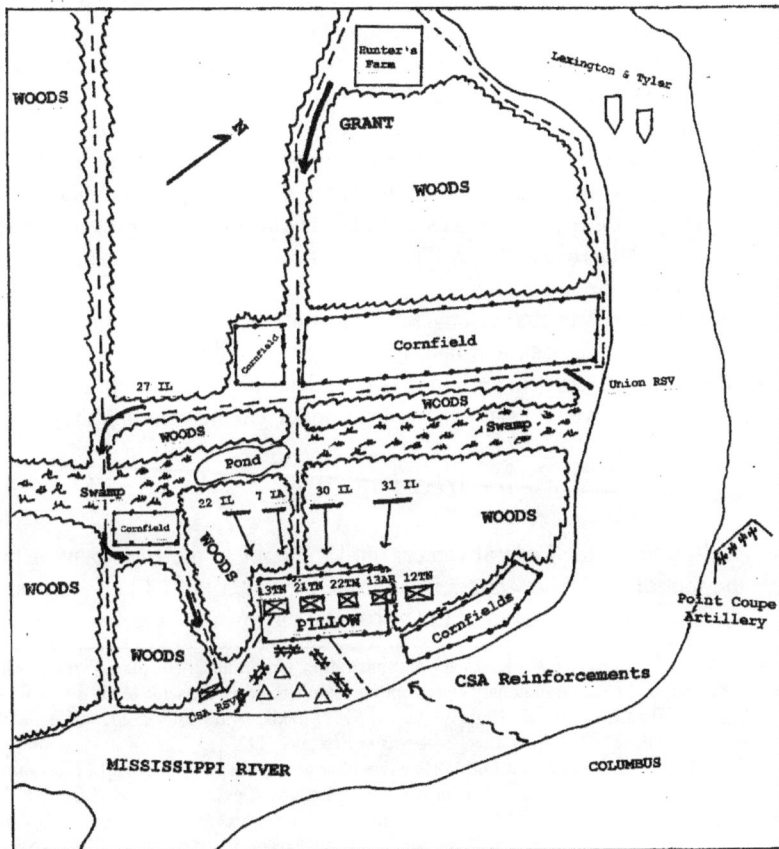

WOODS

Hunter's
Farm

Lexington & Tylar

GRANT

WOODS

Cornfield

Cornfield

27 IL

Union RSV

WOODS

Swamp

Pond

Swamp

Cornfield

22 IL   7 IA

30 IL   31 IL

WOODS

WOODS

WOODS

13TN 21TN 22TN 13AR 12TN

PILLOW

WOODS

Cornfields

Point Coupe
Artillery

WOODS

CSA Reinforcements

CSA RSV

MISSISSIPPI RIVER

COLUMBUS

✕✕ ✕✕ Fallen Trees   △ △ △ Confederate Camp

left Cairo, proceeded by two gunboats and when in Punteuy Bend, about half way from Cairo to Columbus we were ordered to land on the Kentucky shore.[17] The gunboats were stationed in the river below us as a guard. Whilst laying there we were approached by several men, apparently farmers, who were curious as to our number. No particular notice was taken of them, although they were coming and going all night. After daylight we started and every pilot had been ordered to land as close to the *Belle Memphis*, the headquarters boat, as he could find a landing.

In less than 10 minutes after we got under way Grant came up in the pilot-house and asked how close we could lean to Belmont on the Missouri shore, and being out of sight of Columbus. I stated about three miles. Then he asked about the road from where I could land to Belmont. On receiving my answers he ordered me to pick a landing and land where the balance of the boat could have room to tie up.[18]

After the landing was made and the men got on shore, Grant sent for me and ordered me to go with the advance–under [John A.] McClernand–point out the road. Col. [Napoleon B.] Buford was on the right and John A. Logan on the left. When we reached the road and turned to the left I was ordered back to the boat but I kept on until the retreat began.[19]

When the enemy was first discovered, they were anxiously looking and waiting for orders to come back and take the Yankees in the rear in their supposed attack on Columbus. Consequently it was complete surprise. Yet, although taken by surprise, they showed no symptoms of surrender. On the contrary, they

Retired Fighting,

closely followed by the Federal forces, until they got to the river bank a little above the foot of the Willow bar, and opposite the battery of 64-pounders about 600 yards distance, on the point of the hill above the town; where they attempted

---

the position of Secretary of War in Grant's administration. Unfortunately he died six months later on September 6, 1969, of "pulmonary consumption" or tuberculosis, the same as his first wife who died in 1861. Boatner, 681–682; Heitman, vol. 1: 817; Sifakis, *Who Was Who in the Union*, 328; *Union Army*, vol. 8: 207–208' Warner, *Generals in Blue*, 391–392.

17. Punteuy Bend was located near Old Fort Jefferson at the confluence of Mayfield Creek and the Mississippi River. It was about eight miles south of Cairo. Davis, *Civil War Atlas*, plt. 163; Hughes, 50, 54; John Seaton, "The Battle of Belmont," in *War Talks in Kansas MOLLUS* (Kansas City, Mo., 1906; 70 vols., reprint ed. Wilmington, NC,1992), vol. 5: 308, hereafter cited as Seaton, "Battle of Belmont."

18. The Federal Army disembarked at Hunter's farm, near Lucas Bend in the Mississippi River and about three miles from Belmont (Polk placed the distance at five to six miles). They began landing at 8:00 a.m, assembled and marched off to Belmont at 8:30 a.m. *O.R.S.*, pt. 1, 1:266, 269; Hughes, 57, 80; Polk, "Belmont," vol 1:348; "The Battle of Belmont," *Chicago Tribune*, November 12, 1861; Seaton, "Battle of Belmont," 312.

19. For the up coming Battle of Belmont, McClernand commanded Grant's First Brigade; Napoleon B. Buford commanded the 27th Illinois and was in McClernand's Brigade; while John A. Logan was also in McClernand's command leading the 31st Illinois Infantry. See **Appendix C, Selected Officers in Grant's Command**, for further comments on John McClernand, Napoleon Buford and John Logan.

to shield themselves, in the Willows, and fired as fast as they could load. [20] Meantime it was evident that Polk began to guess the true state of the case, and order a force to board the *Henry Hill*, which coming over, saw the Federals firing on the Confederates in the Willows, the latter answering them as fast as they could load and fire.[21] Both sides wore the blue blouses, and consequently as the *Hill* began to straighten up to land, the men on her began firing on their comrades that stood in the Willows. At the same time the Federal brought a field piece and unlimbered on the bank abreast where the *Hill* was going to land and sent a shot into her which caused the pilot to give her a broad sheer to starboard. Then the federal gunners directed their shot at the hull in order to sink her. Three shots opened the eyes of the Confederate commander of the battery on the *Hill* and he then opened on the federal forces of Belmont.[22]

As soon as the battery opened Grant gave orders to fall back to the steamers. This was begun by the troops under McClernand and Logan, and orders were sent to Buford to take the road to Birds Point.[23]

---

20. In presenting his account of the engagement at Belmont, Scott has skipped the bulk of the battle which occurred after the initial contact until the rebels are driven to the banks of the Mississippi. See **Appendix C** for **Extended Comment on Belmont: Federal success at Belmont–10:15 to 1:00 p.m.**

21. While Polk watched the battle develop at Belmont, he awaited word as to the reported Federals coming from Paducah. Between noon and 1:00 P.M., Polk decided that any type of attack on Columbus had been delayed or would not take place; he then ordered Preston Smith's Brigade over to Belmont with two regiments from John P. McGowan's Division to follow. *O.R.*, 3:308, 346, 353.

    The *H. R. W. Hill* or *Henry Hill* was a 602 ton side-wheel steamer, commanded by Captain Tom H. Newell. The *Hill* continued to operate on the Mississippi River until its capture at Memphis on June 6, 1862, while they lay at anchor. The capture was credited to Commodore C.H. Davis. The *Hill* was subsequently towed to Cairo where the vessel was transferred to the Subsistence Department on June 21, 1862. The vessel for the purpose of prize money was noted as worth $6,250. *O.N.R.*, vol. 23:149, 218, 379, 685; Hughes, 136; Thomas Truxtun Moebs, *Confederate States Navy Research Guide: Confederate Naval Imprints Described and Annotated, Chronology of Naval Operation and Administration, Marine Corps and Naval Officer Biographies, Description and Service of Vessels, Subject Bibliography* (Williamsburg, VA, 1991), 332.

22. In his offical report on the battle, General Polk acknowledged that his transports were indeed hit by the Federal artillery "driving shots through two of them at the same time." Of the boats hit, Captain W. L. Trask of the *Charm* noted that his boat was struck several time by the Federal guns with "one ball… passing through the boiler deck." The *Hill*, according to Samuel Clemens, the "cub pilot" of the Hill noted that "Three cannon balls went through the chimney," while "one struck off the corner of the pilot house." Both boats survived the attacks and continued to operate throughout the day. *O.N.R.*, vol. 22:409, 426; Quoted in Hughes, 256 n.9.

23. During a lull in the battle, which happened between 2:00–2:30 p.m., the Federals celebrated, raising the American Stars and Stripes upon Camp Johnston's flagpole. The band of the 22nd Illinois, which had accompanied the expedition as the "hospital corps," had their instruments and struck up a number of patriotic tunes, playing "Dixie," the "Star Spangle Banner," and then "Yankee Doodle," plus several others, all to the delight of the jubliant Unionists. All was cheer before the storm as the Federals seemed to forget about their recently defeated foes and more so, the newly arriving Confederate reinforcements; and then looting began. Meanwhile, rebel General Frank Cheatham had arrived on the scene and buoyed Pillow's defeated men into assuming the offensive. The 11th Louisiana and 15th Tennessee had also been active moving around the flank of Grant's command setting the stage for a reverse of what had previously happened to the rebels at Belmont. Grant,

Grant and our forces made their way to the steamers unmolested, and the only men the Confederates found to oppose them when they returned in force was a lot of stragglers who had scattered to plunder the tents of the regiments that have been stationed there.[24]

The federal forces have been arriving at the boat at least one half hour, and were engaged in getting our guns on board.[25] Owing to the cowardice and traitorism of the captain of one of the steamers, this detained us from keeping his boat still so as to get the guns on board, he would keep backing and (( )) impossible to bring them on board. At length John A. Logan stepped up to him, the captain , and

---

being informed of the rebels landing in his rear, ordered a retreat at the double-quick. It was barely in time. Cheatham struck first, at about 2:30 p.m. with about 1,000–1,500 men of Pillow's previous forces. After fifteen minutes the Unionists buckled and headed for the safety of their boats; all semblance of order appeared lost. The Eleventh and Fifteenth, under Colonel Samuel Marks, to the right of Cheatham moved forward, to block the retreating Federals now trapped in Belmont. Grant ordered his command to cut their way through to the boats. Logan's 31st Illinois led the way, pushing aside Mark's force, as Grant's men hurried to the boats, leaving the road cluttered with their accouterments of war. Harrell, *Arkansas, Confederate Military History*, vol. 10: 62; Hughes, 127, 129–130, 138, 140, 142–145, 148–149, 153, 155; ; Seaton, "Battle of Belmont," 313.

24. Contrary to Scott's account, Grant's command struggle to return to Hunter's Farm being harassed by the rebels who blocked their path. Bringing up the rear Buford's Regiment was "intercepted" by the rebel reinforcements, causing the27th to veer away from the march to Hunter's Farm. Marching farther to the west Buford, who one soldier declared was "as brave as a lion," skirted the rebels and the rest of Grant's command, seeking another path to safety. Buford would finally succeed in reaching the river and safety, passing three miles to the north of their initial landing. As for the rest of Grant's command, they all reached the transports, but in a disorderly state. Colonel Dougherty recorded that the 7th Iowa was "confused" and "scattered" during the retreat; simply speaking his brigade had been "overrun." A member of Taylor's Battery noted that "colonels and officers tried every means to rally their men," as they approached the boats, "but without success." Further, the path of retreat was "strewn with knapsacks, overcoats, etc.," indicating anything but an orderly retreat. "Despite the assertion of Grant and others that 'there was no hasty retreat or running away,' the retreat from Camp Johnston," according to Nathaniel Hughes, "had degenerated into a rout." *O.R.*, vol. 3:284–285, 293; "Another Account," *Chicago Tribune*, November 11, 1861; Hughes, 155–156; G. B. Pickett, "Battle of Belmont," *Rock Island Register*, November 13, 1861.

25. The Federal troops began boarding transports at 2:40 p.m. and were complete by 4:00 p.m., except for the 27th Illinois which took a circuitous rout to the Mississippi River. By 4:00 p.m. Confederate units had arrived at the river and began shooting into the transports with but little effect. To protect the embarkation, the *Lexington* and *Tyler* began shelling the shore, which eventually discouraged the Confederates. Meanwhile, the 27th Illinois, flagged down the transport *Chancellor*, and arranged for the regiment's pickup even as the sun was setting. The Federals for their part lost 128 killed, 350 wounded and 139 missing; total 617 (total excludes naval losses). The Confederates lost 119 killed, 435 wounded and 119 missing; total 673. Grant reported capturing 175 prisoners, while a period newspaper reported the number as 184. Polk reported his missing as 117, killed 105 and wounded as 419; total 641. The discrepancy in the reported losses is the difference between what regiment commanders reported and what the overall commanders reported. Most likely, some of the missing returned and the less wounded were discounted from the final casualty lists. See **Appendix D, Various Orders of Battle, Battle of Belmont**, for details on losses. *O.R.*, 3:272, 281, 285; *O.N.R.*, 22:780; Hughes, 162–163, 184–185; "Our Troops At Belmont," *Chicago Tribune*, November 15, 1861.

Putting a Pistol to His Ear

threatened to shoot him if the vessel was not held still. After this she lay as steady as if she grew to the bank. This I saw from my elevated position in the pilot-house of the *Belle Memphis*, and when turning to look to the shore I saw the Confederate forces crossing the field about a quarter of a mile away, and at the same time I saw Gen. Grant on the bank dismounted , and hallowed to him that the enemy was in sight and coming, when he started down the bank–his horse following him; and as he came on board–his horse still following–the orders were given to let go and push off. At this moment a body of cavalry came through the woods above where we lay and filed down the bank abreast of where we lay, whilst the infantry, cross-ing the fence, passed the cavalry and formed in their front; and all began firing at the steamers.[26]

The position of the *Belle Memphis* was particularly dangerous. Lying with her head against the bank her stern rested against a wrack heap, which required the pilot to go ahead on the outside wheel so as to draw her stern away from the wrack heap and then back out on the shore wheel–stopping going ahead–until clear of the wrack heap, then back on both wheels. The getting the vessel out of the situation gave rise to the story that not less than four pilots were killed on her, while the fact that as soon as the order was given to get out the bell was rung to go ahead on the starboard engine so as to draw her stern out from the wrack heap. The cry arose, "Shoot the pilot!" "Shoots the d--n abolitionist:" and immediately every gun was directed

At the Pilot-House

and the bullets whistled uncomfortably close.[27]

I concluded that if I dropped out of sight they would think the pilot was killed

---

26. Scott's account of Grant boarding the *Belle Memphis* goes contrary to what Grant wrote in his memoirs. It also seems highly unlikely given that Grant's original horse was killed during the battle, leaving him an unfamiliar mount for boarding the boat. Additionally, Hughes in his work on the Battle of Belmont makes no mention of Scott's account, even though he was aware of it.
     Of the incident Grant wrote:
     "The captain of the boat that had just pushed out, but had not started, recognized me and ordered the engineernot to start the engine; he then had a plank run out for me. My horse seemed to take in the situation. There was no path down the bank...My horse put its fore feet over the bank without hesitation or urging, and, with his hind feet well under him, slid down the bank and trotted aboard the boat, twelve or fifteen feet away, over a single gang-plank."
     "The Fight At Belmont," *Chicago Tribune*, November 8, 1861; *O.N.R.*, vol. 22,: 405; Quoted in Hughes, 171.
27. Even though there was no one killed in the attack on the pilot's cabin, Samuel Clemens noted that most thought that he had been killed, but such was not the case. However, the rebel fire did wound several soldiers on the vessel. B.R.K., "Another Account," *Rebellion Record*, vol. 3:Doc-291; Hughes, 235 n. 9; Seaton, "Belmont," 315.

and stop shooting at the pilothouse, so I dropped out of sight, when the rebel yell was raised from thousand throats mingled with the cries "I got him!" "I got him!" And the firing on the pilot-house ceased, only to be renewed as each bell was rung. Meantime the gunboats below us were seeing the attack on the transports started to their relief.

At this time the transports were out in the river and safe from capture unless an accident disabled them. The *Memphis* was the last boat leaving the shore and, as a consequence, in backing down she was inside of the gunboat *Lexington* as it came up to take part in the row.[28] The *Lexington* was about 300 yards from the bank and as she cleared the *Memphis* fired her bow gun obliquely ahead. I was looking to the shore and saw the effect of the two first shots, which was simply terrible. The enemy was standing in compact lines of infantry in front of the cavalry, all forced close to the front of the bank by the fence behind them. The first shot from the Lexington struck near fifty feet below the head of the line and opened a gap at least 50 feet wide leaving

Neither Man Nor Horse Standing.

The second shot struck near fifty feet below the lower line of the upper shot, causing a gap about the same size as the first. The smoke now arose and obscured the view toward the shore, and as the *Lexington* passed ahead the *Memphis* sheered out and went ahead. When she had passed the *Lexington*–that had stopped her engines–neither man or horse stood on the bank, but a number of men had jumped down to the water edge and were firing at the portals of the gunboats, notwithstanding the desperate risk.[29] The transports made the best of their way to Cairo, one of them stopping at the head of the band to take on board Col. Buford and his men.[30]

---

28. The *Lexington* was a wood side-wheel steamer. It was built in 1860, and purchased by government in June 1861, for $20,666.66. It had three boilers, two engines, draft of six feet, and was 177 feet by 36 feet 10 inches. The vessel mounted six guns when first outfitted; "4 8-inch shell guns and 2 32-pounders." *O.N.R.*, Series 2, vol. 1:126–127; Henry Walke, "The Gunboats at Belmont and Fort Henry," *Battles and Leaders*, vol. 1:358; hereafter cited as Walke, "Gunboats at Belmont."

29. The unit that fired at the transports and the gunboats was the 154th Tennessee Infantry. The gun fire was kept up for nearly an hour, according to Marcus J. Wright commanding the 154th Tennessee, ceasing when the boats moved out of range. Overall Wright reported his losses as 1 killed and 12 wounded. It would appear that when the gunboats fired, the rebels fell down behind the river bank and didn't suffer the "great slaughter" or " fly in the greatest of confusion." that Commander H. Walke and others reported. *O.N.R.*, vol. 22: 401; *O.R.*, vol. 3:346, 349; Banasik, *Confederate Tales, 1861*, 157; Walke, "Gunboats at Belmont, 361.

30. Approaching the river near sunset, Colonel Burford noticed that the fleet was heading up river to Cairo. Borrowing a horse from a local resident, Buford sent his Adjutant Captain H. A. Rust galloping up river to flag down the fleet. Getting the attention of the *Chancellor*, the vessel returned to pick up the 27th Illinois, while the *Lexington* and *Tyler* covered the boarding. They then returned to Cario where the fleet arrived about 10:00 p.m. The following day the Belle Memphis returned to the battlefield to discuss the exchange of POWs, and handled the wounded, returning to Cairo

In two or three days after all Oglesby's returned from Bloomfield without a single casualty, and thus one object for which the Belmont battle was fought was fully accomplished. It proved Grant a strategist and afterwards gave him the command of the Tennessee campaign, of which I may say something here after.[31]

C. M. Scott
Pilot of the Belle Memphis.

---

near mid-night the same day. Thus ended the Battle of Belmont except counting the casualties and speculating on the outcome. *O.R.*, vol. 3:285; "Battle of Belmont," *Chicago Tribune*, November 13, 1861; B.C.C., "Another Account," Rebellion Record," vol. 3:Doc-293,

31. Following the battle there was mixed comments from the Federal command as to what had been accomplished and who had won the battle. To be sure according to Grant, and others, Oglesby's command had been saved, assuming he was ever really threatened, but what of the battle. A member of Taylor's Illinois Battery called the whole affair "an awful 'bungle.'" But to Grant "'the object of the expedition the victory was most complete.'" Another, who initially recorded the battle as a loss wrote: upon "further reports it proves to be a decided and valuable victory." The *Louisville Journal* disparaged reports that it was a defeat writing: Belmont appears to "have been one of the most signal and brilliant victories that have graced the pages of our history since the" Mexican War. To a member of the 22nd Illinois, the claim of a Confederate victory was "too preposterous for discussion." And Colonel W. H. L. Wallace wrote of Belmont: Grant and "his friends call it a victory, but if such be a victory, God save us from defeat." "Another Account," *Chicago Tribune*, November 11, 1861; "The Battle of Belmont," *Chicago Tribune*," November 12, 1861; Hughes, 193–194; Seaton, "Belmont," 318; W.C.C., "Louisville 'Journal' Narrative," *Rebellion Record*, vol. 3:Doc- 288.

Appendix A

Assorted Official Documents, Letters and Correspondence

Item: Thomas L. Snead's list of resolutions adopted by a Union meeting held in St. Louis on January 12, 1861.[1]

6. The possession of slave property is a Constitutional right, and, as such, ought to be recognized by the Federal Government. And if the Federal Government shall fail and refuse to secure this right, the Southern States should be found united in its defense, to which event Missouri will share the common duties and common dangers of the South...

8. We cordially approve of the principles of adjustment contained in what are known as the Crittenden Propositions...

10. In the opinion of this meeting, the employment of military forces of the Government to enforce submission from the citizens of the seceding States will inevitably plunge the country in civil war...We therefore earnestly entreat, as well the Federal Government as the seceding States, to withhold and stay the arm of military power, and on no pretext whatever to bring on the nation the horrors of civil war until the people themselves can take such action as our troubles demand.

11. The people of Missouri should meet in convention for the purpose of taking action in the present state of nation's affairs, at the same time to protect the Union of States and the rights and authority of this State under the Constitution.

* * * * * * *

Item: General Frost's letter to Governor Jackson concerning the support of Major William Bell, commanding St. Louis Arsenal.[2]

St. Louis, Mo., January 24, 1861.

His Excellency C. F. Jackson, Governor of Missouri:

Dear Sir: I have just returned from the arsenal, where I had an interview with Major Bell, the commanding officer of that place. I found the Major everything that you or I could desire. He assured me that he considered that Missouri had, whenever the time came, a right to claim it as being on her soil. He asserted his determination to defend it against any and all irresponsible mobs, come from whence they might, but at the same time gave me to understand that he would not attempt any defense against the proper State authorities.

He promised me, upon the honor of an officer and a gentleman, that he would not suffer any arms to be removed from the place without first giving me timely

---

1. Snead, 44–45.
2. Peckham, 43–45.

information, and I, in return, promised him that I would use all the force at my command to prevent him being annoyed by irresponsible persons.

I at the same time gave him notice that if affairs assumed so threatening a character as to render it unsafe to leave the place in its comparatively unprotected condition, that I might come down and quarter a proper force there to protect it from the assaults of any persons whatsoever, to which he assented. In a word, the Major is with us, where he ought to be, for all his worldly wealth lies here in St. Louis (and it is very large)' and then, again, his sympathies are with us.

I shall therefore rest perfectly easy, and use all my influence to stop the sensationists from attracting the particular attention of the Government to this particular spot. The telegrams you received were the sheerest "canards" of persons who, without direction, are extremely anxious to show their zeal. I shall be thoroughly prepared with the proper force to act as emergency may require. The use of force will only be resorted to when nothing else will avail to prevent the shipment or removal of the arms.

The Major informed me that he had arms for forty thousand men, with all the appliances to manufacture munitions of almost every kind.

The arsenal, if properly looked after, will be everything to our State , and I intend to look after it; very quietly however. I have every confidence in the word of honor pledged to me by the Major, and would as soon think of doubting the oath of the best man in the community.

His idea is that it would be disgraceful to him as a military man to surrender to a mob, whilst he could do so, without compromising his dignity, to the State authorities. Of course I did not show him your order, but I informed him that you had authorized me to act as I might think proper to protect the public property.

He desired that I not divulge his particular views, which I promised not to do, except to yourself. I beg, therefore, that you will say nothing that might compromise him eventually with the General Government, whilst he would probably be removed, which would be unpleasant to our interests.

[Thornton] Grimsley, as you doubtless know, is an unconscionable jackass, and only desires to make himself notorious. It was through him that [Charles] McLaren and [James] George made the mistake of telegraphing a falsehood to you.[3]

---

3. Thornton Grimsley, a "hotheaded" and "dedicated secessionist," was born on August 20, 1798, in Bourbon County, Kentucky. He lost both of his parents at age seven and was apprenticed to a saddle maker in 1808. At the age of 18 he moved to St. Louis, completed his indenture-ship. Grimsley married in 1822, opened his own saddle shop the same year. Politically Grimsley was a Whig and a personal friend of Henry Clay,. He was elected a St. Louis alderman in 1826, became a member of the Missouri State Legislator in 1828, and a State Senator in 1838. Militarily Grimsley raised a company in 1832, and fought in the Black Hawk War, and in 1848, he raised a regiment to fight in the Mexican War. Elected colonel, Grimsley's regiment was disbanded as Missouri did not require his command as the war had ended. In the early part of the Civil War, Grimsley made "thousands of dollars out of supplies of harness and saddlery," especially from his military or "dragon saddle," which he invented, and was a favorite with the Union Army. This in turn earned him the animosity of loyal Unionists, who were disgusted that an avowed secessionist, leading "one of the worst secession firms in St. Louis." was becoming wealthy with Union dollars;

I should be pleased to hear whether you approve of the course I have adopted, and if not, I am ready to take any other that you, as my commander, my suggest.

I am, sir, most truly,

Your obedient servant

D. M. Frost

* * * * * * *

Item: List of Delegates to the Missouri Convention on February 28, 1861.[4]

First District: R, B. Frayser, J. G. Waller and G. Y. Bast.

Second District: John B. Henderson, G. W. Zimmerman and Robert Calhoun.[5]

Third District: Warren Woodson, Eli E. Bass and Joseph Flood.

Fourth District: W. J. Howell, John T. Redd and J. T. Matson.

Fifth District: E. K. Sayer, Henry M. Gorin and N. F. Givens.

Sixth District: William A. Hall, Sterling Price, and Theodore Shackelford.[6]

Seventh District: Frederick Rowland, Joseph M. Irwin and John Foster.

Eighth District: A. M. Woolfolk, Jacob Smith and William Jackson.

Ninth District: J. T. Tindall, James McFarren and J. S. Allen.

Tenth District: G. W. Dunn, R. D. Ray and J. H. Birch.[7]

Eleventh District: Robert Wilson, P. L. Higgins and Ellzy Van Buskirk.

---

in other words, according to the Tribune—"every ten dollars given to such men enable them to give one to the cause of treason." During the secessionist crisis, in Missouri, he was one of the leaders of the Minutemen. He died December 22, 1861. Following his death the *Chicago Tribune* wrote that Grimsley "was one of the worst secessionists we have ever had in St. Louis, and has been one of the most objectionable ultra pro-slaver men that the friends of free-labor contended against." In particular "for his active connection, many years ago, with the burning of a [N]egro for stabbing an officer." C., Affairs In Missouri, *Chicago Tribune*, July 24 and October 9, 1861; Gerteis, 81,139, 354 n.27; "Our St. Louis Letter," *Chicago Tribune*, December 26, 1861; Ryle, 198; J. Thomas Scharf, *History of Saint Louis City and County, From the Earliest Periods to the Present Day: Including Biographical Sketches of Representative Men* (2 vols., Philadelphia, PA., 1883), vol. 2: 1858–1859.

Charles McLaren, a wealthy St. Louis businessman, was a member of the St. Louis Police Commission, appointed by Governor Jackson to control the Unionists of the city. He was also the founder and "President of the Minuet Men." McLaren owned a cotton plantation in Mississippi and had some $60,000.00 worth of cotton ready to ship in the fall of 1961. In St. Louis, he owned "one of the finest blocks on Main Street." As a cautious secessionist, McLaren remained in St. Louis during the war, "not wanting to abandoned his business interests," eventually taking the oath of allegiance. C., "Affairs In St. Louis," *Chicago Tribune*, October 5, 1861; Gerteis, *Missouri*, 10, 15; Snead, 136–137; *Union Army*, vol. 4: 240.

Little was found on James George, save he was one of the founders of the Minuet Men As a captain, in the 2nd Regiment St. Louis Missouri militia, George was captured at Camp Jackson and later exchanged and paroled to St. Louis where he reserved the right "should he desire to do so to join General Price and the Missouri State troops." There was no indication that George ever reentered the Confederate Army or joined the MSG. *O.R.*, Series 2, vol. 1: 116, 555; Peckham, 41.

4. Rassieur, 7–8; Webb, 46.

5. John B. Henderson served as a U.S. Senator from 1863–1869. *History of Audrain County*, 40.

6. Sterling Price was Missouri Governor 1852–1855. Ibid., 38.

7. John H. Birch served on the Missouri Supreme Court from 1849–1851. Ibid., 39.

Twelfth District: W. P. Hall, Robert M. Stewart. and R. W. Donnell.[8]
Thirteenth District: A. W. Doniphan, J. H. Moss and E. H. Norton.[9]
Fourteenth District (Independence): James K. Sheeley or Sheley, Abram Comingo and R. W. Brown.
Fifteenth District: Akeman Welch, A. C. Marvin and C. G. Kidd.
Sixteenth District (Lexington): J. F. Phillips, S. L. Sawyer and Vincent Marmaduke.[10]
Seventeenth District: J. J. Gravelly, Nelson McDowell.[11]
Eighteenth District: A. S. Harbin, R. W. Crawford and M. H. Ritchie.
Nineteenth District: Sample Orr, Littleberry Hendricks and R. W. Jamison.[12]
Twentieth District: M. W. Turner, J. W. Johnson and W. L. Morrow.
Twenty-First District: A. W. Maupin, C. D. Eitzen and Zachariah Isbell.
Twenty-Second District: W. C. Pomeroy, V. B. Hill and John Holt.
Twenty-Third District: C. L. Rankin, M. P. Cayse and Joseph Bogey.
Twenty-Fourth District:. C. Collier, Philip Pipkin and W. T. Leeper.[13]
Twenty-Fifth District: Harrison Hough, McCord A. Hatcher and O. Bartlett.
Twenty-Sixth District: N. W. Watkins, J. C. Nowell and J. R. McCormick.[14]
Twenty-Seventh District: J. Proctor Knott, J. W. McClurg and John Scott.[15]
Twenty-Eighth District: William Douglas, J. P. Ross and Charles Drake.
Twenty-Ninth District (St. Louis): S. M. Breckenridge, John How, M. L. Linton, Hudson E. Bridge, T. T. Gnatt, Hamilton R. Gamble, John F. Long, Uriel Wright, Ferdinad Meyer, Henry Hitchcock, Robert Holmes, J. O. Broadhead*, Solomon Smith, Isador Bush and John Shackelford.
* Member of the Safety Committee.

* * * * * * *

8. Willard P. Hall became Governor of Missouri upon the sudden death of H. R. Gamble in 1864. Hall had previously served in the the U.S. House from 1846–1853. Robert M. Stewart was Governor of Missouri from 1857–1860, proceeding C. F. Jackson in the office. Ibid., 38, 40.
9. A Mexican War veteran and leader of the "Doniphan Expedition," to the Mexican State of Chihuahua, Alexander W. Doniphan was offered command of the Fifth Military District, MSG, at the beginning of the war "but declined to serve with the Guard and remained neutral during the war." Duncan, 39; Peterson, et. al., 15, 154.
10. During the Civil War John F. Phillips commanded the 7th MSM Cavalry, playing an important role in Price's 1864 Missouri Expedition. After the war Phillips served in the U.S. Congress in 1874. Banasik, *Confederate Tales, 1864–1865*, 120–121, 140, 144, 147, 153, 331–333; *History of Audrain County*, 41.
11. Joseph J. Gravelly served in the U.S. House from 1866–1868 and was the Missouri Lieutenant Governor from 1870–1872. *History of Audrain County*, 38, 41.
12. Sample Orr was the American Party candidate for Missouri Governor in 1860, and was defeated by C. F. Jackson, losing by 9,863 votes. Rassieur, 3.
13. William T. Leeper served in the 3rd MSM Cavalry participating in operations in southeast Missouri, including the defense of Pilot Knob in 1864. Kyle S. Sinisi, *The Last Hurrah: Sterling Price's Missouri Expedition of 1864* (New York, 2015), 63, 91.
14. James R. McCormach served in the U.S. House from 1866–1873. *History of Audrain County*, 41.
15. Joseph W. McClurg served in the U.S. Congress (1862–1866) and was Missouri Governor 1868–1870. Ibid., 39, 41.

Item: Resolutions, with amendments, that were offered and passed, in the Majority Report to the Missouri State Convention that was held from February 28–March 22, 1861, with comments.[16]

The report was presented by Hamilton R. Gamble, chairman of the Majority Committee. "It was a clear-cut, and conservative report. Its main purpose was to place Missouri irrevocably on the side of the Union and against revolution and war. The report was as follows:"

1. *"Resolved,* That at present there is no adequate cause to impel Missouri to dissolve he connection with the Federal Union, but on the contrary she will labor for such an adjustment of existing troubles as will secure the peace as well as the rights and equality of all the States."
Passed–89 to 1.

2. *"Resolved,* That the people of this State are devotedly attached to the institutions of our country and earnestly desire that by a fair and amicable adjustment all the causes of disagreement, that at present unfortunately distract us as a people may be removed, to that end that our Union may be preserved and perpetuated, and peace and harmony be restored between the North and the South."
Passed–99 to 0

3. *"Resolved,* That the people of this State deem the amendments to the Constitution of the United States, proposed by the Hon. John J. Crtittenden, of Kentucky, with the extension of the same to the Territory hereafter to be acquired by treaty or otherwise, a basis of adjustment which will successfully remove the causes of difference forever from the arena of national politics."
Passed–90 to 4.

4. *"Resolved* [as amended], That the people of Missouri believe the peace and quiet of the country will be promoted by a Convention, to propose amendments to the Constitution of the United States, and the Convention therefore urges the Legislature of the State, and the other States, to take the proper steps for calling such a Convention in pursuance of the fifth article of the Constitution, and for providing by law for the election by the people of such number of delegates as are to be sent to such Convention."
Passed–85 to 9.

5. *"Resolved* [as amended], That in the opinion of this Convention, the employment of military force by the Federal Government to coerce the submission of the seceding States, or the employment of military force by the seceding States to assail the Government of the United States, will inevitably plunge this country into civil war, and thereby entirely extinguish all hope of an amicable settlement of the fearful issues now pending before the country; we therefore earnestly entreat as well the Federal Government as the seceding States to withhold and stay the arm of military power, and on no pretense

16. Rassieur, 9–11; Ryle, 220–221, 230–232.

whatever bring upon the nation the horrors of civil war, and, in order to reflect restoration of harmony and fraternal feeling between the different sections, we should recommend the policy of withdrawing the Federal troops from forts within the borders of the seceding States where there is danger of collision between the States and Federal troops."

Passed–unanimous.

6. *"Resolved,* That when this Convention adjourns its secession in the City of St. Louis, it will adjourn to meet in the Hall of the House of Representatives at Jefferson City, on the Third Monday of December, 1961."

Passed–76 to 19.

7. *"Resolved* [as amended], That there shall be a committee consisting of the President of this Convention, who shall be ex-officio, chairman, and seven gentlemen, one from each Congressional district of the State, to be elected by this convention, a majority of which shall have power to call this convention together at such time prior to the third Monday in December next, and at such place as they may think the public exigencies require; and in the case of any vacancy shall happen in said committee by death resignation, or otherwise during the recess of this Convention, the remaining members or member of said committee shall have power to fill such vacancy."

Passed–By acclamation.

It should be noted that of the 99 members in attendance at the February 28 Convention, not all the members voted on all the resolutions with some being absent or sick.

Further, the Minority Report, though rejected by the Convention recorded that "'while denying the legal right of a state to secede from the Union, we recognize, in lieu thereof, the right of revolution, should sufficient reason arise, therefor; that while, in common with the State of Georgia, we deplore the sectional disregard of duty and fraternity so forcibly presented by her commissioner [Luther J. Glen], we do not despair of future justice, nor will we despair until our complaints have been unavailingly submitted to the northern people; that the possession of slave property is a constitutional right, and as such, ought to be recognized by the Federal government; that if it shall invade or impair that right, the slave-holding states should be united in its defense, and that in such events as may legitimately follow, this state will share the danger and destiny of her sister slave states.'"[17]

* * * * * * *

---

17. Quoted in Rassieur, 9.

Item: Governor Claiborne F. Jackson, response the President Lincoln's call for troops. [18]

Executive Department,
Jefferson City, Mo., April 17, 1861
Hon. Simon Cameron,
Secretary of War:

Sir: Your dispatch of the 15th instant, making a call on Missouri for four regiments of men for immediate service, has been received. There can be, I apprehend, no doubt but the men are intended to form a part of the President's army to make war upon the people of the seceded States.

Your requisition, in my judgement, is illegal, unconstitutional, and revolutionary in its object, inhuman and diabolical, and cannot be complied with. Not one man will the State of Missouri furnish to carry on any such unholy crusade.

C. F. Jackson,
Governor of Missouri

* * * * * * *

Item: Extended comment on why the secession faction failed to remove Missouri from the Union, by William H. Lyon. [19]

"Looking specifically at the actual events of the secession crisis, one sees how complex the situation was. From the events the following conclusions are drawn:

(1). Missourians remained confused and undecided on the issue of union or secession until the late hour–too late for them to make a free and unfettered choice.

(2). Secession ceased to be a major issue after the Camp Jackson affair, but instead it became the sovereignty of the state as opposed to Federal military control. Slavery was not a primary issue, but rural-urban conflict and anti-German sentiment helped shape events.

(3).Governor Jackson was at first pro-Southern, but was forced to turn to neutralism in the North-South crisis at a time when neutrality was impossible. Nor must we forget that before the secession crisis he had a reputation for party loyalty and for compromise, and it would be wrong to call him a thoroughgoing radical secessionist.

(4).The decision to remain in the Union was made by military force–ruthless, determined, vigorous, and uncompromising.

(5). The Missouri radical secessionists failed to organize and dramatize their program in time to accomplish their purpose. A handful of St. Louis Republicans simply out-maneuvered and out-fought them."

---

18. *O.R.*, Series 3, vol 1: 82–83.
19. Lyon, 441.

* * * * * * *

Item: General William S. Harney's Proclamation to Missouri, on May 14, 1861, denouncing the Military Bill; why Missouri should remain in the Union; and justifying the capture of Camp Jackson.[20]

Military Department of the West,
Saint Louis, May 14, 1861.
To the People of the State of Missouri:

On my return to the duties of the command of this department I find, greatly to my astonishment and mortification, a most extraordinary state of things existing in this State, deeply affecting the stability of the Government of the United States as well as the governmental and other interests of Missouri itself.

As a citizen of Missouri, owing allegiance to the United States, and having interests in common with you, I feel it my duty as well as privilege to extend a warning voice to my fellow citizens against the common dangers that threaten us, and to appeal to your patriotism and sense of justice to exert all your moral power to avert them.

It is with regret that I feel it my duty to call to your attention to the recent act of the General Assembly of Missouri known as the "Military Bill," which is the result, no doubt, of the temporary excitement that now pervades the public mind. This bill cannot be regarded in any light other than an indirect secession ordinance, ignoring even the forms resorted to by other States. Manifestly, its most material provisions are in conflict with the Constitution and laws of the United States. To this extent it is a nullity, and cannot and ought not be upheld or regarded by the good citizens of Missouri. There are obligations and duties resting upon the people of Missouri under the Constitution and laws of the United States which are paramount, and which I trust you will carefully consider and weight well before you will allow yourselves to be carried out of the Union under the form of yielding obedience to this Military Bill, which is clearly in violation of your duties as citizens of the United States.

It must be apparent to everyone who has taken a proper and unbiased view of the subject that, whatever may be the termination of the unfortunate condition of things in respect to the so-called "Cotton States," Missouri must share the destiny of the Union. Her geographical position, her soil, productions, and, in short, all her material interests, point to this result. We cannot shut our eyes against this controlling fact. It is seen and its force is felt throughout the nation. So important is this regarded to the great interests of the country, that I venture to express the opinion that the whole power of the Government of the United States, if necessary, will be exerted to maintain Missouri in her present position in the Union. I express to you, in all frankness and sincerity, my own deliberate convictions, without assuming to speak for the Government of the United States, whose authority here

---

20. *O.R.*, vol. 3: 371–372; "Gen. Harney's Proclamation," *Rebellion Record*, vol. 1:Doc. 242–243.

and elsewhere I shall at all times and under all circumstances endeavor faithfully to uphold. I desire above all things most earnestly to invite my fellow citizens dispassionately to consider their true interests as well as their true relation to the Government under which we live and to which we owe so much.

In this connection I desire to direct attention to one subject which, no doubt, will be made the pretext for more or less popular excitement. I allude to the present transactions at Camp Jackson, near Saint Louis. It is not proper for me to comment upon the official conduct of my predecessor in command of this department, but it is right and proper for the people of Missouri to know that the main avenue of Camp Jackson, recently under the command of General [Daniel] Frost, had the name of Davis, and a principle street of the same camp that of Beauregard, and that a body of men had been received into the camp by its commander which had been notoriously organized in the interests of the secessionists, the men openly wearing the dress and badge distinguishing the Army of the so-called Southern Confederacy. It is also a notorious fact that a quantity of arms had been received in the camp which were unlawfully taken from the United States Arsenal at Baton Rouge, and surreptitiously passed up the river in boxes marked "Marble,"

Upon facts like these, and having in view what occurred at Liberty, the people can draw their own inferences, and it cannot be difficult for any one to arrive at a correct conclusion as to the character and ultimate purpose of the encampment.[21] No Government in the world would be entitled to respect that would tolerate for a moment such openly treasonable preparations.

It is but simple justice, however, that I should state the facts that there were many good and loyal men in the camp who were in no manner responsible for its treasonable character.

Disclaiming as I do all desire or intention to interfere in any way with the prerogatives of the State of Missouri or with the function of its executive or other authorities, yet I regard it as my plain path of duty to express to the people, in respectful but at the same time decided language, that within the field and scope of my command and authority the "supreme law" of the land must and shall be

21. Harney was referring too the seizure of the Liberty Arsenal on April 20, 1861. Henry L. Route, an attorney by profession, and a colonel of the Missouri Militia, led a 200-man force against the arsenal, easily taking the facility from the three men, headed by Nathamiel Gant, who manned the arsenal. In all, the Missourians captured 1,180 muskets (including 40 boxes of "smooth-bore muskets"), 243 rifles (40 boxes of Mississippi Rifles), 121 carbines (40 boxes), 923 pistols, 3 brass cannons and 13 iron guns with a large supply of ammunition. The arsenal was built in 1839 (Eakin and Hale say it was built in 1832) and was composed of a main fortress building encompassed by a fence that surrounded two acres of land; the entire arsenal occupied ten acres. Federal authorities abandoned the arsenal and in 1863, sold it at public auction. Adamson, 6; Britton, 25–26; Brooksher, 45; Joane C. Eakin and Donald R. Hale, *Branded as Rebels: A List of Bushwhackers, Guerrillas, Partisan Rangers, Confederates and Southern Sympathizers from Missouri During the War Years* (Independence, MO, 1993), 321; Gary G. Fuenfhausen, *A Guide to Historic Clay County Architectural Resources and Other Historic Sites of the Civil War also Exploits of John C. Calhoun "Coon" Thornton a Clay County Confederate Officer* (Kansas City, MO, 1996), 83–85; Peterson, 158; Snead, 152.

maintained, and no subterfuges, whether in the forms of legislative acts or other-wise, can be permitted to harass or oppress the good and law abiding people of Missouri. I shall exert my authority to protect their persons and property from violations of every kind, and I shall deem it my duty to suppress all unlawful combinations of men, whether formed under pretext of military organizations or otherwise.

Wm. S. Harney,
Brigadier-General, U.S. Army, Commanding.

* * * * * * *

Item: Report of the July 22–31, 1861, Convention to the People of Missouri, supposedly authored by Provisional Governor Hamilton R. Gamble on July 31, 1861.[22]

Address to the People Of Missouri.

"To the people of the State of Missouri:

Your delegates assembled in Convention propose to address you upon the present condition of affairs withing our State.

Since the adjournment of this Convention in March last, the most startling events have rushed upon us with such rapidity that the nation stands astonished at the conditions of anarchy and strife to which, in so brief a period, it has been reduced.

When the Convention adjourned, although the muttering of the storm was heard, it seemed to be distant, and it was hoped that some quiet but powerful force might be applied by a beneficent Providence, to avert the fury, and preserve our country from threatened ruin. That hope has not been realized. The storm, in all its fury, has burst upon the country—the armed hosts of different sections have met each other in bloody conflict, and the grave has already received the remains of thousands of slaughtered citizens. Reason inflamed to madness demands that the stream of blood shall flow broader and deeper; and the whole energies of a people, but a few months since prosperous and happy, are now directed to the collection of larger hosts and the preparation of increased and more destructive energies of death.

Your delegates enjoy the satisfaction of knowing that neither by their action, nor their failure to act, have they in any degree contributed to the ferocious war spirit which now prevails so generally over the whole land. We have sought peace, we have entreated those who were about to engage in war to withhold their hands from the strife, and in this course we know that we but expressed the wishes and feelings of the State. Our entreaties have been unheaded; and now, while war is

---

22. "Address to the People of Missouri," *Rebellion Record*, vol. 2: Doc. 446–450

raging in other parts of our common country, we have felt that our first and highest duty is to preserve, if possible, our own State from its ravages. The danger is imminent, and demands prompt and decisive measures of prevention.

We have assembled in Jefferson [City] under circumstances widely different from those that existed when the Convention adjourned its session in St. Louis.

We find high offices of the State Government engaged in actual hostilities with the forces of the United States, and blood has been spilt upon the soil of Missouri. Many of our citizens have yielded to obedience to an ill-judged call of the Governor, and have assembled in arms for the purpose of repelling the invasion of the State by armed bands of lawless invaders, as the troops of the United States are designated by the Governor in his proclamation of the 17th day of June last.

We find that troops from the State of Arkansas have come into Missouri for the purpose of sustaining the action of our Governor in his combat with the United States, and this at the request of the Executive.

We find no person present. or likely soon to be present, at the seat of Government, to exercise the ordinary functions of the Executive Department, or to maintain the internal peace of the State.

We find that throughout the State there is immanent danger of civil war in its worst form, in which neighbor shall seek the life of neighbor, and bonds of society will be dissolved, and universal anarchy shall reign. If it be possible to find a remedy for existing evils, and to avert the threatened horrors of anarchy, it is manifestly the duty of your delegates, assembled in Convention, to provide such remedy; and, in order to determine upon the remedy, it is necessary to trace very briefly to origin and progress of the evils that now afflict the State.

It is not necessary that any lengthy reference should be made to the action of those States which have seceded from the Union. We cannot remedy or recall that secession. They have acted for themselves, and must abide the consequences of their own action. So far as you have expressed your wishes, you have declared your determination not to leave the Union, and your wishes have been expressed by this Convention.

Any action of any officer of the State in conflict with your will thus expressed is an action in plain opposition to the principle of our Government, which recognizes the people as the source of political power, and their will as the rule of conduct for all their officers. It would have been but a reasonable compliance with your will, that after you had, through this Convention, expressed your determination to remain in the Union, your Executive and Legislative officers should not only have refrained from any opposition to your will, but should have exerted all their powers to carry your will into effect.

We have been enabled to ascertain by some correspondence of different public officers, accidently made public, that several of these officers not only entertained and expressed opinions and wishes against the continuance of Missouri in the Union, but actually engaged in schemes, to withdraw her from the Union, contrary to your wishes.

After the adjournment of your Convention, which had expressed your purpose to remain in the Union, Governor Claiborne F. Jackson, in a letter addressed to David Walker, President of the Arkansas Convention, dated April 19, 1861, says: "From the beginning, my own conviction has been that the interest, duty, and honor of every slaveholding State demanded their separation from the non-slaveholding States." Again, he says: "I have been, from the beginning, in favor of decided and prompt action on the part of the Southern States, but the majority of the people of Missouri, up to the present time, have differed with me." Here we have the declaration of his opinion and wishes, and the open confession that a majority of the people did not agree with him[23].

Bur he proceeds: "What their future action (meaning the future action of the people) may be, no man with certainty can predict or foretell; but my impression is, judging from the indications hourly occurring, that Missouri will be ready for secession in less an thirty days, and will secede if Arkansas will only get out of the way and give her a free passage."

It will presently be seen, by an extract from another letter, what the Governor

23. David Walker was born in Todd County, Kentucky, on February 19, 1806, and moved to Arkansas, living initially in Little Rock. A lawyer by profession, Walker moved to Fayetteville, settling on a farm just south of the city. Considered an "honorable, high-minded man," Walker was politically a Whig, being elected prosecuting attorney in 1833, and served for four years. Popular with Washington County, Walker was elected a member of the First Arkansas Constitutional Convention and in 1840, was elected as a State Senator (1840–1843). Following his term us an Arkansas Senator, Walker ran for the U.S. Congress, in 1844, but lost to Archibald Yell by 3,529 votes. In 1848, he was elected the Arkansas Supreme Court and served until he retired in 1855. Returning to his farm, Walker opened up a law office, serving the local area until the secession crisis of 1860–1861. In 1861, Walker, as a Conditional Unionist, was elected to represent his county at the Arkansas Secession Convention. During the March convention, Walker, who was now considered "among the most influential citizens of the state," was elected President. The March Convention came to an abrupt halt, following a rancorous debate on secession, which was turned down by five votes. The Convention then adjourned to reassemble on the fist Monday in August; however, Judge Walker was given to sole power to call for the Convention to reassemble if "public events required him to do so." With the firing on Fort Sumpter and President Lincoln's call for troops, Walker recalled the Convention, to meet on May 6. By a vote of 69 in favor to one opposed a secession ordinance passed. During the war Walker served for a time as Judge Advocate on General Price's staff, was capture in June 1862, took the oath of allegiance, paying a $10,000 to guarantee his compliance. With the capture of Little Rock, in September 1863, Walker relocated to the city, becoming a founding member of the Arkansas Historical Association the same year. Following the war Walker served on the Arkansas Supreme Court (1866); however, the position was vacated because of reconstruction. He was re-appointed to the court for a third time in 1874, and served until his retirement, in 1879, due to ill health. He died in a buggy accident on September 30, 1879. *O. R.*, vol. 13: 451–452; Albert W. Bishop, *Loyalty on the Frontier or Sketches of Union Men of the Southwest With Incidents and Adventures in Rebellion on the Border* (St. Louis, 1863), 21–22, 25; James J. Johnston, "Letter of John Campbell Unionist," Arkansas Historical Quarterly 29 (Summer, 1970), 180 n. 6; Internet site, www.geni.com., key word "Judge David Walker"; Margaret Ross, *Arkansas Gazette: The Early Years 1819–1866* (Little Rock, AR 1969), 203, 208, 354, 383; Robert E. Waterman and Thomas Rothrock, eds., "The Earle-Buchanan Letters of 1861–1876," *Arkansas Historical Quarterly* 33 (Summer, 1974), 116 n. 47, 123; Ted R. Worley, "Letters to David Walker Relating to Reconstruction In Arkansas, 1866–1874," *Arkansas Historical Quarterly* 16 (Autumn, 1957), 319.

means by being ready for secession; but it is very remarkable that he should undertake not only to say that she would be ready to secede in thirty days, but further, that she will secede, when in fact your Convention, at that time, stood adjourned to the 3d Monday of December next. His declaration, that the State would secede is made, doubtless, upon some plan of his own, independent of the Convention.

Nine days after this letter to the President of the Arkansas Convention, he wrote another, addressed to J. W. Tucker, Esq., the editor of the secession newspaper in St. Louis.[24] This letter is dated April 28, 1861. The writer says: "I do not think Missouri should secede to-day or to-morrow, but I do not think it good policy that I should so openly declare. I want a little time to arm the State, and I am assuming every responsibility to do it with all possible despatch."

Again he says: "We should keep our own counsels. Everybody in the State is in favor of arming the State, then let it be done. All are opposed to furnishing Mr. Lincoln with soldiers. Time will settle the balance. Nothing should be said about the time or the manner in which Missouri should go out. That she ought to go, at the proper time, I have no doubt. She ought to have gone last winter, when she could have seized the public arms and public property, and defended herself."

Here we have the fixed mind and purpose of the Governor, that Missouri should leave the Union. He wants time–a little time to arm the State. He thinks secrecy should be preserved by the parties with whom he acts in keeping their counsels. He suggests that nothing should be said about the time or manner of going out; manifestly implying that the time and manner of going out, which he and those with whom he acted, proposed to adopt, were some other time and manner other than such as were to be fixed by the people through their Convention. It was no doubt to be a time and manner to be fixed by the Governor and the General Assembly, or by the Governor and a military body to be provided with arms during the little time needed by the Governor for that purpose.

There have been no specific disclosures made to the public of the details of this plan, but the Governor expresses his strong conviction that at the proper time the State will go out.

The only correspondence of the Governor occurred at a time when there was no interference by the soldiers of the United States with any part of the citizens, or with the peace of the State. The event that produced exasperation through the State, the capture of Camp Jackson, did not take place until the 10th of May. Yet, the evidence is conclusive that there was at the time of this correspondence a

---

24. J. W. Tucker was born in 1832, in South Carolina, where he was a lawyer, and later immigrated to St. Louis following financial troubles. Tucker was a decided supporter of secession and his newspaper, the *St. Louis Journal* reflected his views on the same. As the war began Tucker's newspaper was suspended, he was arrested, paid a bail, but then fled St. Louis for southwest Missouri. Tucker eventually ended up in Mobile, Alabama, where he completed his Civil War Service, editing a newspaper and organizing a group of saboteurs to attack shipping on the western waterways. Final disposition unknown. See **Appendix B** for a complete biography. Piston & Sweeney, *Portraits of Conflict, Missouri,* 195.

secret plan for taking Missouri out of the Union without any assent of the people through their Convention.

An address to the people of Missouri was issued by Thomas C. Reynolds, the Lieutenant Governor, in which he declares that in Arkansas, Tennessee, and Virginia his efforts have been directed unceasingly, to the best of his limited abilities, to the promotion of our interests, indissolubly connected with the vindication of our speedy union with the Confederate States. Here is the second executive officer of Missouri avowedly engaged in traveling through States which he must regard while Missouri continues in the Union as foreign States, and those States endeavoring as he says, to promote the interests of our State.

The mode of promoting our interests is disclosed in another passage of the address, in which he gives the people assurance that the people of the Confederate States, though engaged in a war with a powerful foe, would not hesitate still further to tax their energies and resources at the proper time, and on a proper occasion in aid of Missouri. The mode of promoting our interests, then, was by obtaining military aid, and this while Missouri continued in the Union. The result of the joint action of the first and second executive officers of the State have been that a body of military forces of Arkansas have actually invaded Missouri, to carry out the schemes of your own officer, who ought to have conformed to your will, as you had made it known at elections, and had expressed it by your delegates in Convention.[25]

Still further to execute the purpose of severing the connection of Missouri with the United States, the General Assembly was called, and when assembled sat in secret secession, and enacted laws which had for their object the placing in the hands of the Governor large sums of money to expend in his discretion for military purposes, and a law for the organization of a military force which was to be sustained by extraordinary taxation, and to be absolutely subject to the orders of the Governor, to act against all oppressors, including the United States. By these acts, schools were closed, and the demands of humanity for the support of lunatics was denied, and the money raised for the purpose of education and benevolence may swell the fund to be expended in war.[26]

Without referring more particularly to the provisions of these several acts, which are most extraordinary and extremely dangerous as precedents, it is sufficient to say that they display the same purpose to engage in a conflict with the General Government, and to break the connection of Missouri with the United States which had before been manifested by Gov. Jackson. The conduct of these officers of the Legislative and Executive Departments has produced evils and dangers of

---

25. Arkansas troops entered southwest Missouri on July 4, capturing Neosho and taking 137 prisoners, seven wagons and 150 small arms the following day. Following the engagement at Neosho the Arkansas troops pulled back to northwest Arkansas. They, with additional troops from Texas would return to Missouri for the Battle of Wilson's Creek on August 10, 1861, after which they left the state. *O.R.*, vol. 3: 607; Piston & Sweeney, "Missouri State Guard," 22.

26. See Note 56, Chapter 1 for details.

vast magnitude, and your delegates in Convention have addressed themselves to the important and delicate duty of attempting to free the States from these evils.

The high executive officers have fled from the Government and from the State, leaving us without the officers to discharge the ordinary necessary executive functions. But, more than this, they have actually engaged in carrying on a war with the State, supported by the troops from States in the Southern Confederacy; so that the State, while earnestly desirous to keep out of the war, has become the scene of conflict without any action of the people assuming such hostility. Any remedy for our present evil, to be adequate, must be one which shall vacate the offices held by the officers who have thus brought our trouble upon us.[27]

Your delegates desire that you shall by election fill these offices, by process of your own choice, and for this purpose they have directed by ordinance, that an election shall be held on the first Monday in November. This time rather than one nearer at hand, was selected, so as to conform to the spirit of the provision in the Constitution which requires three months notice to be given of an election to fill a vacancy in the office of Governor. But, in the mean time, much damage might happen to the State by keeping the present incumbents in office, not only by leaving necessary executive duties unperformed, while they prosecute their war measures, but by continuing and increasing the internal social strife which threatens the peace of the State.

Your delegates judged it necessary that, in order to preserve the peace, and in order to arrest invasions of the State, these executive offices should be vacated at once, and be filled by persons selected by your delegates, until you could fill them by election. They have, therefore, made such selections as they trust will be found to be judicious in preserving the peace of the State. The office of Secretary of State has not been mentioned before, and it is sufficient to say that Benjamin F. Massey, the present incumbent, has abandoned the seat of government, and has followed the fortunes of the Governor, taking with him the Seal of State as an instrument of evil. He may be employed by the Governor in action deeply injurious to the State; and he has been dealt with by your delegates in the same manner as the Governor and Lieutenant Governor.[28]

---

27. Conveniently absent from the discussion of the Governor's actions was the capture of Camp Jackson, on May 10, 1861. The capture subsequently brought about the bulk of the legislation that the Convention disagreed with, while exonerating the actions of General Lyon and Frank Blair in taking the duly assembled Missouri Militia. Further, even though the Convention will argue that Governor Jackson wanted to take the arsenal, they clearly state in the Governor's correspondence that the time was not yet ready to secede. And still further, the Convention makes no mention that by the time of Camp Jackson the arms that Governor Jackson desired had already been removed from the arsenal on April 26 and May 1, and sent to Illinois, negating the necessity to capture the camp. Lyon, 434; McElroy, 67; Peckham, 119; Snead, 157.

28. Benjamin F. Massey was born in Kent County, Maryland in 1811, and moved to St. Louis in 1831, where he became a business man. He moved again to Fayette, Howard County, Missouri, in 1837, where he remained for two years, being "engaged in merchandising." Next Massey moved to Jasper County, making his residence in Sarcoxie. Elected Secretary of State, as a Democrat, in 1856, Massey served a four year term. He was reelected in 1860, for a second term; however, his

In regards to the members of the General Assembly, it is only necessary to say that by the enactment of the law called the Military Bill, which violates the Constitution, and places the entire military strength of the State at the almost unlimited control of the Executive, and imposes onerous burdens upon the citizens for the support of the army, and by the passage of general appropriation acts which give to the Executive the command of large funds to be expended at his discretion for military purposes, thus uniting the control of the purse and the sword in the same hands, they have displayed their willingness to sustain the war policy of the Executive, and place the destinies of the State in the hands of the Governor.

The offices of the members of the General Assembly have therefore been vacated and a new election ordered, so that you may have an opportunity of choosing such Legislative Representatives as may carry out your own views of policy.

In order that the schemes of those who seek to take Missouri out of the Union may not further be added to by the late secret legislation of the General Assembly, your delegates have by ordinance amended the Military law, and such other acts as were doubtless passed for the purpose of disturbing the relations of the State with the Federal Government.

These are the measures adopted by your delegates in Convention for the purpose of restoring peace to our disturbed State, and enabling you to select officers for yourselves to declare and carry into effect your views of the true policy of the State. They are measures which seem to be imperatively demanded by the present alarming condition of public affairs, and your delegates have determined to submit them to you for your approval or disapproval, that they may have the authority of your sanction, if you find them to be adapted to secure the peace and welfare of the State.

There are some who question the power of the Convention to adopt these measures. A very brief examination of this question of power will show that the power exists beyond a doubt. It is one of fundamental principles of our Government, that all political power resides in the people; and it is established beyond question, that the Convention of Delegates of the people, when regularly called and assembled, possess all the political power which the people themselves possess, and stands in the place of the assemblage of all the people in one vast mass. If there be no limitation upon the power of the Convention, made in the call of the body, then the body is possessed of unlimited political power.

If it be a State Convention, then there is a limitation upon it, imposed by the Constitution of the United States. If we state the position of the opponents of the power now exercised by the Constitution in the strongest form, it is this: The Convention was called by an act of the General Assembly for specific purpose declared in the act, and, therefore, the people in electing delegates under that act intended to limit the Convention to the subjects therein specified, and this action

---

position was vacated by the Missouri Convention on July 31, 1861. No further record was found on Massey after he fled Jefferson City in May 1861. Hale, 203; History of Audrain County, 39; Phillips, *Missouri's Confederate*, 163; Ryle, 142.

taken by the Convention, in vacating State offices, is not within the scope of the subjects thus submitted to the Convention.

It is very well understood by all that a Convention of the people does not derive any power from any act of the Legislature. All its power is directly the power of the people, and is not dependent upon any act of the ordinary functionaries of the State. It cannot be claimed, in the present case, that we are to look at the act of the Assembly referred too for any other purpose than to find whether there is any limitation imposed by the people upon the powers of the Convention, by electing the Convention under the act. If it be examined with that view, and if it be conceded that any of its provisions were designed to limit the powers of the convention, it will be seen that all the Convention has done comes clearly within the scope of the powers designed to be exercised. The 5th section of the act provides that the Convention, when assembled, shall proceed to consider the then existing relations between the Government of the United States, the people and governments of the different States, and the government and people of the State of Missouri, and to adopt such measures for vindicating the sovereignty of the State and the protection of its institutions as shall appear to them to be demanded. The measures to be adopted are to be such as the Convention shall judge to be demanded in order to vindicate the sovereignty of the State and protect its institutions; those measures are left to the judgement of the Convention, and may reach any officer or any class of persons. Let us take the case, then, of an armed invasion of the State by troops from Arkansas, neither invited nor headed by the Governor of Missouri.[29] The vindication of the sovereignty of the State may demand that such invasion be repelled by force, and every person can see that, while the forces of Missouri may be employed in repelling the invasion, it is perfectly obvious that the vindication of our sovereignty requires that the Governor, who is, by the Constitution, Commander-in Chief of the Army of the State, must be removed from that office when he is actually engaged in leading or inciting the invasion. To consider the relations existing between the people and Government of Arkansas and the people and Government of Missouri, and to adopt measure to vindicate our sovereignty, imperatively demands in the case supposed, and which actually

---

29. Not true. The supporting troops from Arkansas were invited by Governor Jackson to help "free themselves from the yoke which has been placed upon them" by the Federal Government, represented by General Lyon. On the train ride back from the June 11, meeting with General Lyon, Governor Jackson "began to formulate plans. Price would take command of all state troops that could be put in the field, and the Confederate government would be asked to send a co-operating army into Missouri as quickly as possible." In Arkansas, Governor Jackson had already forwarded Colton Greene to northwest Arkansas to request aid from Arkansas. On June 14, Ben McCulloch, commanding in northeast Arkansas acknowledge the request for aid, forwarding correspondence to the Confederate Secretary of War for guidance. Twelve days later the Richmond government responded and "authorized" McCulloch to "give such assistance to Missouri as will subserve the main purpose of your command." On July 5, McCulloch entered Missouri, proceeding northward to aid the Missouri forces, which were falling back to Cowskin Prairie to regroup and train. *O.R.*, vol. 3: 594, 599, 606; Adamson, 129, 135; Bearss, "Fort Smith, 324; Brooksher, 81, 95; Phillips, *Missouri's Confederate*, 257–258, 262; Shalhope, 166–167.

exists, that the commander in the State of Missouri be removed from his office. This case is stated merely as an illustration of the principles upon which the action of the Convention rests. It is clearly an action demanded by the duty of vindicating the sovereignty of the State, and it applies to the other persons removed from office by the Convention upon the ground that they are all involved in the same scheme for assailing the sovereignty of the State.

In relation to the members of the General Assembly, the Convention are aware that all the members did not participate in the action which is regarded as an attempt to destroy the institutions of the State by destroying the connection with the Union, and thus overturning the institutions which she has as one of the United States. But no distinction could be made among the members on account of their individual opinions. The body was necessarily located collectively.

And now, having stated the necessity for the action of the Convention, and the principles which have governed the action, your delegates submit the whole for your consideration and calm judgement. They have felt their own position and that of the State to be peculiar. They have looked over Missouri and beheld the dangers that threaten her. They desire to avert them. They desire to restore peace to all her citizens. They have adopted the measures which, in their judgement, gave the highest promise of peace and security to all her citizens. If the measures adopted should have the desired effect, your delegates will feel that gratification which always attends the success of a well-intended effort. If the measures fail to restore peace, your delegates will find consolation in the fact that they have done what they could.

The report of the Convention was agreed to.

* * * * * * *

Item: The Prose and Songs from Wilson's Creek.

A. A poem on the Battle of Wilson's Creek, by F. D. Ten Eyck.[30].

By the Graves At Wilson's Creek

An hour, a flower, a memory, perchance a tear or two;
These give you from your life to them, Nation!
What gave they you?
What of silent partings, that lie to deep for tears?
What of yearning sighings, which only the night wind hears?
What of the walking picket, guarding the nation's sleep?
What of the cold and hungry–what of the thirst and heat?
What of the midnight marching, where weary, footsore and drenched?
The pallid, weeping morning shows the enemy entrenched?
What of the shriek of the battle–what of the after hours?

30. F. D. Ten Eyck, "By the Graves At Wilson's Creek," *Missouri Republican*, June 5, 1886.

Oh, men! In the name of God, can ye heal such wounds with flowers?
Look to your lilies, Columbia; stainless they should be as snow,
To rest on hearts burned while in battle's furnace glow;
And your roses red as the blood which flowed on fields of death,
And their fragrance that can never stifle the scent of the battle's breath.
Alas if flowers were all that were laid on each nameless grave;
Alas for us and for them and the sacrifice they gave.
But over those lonely hillocks, as over the hills of God.
A glory shines from the flower-cups withering on the sod;
For they are the pledge of the promise: What you gave to us we will keep–
The oath of the country's waking sons to her sons who are asleep.

F. D. Ten Eyck,

/ / / / / / /

B. Songs and Poetry related to the Battle of Wilson's Creek and Franz Sigel, in Stephen Engle's *Yankee Dutchman*.[31]
No. 1 (A Song on supporting General Franz Sigel):

When I came from der Deutsche countree
I vorks sometimes at baking,
Den I keeps a lager beer saloon,
Und den I goes shoe making,
But now I was a soger been
To save the Yankee Eagle,
To schauch dem tam secession volks
I'm going to fight mit Sigel

/ / / / / / /

No 2 (A Poem idolizing General l Franz Sigel):

I Fights Mit Sigel

I met him again, he was trudging along,
His knapsack with chickens was swelling,
He'd "Blenkered" these dainties, and thought it no wrong,
From some secessionist's dwellin
"What regiment's yours? And under whose flag
Do you fight?" said I, touching his shoulder:
Turning slowly around he smilingly said,
For the thought made him stronger and bolder;
"I fights mit Sigel."

---

31. Engle, 83–84,

The next time I saw him his knapsack was gone,
    His cap and canteen were missing,
Shell, shrapnel, and grape, and the swift rifle-ball
    Around him and o'ver him were hissing
"How are you, my friend, and where have you been,
    And for what and for whom are you fighting?"
He said, as a shell from the enemy's gun
    Sent his arm and musket a "kiting,"
        "I fight mit Sigel."

And once more I saw him and knelt by his side,
    His life blood was rapidly flowing:
I whispered of home, wife, children, and friends,
    The bright land to which he was going:
And have you no words for the dear ones at home.
    The "wee one," the father or mother?
"Yaw yaw,"said he, "tell them oh tell them I fights"–
        "I fight mit Sigel."

We scraped out a grave, and he dreamlessly sleeps
    On the banks of the Shenandoah River;
His home and his kindred alike are unknown,
    Hid reward in the hand of the Giver
We placed a rough board at the head of his grave,
"And we left him alone in his glory,"
    But on it we marked ere we turned from the spot,
The little we know of his story–
        "I fights mit Sigel."

/ / / / / / /

C. A Poem on Nathaniel Lyon as found in Frank Moore's *The Civil War in Song and Story*.[32]

Lyon

Sing birds, on green Missouri's plain
    The saddest song of sorrow;
Drop tears, O clouds, in gentlest rain
    Ye from the winds can borrow;
Breath out, ye winds, your softest sigh,
    Weep, flowers, in dewy splendor,

32. Frank Moore, The Civil War in Song and Story. 1860–1865 (New York, 1889), 97.

For him who knew well how to die,
    But never to surrender.

Up rose the serene the August sun
    Upon that day of Glory;
Up curled from musket and gun
    The war-cloud gray and hoary;
It gathered like a funeral pall,
    Now broken and now blended,
Where rang the angry buffalo's call,
    And rank with rank contended.

Four thousand men, as brave and true
    As e'ver went forth in daring,
Upon the foe that morning threw
    The strength of their despairing,
They feared not death–men bless the field
    That patriot soldiers die on–
Fair freedom's cause was sword and shield,
    And at their head was Lyon!

Their leader's troubled soul looked forth
    From eyes of troubled brightness;
Sad soul! the burden of the North
    Had pressed out all the lightness.
He gazed upon the unequal fight,
    His ranks all rent and gory,
And felt the shadows close like night
    Round his career of glory.

"General, come, lead us!" loud the cry
    From a brave band was ringing–
"Lead us, and we will stop, or die,
    That battery's awful singing."
He spurred to where his heros stood,
    Twice wounded,–no wounds knowing,–
The fire of battle in his blood
    And on his forehead glowing.

O, cursed for aye that traitor's hand,
    And cursed that aim so deadly,
Which smote the bravest of the land,
    And dyed his bosom redly!
Serene he lay while passed him pressed

The battle's furious billow,
As calmly as a babe may rest
        Upon its mother's pillow.

So Lyon died! And well may flowers
        His place of burial cover,
For never has this land of ours
        A more devoted lover.
Living, his country was his bride;
        His life he gave her, dying;
Life, fortune, love—he nought denied
        To her and to her sighing.

Rest, Patriot, in thy hillside grave,
        Beside her form who bore thee!
Long may the land then diedst to save
        Her bannered stars wave o'er thee!
Upon her history's brightest page,
        And on Fame's glowing portal,
She'll write thy grand, heroic page,
        And grave thy name immortal!

* * * * * *

Appendix B
Selected Biographies

James Buchanan Eads

He was born on May 23, 1820, in Lawrenceburg, Indiana, and moved to St. Louis in 1833. With no formal education, Eads "learned mathematics and sciences on his own" and worked as either a clerk or on the local steamboats that plied the Mississippi River. He married his first wife, Martha, in 1842, against the wishes of her father; however the marriage ended suddenly in 1852, when Martha died of cholera..

Eads's love for the river and his desire to better himself resulted in a partnership with two St. Louisians to clear "snags from the rivers and salvaging cargo." To that end the inventive Eads developed a diving bell, at the age of twenty-two that allowed him to salvage wrecks in the rivers and recover75 % of the cargos

James B. Eads

value from the insurers. Over time, as Eads worked the Mississippi River from Iowa to the Gulf of Mexico, he became quite well known for his knowledge of the Mississippi River; this in turn earned him the honorary title of "captain." Further, Eads' work as a salvager earned him a "solid fortune." though it did imperil his health, causing him to refrain from further diving in the 1850's.

Eads married for a second time in 1861, even as the secession crisis boiled over. An Unconditional Unionist, Eads recognized the importance of the river system that permeated the South and believed that a strong river navy was essential to the Union victory. With the help of his friend, Attorney General Edwin Bates, Eads submitted a proposal to build what became the "City Class Ironclads," in August 1861. As the lowest bidder, of seven submitted, Eads won the contract to build seven of the ironclads, which he agreed to complete within 65 days; however the first boat was not completed on October 12, 1861–a few days late–and four more were delivered by mid-October. And by the end of the war he had built 30 of the iron monsters. Overall Eads contribution to the Union war effort produced what one author credited "for the early victory in the West."

Following the war Eads took up a new challenge–engineering and building the first bridge across the Mississippi River. He completed his plans in 1868 and finished the bridge in 1874–the first steel bridge across the river. Today the bridge still stands and is noted as a "National Historical Landmark."

Eads moved to New York in 1883. He died on March 8, 1887, in Nassau, Bahama Islands from tuberculosis; however, a modern-day historian recorded that Eads probably died from the "bends," caused by his frequent diving operations. And by the time of his death, this self educated man held more that 50 patents.[1]

* * * * * * *

Thomas Clement Fletcher

Thomas Clement Fletcher was born on January 22, 1827, in Herculaneum, Missouri. He received a basic public school education and was elected the county clerk of Jefferson County, Missouri, in 1849, and served until 1856. Fletcher moved to St. Louis in 1856, and became a lawyer and friend of Frank Blair. With Blair, Fletcher helped organize the Missouri Republican Party. In 1860, he served as a delegate to the Republican National convention.

With the outbreak of the Civil War, General Nathaniel Lyon appointed Fletcher as Assistant Provost Marshall of St. Louis. He organized and recruited the 31st Missouri Infantry, being appointed colonel of the regiment on October 7, 1862. Fletcher lead his command at the Battle of Chickasaw Bluff (December 29, 1862), where he was wounded and captured. After spending five months in Libby Prison, Fletcher was exchanged in May 1863, and returned to his command, then sieging Vicksburg, Mississippi. Fletcher continued to operate in the Western Theater until illness forced him to resign on June 16, 1864, and return to St. Louis to recover.

During Price's 1864 Missouri Raid, General William Rosecrans, commanding the Department of Missouri, asked Fletcher to organize a regiment to assist in the defense of Missouri. On August 15, Fletcher completed the organization of the 47th EMM, of which he was appointed colonel on September 17. Fletcher successfully led his command at Pilot Knob, after which he was elected the 18th Governor of Missouri (1865–1869), as the Radical candidate, on November 8. He resigned from the army on November 18, but was later promoted to brevet brigadier general for "gallant services at Pilot Knob."

During his tenure as governor Fletcher "issued an emancipation proclamation with

Thomas C. Fletcher

---

1. Gerteis, *St. Louis*, 236–240; Sifakis, *Who Was Who in the Union*, 123; Wikipedia, keyword "James Buchanan Eads"; Winter, 33–78, 130.

a 60-gun salute on January 14,1865." Slaves were to be freed "without compensation tor the owners." And on March 7, 1865, he ended martial law in Missouri. After the war, to keep the Radicals in power, Fletcher supported limited "Universal Suffrage," that allowed Negroes to vote while denying ex-Confederates the same right.

After his term expired Fletcher opened a law office in St. Louis, where he became a successful lawyer. Fletcher later moved to Washington, DC where he died on March 25, 1899, and was later buried in St. Louis. Prior to his death Fletcher wrote a biography titled Reminiscences of Wm. T. Sherman (1891).[2]

* * * * * * *

Hamilton Rowan Gamble

H. R. Gamble was born in Winchester, Virginia, on November 29, 1798, graduated from Hampden-Sydney College, Virginia in 1815, after which he was admitted to the bar. He practiced law in Virginia and Tennessee for three years before moving to St. Louis to join his brother Archibald in 1818.

Gamble quickly became involved in the local judiciary, serving first as a county clerk and then prosecuting attorney before receiving a political appointment as the Missouri Secretary of State in 1824, serving under Governor Frederick Bates. After a two year term Gamble returned to the law, but reentered politics in 1846, being elected to the Missouri Legislature for a single term. In 1851, he was elected as a moderate Whig to the Missouri Supreme Court, being advanced to lead the court by the other two justices upon taking his seat. As a justice, Gamble presided over the Dred Scott case, offering the only dissenting opinion, believing that Scott should be freed. Gamble retired from the court in 1854, due to ill health. Spending the next four years in Missouri, Gamble then moved to Norristown, Pennsylvania, in 1858, "in order to provide adequate educational facilities for his children." There he remained until the secession crisis.

Returning to Missouri in early 1861, Gamble made his first public address on January 12 at the meeting of the Conditional Unionists that was held at the St. Louis courthouse. A brother-in-law to Edward Bates, the U.S. Attorney General, Gamble was nominated for the February 28 Convention by both the Conditional and Unconditional Union Parties. Elected to the February 28 Convention, Gamble was appointed Chairman of the Committee to prepare a report on Missouri's future relationship with the Federal Union. In the end, Gamble proved instrumental in drafting the seven proposals that the Convention eventually adopted.

Upon the outbreak of hostilities, the Convention was again called into session

---

2. Boatner, 285; Carter, 156, 235,180; Thomas C. Fletcher, "The Battle of Pilot Knob, and the Retreat to Leasburg," in *War Papers and Personal Reminiscences. 1861–1865. Read Before the Commandery of the State of Missouri, MOLLUS* (St. Louis, 1892.; reprint ed., Wilmington, NC,, 1992), vol. 14: 30–32; Gerteis, *St. Louis*, 309, 334; Heitman, vol. 1: 425; Hunt & Brown, 207; Smith, *Blair Family*, vol. 2: 346–347, 432; Wikipedia, key word "Thomas Clement Fletcher"; Winter, 127.

on July 22, 1861. Initially the *Chicago Tribune* questioned the wisdom of appointing Gamble to the Committee to decide Missouri's future, writing: "Although Judge G. is an able man, and has a clear Union record, his personal affiliations are not those of a first rate Union man." However, when the Convention completed their work and elected Gamble the Provisional Governor of Missouri the *Tribune* accepted him as the new governor recording that he was elected because of his "unquestionable ability and doubtless fitness for the position."

As to why Gamble was elected Governor of Missouri, Marguerite Potter wrote of him in his biography that he was always "Calm, dignified, self-possessed, [and] always perfectly at ease. The confidence which he had in himself caused others to place their confidence in him. He was slow and deliberate in his speech, yet so logical, clear and forceful that he never left a jury in doubt about the strong points of his own testimony and the weak points of his opponent's. In no sense of the word was he a spectacular orator, for he disliked and avoided all kinds of show. His modesty and utter lack of pretension led many to undervalue his real ability, but they changed theat opinion once they met him at the bar. Gamble was motivated by high principles from which he would not deviate for personal gain and which he displayed not only in his profession, but in all relationships of his life... He left a splendid example of integrity in the law."

Despite Gamble's election, the legitimacy of the Convention's actions to declare "the state offices vacant and appoint a provisional government was questioned" by the legal minds of the day, with the Missouri Supreme Court unanimously ruling that the appointment was illegal. "However, Abraham Lincoln's administration quickly recognized the provisional government, giving it legitimacy."

As Governor, Gamble reorganized the Missouri Militia calling for 42,000 volunteers and negotiated with the Federal Government to pay for the arming and support of the command. However, only 6,000 answered the call necessitating additional call for troops as the war progressed. He also continued to support slavery, in an attempt to mollify the slave holders of the state, but by 1863, Gamble had changed his position, passing legislation to gradually eliminate the practice.

Continued ill health and the "strain of bitter personal abuse and oppressive official responsibilities, plagued Gamble throughout his term of office as well as some bad luck. On December 17, 1863, Gamble slipped on the State Capital steps, re-fracturing an old injury, after which pneumonia set in that ended with his death on January 31, 1864.

Upon his death the *Missouri Republican* noted that "'A good man is dead.'" Overall Gamble "had returned to Missouri at a time when the Union cause needed him. He was an advocate of peace, when hotheads called for war...To keep Missouri loyal, prevent anarchy, rebuild civil government, ward off military control, repel invasion, reconstruct state finances, and pacify the people were only a few of the herculean tasks to which Gamble set his hand." And Marguerite Potter wrote that to "Hamilton Rowan Gamble...more than any other man, belongs the credit for keeping Missouri in the Union."[3]

* * * * * * *

John William Reid

John W. Reid (not Reed) was born in Lynchburg, Virginia, on June 14, 1821, educated at "common schools,"moved to Missouri in 1840, settling in Lexington, Lafayette County. Professionally, he was a teacher, studied the law in his spare time and was admitted to the Missouri bar at Jefferson City in 1844. Described by Jay Monaghan as "a six-foot giant weighing two hundred pounds," Reid was married twice, fathered one daughter and two sons, was a slave owner and politically a Democrat,.

With the beginning of the Mexican War, Reid "distinguished himself under [Alexander W.] Doniphan at Sacramento," where he served in the 1st Missouri Mounted Regiment as a 1st Lieutenant and then a captain commanding Company D, Lafayette County Company. Reid was noted for bravery at the Battle of Bracito (December 25, 1846), near El Paso, Texas, and at the Battle of Sacramento (February 28, 1847), near Chihuahua, Mexico, where he led a charge that captured an enemy battery. In May 1847, Reid participated in a raid against a band of Comanches (not Navajos as mentioned in Wikipedia), where he was wounded twice and successfully rescued 19 girls and boys that had been taken prisoners by the renegades.

After the Mexican War, Reid returned to Missouri, where he was elected to the Missouri House (1854–1856) as an "anti-Benton Democrat," and, in 1856, during the Bleeding Kansas days, served as a "general" commanding a portion of a 1,500-man Missouri Militia force that invaded Kansas in the summer. Reid's force consisted of 250 men which took Osawatomine, Kansas, on August 30, suffering the loss of five men wounded (two later died), while killing six including the son of John Brown–Frederick Brown. Reid then burned the town and moved to Lawrence, where he participated in the sack of the town in September before pulling back to Missouri.

During the secession crisis, of 1860, Reid was considered a leading secessionist, being elected to the U.S. Congress (1860–1861), taking his seat on March 4, 1861, but surrendered the office on August 3, having joined the MSG. Reid was appointed the MSG Chief of the Subsistence Department, on May 21, 1861, serving under Sterling Price. Toward the end of June 1861, Reid departed Price's headquarters and journeyed, with James Harding and others, to Ft. Smith, Little Lock and Memphis in search of supplies for the MSG. Reid rejoined the army at Lexington on the day that the city surrendered (September 20, 1861), where

---

3. Boatner, 322; C., "Affairs In Missouri," *Chicago Tribune*, July 31 and August 7, 1861; Carter, 239; James G. Downhour, "Gamble, Hamilton Rowan," in *Encyclopedia of the Civil War*, 805–806; Faust, 297; Gerteis, *St. Louis*, 26; Potter, "Hamilton R. Gamble," 66, 75–76, 99–101; Sifakis, *Who Was Who in the Union*, 147; Smith, *Blair Family*, vol. 2: 24; Winter, 120–121.

he served as either Commissary General, Subsistence General or Commissary of Subsistence. In December 1861, Reid departed the Guard, on leave, and went to Jackson County, Missouri, for a short visit to the residence of J. F. Stonestreet. Also, in December on Reid was officially expelled from the U.S. Congress, on the 2nd for joining the rebel cause.

Reid returned to the rebel army by early January 1862, and was at thee Battle of Pea Ridge (March 6–8,1862), being with the army's train. Upon reorganization of Earl Van Dorn's Army at Van Buren, Arkansas, following Pea Ridge, Reid joined the Confederate Service, as a member of Price's staff on March 22, 1862. When Price relocated to the east side of the Mississippi in the late Spring 1862, Reid probably went with him but later returned in the Summer of 1862, going to Missouri on recruiting service. Captured near Lone Jack, in mid-July 1862, during the Missouri Guerrilla War of 1862, Reid was sent to Gratiot Street Prison, in St. Louis, where he arrived on August 19 and on September 12, he was transferred to Alton, Illinois Prison. Reid was released from prison in late Spring or early Summer of 1863, under the condition that he "take no further part in the war." Returning to Arkansas, Reid promptly rejoined General Price's staff.

Reid was at the Battle of Helena, Arkansas (July 4, 1863), after which Price recommended him for promotion; however he was never promoted. During his time in the army Reid attained the rank of colonel in the Guard and later a major in the Confederate Army. At the end of the war, Reid surrendered at Shreveport, Louisiana, as a member of the 10th Missouri Infantry (CSA), while Price fled to Mexico.

Returning to Missouri, Reid was pardoned for his part in the war and settled on a piece of land that he owned near the Kansas and Missouri Rivers. In his post-war years, Reid was instrumental in the construction of the first bridge across the Missouri River, while opening a successful law practice in Kansas City, Missouri. He was also a successful banker. By the time of his death on November 22, 1881, at Lees Summit, Missouri, Reid had rebuilt his fortune. He was buried in Kansas City.[4]

* * * * * * *

Thomas Caute Reynolds

Born on October 11, 1821, in Charleston, South Carolina, Reynolds moved to Virginia, at a young age, where he was educated at the University of Virginia.

4. *O.R.*, vol.13: 339; *O.R.*, vol. 22, pt. 1: 416; *O.R.*, vol. 22, pt. 2: 811; Bartels, *Confederate Surrender*, "Reed, J" entry; Bartels, *Trans-Mississippi Men*, 3, 161; Bevier, 68; Crute, *Confederate Staff*, 158; Duncan, 8, 15, 21–22, 25, 27, 36 ; Eakin, *Missouri Prisoners of War*, "Reid, John W." entry; Edwards, 449; 158; Etcheson, 55, 122, 364; Goodrich, 158–161; Hale, 270, 312; Heitman, vol. 2:65; *History of Audrain County*, 40; Lademann, "Prisoner of War," 441; McGhee, *Letter and Order Book*, B, 11–12, 168, Index "Reid, John W." entry; McGhee, *Service With the Guard*, 20, 38–39, 44, 51–52, 64–65; Monaghan, 80–81; Nichols, 157; Peterson, et.al., 15, 34; Rassieur, 7; Wikipedia.org, keyword, "John William Reid; Ryle, 73; Welch, 5–7.

Reynolds graduated in 1842 and obtained a law degree two years later. After graduation, he traveled extensively in Europe, where he gained a proficiency in French, German and Spanish. In 1846, he was in Madrid, Spain, serving in the U.S. Legation and upon termination of his appointment he returned to the United States, settling in St. Louis in 1850.

Reynolds was described as a "short, full-bodied man" or "short stocky man with jet black hair, and eyes habitually shaded by gold-rimmed spectacles." Another contemporary supporter noted that Reynolds was "a man of medium height and compact mould, with regular features that were at once refined and strong–a rather handsome man. His jet black hair and beard were closely cut." Another recalled that "Politically" he was "a hardline secessionist Democrat," who severed as the U.S. District Attorney for Missouri (1853–1857), during which time he befriended C. F. Jackson, the future Governor of Missouri. As an attorney "he was possessed of great natural ability, and his mind was both vigorous and acute. He was of an unusually calm, well-balanced temperate, self possessed and not easily excited." Despite his love for the law, Reynolds was drawn into the fierce political debate that permeated Missouri in the years proceeding the Civil War, causing him to spend a large amount of his time involved in politics. Being "a cultivated scholar and a fluent speaker" propelled Reynolds forward in the Missouri political arena, though above all else he excelled "in council and action."

In 1860, Reynolds aligned himself with C.F. Jackson, running for lieutenant governor of Missouri. To Reynolds, "A radical and extreme 'fire-eater'" the reason for running for office were rather simple–he realized "the actualities and the possibilities of that position in the trouble times." In August 1860, he was elected lieutenant governor by 14, 687 votes, over his nearest opponent which also made him speaker of the Missouri Senate. Upon taking office as lieutenant governor on January 3, 1861, Reynold, "the leading proponent of secession in Missouri," moved quickly to assert his position. Holding a meeting with like minded individuals, Reynolds caused the introduction of three pieces of legislation, that were meant to remove Missouri from the Union: First–The Military Bill, giving the Governor "absolute control of the State." Second–An Act Creating a Board of Police Commission, which gave the Governor and his agents "power to suppress mobs," thus limiting the power of local Unionist officials of St. Louis. Third–An Act Calling for a State Convention to consider the secession question. Of the three bills, the second and third passed while the first bill was held up by political maneuvering.

As the lieutenant governor, according to one author, Reynolds "had a brilliancy of planning and boldness of execution that Governor Jackson lacked. In fact he prepared many of Jackson's papers for him and put out a number of his own initiatives." Reynolds was considered "the most accomplished, the clearest-headed and the strongest man connected with the " Missouri State Government. Governor Jackson, as a result, used Reynolds as a diplomat to the Southern states, seeking aid in Missouri's bid for secession. In the end Reynold's efforts would gain support for their sister Southern states, but would prove to no avail. The State Convention was held on February 28, 1861, and completed its work on March 22–Missouri would remain in the Union.

With the beginning of the Civil War, Missouri attempted to remain neutral, but that all vanished when Federal forces captured Camp Jackson, in St. Louis, on May 10, 1861. The Military Bill was resurrected in the Missouri Legislature and passed easily. General Lyon, commanding Federal forces in Missouri, captured Jefferson City, causing Jackson and Reynolds to flee. Reynolds would remain on as the lieutenant governor of Confederate Missouri, until the death of Governor Jackson on December 7, 1862.

During the war Reynolds continued Missouri's government in exile, operating out of Marshall. Texas. Upon formation, of the "Committee of Public Safety," by the governors of the Trans-Mississippi, Reynolds was elected Chairman of the Committee. His selection as chairman was "indication of his standing with his fellow" governors, according to Arthur Kirkpatrick– indeed the position "made him, next to General Smith, the most important official in the Trans-Mississippi." In 1864, he supported Sterling Price leading an expedition into Missouri and subsequently accompanied the expedition, serving as an aide-de-camp to General J. O. Shelby. Reynolds served as the Confederate Missouri Governor until the end of the war. At the conclusion of the war Reynolds refused to send a telegram to E. Kirby Smith "with instructions to surrender the Trans-Mississippi Department"– the only governor to refuse to surrender. The surrender completed, Reynolds fled to Mexico, where he remained until 1868, when he returned to St. Louis.

Reynolds post-war activities included, reopening his law office, a term in Missouri's Legislature (1874) and an appointment as a diplomat to South and Central America (1886). In "declining mental and physical health" and "plagued by 'persistent melancholy' and 'hallucinations' he died in 1887 [March 30] from a fall down an elevator shaft, a presumed suicide."[5]

* * * * * * *

Charles E. Salomon

Charles E. Salomon was the eldest of three brothers, who immigrated to the United States following the 1848 German Revolution. Charles, who spoke English, French and German, was born on June 21, 1822, in Stemmern, Prussia, while his brother Edward, the Governor of Wisconsin, was born in 1828, and

5. Banasik, *Confederate Tales of the War,1864–1865*, 253–254; Banasik, *Missouri in 1861*, 352; Faust, 626–627; Gerteis, *St. Louis*, 334; Arthur Roy Kirkpatrick, "Missouri In the Early Months of the Civil War," *Missouri Historical Review* 55 (May, 1961), 248; Kirkpatrick, "Missouri on the Eve of Civil War," 100, 104–106; Kirkpatrick, "Missouri Secessionist Government," 134; Laughlin, 586; McElroy, 27, 32–33; Moore, *Missouri, Confederate Military History*, 14; Peckham, 27; Thomas C. Reynolds, "Circular," dated August 20, 1863, in Washington Telegraph (October 7,1863); Ryle, 146 n. 155, 175, 181–182; Smith, *Blair Family*, vol. 1:496; Snead, *Fight for Missouri*. 30–33.

Frederick was born in 1826. An engineer by profession, Charles Salomon served in the Prussian Army as an engineer officer, fought in the 1848 Revolution, on the losing side, and subsequently fled to the United States in 1849, settling in St. Louis in 1850, where he worked as a surveyor, and, in 1860, he defeated U.S. Grant for the position of County Engineer. With the coming of the Civil War, Salomon was elected a captain on May 4, 1861 of his company, and then colonel of the 5th Missouri Infantry (Three months), on May 18, 1861. Salomon led his regiment at Carthage and Wilson's Creek, avoiding capture following Sigel's defeat in the early part of the August 10 battle. Following Wilson's Creek the 5th returned to St. Louis where the regiment and Salomon were mustered out on August 26. Salomon was heavily criticized for his performance at Wilson's Creek by the local German newspapers, which unfairly labeled him a coward. Returning to civilian life, Salomon re-entered the army in the Summer of 1862, following the promotion of his brother Frederick to brigadier general in June–his brother, the governor of Wisconsin, appointed Charles colonel of the German-speaking 9th Wisconsin Infantry effective September 26, 1862. Charles joined his new command at Sarcoxie, Missouri, in late September 1862, remaining with it until the unit attained veteran status in 1864. The highlight of Salomon's career occurred on April 30, 1864, when he assumed command of his brigade at the Battle of Jenkin's Ferry and "led it through the heaviest part of the action, and by his presence and personal disregard of danger, encouraged his men in the performance of their whole duty." General Frederick Steele further noted that Salomon "managed the [brigade] with skill." Following the Camden Expedition, Salomon, with the non-veterans of the 9th Wisconsin, were mustered out of the service on November 17, 1864, at Little Rock. Arkansas. Returning to Wisconsin, Salomon left the army on December 4. For his service Salomon was breveted a brigadier general on March 13, 1865, "for meritorious service during the war." Nothing is known of his post-war years other than he died in Salt Lake City, Utah on January 9, 1881.[6]

* * * * * * *

Joseph Wofford Tucker

Joseph W. Tucker, "a gentleman of great intelligence," was born in 1832, in South Carolina, where he "enjoyed a successful career" Of his many accomplishments, "he practiced law, was elected to the state legislature, edited the *Carlina Spartan*, and became president of the Spartanburg Female College."

Following financial difficulties Tucker immigrated to St. Louis where he was

---

6. *O.R.*, vol. 3:15–18, 86–88; *O.R.*, vol. 34, pt.1: 671, 690; Gerteis, *Missouri*, 18; Heitman, vol. 1: 857; Hunt & Brown, 531; Piston & Hatcher, *Wilson's Creek*, 189, 255, 323; Edwin Bentlee Quiner, *Military History of Wisconsin; A Record of the Civil and Military Patriotism of the State in the Late War for the Union, With A History of the Campaigns in Which Wisconsin Soldiers Have Been Conspicuous—Regimental Histories—Sketches of Distinguished Officers—The Roll of the Illustrious Dead—Movements of the Legislature and State Officers, etc.* (Chicago, 1868), 542, 545, 547; Sifakis, *Who Was Who in the Union*, 351; *Union Army*, vol. 4: 258; Winter, 124.

the owner and editor of the St. Louis *Missouri State Journal*–a decided, extreme, Southern newspaper. In addition to his newspaper business, Tucker was also an ordained Southern Methodist minister, being often referred too as "deacon." On July 12, 1861, the *Journal* was suppressed by order of General Lyon, "a blow in the right direction [which]...ought to have been done a month ago," according to the *Chicago Tribune*. And two days later Tucker was arrested for treason, paid s $10.000 fine and then fled St. Louis for southwest Missouri

After Tucker was arrested his office was searched and a letter, supposed to have been written by Governor Jackson to Tucker, was found. The letter, according to James Peckham, "more than any other document...justified the policy of Lyon" in taking Camp Jackson, proving Lyon "to be a man of great foresight and knowledge." However, Christopher Phillips, biographer of Governor Jackson, raises several concerns about the letter, following an analysis of the hand writing, as well as the circumstances of its seizure. Despite having used the letter in the past in a different article on Jackson, Phillips no longer chose to "use it as evidence of Jackson secessionist impulses." The letter was subsequently offered as evidence in the trial of Tucker, but ruled inadmissable and given to "one of the United States judges, and by them detained , so that no copy of it could be obtained for publication." However, even as the July Missouri Convention was opened the letter was published in the *New York Tribune* and used as justification to vacate the three chief officers of Missouri.

Following his escape from St. Louis, Tucker joined Price's Army at Neosho and partnered with William F. Wisely to publish a series of army newspapers, beginning with the *Platte City Missouri Argus*. And when Price's Army crossed the Mississippi, in April 1862, so did Tucker and Wisely, the pair being referred too as the army's "printer and editors." Known as Price's "organ" or mouthpiece, the *Argus and Crisis* was next published in Jackson, Mississippi, but when Price returned to the Trans-Mississippi, Tucker moved to Mobile, Alabama, with his partner, where they continued publishing the *Argus and Crisis* in January 1864, and Tucker was appointed or assumed the title of "Judge."

Wanting to do more for the Confederate cause, Tucker took on the role of a rebel saboteur, attacking Federal shipping on the western rivers with a small band of followers. As the war progressed Tucker's band proved to be most successful, "in the destruction of so much valuable property and life,"sinking a minimum of 13 vessels in 1863. In February 1864, Tucker went to Richmond, Virginia, with the support of Senator John B. Clark, Sr., to lobby the War Department to sanction his activities. Tucker desired either a commission or a simple order for him and his men to organize an official "secret service" that would target a variety of targets including river shipping, naval yards, stores and transports. Not having a reply from the War Department, Tucker wrote a private letter to Jefferson Davis on March 14, outlining his plan. On March 21, 1864, the Secretary of War, James A. Seddon approved Tucker's plan.

By April 1865, the Federal authorities, admitted that it was "impossible to obtain a correct amount of the property destroyed" by Tucker's command "during the war," though the loss of the seventy steamboats in St. Louis, alone, would seem to indicate that it was substantial. Tucker was never caught, he survived the war, though his final disposition was not known.[7]

7. *O.R.*, vol. 24, pt.3: 1066; *O.R.*, vol. 32, pt. 2: 13; *O.R.*, vol. 48, pt. 2:194–196; *O.R.*, vol. 52, pt. 2: 763; *O.R.*, Series 2, vol. 8: 516; *O.R.*, Series 4, vol. 3: 125–126, 239; C. "Affairs In Missouri," *Chicago Tribune*, July 10, 18, and 24, 1861; Carolyn M. Bartels, *True Tales: Civil War in Missouri* (Independence, MO, 2002), 150–152; Castel, 133,194; Hale, 32; Library of Congress. *Newspapers in Microform*, vol. 1:8; Peckham, 286–287; Phillips, *Missouri's Confederate*, 249–250 n. 10; Piston & Sweeney, *Portraits of Conflict, Missouri*, 195; Robert G. Schultz, ed., *General Sterling Price and the Confederacy* (St. Louis, 2009), 48, 54–55, 266 n.40; "The Struggle in Missouri," *Charleston Mercury* (Charleston, SC), January 14, 1862; William F. Swindler, "The Southern Press In Missouri," *Missouri Historical Review* 35 (July, 1941), 396, 398–399.

Appendix C
Extended Comments

Item: The court-martials of David Murphy and why he left the army in 1861.[1]

During the course of his service, Murphy was court-martialed three separate times; all of which were connected to drinking.

Within days of entering the army, on July 1, 1861, Murphy had a confrontation with a private from his company, who was not performing as was expected. Murphy then called the private a "damned son of a bitch," threw stones at him, and hitting him with his scabbard. Murphy was charged with "conduct unbecoming an officer" on July 11. Unknown as to final outcome.

On May 26, 1862, while his company was garrisoning Sedalia, Missouri, Murphy was informed that his men tried to purchase some liquor from a local merchant, but were denied. Murphy then went to the merchant, forcing him to sell the brew. Returning to his camp Murphy and his company got drunk and returning to town came into conflict with the men of the 26th Indiana Infantry. As to what happened next Thomas J. Keith of the 26th recorded the following:

> This afternoon there was a riot in town between members of the 1st Mo. Battery [Company F] and the soldiers of the 26th [Indiana Infantry]. The artillerists came into town with their Capt. [David Murphy] got drunk and commenced an attack on the Indianans. The fight soon became general. The artillerists fighting with their pistols and the infantry with knives and stones[.] [F]inally the artillerists getting the worst of it, went to their camp and brought down four pieces of cannon with the avowed intention of shelling the town, and our camp, simultaneously[.] [O]ur Reg't was called out under arms to quell the riot, and for a while a general fight seemed immanent, but the coolness & courage of Col. [William M.] Wheatly saved further loss of blood. The force on each side went to their respective quarters. The result of the whole thing was the wounding of several men on each side some of whom will die and the badly scaring of the citizens of Sedalia, who fled in dismay, and [in] the most abject terror from the time on[.] All together it was a lamentable thing and is to be traced to intoxicating drink.

Overall two men were killed and two were wounded. And as before, the results of the trial were unknown.

The third recorded incident of Murphy's insubordination occurred in July 1862, when his battery was stationed in Springfield, Missouri. A drunken Murphy

---

1. National Archives, Record Group 405, roll no. 310, Union Compiled Service Records, 1st Missouri Artillery Regiment; Thomas C. Keith Diary, August 1861–June 1862, Missouri Historical Society (St. Louis).

had proceeded to General E. B. Brown's headquarters and insulted the general. He was immediately arrested and placed under arrest. The following day Murphy begged forgiveness citing the fact that he had imbibe too much liquor—the results of the subsequent court-martial are unknown.

As to why Murphy left the army, following the capture of Vicksburg on July 4, 1863, it was found that Murphy seemed to have been discouraged as to his future in the service. On July 8, 1863, he submitted his resignation; two days later it was accepted. In submitting his resignation Murphy cited four reasons:

1. All the batteries in the 1st Missouri Artillery Regiment were parceled out to the various brigades, negating the need for field officers unnecessary in the regiment.
2. As a volunteer major in the U.S. Army he was ineligible to enter the Regular Army except by special appointment.
3. The Chief of Artillery, in the division, could be handled by a captain.
4. He couldn't find another position in the army so he would look elsewhere for a post "which I [can] conscientiously serve my country."

Following the acceptance of his resignation Murphy returned to St. Louis where he resumed his civilian life; however, there was probably more to Murphy's departure from the army, which may have caused him to be unacceptable as noted by his personal behavior.

* * * * * * *

Item: The Battle of Carthage—The Engagement at Dry Fork Creek (12:00 a.m. –2:00 p.m.).[2]

In withdrawing his command to the south side of Dry Fork Creek, during the noon hour, Sigel divided his force into two parts; Lieutenant Colonel Hassendeubel led his 1st Battalion, 3rd Missouri, with Wilkin's Artillery to supplement the train guard, and Lieutenant Colonel Christian D. Wolff led the 1st Battalion, 5th Missouri, following behind Hassendeubel across Dry Fork Creek. The remainder of Sigel's command, under Colonel Charles E. Salomon took their position on the south side of Dry Fork Creek, covering the only ford across the stream. Essig's artillery covered the ford of the creek, supported by a company from his regiment of his left and another two from the 3rd Missouri on his right. Two additional companies from the 5th served "as a reserve behind both wings."

Hassendeubel's detachment, with Essig's Battery pulled out of the line first, according to M. M. Parsons (Adamson says it was Salmon's detachment), while

---

2. *O.R.*, vol. 3: 18, 23–24, 30–31, 35–36; Adamson, 151; Banasik, *Missouri in 1861*, 203; Biever, 37–38; Brooksher, 122–123; "Col. Burbridge's Regiment," 21–22; Gerteis, *Missouri*, 47; "Great Battle In South Western Missouri," *Waukegan Weekly Gazette*, July 11, 1861; Hinze & Farnham, 143–162: Ingenthron, 47; Moore, *Missouri, Confederate Military History*, 49; Pollard, 158; Schrantz, 37–38; *Rebellion Record*, Vol. 2: Diary 20; Snead, *Fight for Missouri*, 226–227; Union Army, vol. 5: 228.

Salomon's command acted as the rear guard, retiring slowly, to cover Hassend-eubel's detachment which was hurrying off to the train. Crossing Dry Fork Creek, Hassendeubel continued southward to link up with the train, while Essig placed his guns, "masking" their position, in the woods to cover the retreat of the other troops. It was about noon and "Sigel's men were well across the ford when Jackson's forces left the ridge and rolled down the hill" toward Dry fork Creek.

On the northern slope of Double Trouble Creek there was an initial hesitation as to what to do when the Federals pulled back. Colonel Richard Weightman extended his line on his right adding Colonel Edgar Hurst's regiment. His line fully extended, Weightman ordered an advance toward Dry Fork Creek, without orders, and seemingly without any direction from Governor Jackson. To Weightman's left General Slack's infantry followed suit On the far left of the Guard line General Clark, seeing Weightman and Slack advance, consulted with General Parson and they too joined in the advance, the whole line being "in some disorder," according to Thomas Snead. At 400 yards from the creek Essig's Battery opened fire, momentarily halting the rebel advance.

Upon receiving fire from the enemy,, the Guard raced on forward, across the open prairie, and field, with their first "rebel yell," finally reaching the cover of the timber on the northern bank of Dry Fork Creek. And at close range, from 40–50 yards, the two sides traded small arms fire while, Essig's Battery pelted the Guard line with grape and canister. Even with their superior numbers, the State troops were unable to cross the 30-foot wide stream, due its depth, causing Weightman and Slack to halt, while John Graves and Hurst's Regiments looked for a crossing farther up stream. To Slack's left Parsons and Clark also experienced stiff resistence, the fire "incessant and fierce" in the face of "obstinance" Union resistance. And even as the Guard infantry opened fire, Bledsoe's Battery wheeled into position and joined in, using the small amount of cannister and grape that they had for the first time–it was 1:00 p.m.

In the meantime, troops on the Guard left, probably Colonel Burbridge's command (or possibly Grave's or Hurst's Regiments on the right), "threw a quantity of timber into the stream and commenced crossing in large numbers." With their position turned, the Federals abandoned the Dry Fork line, leapfrogging their artillery to provide covering fire while they pulled back to their trains which were already engaged with the flanking Guard cavalry. However this time the retreat "was not conducted in as good order as the former one," according to George Taylor. In fact, the *Waukegan Weekly Gazette* further reported that Sigel's "lines were nearly broken, when ...the arrival of 200 Union men from Shoal Creek" saved the Union position, losing five killed and two mortally wounded.

Overall the engagement at Dry Fork Creek had lasted about two hours; It was near 2:00 p.m. when Sigel retreated from Dry Fork Creek and hurried back to his train which was already under fire from rebel cavalry to his rear.

* * * * * * *

Item: Lyon's march to Springfield, Missouri, July 3–13, 1861

Following his capture of Boonville, on June 17, Lyon had difficulty obtaining transport and supplies for the journey to Springfield. On June 23 "eleven boat-loads of supplies finally arrived in Boonville," however, the number of wagons were still lacking, having only one hundred teams and wagons by June 27. The State troops had previously "taken the best animals," leaving him a lot of "decrepit animals" which one participant described as "sick and lame." And the conveyances were no better, being nothing more than "broken down and rickety vehicles." Finally, after spending $20,000, according to one source, which Lyon was not authorized to spend, he secured about 150 wagons or half of what he needed. General Lyon departed Boonville on July 3. At 10:00 a.m.,"with drums beating and flags floating," Lyon headed to Springfield, the day being "hotter than the fever heat of the infernal regions," while a herd of cattle brought up the rear.

For their first day of the march the command made about 12–15 miles, camping at 4:00 p.m. July 4 was a normal day for Lyon's men–"Not a gun was fired, nary [a] speech, no firecrackers, nobody to speak, and nothing to drink in honor, etc. of the day" as Lyon refused to even fire a customary salute–still 16–19 more miles were logged by the Lyon's troops. Rain greeted Lyon's command on July 5, as they made only 12 miles, camping at noon, being greeted by "terrific lightening" in mid-morning. The sky was clear on the 6th with the command making 20–23 miles, having started at 5:00 a.m., camping at 2:00 p.m. to avoid the heat of the day. July 7, continued the hot spell, with no rain, as Lyon reached the Grand River, following a twenty mile tramp, camping a short distance from Clinton about noon, where he found Sturgis command waiting.[3]

The day before Lyon met Price at the Planter's house, on June 11, he had ordered Major Samuel Sturgis to Kansas City, to break up a rebel band that was reported in the area. On June 10, Sturgis relocated his command, of U.S. Regulars from Ft. Leavenworth, with the 1st Kansas Infantry (Three months), to Kansas City, and, upon arrival, found the city empty of any rebel forces. And with the capture of Boonville, on June 17th, Lyon further directed Sturgis to march his 2,200-man Kansas command to join him at the Clinton, Missouri bridge which crossed the Grand River about a mile from Clinton.

Before Sturgis headed for Clinton, he was joined by the 2nd Kansas Infantry (Three months), on June 19, and mustered the unit the following day. With his command assembled and the necessary supplies obtained, Sturgis departed Kansas City, at noon, on June 24 (others have the date as June 26). Sturgis's

---

3. Note: The milage specified varied depending on whose account was used. Ware's account was the higher number while Jacob Ritner (Larimer's book) was the lower number. Banasik, *Missouri in 1861*, 101–103; Britton, 70–71; Brooksher, 104, 117–118; Burke, 4; Larimer, 38–42; Kathleen White Miles, *Bitter Ground: The Civil War in Missouri's Golden Valley Benton, Henry, and St. Clair Counties* (Warsaw, MO, 1971),67, hereafter cited as Miles; Monaghan, 146; Phillips, *Damned Yankee*, 225–226, 228; Piston & Hatcher, *Wilson's Creek*, 74; Ware, 159, 161, 165, 168, 170, 175; Woodard, 290–292.

command, like Lyon's column, experienced the same "unfavorable weather" which delayed the march–still, an advance party of Sturgis's force arrived at the Clinton bridge on July 3. The remainder of Sturgis boys arrived early on July 4, where they established Camp Washington, there to await the arrival of Lyon; the "water still being too high in the bottom to gain access to the bridge." And while they waited for the "bridge guard," Sturgis' boys celebrated the "85th Anniversary of American independence" by firing a 34 gun salute "to arouse in the heart such patriotic feelings as former civic celebrations had never done." The bridge guard arrived on July 7, however, the water was still too high, so Sturgis moved his command "down river about nine miles to the ferry" where they united with Lyon in the early afternoon near what was known as "Big Ripple" or the Thornton Ferry. And even as Sturgis arrived at Lyon's location, the work had already begun at crossing the Grand River.[4]

To cross the Grand River, three men from the 1st Iowa swam the river, pulling cords attached to a two inch thick rope or "ferry ropes" that formed the basis for pulling boats across the river. After attaching the thick ropes to trees on the opposite bank, several more men crossed the Grand using the rope as their guide to serve as a guard, ensuring the security of the rope line. By nightfall on July 7, scouts had returned with one large and one small flat boat to serve as the ferry in addition to several small "skiffs." Additionally, the river bottom leading to the river was covered with water necessitating the building of a corduroy road to get to the ferry. And so the work of ferrying the joint command continued day and night, with bonfires providing the necessary light to make the crossing. And to make matters worse, it rained beginning at 3:00 a.m. on July 8, soaking the command as it crossed. It would take days for Lyon's command to cross the Grand, as the large boat or "scow" could only carry forty troops at a time or one wagon at the rate of only three conveyances per hour.[5]

On July 8, with Sturgis' cavalry and the infantry from his original column, Lyon crossed the Grand River, while the 1st Iowa came over last. Lyon then sent his cavalry forward to the Osage River, with an infantry regiment, to secure the ferry over the Osage River near Osceola. At 7:00 p.m., on July 8, a messenger arrived in camp (Adamson, Phillips, Snead and other writers say this occurred on July 9) alerting General Lyon to Sigel's defeat at Carthage. Lyon immediately determined to come to the Sigel's aid by making a forced march to Springfield with a portion of his command while the rest would follow as best they could. During the night additional rafts were built in the Kansas commands to ferry the troops across the Grand as quickly as possible; however, the rafts proved unsuccessful and Sturgis's infantry, artillery and wagons were slow in crossing, having to take the flat boats. The 1st Iowa was the last of Lyon's original troops to head for the

---

4. *O.R.S.*, pt.1, vol. 1: 239; Brooksher, 94; Burke, 4; Crawford, 25; Fry, 19,23; Miles,71; Phillips, *Damned Yankee*, 223; Piston & Hatcher, *Soldiers' Letters*, 37–38, 45–48; Piston & Hatcher, *Wilson's Creek*, 69–70; Ware, 165, 176; *War in the West*, 160.

5. Adamson, 156–157; Miles, 70; Ware, 176–177; Woodard, 292.

Osage. They were up at 3:30 a.m. on July 9, and by 6:00 a.m. were on the road, even as Sturgis' infantry continued to cross the Grand River. Following a march of 18–25 miles, the Iowa troops finally caught up with Lyon's column at the Osage River, who were already crossing.[6]

Crossing the Osage proved to be less troublesome than the Grand River, as Lyon's advance captured the ferry boat when they arrived at the river on the evening of July 8. And by mid-night of July 10, the last of Lyon's column had crossed the Osage and they in turn were followed by Sturgis' Kansans. Three hours after getting his column across the Osage, Lyon broke camp on July 11. and forced marched to Springfield. Twenty miles from the Osage, the Sac River was crossed near noon, the column then stooped briefly for lunch, at 3:00 p.m., then continued their march until sundown, rested but a short time and moved on, marching through the night. At noon, on July 12, Lyon finally halted his command, having marched about 50 miles, with but a two hour rest in the last two days. On the 13th Lyon rode ahead with his staff and a "small escort," of ten men from the 1st U.S. Cavalry, arriving in Springfield in the "early evening hour," while his command lagged about three hours behind, camping about 12–15 miles from the city, near Little York. There, the command would await the arrival of the Kansas troops which finally caught up with the rest of Lyons' troops by the 13th, just a few hours behind the bulk of Lyons' column. As it turned out Springfield was in no danger, Sigel having successfully disengaged from the State troops at Carthage.[7]

For now Lyons' joint command rested–Lyons' and Sturgis' men camped near Little York, west of Springfield, while Sigel's troops were located south of the city on the Forsyth Road, all awaiting the inevitable showdown with the rebel troops at Wilson's Creek

* * * * * * *

Item: The Skirmish of Dug Springs, August 2, 1861.[8]

On August 1, General Lyon received information that the rebels were advancing on Springfield, in three separate columns. Hoping to attack and defeat the center column, before engaging the other two weaker forces. Lyon departed

---

6. Adamson, 158; Brooksher, 128–129; Larimer, 44; Moore, *Missouri, Confederate Military History*, 50; Phillips, *Damned Yankee*, 228–229; Piston & Hatcher, *Soldiers' Letters*, 53; Snead, *Fight for Missouri*, 249; Snead,"First Year," 269; Ware, 179, 183–185.

7. *O.R.*, vol. 3: 394; Adamson, 159–162; Britton, 71; Holcombe & Adams, 8; Larimer, 46; Moore, *Missouri, Confederate Military History*, 51; Phillips, *Damned Yankee*, 230; Snead, *Fight for Missouri*, 249; Ware, 193–194 , 196, 205; Woodard, 291–294.

8. *O.R.*, vol. 3: 47–52; *O.R.S.*, pt.1, vol. 1: 226–227, 239–240; Banasik, *Missouri in 1861*, 132–133,135; Bearss, *Wilson's Creek*, 14–16, 24–26; Britton, 80–81; Crawford, 27–28; Dyer, 709; "Fight At Dug Springs," *Rebellion Record*, vol. 2: Doc. 468–471; Holcombe & Adams, 12; Piston & Hatcher, *Wilson's Creek*, 139–141; Ware, 269–270, 272; Wherry, "General Lyon," 81–82; Woodard, 206–208.

Springfield between 5:00–6:00 p.m.,marched into the night, camping ten miles past Springfield, on the Fayetteville Road, near Wilson's Creek. The last units to arrive came from near Little York, and encamped at 3:00 a.m. on August 2. Three hours later the camp was awaken by various personnel, the bugle and drum being quiet as they "were in the presence of the enemy."

The advance on August 2, was led by Captain Frederick Steele's Infantry Battalion, supported by James Totten's Artillery. The day was exceedingly hot, with the temperature rising to 110° before the end of the day and with the sacristy of water, "the thirst of the men was unendurable,"causing many to drop out of the march. Still, on they marched , buoyed by the prospects of engaging the enemy.

The skirmish at Dug Springs began at 9 A.M., according to Franc Wilkie, a newspaper correspondent, traveling with the advance. A rebel instigated the skirmish, according to Wilkie, with a long range shot that fell well short of his intended target. With rebel cavalry in their front Captain Steele deployed his battalion of the 2nd U.S. Infantry; two companies on each side of the road, with Totten's Battery in support. Totten's command responded to the sentry's shot, scattering the rebels in the distance with a couple of rounds from a six-pound gun.

Following the initial contact with the rebel pickets, Steele's Federal troops advanced cautiously forward trying to develop the position and strength of the enemy. Supporting Steel's regulars was a troop of cavalry under Captain D. S. Stanley. Meanwhile, General Lyon with the remainder of the army pulled back about a mile and a half to encamp at the Hayden farm near the water as his men craved the precious liquid desperately. As the day progressed both sides continued to pop away at each other with no appreciable results.

With arrival of James Rains' MSG men, near 5:00 p.m., the rebels pushed forward, with Colonel Jesse Cravens leading 150 men into the fight. The move unhinged the Unionists, who retreated a bit to the safety of their artillery and their reserve units. General Rains reported driving the Feds "back in utmost confusion," but such was not the case--as the Union skirmishers did what they were supposed to do when confronted with a superior force; retreat to their main body.

The advancing rebels were then met a 25-man platoon of Company C, 1st U.S. Dragoons, commanded by Lieutenant Michael J. Kelly. According to William Wherry, an aide to General Lyon, Kelly's command had been goaded into action to protect the Federal skirmishers who were falling back. A Sergeant Sullivan moved

Captain James Totten

the men forward, against orders, and was quickly followed by the impetuous Kelly, who took over from Sullivan. Captain Stanley, commander of Kelly's unit, ordered recall sounded, but Kelly ignored the bugle and made his attack anyway. After the battle Stanley disciplined the young Kelly, but Lyon commended him for the action and further, recommended Kelly for promotion.

When Kelly made his charge, which Ashbel Woodard described "as brilliant in results as rash in conception," he did so to thwart a Confederate move around the Union left, which was pushing back the Union infantry. Rains in his official report admits that he tried to flank the enemy at this time, but Totten's artillery opened upon Rains' flanking column, "a portion of whom, became panic stricken and retired in the utmost confusion." Steele, for his part, claims that Kelly made his charge after the rebels were routing from the field. Franc Wilkie, Union reporter, supports Rains' account of the incident–either way the results were the same; the rebels were driven from the field in confusion.

After Kelly's charge the skirmish abruptly ended. Steele did not follow up the retreating rebels, being ordered by General Lyon to fall back to a new position. The Confederates, for their part, regrouped and continued to monitor the front. Captain James McIntosh, who was called upon for support, never arrived, as he "respectfully declined," to support Rains, because Rains had "unadvisedly" engaged the enemy.

Losses on both sides at Dug Springs were minor; the Federals reported losing four killed and seven wounded. However, in Dyer's *Compendium*, Federal losses were reported as 4 killed and 37 wounded, and Surgeon Phillip C. Davis, of the Regular Army, recorded Federal losses as "twelve or fourteen killed, and about forty wounded." Additionally, General Frémont, the department commander, reported the Federal losses as 8 killed and 30 wounded while causing the rebels 40 killed and 44 wounded. Since the Federals gave up the field immediately after the battle, and went into camp, this last comment seems a bit far-fetched, considering General Rains, reported his loss as six wounded. That said, Franc Wilkie, a newspaper correspondent traveling with Lyon's command reported finding one dead rebel and 18 wounded in houses close to the battlefield on the day following the engagement. Other news reporting, at the time, put the Confederate losses at "twenty-five killed and sixty to one hundred wounded.".

Overall the real impact of the August 2 engagement, according to William Piston and Richard Hatcher, was "on the relationship between the Missouri State Guard and the rest of the Southern forces. Honor was all-important to these men, and 'Rains's Scare' as the episode became known, reflected negatively on the Missourians." Soldiers' letters home labeled the Missourians "'dastardly cowards,'" noting in another case that they "ran like cowards." To many in the regular Confederate forces the MSG had yet to prove their worth, but Wilson's Creek would change all that.

* * * * * * *

Item: The problems that Frémont faced upon his arrival in St. Louis.

According to Frémont, when he arrived in Missouri, he "found himself in the enemy's county...and the State of Missouri was in active rebellion against the national authority." Further, he was on his own hook in Missouri, with little support coming from the Federal Government, and, the weapons, which he had procured in New York, were stripped from him and given to Eastern troops. And upon reviewing his command, Frémont found he had 23,000 troops, 8,000 of whom were three months' men, whose term of service was about to expire. Further, of the eight regiments at Cairo, which Frémont considered a key to holding Missouri, six regiments were three months' men, whose terms expired on July 28, three days after Frémont's arrival. Also, at the time of his arrival, Frémont was threatened with the real possibility of an invasion from southeast Missouri, and western Kentucky, by rebels under General Polk, who realized that he had an excellent chance of taking St. Louis because of Lyon's absence.

To counter Polk's movements Frémont led a small fleet of river boats to Cairo on August 1, with "what troops he could gather [about 3,800]." The movement was made "with as much display as possible, in order to increase the apparent size of his small force," according to Frémont's Adjutant John C. Kelton. Of the remaining troops, under Frémont, some were with General John Pope securing north Missouri, others garrisoned important Missouri cities like Boonville, Jefferson City, Rolla and Lexington. And Lyon's command, which had over extended its line of communication, was located in southwestern Missouri, where the combined rebel force numbered about 15,000, including 2,000 unarmed recruits.[9]

Further compounding Frémont's problems was the lack of funds to run the Department, which Isaac H. Sturgeon, Assistant Treasure of the United States, refused to release the funds under his care. Writing to the President on July 30, Frémont noted that troops had not been paid "and some regiments ...[were] in a state of mutiny, and the men whose term of service,,, [had] expired generally refuse[d[to enlist."[10]

To Frémont, his priority was to secure St. Louis, which was directly threatened from southeast Missouri and Columbus, Kentucky, where the Confederates number about 22,000, and, according to Chester Harding of Lyon's staff, "no adequate preparation was made to meet it," prior to Frémont's arrival. Local newspapers also noted that a "greatest of anxiety" existed in St. Louis for Cairo and Bird's Point; In other words "there are not men enough for active operations in" Missouri. And the key to securing St. Louis, according to Frémont, was holding Cairo, Illinois, at the confluence of the Ohio and Mississippi Rivers.

However, Major John M. Schofield, Lyon's Adjutant General, believed that

9. *O.R.*, vol. 3:400–403, 411, 420,608; Adamson, 177, 180; Bearss, *Wilson Creek*, 21; C., "Affairs In Missouri," *Chicago Tribune*, August 7, 1861; Crawford, 29; Frémont, 278–280; Gerteis, *Missouri*, 55–57; Holcombe & Adams, 18; O'Flaherty, 74–75; *War in the West*, 95, 99.

10. *O.R.*, vol. 3: 416–417; Frémont, 280.

Lyon's requests for reenforcements should have been given priority and that St. Louis could be defended by the Home Guard. To author James Peckham, any threat coming from southeast Missouri or Columbus, Kentucky, was nothing more than "balderdash" and "Springfield was the place to defend St. Louis."[11].

Disagreeing with Schofield and Peckham, Anselm Albert of, Frémont's staff, testified before Congress that Frémont had no "troops to spare in St. Louis, and every place in Missouri was threatened by attack of the enemy." Albert further stated that "Bird's Point and Cairo were very important places to be taken care of."[12]

Overall, General Lyon had over extended his command and had he ended his campaign following the capture of Boonville "it would have been viewed as an unquestionable success," having "accomplished all that was strategically necessary to secure Missouri. However, Lyon "was now leading a punitive crusade... to deal summarily" with the secessionists in Missouri. And through his actions Lyon was trying to force Frémont to send him help which Frémont simply did not immediately have. Eventually, Frémont did order troops to Lyon, in Springfield, on August 5; however there was no way for them to reach Lyon on time.[13]

* * * * * * *

Item: Lyon's decision to attack at Wilson's Creek.[14]

Brigadier General John M. Schofield

In reviewing the decision to attack on August 10, John M. Schofield, who had been then Commander-in-Chief of the United States Army (!888–1895), would put forth a counter argument as to why Lyon's decision to attack was a poor choice. Writing in 1897 Schofield noted:

Lyon's personal feelings was so strongly enlisted in the Union cause, its friends were so emphatically his personal friends and its enemies his personal enemies, that he could not take the cool, soldierly view of the situation which should control the actions of a national army. If Lyon could have foreseen how many times the poor people of that section were destined to

11. Peckham, 323, 326–327; Snead, *Fight for Missouri*, 250–250.
12. *War in the West*, 265.
13. *O.R.*, vol. 3:425; Brooksher, 91–93; Peckham, 321–322; Phillips, *Damned Yankee*, 221–222.
14. Heitman, vol. 1: 865; Schofield, 39.

be overrun by the contending forces before the contest could be finally decided, his extreme solitude at that moment would have disappeared. Or if he could have risen to an appreciation of the fact that his duty, as the commander in the field of one of the most important of the national armies, was not to protect a few loyal people from the inevitable hardships of war (loss of their cattle, grain, and fences), but to make as sure as possible the defeat of the hostile army, no matter whether to-day, to-morrow, or the next month, the battle of Wilson's Creek would not have been fought."

* * * * * * *

Item: Lyon's Column at the Battle of Wilson's Creek on August 10, 1861.

Of the two Federal columns that marched to Wilson's Creek on the evening of August 9, Lyon's column was the largest, containing three of Lyon's four brigades: Major Samuel Sturgis's 1st Brigade was the smallest with 684 men; Lieutenant Colonel George L. Andrews 3rd Brigade fielded 1,116 men and Colonel George W. Deitzler's 4th Brigade contained the bulk of the command with 2,400 men.. Additionally, each of the regiments, battalions or batteries was guided by one of 20 men from the local area. In all, the column, including guides, staff, and Voerester's Pioneer Company numbered 4,334 officers and men (See Appendix D for details).[15]

Prior to departing for the rebel encampment Lyon addressed his command, according to Eugene Ware of the 1st Iowa Infantry, going to each of the various commands one after the other. "It was a tactless and chilling speech, there was nothing in it of dash, vim, or encouragement." And Private Ironquill, also of the 1st Iowa, noted that Lyon's "tone of voice was so low that it appeared as if he was talking under exhaustion." As best as Ware recalled Lyon said:

> Men, we are going to have a fight. We will march out in a short time. Don't shoot until you get orders. Fire low–don't aim higher than the knees; wait until they get close; don't get scared; it's no part of a soldier's duty to get scared.

Following Lyon's speech, muster rolls were taken, ammunition was distributed and two days' rations issued, in the form "loaves of bread [that] were about the size of an ordinary bucket." With all in readiness, the column departed Springfield at 5:00 p.m., led by Captain Charles C. Gilbet's , Company B, 1st U.S. Infantry, Plumber's Battalion of Sturgis' 1st Brigade. The column marched westward into the twilight, their artillery wheels muffled by blankets, for about five miles before heading south toward the unsuspecting rebels at Wilson's Creek. Near 1:00

---

15. Bearss, *Wilson's Creek*, 51; Banasik, *Missouri in 1861*, 376–378.

a..m. on August 10, the Federal column spied rebel camp fires about two miles to their front and halted, awaiting the dawn.[16]

At "a slight flush of dawn" Lyon resumed his advance–the time was 4:00 a.m. Led yet again by Gilbert's Company, the remainder of Sturgis' Brigade followed in column, as did the rest of Lyon's troops. Within half a mile the Unionists encountered foragers from James Rains MSG Division, who quickly retreated to the rebel camp, giving the warning of the approaching Federals. Rains in turn sent riders to General Price's headquarters, where they relayed their message of the approaching Yankees. And still later, when General McCulloch heard the report of Rains' foragers, he considered it just another of "Rains' Scares," though he did ride over to Price's headquarters to confer with the Missouri commander–the time was about 5:00 a.m.[17]

Meanwhile, Lyon's troops deployed, moving rapidly forward, with Plummer's Battalion on the left, Gilbert's boys on the right, with the 1st Missouri and Totten's Artillery forming in the center, with the remainder following. Shortly before 5:00 a.m., Lyon's advance made contact with James Cawthorn's Brigade, from Rains' command, which had positioned themselves on the northern spur of Oak Hill. Firing erupted ten minutes later, according to John McElroy, with Totten's command firing their first shots of the battle, while the rest of the line moved forward, driving Cawthorn's men from spur at 5:30.[18]

After the initial contact with Cawthorn's Brigade, Lyon reenforced his advance to secure Oak Hill. The 1st Kansas Infantry moved to the left of the main Federal line while the 1st Missouri was to the right; Totten's Battery was positioned in the center between the two infantry commands. Plummer's 1st U.S. Infantry Battalion moved off to the far left near Gibson's Mill. As the line pushed Cawthorn back across Oak Hill, Osterhaus' 2nd Missouri Battalion deployed to the right of the main Federal line. The 1st Kansas and 1st Missouri maintained their relative positions, while Totten's Battery moved to the top of Oak Hill, which placed the 1st Kansas Infantry to their left front. The 1st Iowa, the 2nd Kansas and Frederick Steele's Battalion, with DuBois' Battery were held in reserve.[19]

Even as Lyon was securing Oak Hill, he directed Joseph Plummer to cross Wilson's Creek with his battalion of regulars and Clark's Home Guard command, to assault the rebels from that quarter. Spying the move, Ben McCulloch shifted the 3rd Louisiana (Louis Herbert's Regiment) and the 2nd Arkansas Rifles (James McIntosh's command) to meet the Federal threat. Hiram Bledsoe's Missouri and William Woodruff's Arkansas Batteries, with D. McRae's Arkansas Battalion, supported the rebel move to counter Plummer's advance. When the 3rd

---

16. The speech given by Lyon was similarly reported by Private Ironquill of the 1st Iowa Infantry. Beass, *Wilson's Creek*, 52–53; Holcombe & Adams, 28–29; Moore, *Missouri, Confederate Military History*, 55; Prentis, 70–71, 74; Ware, 310–313.

17. *O.R.*, vol. 3: 60; Holcombe & Adams, 31–32; Piston & Hatcher, *Wilson's Creek*, 201–202; Prentis, 75.

18. McEroy, 168; Piston & Hatcher, Wilson's Creek, 193, 196–198.

19. Bearss, *Wilson's Creek*, 60–61, 82–83; Holcombe & Adams, 32; McElroy, 168; Peckham, 335.

Louisiana came into the open John V. DuBois' Battery momentarily drove them back into the brush. Reorganized, the rebels came again and by 7:00 a.m. had driven Plummer back across Wilson's Creek. Only the intervention of DuBois' Battery a second time prevented the Unionists from being captured.[20]

Back at Oak Hill or "Bloody Hill" as it would be known, both sides established their lines by 6:30 a.m. And even though Lyon's column had taken the rebel army by complete surprise on the morning of August 10, it was with "truly remarkable speed," wrote Daniel O'Flaherty, that "Price whipped his Missourians into line at Wilson's Creek, [and] undoubtedly saved the day at Bloody Hill." For it took Price less than twenty minuets, recalled a member of the MSG, after the first cannon shots from Totten's guns to form his initial line at the base of Oak Hill–it consisted of the remnants of Cawthorn's Brigade, which occupied the far right, next came W.Y. Slack's command, then John B. Clark's Division followed by M.M. Parson's small division and finally James McBride's men. In all, the initial rebel line contained about 2,000 men.[21]

Having pushed Cawthorn's men off of Bloody Hill, Lyon ordered his men to continue the advance, even as Plummer's command crossed Wilson's Creek to the east. Lyon's main force was met by a crushing volley from Price's Missourians, which brought the Federal movement to a halt. For thirty minutes, the two sides traded volleys, even as James McBride was moving on the right flank of Lyon's main line anchored by 1st Missouri Infantry. Lieutenant Colonel George Andrew's, commanding the 1st Missouri, sent word to Lyon of the rebel movement, on his right flank. Lyon then directed Totten to move George Sokalski's section of artillery to support Andrew's right flank. By 7:00 a.m., Richard Weightman's Brigade had joined Price's line, closing a gap between Slack's and Cawthorn's commands, increasing the rebel numbers to about 3,300 men against about 2,800 Federals atop Oak Hill.[22]

About 7:30 a.m., Price launched his first of many assaults, to take Oak Hill. Most accounts have McBride's over anxious division leading the assault, which in turn caused Price to commit the rest of his line. The rebel troops "fought with great bravery and determination...Many times the firing was a continuous roar" with the sides at times but "thirty of forty yards apart." As McBride's men advanced they were first greeted by some rounds from Totten's Battery, became momentarily disorganized, rallied and advanced to the summit of Oak Hill. Cresting Oak Hill, McBride found himself on the flank of the 1st Missouri Infantry, where they delivered a well "directed and effective fire in the enemy's ranks." George L. Andrews, commanding the Unionists, seeing McBride's flanking move, shifted half of his regiment to confront the rebels and "drove them back." Piston and Hatcher saw

20. *O.R.*,vol. 3: 61, 112; Bearss, *Wilson's Creek*, 75–76, 82, 84–85; Holcombe & Adams, 34; Piston & Hatcher, *Wilson's Creek*, 213–214; Snead, *Fight for Missouri*, 277–278.
21. Bevier, 43.
22. *O.R.*, 3:74, 76; Bearss, *Wilson's Creek*, 79–80, 82; Duncan, 89; Moore, *Missouri, Confederate Military History*, 57; O'Flaherty, 83; Piston & Hatcher, *Wilson's Creek*, 207, 234, 242.

this move by McBride, though unsuccessful, as the turning point in the battle for Oak Hill, as the Federals had stopped advancing and for the remainder of the battle would essentially be fending off Confederate attack, after attack, until the battle closed. Between 7:30–8:00 a.m. Lyon's charge and Price's counter charge had petered out and both sides adjusted their lines for the continued action.[23]

Though repelled, McBride's rebel Missourians renewed their attack a second time which gained a small prominence which the Confederates steadfastly held despite the pounding they were taking from Totten's section and the Federal Missourians. Shortly after McBride's men gained their foothold, General Mosby M. Parsons led the third assault on Andrews' 1st Missouri Infantry. About 9: 00 a.m., the 1st Kansas Infantry began to buckle, and Lyon rode forward to rally the Kansans. Reenforcing the line with a battalion of four companies from the 1st Kansas, Lyon positioned them to the left of the 1st Missouri, and adjacent to the other companies of the 1st Kansas. In the process, Lyon was wounded in the head and leg and shortly thereafter the Union commander confided in his adjutant, John Schofield, that he feared the day was lost. Between 9:00 and 9:30 a.m., the 1st Iowa relieved the 1st Kansas, while the 2nd Kansas took the place of the 1st Missouri Infantry.[24]

By most accounts General Lyon was killed about 9:30 a.m. while leading a portion of the 1st Iowa Infantry forward, which was only partially true. At the same time that Lyon moved forward, Colonel Robert Mitchell, also led the 2nd Kansas Infantry into the fray. As the 2nd Kansas crested Oak Hill, they were met by a crushing volley; Lyon "was struck in the left breast from by a ball from a squirrel rifle"and died within seconds, falling into the arms of his orderly Edward Lehman, muttering as he fell to Lehman, "'I am killed; take care of my body.'" In the same volley Colonel Mitchell took rounds in his thigh and calf, survived the battle, but turned the command of his regiment over to Lieutenant Colonel Charles Blair, who finished the battle unscathed. Some accounts have Lyon leading the 1st Iowa forward, which on the surface could easily be misunderstood as Lyon was close to the 1st Iowa Infantry when the reenforcing commands moved forward. One of the best accounts of Lyon's death came from Samuel Crawford, who commanded Company E, 2nd Kansas. According to Crawford, who was only ten paces away when Lyon was stuck, his unit fired a volley into the rebels, "over Lyon's body." Still another account by William Wherry, Lyon's aid-de-camp, has Lyon leading both the 2nd Kansas and two companies of the 1st Iowa forward. However, yet another member of the 2nd Kansas, stated that the "First Iowa was some distance down the hill" when Lyon was killed–"It is not possible," continued

23. *O.R.*, vol. 3: 62, 76; *O.R.*, vol. 53: 434–435; Banasik, *Missouri in 1861*, 379; Bearss, *Wilson's Creek*, 66, 82, 104; Piston & Hatcher, *Wilson's Creek*, 206–207, 232, 239–242; Wherry, "Wilson's Creek," vol. 1: 292.

24. *O.R.* vol. 3:61; Adamson, 257; Bearss, *Wilson's Creek*, 60, 82, 99–101, 104, 132; Peckham, 336; Wherry, "General Lyon,"84; Wherry, "Wilson's Creek," 293.

the member of Company G, that Lyon "could have been leading them [First Iowa] on to a charge as stated in the [*Missouri*] *Democrat.*"[25]

The death of Lyon could have been catastrophic to the Union morale had not a quick thinking William Wherry, of Lyon's staff, not covered the face of the fallen general as he was carried to the rear. Further, Wherry ordered Edward Lehman, Lyon's orderly to "stop crying like a child...to suppress the news that the general had been killed."[26] Most men of Lyon's command had no idea that Lyon had been killed, while Captain George H. Fairchild, commanding Company K, 1st Kansas noted of the moment:

The effect of Lyon's death upon our troops was terrible. A feeling of consternation spread through the ranks and dispirted itself in every countenance. At that moment, had the enemy made a charge, our troops would have hardly resisted it with success, and their defeat might have been easy. But soon every feeling gave way to a feeling of revenge and deadly determination.[27]

Following Lyon's death the command of the army fell upon Major S. D. Sturgis, as he was the only unwounded brigade commander remaining in Lyon's column; a "senior officer of military education and experience." further, Sweeney and Detzieler, the other brigade commanders, were both severely wounded. Besides, according to John Schofield, "Who was the actual senior in rank on the ground was not easy to ascertain in the midst of a fierce engagement. It was no time to make experiments with untried military genius." With Sturgis in command the battle continued unabated, while he assessed the situation.[28]

About 10:00 a.m. (Gerteis has it as 9:00 a.m.), Colonel Greer with five companies of his Texas cavalry regiment (about 450 men) was ordered to attack the Union right flank. Greer moved his command, undetected, across the front of Oak Hill, picking up DeRosey Carroll's Arkansas Cavalry Regiment as he went and successfully positioned his command in the Union rear and on their right flank. Having no sabers, Greer ordered his men to draw pistols and charge. With a loud "shout for Texas," the Texans charged up Oak Hill, completely surprising the Federals in that quarter. Unfortunately for the rebels, the attack was poorly executed, even though it did scattered some of Totten's men and a Union company which was skirmishing on that flank. Greer's attack quickly evaporated following

---

25. Note: Adamson, Brooksher with Piston & Hatcher have Lehman's name as Albert, while Bearss with Holcombe & Adams have the name as Edward Lehman of Company B, 1st U.S. Cavalry. Adamson, 257; Banasik, *Missouri in 1861*, 149; Bearss, *Wilson's Creek*, 108; Britton, 98; Brooksher, 213; Burke, 17; Crawford,, 32–33; Duncan, 90; Fry, 23; Gilmore, 121; Holcombe & Adams, 36, 97; Ingenthron, 86; McElroy, 171; Piston & Hatcher, *Soldiers' Letters*, 73–74; Piston & Hatcher, *Wilson's Creek*, 265, 268–269; Wherry, "General Lyon," 85; Wherry, "Wilson's Creek," vol. 1:295–296; Woodward, 319.,

26. Piston & Hatcher, Wilson's Creek, 97:

27. "The News From Missouri," *The Daily Bulletin* (Charlotte, NC), August 23, 1861.

28. Schofield, 45–46.

a devastating volley from Company K, 2nd Kansas Infantry, commanded by Lieutenant Gustavus Schroyer, and Totten's artillery. Carroll, who was following, did little better. Both units subsequently rallied and redeployed on the Confederate left flank to continue the battle. Of the attack, Captain Totten wrote: "This was the only demonstration made by their cavalry, and it was no *effete* and effectual in its force and character as to deserve only the appellation of child's play." An Iowan called the attack "disorderly" and made by a "crowd of cavalry." The assault had the potential to have seriously affected the Union forces, but the lack of proper preparation and control resulted in a non-event.[29]

Greer's ill-fated charge was followed by yet another charge of some fresh rebel troops under N.B. Pearce, who had just arrived on the scene having been in reserve supporting the rebel artillery. John Gratiot's 3rd Arkansas Infantry Regiment (State Troops) led the rebel final assault, being cheered by their rebel brethren as they moved forward. After about fifty paces, Gratiot's boys went to the ground being ranked by artillery and musket fire from the Federals upon the hill; but they held their ground, being "cut down like grass." In about thirty minutes, Gratiot's Regiment lost 110 men of 571 engaged or about twenty percent of his command, including his quartermaster killed, his Commissary wounded, his major's arm broken, while Gratiot and his lieutenant colonel both lost their horses. Though failing to drive the Unionists off Bloody Hill this last assault "proved to be the decisive engagement" in the battle, according to N. B. Pearce. About 11:30 a.m., following a lull in the battle the Unionists began to pull back, their ammunition nearly exhausted; they had held Blooding Hill until ordered to withdraw, but the battlefield and the victory rested with the Confederate troops.[30]

Following the retreat of Lyon's column, the Confederates failed to immediately follow up the retreating Unionists. According to a member of Thomas Churchill's Regiment "our men were so worn out and exhausted that they could do nothing in the way of taking prisoners. Feeble, faint, and wearied, our soldiers threw themselves on the ground among the dead and wounded to rest." The men, continued Robert Emmanuel, "seeing the enemy fleeing, and yet to near dead to pursue them."[31]

* * * * * * *

29. *O.R.*, 3:74, 118–120, 126, 390; Bearss, *Wilson's Creek*, 103–104, 117–118; Britton, 103–104; Crawford, 34; Fry, 22; Gerteis, *Missouri*, 72; Piston & Hatcher, *Wilson's Creek*, 270–271; Prentis, 80–82; Ware, 322; Woddward, 315–316.
30. *O.R.*, 3:121; Bearss, *Wilson's Creek*, 126–128, 130; 302–303; Moore, *Missouri, Confederate Military History,* 59–60; N. B. Pearce, "Arkansas Troops in the Battle of Wilson's Creek," *Battles and Leaders of the Civil War* 4 vols. (New York, 1887–1888), vol. 1:302–303.
31. Robert Emmanuel, "The Battle of Oak Hills," *The Daily Sun* (Columbus, GA), October 19, 1861.

Item: Selected Officers and Captains of the 3rd Texas Cavalry.

Regimental Commander:

A Mexican War veteran, Elkanah B. Greer was born on October 11, 1825, in Paris, Tennessee. He moved to Marshall, Texas, in 1848, where he owned a plantation. At the beginning of the Civil War he was elected the colonel of the South Kansas and Texas Regiment (also known as the 3rd Texas Cavalry). Greer led his command at Wilson's Creek and Pea Ridge, Arkansas (March 6–8, 1862), being promoted to brigadier general on October 8, 1862. The Governor of Texas considered Greer "a gentleman worthy of the highest confidence." At war's end, Greer was the Chief of the Conscription Bureau of the Trans-Mississippi Department, a post he held since his promotion to general officer. He died at DuVall's Bluff, Arkansas, on March 25, 1877, while visiting a sister and was later buried in Memphis, Tennessee.[32]

Company A:

Captain Thomas W. Winston was born in Alabama, in about 1829, a resident of Harrison County, Texas, at the beginning of the Civil War, and the owner of a cotton plantation that employed some 31 Negroes. He raised Company A, 3rd Texas, from an "elite class of cotton planters" in eastern Harrison County, being mustered into the service on June 12, 1861. He fought at Wilson's Creek and Pea Ridge, where he was noted for his "gallant bearing and conduct throughout the entire engagement." His command transferred to the east side of the Mississippi River in April 1862, and in May the regiment reorganized, while Winston resigned on May 16, 1862, and returned to Texas. Final disposition unknown.[33]

Company B:

Robert H. Cumby was born on August 24, 1824, in Charleston County, Virginia, moved to Mississippi at the age of 12, where he was was raised in Lafayette County, and later married. In 1849, Cumby moved to Rusk County, Texas, became a large plantation owner, employing 30 slaves. By the beginning of the Civil War, Cumby was the richest planter in county and was elected to the Texas Legislature, serving from 1859–1861. He entered the military service on May 7, 1861, and organized Company B. 3rd Texas Cavalry on June 13, 1861. In addition to Wilson's Creek, where he acted his "part well," Cumby fought at Pea Ridge, where he served with "'great gallantry,'" after which his command was transferred to Mississippi. Cumby was elected colonel of the 3rd Texas, on May 20, 1861, but resigned on June 12, due to chronic diarrhea and returned to Texas. Recovering his health, Cumby joined General E. Greer's staff, being appointed a major and Chief-of-Staff, on May2,1863. Cumby completed his service as a general of Texas

---

32. Warner, Generals in Gray, 118; Confederate Military History: vol. 11: Texas, by O. M. Roberts, vol. 11: 233, hereafter cited as Roberts, Texas, Confederate Military History.

33. *O.R.*, vol.8: 295; *O.R.S.*, pt. 2, vol. 67: 702; Hale, *Third Texas Cavalry*, 28–29.

State Troops, commanding the 4th Brigade (1864–1865). Following the war, having lost everything, Cumby became a grocer in Sulphur Springs, Texas, where he died on November 10, 1881.[34]

Company C:

Francis M. Taylor was born in Alabama, in about 1828, and a resident of Cherokee County, Texas, at the beginning of the Civil War. The District Clerk of Cherokee County, Taylor commanded Company C, 3rd Texas Cavalry. And like all captains of the regiment was a slave owner. Taylor was known as "'a noble, brave and patriotic man'" who was "especially popular with the troops despite his reputation as a disciplinarian." Following the Battle of Wilson's Creek, Taylor's company, with the remainder of the 3rd found themselves camped near Carthage, Missouri, where the regiment was ravaged with measles and typhoid. On December 5. 1861, Captain Taylor died, a victim of typhoid.[35]

Company D:

Stephen M. Hale was born about 1814, in Alabama, and a resident of Greenville, Texas, Hunt County at the beginning of the Civil War. A small farmer, Hale owned one slave, and, in June 1861, raised what became Company D, 3rd Texas Cavalry, from Hunt and Fannin Counties, Texas. Hale was the poorest and oldest of all the officers in the 3rd Texas when the regiment organized on June 13, 1861. "Known for his rustic manners and irregular grammar," Hale was the exact opposite of his fellow captains who were of the "planter-political class." Hale fought at Wilson's Creek and Pea Ridge and upon reorganization of the regiment in May 1862, he was not re-elected captain of his command, being dropped from the rolls effective May 20, 1862. Returning to Texas, Hale appears to have had no further service in the army. Final Disposition unknown.[36].

Company E:

Daniel M. Short, was born in about 1819, in Delaware. A lawyer by profession, Short, a slave owner, lived in Shelbyville, Shelby County, Texas, at the beginning of the Civil War. Prior to the Civil War, he saw action fighting Indians as a member of the Texas Rangers. At the beginning of the war, Short raised Company E, 3rd Texas Cavalry, in San Augustine and Shelby Counties. In addition to Wilson's Creek, Short also fought at Chustenahlah, Indian Territory (December 26, 1861), where his company led the advance. After the command moved to Mississippi, the regiment reorganized and Short was not elected captain of the unit

---

34. *O.R.S.*, pt. 2, vol. 67: 702: Allardice, Confederate Colonels, 118; Allardice, More Generals In Gray, 68; Douglas John Cater, As It Was: Reminiscences of a Soldier of the Third Texas Cavalry and the Nineteenth Louisiana Infantry (Austin, TX, 1990), 94, 132, hereafter cited as Cater, As It Was; Hale, Third Texas Cavalry, 28–29, 115; Sifakis, Who Was Who in the Confederacy, 114.
35. *O.R.S.*, pt.2, vol. 67: 702; Hales, *Third Texas Cavalry*, 28–29, 31, 73.
36. *O.R.S.*, pt. 2, vol. 67: 703; Hale, *Third Texas Cavalry*, 28–29, 31; Ralph A. Wooster, *Lone Star Regiments in Gray* (Austin, TX, 2002), 71, hereafter cited as Wooster

and was subsequently dropped from the rolls. Returning to Texas, Short survived the war and was subsequently elected to the Texas Legislature. Final disposition unknown.[37]

Company G:

Hinche Parham Mabry was born on October 27, 1829, in Laurel Hill, Georgia (Simpson says it was North Carolina–where his father was born). He was educated at the University of Tennessee, moved to Jefferson, Texas in 1851, where he studied the law while working as a merchant. Admitted to the Texas Bar in 1856, Mabry served as a Texas Ranger, was elected to the Texas Legislature (1856–1860), and was a member of the Texas Secession Convention. Mabry joined the Confederate Army on June 13, 1861, commanding Company G, 3rd Texas Cavalry. In addition to Wilson's Creek, Mabry also fought at Pea Ridge in March 1862, after which his command was transferred to the East side of the Mississippi River, where he was promoted to lieutenant colonel on May 8, 1862, and colonel on June 12,1862. Mabry remained in the East until March 1865, when he returned to the Trans-Mississippi and was apparently promoted to a general officer by E. Kirby Smith in the waning days of the war. Mabry was paroled in Shreveport, Louisiana, on June 22, 1865. Following the war he returned to Jefferson, Texas, took up the law, was elected judge and opposed Reconstruction by obstruction of "the functions of the courts." Mabry was also the "leader of a Ku Klux Klan affiliate (the "Knights of the Rising Sun"). " Following a lynching incident, he fled to Canada, but eventually returned to Texas, settling in Fort Worth in 1879. A victim of an accidental shooting. Mabry died in Sherman, Texas, on March 21, 1884 (Simpson say he died in Fort Worth in 1885).[38]

Company H:

Jonathan L. Russell was born about 1826, in North Carolina, and a resident of Upshur County, Texas, at the beginning of the Civil War. A farmer, who owned but two slaves, Russell also served for a time as a senator in the Texas Legislature. On June 13, 1861, Russell was mustered into the Confederate Service, commanding Company H, 3rd Texas Cavalry, a position he held until May 20, 1862, when he was not re-elected to command the company upon its reorganization. Returning to Texas, it appears that Russell saw no additional service, survived the war and in 1876, helped "frame the new constitution" of Texas. Final disposition unknown.[39]

* * * * * * *

---

37. *O.R.*, vol. 8: 22–23, 29; *O.R.S.*, pt. 2, vol. 67: 703; Hale, *Third Texas Cavalry*, 28–29, 31, 284; Wooster, 71.
38. *O.R.*, vol. 53: 425; Allardice, *Confederate Colonels*, 247; Allardice, *More Generals in Gray*, 146–147; Cater, *As It Was*, 97; Hale, *Third Texas Cavalry*, 284; Roberts, *Texas, Confederate Military History*, vol. 11: 37; Simpson, 86.
39. *O.R.S.*, pt. 2, vol. 67: 704; Hale, *Third Texas Cavalry*, 28–30, 284.

Item: Selected Officers in Grant's Command.

John Alexander McClernand was a Kentucky native being born near Hardinburg on March 30,1812. He moved to southern Illinois at the age of four following the death of his father. Self educated, he passed the Illinois Bar in 1832, fought in the Black Hawk War (served only sixty days), first as a private then as "assistant brigade quartermaster with the rank of colonel;" this was his only military experience prior to the Civil War. A Jacksonian Democrat, McClernand was elected to the U.S. Congress 1843, served until 1851, and served again in 1859–1861. Reigning from Congress, McClernand was appointed a brigadier general effective May 17, 1861, by President Lincoln in a large part for his political affiliation. For the Battle of Belmont, he commanded Grant's First Brigade. With the exception of Belmont and Arkansas Post McClernand served the majority of his military career east of the Mississippi River. He was promoted to major general on March 21, 1862, was relived of command, by Grant on June19, 1863, reinstated by President Lincoln in January 1864, eventually leaving the army, on November 30, 1864, because of health (probably from the malaria he contracted while serving in Louisiana). Returning to Illinois, he resumed his previous political activities. He died on September 20, 1890, in Springfield, Illinois, where he was buried. According to one source, John McClernand, was "ambitious and untactful," one who "disliked West Pointers and never forgot his political fences in Illinois." Overall, McClernand "mixed war and politics and was unable to separate politics from the military...He habitually circumvented the military chain of command and wrote directly to political figures, most frequently to President Lincoln." This led to his dismissal by Grant and his dislike by his many of his fellow officers.[40]

Napoleon Bonaparte Buford was born in Woodford County, Kentucky, on January 13, 1807, educated locally before entering West Point in 1823, graduating number six of thirty-eight in the Class of 1827. Assigned to the artillery, Buford was granted permission to study law at Harvard in 1831, then returned to the Point as an instructor until he resigned on December 31, 1835, to enter private business in Kentucky. Moving to Rock Island, Illinois, in 1843, Buford was a successful banker, merchant, and railroad president; however he experienced financial problems just prior to the war, causing him to enter bankruptcy in 1861. With the beginning of the Civil War, Buford was mustered into the 27th Illinois Infantry on August 10, 1861, and subsequently led the unit at Belmont as part of McClernand's Brigade. In addition to Belmont, Buford was also present at Island No. 10, his last Trans-Mississippi engagement, in March 1862. He was promoted to brigadier general effective Aptil15, 1861, and brevet major general on March 13, 1864, "for gallant and meritorious service during the war." For most of the remainder of the war he served east of the Mississippi until the end when he

---

40. Boatner, 525; Christopher C. Meyers, "McClernand, John Alexander," in *Encyclopedia of the Civil War*, 1277–1279; Sifakis, *Who Was Who in the Union*, 250–251; *Union Army*, vol. 8:165; Warner, *Generals in Blue*, 293–294.

commanded the District of Eastern Arkansas, in Helena (September 1863-March 1865). Following the war he worked for the government serving as an Indian agent and inspector of the Union Pacific Railroad. He died on March 28, 1883, in Chicago, Illinois. His half brother was John Buford of Gettysburg fame. [41]

John Alexander Logan, who Ezra Warner banded"perhaps the Union's "premier civilian combat general," was born on February 9, 1826, in Jackson County, Illinois. At the age of sixteen he attended Shiloh Academy, in Randolph County, Illinois, and five years later enlisted in the 1st Illinois Infantry, fighting in the Mexican War as a lieutenant. Returning to Illinois, he studied law in Louisville, Kentucky, graduating in 1851. Finding he had a knack for politics, Logan ran for the U.S. Congress in 1858, and was elected. At the beginning of the Civil War he joined a Michigan regiment as a volunteer as it marched to the Bull Run battlefield, in July, after which he returned to Southern Illinois where he recruited the 31st Illinois Infantry Regiment. Commissioned the colonel of the 31st on September 18, 1861, Logan or "Black Jack" as he was known, led the command at Belmont, his only Trans-Mississippi battle. He was promoted to brigadier general on March 21, 1862, following Grant's Henry and Donelson Campaign, By the end of the War Logan had been promoted to major general, effective November 29, 1862. Awarded the Congressional Medal of Honor (inscribed "Vicksburg July 4, 1863") for his performance at Vicksburg, Logan completed his service participating in the Atlanta Campaign and Sherman's Carolina Campaign. Following the war Logan returned to politics serving in both houses of Congress. A founding member of the "Grand Army of the Republic," Logan died while still in the Senate on December 26, 1886.[42]

* * * * * * *

Item: Extended Comments on the Battle of Belmont: Federal success–10:15 to 1:00 p.m.

Note: See battle map for the deployment of the two commands to correspond with the narrative below.

The main fighting during the Battle of Belmont began about 10:15 A.M., as Grant's forces moved toward the main rebel line and engaged Pillow's skirmishers. Grant, like Pillow, had no effective reserve as both commanders deployed their entire force on line. Pillow, for his part, had one company of the 13th Tennessee Infantry, which served as a flank guard and acted as a extremely small reserve. Grant had Detrich's make-shift battalion a mile to his left rear, which in the course of the battle, Grant seemed to have forgotten about until it was time to leave. By

41. Boatner, 97–98; Heidler, "Buford, Napoleon Bonaparte,"in *Encyclopedia of the Civil War*, 310–312; Heitman, vol. 1: 260; *Union Army*, vol. 8: 42; Warner, *Generals in Blue*, 53–54.

42. Heitman, vol. 1: 638; Dane Magon,"Logan, John Alexander," in *Encyclopedia of the Civil War*, 1203–1205; Sifakis, *Who Was Who in the Union*, 239–240; *Union Army*, Vol. 8:153–154; Warner, *Generals in Blue*, 282–283

11:00 a.m. the rebel skirmishers had been driven back to their commands and the battle proper began.[43]

Between 11:00 a.m. and noon, the two opposing lines began to exchange fire in earnest. The 31st Illinois occupied the Union left opposite the 13th Arkansas and 12th Tennessee Infantries. After receiving fire into their left flank, Colonel John Logan, commanding the 31st Illinois, adjusted his line to the left to better confront the 12th Tennessee, which actually overlapped the Unionist line and was charging the Federal left. Within a short time the 12th Tennessee halted their charge, began firing and was quickly out of ammunition, having only twenty rounds per man at the start of the contest. In the center, the 21st and 22nd Tennessee Infantries were in a cornfield and exposed to concentrated fire from the 7th Iowa, the 22nd and 30th Illinois infantries. Toward 11:30, the center under Gideon Pillow's direction, launched a bayonet charge that rippled down the line, but accomplished little. Union artillery, now planted in the center of their line, began pounding the two rebel units in the Confederate center. By twelve the line was still holding, though a "regiment and a battalion," were without ammunition. However, a dramatic change would take place over the next thirty minutes.[44]

While the right and center of the rebel line was being punished by the unseen Yankees in the woods beyond the cornfield, the far left was also in a similar quandary. By noon the 13th Tennessee faced the same problems--low ammunition and a constant flow of casualties against a largely unseen foe. While the Thirteen gamely held the left of the rebel line, they were startled to hear gunfire to their rear. Their one detached company, Pillow's sole reserve, became engaged by the 27th Illinois which had approached the rebel rear via another road. Colonel John Wright, commander of the 13th Tennessee, immediately communicated the information to General Pillow. "Finding it impossible longer to maintain" his position, Pillow "ordered the whole line to retreat to the river bank." With his line broken and troops "mingled together," back went the 13th as did the rest of the line. On the right, the 12th Tennessee was out of ammunition and retreated to the river bank to resupply. In the center the 21st and 22nd Tennessee followed suit. Smelling blood the victorious Federals pressed the attack; panic set into the rebel lines as they rushed to the rear and the safety of the river bank and the Columbus, Kentucky, artillery.[45]

Pressing forward Grant's men reached the rebel camp and prepared for the final assault. Firing several volleys they pressed into Camp Johnston, seized the Watson Battery and drove the rebel mob back to the safety of the levee. Still other rebels headed north, along the river to get away from the Federal attack; the time was 1:00 p.m. Meanwhile, rebel reinforcements had arrived and were organizing for a counter stroke. The 2nd Tennessee Infantry, under Colonel J. Knox Walker

---

43. O.R., 3:307; Harrell, Confederate Military History: Arkansas, 62; Hughes, Battle of Belmont, 85–86, 92.

44. O.R., 3:326; O.R.S., pt. 3, 1:462; Hughes, Battle of Belmont, 94–97, 100, 103.

45. O.R., 3:326, 333–334; O.R.S., pt. 3:462; Hughes, Battle of Belmont, 109–113, 116–117.

delivered the first blow halting the Federal pursuit in its tracks. In turn, the 2nd was devastated by Union artillery, including the recently captured Watson Battery, which stopped the Confederate counter thrust. However, Walker's attack did sty-mie the Union forces, allowing time for more troops to arrive from Columbus and more importantly, permit the recently routed rebel units to reform. It also turned the Unionist's attention away from Pillow's demoralized troops which hugged the banks of the Mississippi River. By 1:30 p.m., Camp Johnston was burning followed at about 2:00 p.m. by "an eerie lull" that settled over the battlefield and lasted for thirty minutes.[46]

* * * * * * *

46. *O.R.*, 3:308, 343; Hughes, *Battle of Belmont*, 117–119, 121–124, 127.

Appendix D
Various Orders of Battle

Abbreviations:

Bn. = Battalion	Brig. = Brigadier
Indpt. = Independent	Inf. = Infantry
Cav. = Cavalry	Cdr. = Commander
K = Killed	lb = Pound
Co. = Company	Col. = Colonel
Lt. = Lieutenant	M = Missing
Detch. = Detachment	Div. = Division
Mtd. = Mounted	MW = Mortally Wounded
(E) = Estimate	EFF = Effectives
Regt. = Regiment	SB = Smoothbore
Gen. = General	How. = Howitzer
W = Wounded	WIA = Wounded In Action

* * * * * * *

Order of Battle, Carthage, Missouri
July 5, 1861

General References:
1. "Battle of Carthage," *Rebellion Record*, vol. 2: Doc. 247.
2. Britton, 53–54.
3. Hinze & Farnhan, 221–222.
4. Moore, Missouri, Confederate Military History, 47–48.
5. Schrantz, 32–33.

* * * * * * *

Missouri State Guard Order of Battle
General Information Missouri State Guard:

Organizing the Guard At Lamar–On July 4, the MSG was organized at Lamar, Missouri, on the eve of the Battle of Carthage. At the time, Governor Jackson and his various generals had no idea that General Sigel's Federal command was approaching the area from the south, until about 6:00 p.m. that evening. And prior to that notice, Governor Jackson issued General Orders No. 16, directing "The several brigadier generals now in the field will proceed forthwith to the organization of the forces of their various districts." As part of that organization units from the Second District (General Tom Harris) were attached to General John

B. Clark's Third Division, while those of the Fifth District (General A. E. Steen) were attached to General William Y. Slack's Fourth Division.[1]

Losses–Loses were generally reported by all the participating divisions, with the killed and wounded listed; the only exception being the Third Division, which combined the killed and wounded into one number. And based upon the losses in the other commands the killed and wounded in the Third Division can be estimated–See the Third Division, note no. 20 for details.

Strength–The effective strengths of the various commands is generally known, with the exception of Parsons' Sixth Division as well as some units that were previously excluded from the sources listed above. A review of *Official Records* shows that some commands, and their effective strengths, were not enumerated in the various Order of Battles listed under General References (See notes nos. 11 and 14 below). Additionally, I've included the divisional and brigade staff strengths of the various commands which were never mentioned in any accounts of the battle, excluding only the surgeons of the commands.

* * * * * * *

Missouri State Guard (Governor Claiborne F. Jackson)[2].

Gen. Staff: EFF = 8
Patriot Army of Missouri (Maj. Gen. Sterling Price; absent in SW
  Missouri)[3]

Second Division, MSG. James Rains' Division should be called the Eighth Division, according to David Hinze and Karen Farnham, because Rains commanded the Eighth Military District, while Ward L. Schrantz labeled Rains' command as the "Second and Eighth Divisions Missouri State Guard." However, at the Battle of Carthage Rains' Division was known as the Second Division, despite the District designation. Further, following the engagement at Carthage, per General Orders No. 3 (July 11, 1861), Headquarters MSG, Rains' command was officially designated as the Second Division, and continued to use that designation through the Battle of Wilson's Creek on August 10 and the Siege of Lexington on September 20. Rains was finally designated the commander of the Eighth Division, MSG on December 4, 1861, while the army was camped on the Sac River.

  At Carthage, Rains staff consisted of at least 16 members, including himself, and one surgeon. Units strength and losses come from the *Official Records*, unless otherwise noted. All the units listed below, except where noted, come from the

---

1. *O.R.*, vol. 53: 705.
2. The General Staff includes Governor Jackson, but excludes the Medical Director. Peterson, et. al., 32–22.
3. Price was absent, having gone to Arkansas to enlist the help of General Ben McCulloch. O'Flaherty, 66; Pollard, 157.

Eight Division, MSG, though for the Battles of Carthage and Wilson's Creek they were considered part of the Second Division, MSG.[4]

    2nd Division (Brig. Gen. James S. Rains):
    Staff: EFF = 16
        1st Brigade (Col. Richard Weightman):[5]
        Staff:EFF = 8 [no losses]
            Inf. Detch. (Capt. F. W. McKinney) EFF = 16 [losses uknown].
            2nd Regt. (Col. John R. Graves)[6] EFF = 271 [losses unknown].
            3rd Regt. (Col. Edgar V. Hurst).EFF = 521 [losses uknown].
            4th Inf. Bn. (Lt. Col. Walter S. O'Kane)[7] EFF = 350
                [2K, 20 W, 0 M].
            Artillery (Capt. Hirman Bledsoe; WIA)[8] 3 guns; 1, 12-pd. How. and
                2, 6-lb SB EFF = 46 [0 K, 10 W, 0 M].
            Brigade Total = 1,212 [2 K, 38 W, 0 M].

        Cavalry Command (Col. R.Y. L. Peyton):[9]
            3rd Cav. Regt. (Cos. A, B, and part of H–Col. Robert Y. L. Peyton)[10]
                EFF = 115 [0 K, 1 W, 0 M].
            3rd Cav. Regt. (Cos. C, E, F, G, part of H–Lt. Col Martin White)[11]
                EFF = 66 [0 K, 1 W, 0 M].

4. *O.R.*, vol. 3: 20, 22, 127, 188; *O.R.*, vol. 53: 710; Carolyn Bartels, *The Forgotten Men Missouri State Guard* (Shawnee Mission, 1995) 12 (James Barkley entry); Hinze & Farnham, 253 n. 3; McGhee, *Letter and Order Book*, 17–18, 60–61, 91; Peterson, et. al., 209–212; Schrantz, 32.
5. Weightman's command staff, including himself and aides, consisted of at least eight individuals that were not included in the 1,204 figure that Weightman gave as his brigade's strength. This would give his brigade 1,212 men of all types, including the artillery command. Only two units in the brigade have known losses–O'Kane's Battalion and Bledsoe's Artillery–their losses comprising all but ten of the wounded that were listed by Weightman in his Official Report. *O.R.*, vol. 3:24- 25.
6. Peterson, et. al., 221, 227.
7. The command organized as a battalion on July 4, and became a regiment when it added two more companies in October 1861. When organized on July 4, it was known as the 4th Battalion. *O.R.S.*, pt. 2, vol. 38: 686, 695–696; Adamson, 135; Peterson, et. al., 232, 235.
8. General Rains has the command with only 40 men, while Colonel Weightman has it at 46, which is the correct amount to get to the total of 1,204 men in the brigade, which both Rains and Weightman listed. *O.R.*, vol. 3: 20, 22.
9. Ibid., 27.
10. In addition to the companies from the 3rd Cavalry Regiment, Companies A (Captain Thomas E. Owen), and D (Captain David C. Stone) of the 2nd Regiment, Cavalry Brigade, Eighth Division MSG and were part of the 115 effectives listed above. However, at Carthage they were part of the 1st Battalion Independent Cavalry. Also, the remaining companies of Peyton's 3rd Regiment were at Carthage; however, they were armed but had no ammunition and were counted among the "unarmed" men of the MSG. Further, Peyton reported losing one man wounded and another injured–only the wounded man is listed under the casualties. Ibid., 27–28; Peterson, et. al., 248, 250.
11. As the battle progressed on July 5, a number of men from the 3rd Regiment managed to obtain ammunition and were able to participate in the battle under the command of Lieutenant Colonel Martin White on "different parts of the field." *O.R.*, vol. 3: 28.

1st. Bn. Indt. Cav. (Lt. Col. James McCown)[12] EFF = 250
[1 K, 2 W, 0 M].
7th Cav. Regt. (Cos. A, B, C and D–Lt. Col. Richard A. Boughan)[13]
EFF = 200 [0 K, 1 W, 0 M].
1st Cav. Regt., 5th Div. MSG (attached–Lt. Col. Charles P. Hyde)[14]
EFF = 100 [0 K, 0 W, 0 M].
Ranger Co. (Capt. Joe. O. Shelby) EFF = 43 [0 K, 1 W. 0 M].[15]
Cavalry Command Total = 774 [1 K, 6 W, 0 M].
Division Total = 2,002 [3 K, 9 MW, 32 W, 0 M].[16]= 1,200
unarmed [probably no losses].[17]

* * * * * * *

Third Division, MSG. There was some confusion surrounding the strength and units of John B. Clark's Division at Carthage on July 5. Clark in his official report on the engagement stated that he had "365 men, rank and file," further implying that he had both mounted and dismounted men. This would suggest that he had some cavalry at the battle.

William Piston and Richard Hatcher stated that Clark had two commands that were organized or available on July 3, upon their arrival at Lamar–John Q. Burbridge's Regiment, with 270 officers and men, in addition too Lieutenant Colonel James P. Major, who commanded "the division's 273 mounted men." Louis Gerteis further supports Piston and Hatcher, citing their work in his book on *The Civil War In Missouri*. However, that was not correct–Piston and Hatcher failed to list the source of the two units' strength, which upon investigation, were the numbers that Thomas L. Snead listed as Burbridge's and Major's strength at Wilson's Creek on August 10.

12. In addition to the casualties listed, Colonel McCown also noted that "several [were] slightly wounded." Ibid., 26; Peterson, et. al., 247, 252.
13. Name was misspelled in the *Official Records* and Ward Schrantz, in his book on Jasper County, Missouri, lists Boughan as the correct spelling verses Voughn in the *Official Records*. *O.R.*, vol. 3: 29; Schrantz, 32.
14.In his report of the Battle of Carthage General Rains does not mention Hyde's command at the battle; however, Richard Boughan noted in his official report that Hyde's 100-man command was attached to his 200-man battalion. *O.R.*, vol. 3: 20–22, 29; Preston Filbert, *The Half Not Told: The Civil War in a Frontier Town* (Mechanicsburg, PA, 2001), 30; Peterson, et. al., 156–157.
15. Shelby had one man wounded in the initial contact with the enemy, per George W. Taylor, Rains' Medical Director. Banasik, *Missouri in 1861*, 202.
16. The Division's Medical Director, George W. Taylor initially recorded the losses as seven killed with 36 wounded. Of the wounded Taylor noted that five of the mortally wounded died by July 20, giving the command a loss of 12 killed with 31 wounded–total 43. Rains' reported losing 3 killed and 41 wounded. The one man difference in losses recorded by Rains and his Medical Director was probably the one man from Shelby's Company, who received a "flesh wound," but returned to the fight. *O.R.*, vol. 3: 22; Banasik, *Missouri in 1861*, 202, 204.
17. Duncan put the number of unarmed at 800, while Gerteis and Snead have the unarmed number as 1,200. Duncan, 77; Gerteis, *Missouri*, 42; Snead, *Fight for Missouri*, 218–219.

Using Burbridge's strength at Wilson's Creek and his reported losses for Carthage will give a fairly accurate strength for Burbridge's Regiment at Carthage, less any cavalry that were dismounted and operated under the command of Burbridge and his staff. At Carthage, General Clark reported Burbridge's losses as ten killed and wounded (probably severely wounded and not available at Wilson's Creek). In an account from a member of Burbridge's command, Burbridge's loss was reported as five killed and fifteen wounded. The difference in the reported loss was probably slightly wounded–or ten men slightly wounded, who would have been part of the 270 men available at Wilson's Creek, while the dead and severely wounded at Carthage would be added to the reported strength at Wilson's Creek, increasing the strength of the regiment at Carthage on July 5. This would suggest that Burbridge's Regiment carried 280 (270 + 10 = 280) effective officers and men into the engagement at Carthage.

General Clark in his report on the engagement at Carthage listed his command with 365 rank and file members with guns. Subtracting Burbridge's strength from Clark's reported armed men would suggest that Clark's command contained 85 (365 - 280 = 85) cavalry.

A review of Peterson's book on *Sterling Price's Lieutenants* sheds some light on the issue. The 1st Cavalry Battalion, Third Division, MSG was noted as serving at Carthage, referring the reader to the companies in the 1st Cavalry Regiment. Of the companies within the 1st Regiment, four were noted as having formed before the engagement at Carthage–Company A (reconstituted)–Captain John Poindexter; Company D (Captain L. L. Maughan), Howard County Volunteers (Captain Gustavus A. Elgin) and a fourth unnamed company (Captain Harvey G. McKinney); and another, the Windsor Guards, also known as Company A of the battalion was with the battalion. Of the units listed ,only the Windsor's Guards and the Howard County Volunteers appeared to have fought at Carthage, while the others were probably part of the unarmed portion of Clark's Division. Also note, that the 1st Cavalry Battalion did not organize under Lieutenant Colonel J. P. Major until July 28, 1861.[18]

  3rd Division (Brig. Gen. John B. Clark, Sr.):[19]
  Staff: EFF = 13 [losses probably zero].
    1st Inf. Regt. (Col. John Q. Burbridge) EFF = 280
    [5 K, 15 W, 0 M].[20]

---

18. *O.R.*,vol.3: 30–31; "Col. Burbridge's Regiment," 22; Gerteis, *Missouri*, 43, 216–217 n. 17 & n. 18; J. S. Kelly Letter (February 20, 1914), Skaggs Collection, Arkansas History Commission, hereafter cited as T. S. Kelly Letter; Peterson, et. al., 110–112; Piston & Hatcher, *Wilson's Creek*, 85, 352 n. 21; Wayne S. Schnetzer, *More Forgotten Men: The Missouri State Guard* (Independence, MO, 2003), 73, hereafter cited as Schnetzer; Snead, *Fight for Missouri*, 313.

19. Staff and commander not include in previous accounts of men in the Third Division, MSG. Of the 16 three were surgeons. Peterson, et. al., 107–110.

20. Clark reported his losses as 10 killed and wounded; however, Colonel Burbridge recorded his losses as five killed and fifteen wounded, "the heaviest loss" of Jackson's command. The

1st Cav. Bn. (unorganized–led by 1st Inf. Regt. command staff)[21]
EFF = 85 [losses under 1st Regt.].
Division Total = 378 [5 K, 15 W, 0 M].

* * * * * * *

Fourth Division, MSG. According to John C. Moore, Slack's Division had 700 infantry commanded by John T. Hughes and John C. C. Thornton; however, Thornton, who was normally assigned to the Fifth Division MSG, was temporarily assigned to the Fourth Division. On June 22, when the division was organized the roster shows that Hughes's command numbered 431 men. This would suggest that Thornton's battalion numbered about 269 men.

Also, Thomas McCarty's Battalion, of three companies, from the Fifth Division, MSG was "attached" to Hughes's command and not listed as a separate unit within Slack's Division in the official report of the battle. Its unknown as to whether McCarty's Battalion was part of Hughes's 471-man command or part of Thornton's Battalion or a unit of previously unknown strength. Based upon Thornton's five-company battalion its estimated that McCarty's Battalion would of had 132 (269 / 5 = 54, or 3 x 54 = 162 officers and men per company) if it were a separate unit..[22]

4th Division (Brig. Gen. William Y. Slack):[23]
Staff: EFF = 7 (E) [Loses probably zero].
    1st Inf. (Col. John T. Hughes). EFF = 431 [2 K, 6 W, 0 M].
    1st Inf. Bn., 5th Div., MSG (Maj. John C. Calhoun Thornton).[24] EFF
       = 269 [losses embraced under 1st Inf.].
    Extra Bn., 5th Div., MSG (Capt. Thomas McCarty).[25] 1st Cav. Regt.

difference, between Clark's report and Burbridge's report was probably 10 slightly wounded. *O.R.*, vol. 3: 31; "Col. Burbridge's Regiment," 22.
21. Unit probably composed of the Windsor Guards (Captain J. P. Major) and the Howard County Volunteer Company (Captain Gustavus A. Elgin). Also note that horse holders were not considered as there were sufficient unarmed men to hold the mounts of the armed men. Peterson, et. al., 111–112; J. S. Kelly Letter; Schnetzer, 73.
22. Eakin & Hale, 137; Moore, *Missouri Confederate Military History*, 48; Peterson, et. al., 143; Schnetzer, 67; Shelton Reminiscence, 7.
23. Staff not specified and estimated at seven, including the division commander but excluding the surgeon. Divisional losses per Slack. *O.R.*, vol. 3: 33; Bevier, 70; Peterson, et. al., 136–137.
24. Of Thornton's five companies, two are known to have not been formed by the Battle of Carthage–Lewis B. Dougherty's and John S. Groom's commands. As such, McCarthy's Battalion, which was noted by Peterson as at Carthage, probably served under and was part of Thornton's command at the Battle of Carthage. Additionally, since both McCarthy's and Thornton's Battalions were part of the Fifth Military District, it makes sense that Thornton would have commanded both units at Carthage under Hughe's command. Losses embraced in Hughes' command. Peterson, et. al., 158–159, 167–168.
25. Unit noted as "attached" to Hughes' Regiment. Effectives and losses embraced in Hughe's Regiment or Thornton's Bn. Ibid., 167–168; Shelton Reminiscence, 7.

(Col. Benjamin A. Rives) EFF = 500 EFF
[4 K, 0 W, 1 M].Division Total = 1,207 EFF [6 K, 6 W, 1M]

* * * * * * *

Sixth Division MSG. Most sources are in general agreement as to the strength of the various MSG Divisions, with the exception of Parsons' Sixth Division. In his Official Report, Parsons gives no indication as to his strength; however, the various sources are divided as to Parsons' strength at Carthage. Those that listed Parsons' strength place it at "about 650." However, Wiley Britton and John McElroy, citing "official sources" or "official returns" place Parsons' command at 1,000 effectives, excluding the artillerymen, while the overall MSG effective strength was 4,375. Further, a member of the Third Division also places the overall strength of the Guard 4,500.

Excluding staff, and artillery, from the army, the Second (1,940), Third (365) and Fourth (1,200) Divisions with attachments numbered 3,505 (1,940 + 365 + 1,200 = 3,505). This would suggest that Parsons' Division numbered 870 (4,375 - 3,505 = 870) officers and men, excluding staff and artillery.[26]

Removing Brown's strength, which H. C. Adamson places at 250, from the 870 figure leaves 620 (870- 250 = 620) officers and men for Kelly's Regiment, Dills' Battalion and the two mounted infantry companies. Within the *Supplement to the Official Records*, five companies are known to have muster in totals for officers and men, totaling 230 officers and men. Additionally, a review of five other regiments or battalions with known companies that were at Carthage shows that their strength at the engagement at Carthage was 1,456 for 27.5companies. IE: O'Kane's Battalion had Companies A, B, C, D, and E; Grave's Regiment had Companies A, C, D, E, G, and I ; Hurst's Regiment had ten companies; Peyton's partial regiment had two and a half companies; and Boughan's Regiment had four companies. Overall, considering the *Supplement to the Official Records* companies and those of known strength at Carthage would suggest that the average company size was about 51.82 or 52 (230 + 350 + 271 + 520 + 115 + 200 = 1,686 / 32.5 = 51.82) officers and men per company.

This would suggest that Kelly's Regiment, which contained seven and a half companies (See note no. 29 below) contained 390 (52 x 7.5 = 390) officers and men; Alexander's and Chews' Companies would total 52 officers and men each, for 104; and Dills' Battalion of an unknown number of companies would contain the remaining or 126 (620 - 390 - 104 = 126) officers and men–about two and a half companies worth of men.[27]

---

26. Adamson, 136; Britton, 54; "Col. Burbridge's Regiment," 22; McElroy, 138; Moore, *Missouri, Confederate Military History*, 48; Snead. *Fight for Missouri*, 219;

27. *O.R.S.*, pt. 2, vol. 38: 688, 692–694; Adamson, 136, 147; Bartels, *Forgotten Men*, 68 (Connor entry); Peterson, et. al., 184–185, 190, 221- 227, 232–235.

6th Division (Brig. Gen. Mosby M. Parsons):[28]
Staff: EFF = 16.
    1st Rifle Regt. (Col. Joseph M. Kelly)[29] EFF = 390 (E)
    [0 K, 2 W, 0 M].
    Dills' Inf. Bn.(Maj. George K. Dills) EFF = 126 (E)
    [0 K, 4 W, 0 M].
    1st Cav. Regt. (Col. William Benjamin Brown)[30] EFF = 250
    [1K, 0 W, 0 M].
    Alexander's Mtd. Inf. Co. (Capt. Charles B. Alexander)[31] EFF = 52
    (E) [0K, 0 W, 0 M].
    Chews' Mtd. Inf. Co. (Capt. Charles L. Chews)[32] EFF = 52 (E)
    [0 K, 1 W, 0 M].
    Artillery (Capt. Henry Guibor).[33] 4 guns; model 1841, 6-lb SB
    EFF = 61 [0 K, 2 W, 0 M][34]
    6th Division Total = 947 (E) [1 K, 9 W, 0 M].[35]= 800 unarmed.[36]

* * * * * * *

Patriotic Army of Missouri Summary
    Army Command Staff = 8 EFF.
    2nd Division = 2,002 EFF.
    3rd Division = 378 EFF.
    4th Division = 1,207 EFF.
    6th Division = 947 EFF.
    MSG Total = 4,542 [24 K or MW, 62 W, 1 M].[37]

28. The staff includes one surgeon, who was excluded from the totals, and Parsons as the commander. Peterson, et. al., 172–174
29. It is unclear as to how many companies Kelly carried into the engagement at Carthage. A review of Peterson shows that six (A, C, D, E, McCarthy's, and the St. Louis Company) of Kelly's eleven companies were at Carthage; one company (Jackson Guards) was part of Dills' command, and Company F, did not organize until after Carthage. while three are unknown–say one and a half were at Carthage, while the remaining were probably organized after July 5. Bartels, *Forgotten Men*, 348 (R.W. Stuart entry); Peterson, et. al., 181–184.
30. Adamson, 136.
31. *O.R.*, vol. 3: 35.
32. Ibid.
33. Based upon the strength of Bledsoe's Battery of three guns which required 15.33 (46 / 3 = 15.33) officers and men for each gun would give the Guibor's Battery 61 (4 x 15.33 = 61.33) officers and men. Peterson, et. al., 191.
34. Patrick, "Guibor's Battery," 32.
35. Two of the wounded were noted as "slightly" and belonged to Guibor's Battery, while Parsons did include slightly wounded in his total, he failed to include Guibor's command in the losses. *O.R.*, vol. 3: 37; Patrick, "Guibor's Battery," 32.
36. This figure also includes the unarmed men from Slacks' and Clark's Divisions. Gerteis, *Missouri*, 43; Snead, *Fight for Missouri*, 219.
37. See also EDITOR NOTE–Aftermath of the Battle of Carthage in Chapter 2 for additional comments on the Guard losses. *O.R.*, vol. 3: 10; Adamson, 151; Banasik, *Missouri in 1861*, 204;

$= 4,375$ [Staff and Artillerymen removed].[38]
$= 2,000$ unarmed.

* * * * * * *

Union Order of Battle
Battle of Carthage, July 5, 1861

Introduction

General Information, Second Brigade, Army of the West. In reviewing the various accounts and previously published Order of Battles for the Union Army at Carthage, it was universally accepted that Franz Sigel's command had only three units at the battle–the 3rd and 5th Missouri Infantries (Three months) and Backof's Battalion of two artillery companies. And the generally accepted strength of Sigel's command ran from 950 "engaged" to 1,100 men of all types, with eight pieces of artillery. However, period and secondary accounts written after the engagement tell a different story of the units that Sigel had available as well as the strength of his brigade.

Units not previously identified. Otto Lademann, whose account relates the tale of the Battle of Carthage, also penned another account of the battle, in 1907, that appeared in the MOLLUS series, which was also entitled "The Battle of Carthage." In this latter account, Lademann identifies Captain Foerester's Pioneer Company (The command was actually Voerester's Pioneer Company), which guarded the brigade's trains, in addition too a "couple of squads of mounted Home Guards" which joined the brigade at Springfield. Further, George Taylor, a rebel doctor also noted in his report of the battle that Sigel's command contained "two companies of cavalry." John Edwards, Joe Shelby's biographer, further supports the idea that Sigel had some mounted troops, recording that Shelby's cavalry company was the first to engage Sigel's forces, "receiving fire from Sigel's outlying dragoons." Other sources also noted that Sigel's command was supported by a number of teamsters, who drove the wagon train, as well as "some cavalry," "a small body of regulars," or "a company of regulars," which had joined at Springfield. All of these commands plus any of 3rd and 5th Missouri companies, who were not "engaged" at Carthage, but were "present, would have added to the Sigel's "available" verses his reported "engaged" strength.[39]

"Battle of Carthage," *Rebellion Record*, vol. 2: Doc. 247; Britton, 63; Hinze & Farnham, 205; "Great Battle in South-Western Missouri," *Waukegan Weekly Gazette*, July 13, 1861; McElroy, 141; "New York 'World's Narrative," *Rebellion Record*, vol. 2: Doc. 248; "New York Times Narrative," *Rebellion Record*, vol. 2: Doc. 250; *Rebellion Record*, vol. 2: Diary 20; Schrantz, 40; *Union Army*, vol. 5: 228
38. This was the figure cited by Britton and McElroy. Britton, 54; McElroy, 138.
39. *O.R.*, Series 3, vol. 1: 794; *O.R.S.*, pt. 2, vol. 50: 102–103; Banasik, *Missouri in 1861*, 204; "Battle of Carthage," *Rebellion Record*, vol. 2: Doc. 247; Edwards, 31;. Ingenthron, 44; Lademann,

Strength of the command. Following the engagement at Carthage, Sigel sent Lieutenant Max Tusk or Tosk with dispatches to St. Louis to report on his movements and the Battle of Carthage. In Tusk's account of the Carthage affair, he stated that Sigel's force amounted "to about eleven hundred men." Other authors also placed Sigel's forces at 1,100, with a few placing his total as low as 1,000 men with eight pieces of artillery, implying the difference of 50–150 men were for the artillery commands. Still others, including the editors of the *Union Army* series, put Sigel's force with 1,200 to 1,500 men of all types. In the *Union Army* account, the editors acknowledge Sigel's reported numbers for the 3rd and 5th Missouri, as 950, "and two batteries of 4 guns each, numbering in all about 1,500 men." So who were the missing 550 men that Sigel had at the engagement, who were not "engaged?" Sigel was clearly misleading in stating the force that he had available verses what he had engaged at Carthage, leaving out the men who manned his artillery as well as others. Even Otto Lademann recorded that when Sigel left St. Louis his force numbered 2,000. This was supported by a modern-day author Donald Gilmore, who wrote that Sigel's command numbered 2,000 men, at Carthage, citing John M. Schofield's report in the *Official Records*, which stated that "Price had about twice Sigel's number of men," implying that Sigel had at least 2,000 men. John C. Moore, a period author of the *Missouri, Confederate Military History*, also places Sigel's strength at Carthage as 2,000. And finally, the *Official Records* gives the strength of Sigel's command strength on June 1, as 2,282–1,103 for the 3rd Missouri; 926 for the 5th Missouri and 253 for Backof's Artillery Battalion of three companies. So what happened to the difference in men that Sigel reported at Carthage verses the amount that he left St. Louis with on June 14?[40]

When Sigel's command left St. Louis they took trains to Rolla, where they rested for a few days assembling the necessary supplies and transportation for the expedition to Springfield. When the command finally departed Rolla they sustained a relatively easy march to southwest Missouri, making about 15 miles a day–hardly a fatiguing march that would have reduced the command's overall strength by 40 percent. However, according to John Beugel, a member of the 3rd Missouri, his command appeared to be in a "deplorable condition" when they arrived in Springfield, resembling "a rabble more than soldiers"; that said, despite their appearance, Hinze and Farnham noted that Sigel's command "endured the march fairly well"–and that, despite the last few days being through a "driving rain storm." Sigel's column then rested for several days allowing them to recover any strength they had lost during the march to Springfield. So a closer look is

---

"Battle of Carthage," 132–133, 138; Monaghan, 154; Moore, *Missouri, Confederate Military History*, vol. 9: 48; O'Flaherty, 67.

40. *O.R.*, vol. 3: 94; *O.R.*, Series 3, vol. 1: 794; "Battle of Carthage," *Rebellion Record*, vol. 2: Doc. 246; Engle, 63–64; "Col. Burbridge's Regiment," 9; "Great Battle in South-Western Missouri," *Waukegan Weekly Gazette*, July 13, 1861; Gilmore, 119; Hinze & Farnham, 222; Ingenthron, 44; Lademann, "Battle of Carthage," 134; Moore, *Missouri, Confederate Military History*, 49; Monaghan, 151; Peckham, 293–294; *Rebellion Record*, vol. 2: Diary 19; Schrantz, 31; Snead, 225; *Union Army*, vol. 5: 228; *War in the West*, 267.

required to see what force Sigel had available for the engagement at Carthage, allowing adjustments for the effects of the march and for men who were present but not effective; say five percent for the march and seven percent for the men present and not effective according to Thomas L. Livermore. Also an accounting must be made for any known detachments that Sigel made prior to July 5.[41]

* * * * * * *

Note: Within the various commands the number within ( ) represents the number of men present, while the un-bracketed number represents number of men engaged.

Second Brigade, Army of the West (Col. Franz Sigel):
Staff = 6 (6) EFF[42] [no losses].

* * * * * * *

Third Missouri Infantry (Three months). When the 3rd Missouri (Three months) was organized in contained twelve companies. A review of the *Supplement to the Official Records* identifies eleven of the companies in the 3rd Missouri, with Company B, commanded by Captain Joseph Conrad, not being listed, even though it was part of the command and captured at Neosho on July 5. Of the eleven companies in the *Supplement* ten were listed as at Carthage, where most sources have only eight or nine companies at the engagement. Of those eleven companies listed in the *Supplement to the Official Records*, six companies–A, A (Rifle Battalion), B, C, G and H were noted as "engaged" at Carthage, the same words that General Sigel used to portray the presence of the 3rd Missouri at the engagement Of the remaining five companies, three were noted as "took an active part in the engagement,"–Company F; or "In battle at Carthage"–Company I; or "was present and acting in the battle"–Company K.. Of the two remaining commands, Companies D and E, Otto Lademann of Company E, recorded that his command managed to fire a small volley toward the end of the battle, meaning that it was engaged, though apparently only briefly, before it "skedaddled." The eleventh company–D–had no entry in the *Supplement*, though Hinze and Farnham and the *Rebellion Record* both recorded that it was one of the listed companies at the battle on July 5; however there was no indication that it was engaged.[43]

41. Bek, "Beugel Diary," 311; Hinze & Farnham, 66–67; Thomas L. Livermore, *Numbers & Losses in the Civil War in America: 1861–1865* (Bloomington, IN, 1957), 69, hereafter cited as Livermore.

42. The *Rebellion Record* listed Sigel's staff with three members, not including Sigel. Additionally, Sigel also had two aid-de-camps for a total staff, with commander, of six. *O.R.*, vol. 3: 19; "Battle of Carthage," *Rebellion Record*, vol. 2: Doc. 247.

43. It should be noted that within the *Supplement*, Company A embraces two commands; Captain John Cramer's Company A and Lieutenant Leopold Helmle's Company A (Rifle Battalion). Also, Captain Henry Zeis' Company B (Rifle Battalion) is listed, while Captain Joseph Conrad's Company B is not listed, though we know it was part of the 3rd Missouri (Three months). *O.R.*, vol.

When the 3rd Missouri left St. Louis its present for duty strength was 1,103, two weeks prior to heading for Rolla. Allowing a five percent loss for the march and another seven percent for present, but non-effective men would give the regiment 971 (1,103 x .88 = 970.64) effective officers and men. Allowing a command staff of 5, including Colonel Sigel, and the two regimental surgeons, would leave the regiment with 964 (971 - 7 = 964) officers and men. On July 4, Sigel detached Captain Joseph Conrad's Company B, reducing the regiment by 94, leaving 870 (964 - 94 = 870) effective officers and men, if they were all engaged. Each company of the remaining eleven would number 79 (870 / 11 = 79.09) officers and men. Assuming that four of the regiment's companies were not engaged, as shown above, would reduce the engaged strength to 554 (79 x 4 = 316 ; or 870 - 316 = 554) officers and men–almost identical to what Sigel reported. See Order of Battle below for the final breakdown for the regiment at Carthage.[44]

3rd Missouri Inf. (Three months–Lt. Col. Francis Hassendeubel):[45]
Staff: EFF = 4 (6).[46]
   1st Bn. (Lt. Col. F. Hassendeubel):
   Co. A (Capt. John F. Cramer) EFF = 79 (E–79) [unknown].
   Co. A (Rifle Bn.–1st. Lt. Leopold Helmle)[47] EFF = 79 (E–79)
      [2 K, 6 W, 0 M].[48]
   Co. B (Rifle Bn.–Capt. Henry Zeis) EFF = 79 (E–79) [1 W; losses
      incomplete].[49]
   Co. C (Capt. Jacob Hartman) EFF = 79 (E–79) [1 K, 0 W, 0 M].[50]
   Co. D (Capt. August Hackman) EFF = 0 (E–79)
      [unknown–though probably 0].
   1st Bn. EFF = 316 (E–395) [3 K, 7W, 0 M–losses incomplete].[51]

3: 19; *O.R.S.*, pt. 2, vol. 36: 437–432; "Battle of Carthage," *Rebellion Record*, vol. 2: Doc. 247; Britton, 53; Peckham, 121–122.

44. *O.R.*, Series 3, vol. 1: 794; Peckham, 121.

45. The *Rebellion Record* has the same commanders for the various companies as presented below; however they are listed commanding different companies; i.e., the *Rebellion Record* has Captain Hackman at Carthage, but commanding Company G, while Company D, Hackman's command, was led by Captain Zeis. And the same is true of the other companies. For this Order of Battle I will use Peckham, the same that Hinze & Farnham used. Also, the regimental staff, in addition to the commander, contained an adjutant, quartermaster and an ordnance officer. *O.R.S.*, pt. 2, vol. 36: 436–442; "Battle of Carthage," *Rebellion Record*, vol. 2: Doc. 247; Hinze & Farnham, 221; Peckham, 121–122.

46. The effectives include Lieutenant Colonel Hassendeubel, the major, adjutant, and quartermaster; those present also includes the regimental surgeons. Peckham, 121.

47. Captain Joseph Indest did not command Company A (Rifle Battalion), as recorded by Hinze and Farnham, but commanded Company H, according to Colonel Sigel. First Lieutenant Leopold Helmle commanded the company according the *Supplement to the Official Records*, effective June 17, 1861. *O.R.*, vol. 3: 17; *O.R.S.*, pt. 2, vol. 36: 437–438.

48. *O.R.S.*, pt. 2, vol. 36: 438.

49. Company B had at least one man wounded –Lieutenant Henry Bischoff. *O.R.*, vol. 3: 19.

50. *O.R.S.*, pt. 2, vol. 36: 438.

51. Lieutenant Colonel Francis Hassendeubel and staff counted in the regimental total.

2nd Bn. (Maj. Henry Bischoff):
Co. E (Capt. John Strodkamp; WIA)[52] EFF = 79 (E–79)
[0 K, 4 W, 0 M].
Co. F (Capt. Hugo Glomer) EFF = 0 (E–79)
[unknown–though probably 0].
Co. G (Capt. Adolph Dengler) EFF = 79 (E–79) [unknown].
Co. H (Capt. Joseph Indest)[53] EFF = 79 (E–79) [unknown].
Co. I (Capt. Carl or Charles H. Mannhardt)[54] EFF = 0 (E–79)
[unknown–though probably 0].
Bn. EFF = 237 (E–395) [4 W–losses incomplete].

Bn. Unknown.
Co. B (Capt. Joseph Conrad)[55] EFF = 0 (94–At Neosho)
[0 K. 0 W. 94 M].
Co. K (Capt. Theodore Menmann)[56] EFF = 0 (E-79)
[unknown–though probably 0].
Bn. EFF = 0 (E–79)[57] [unknown–though probably 0].
Regiment Total = 557 (E–875) [58]
[3 K, 11 W, 0 M–losses incomplete],

* * * * * * *

Fifth Missouri Infantry (Three months). Most accounts have the 5th Missouri (Three months) carrying seven companies into the Battle of Carthage. En route to Springfield in mid-June, 1861, the regiment left Company K at Lebanon, where it was detached to guard the "road" to Springfield. And when the regiment left Springfield it left Companies B and H to protect the town, pending the arrival of

52. Otto Lademann says that his company was part of Hassendeubel's Battalion, while the *Rebellion Record* has the command as part of Bischof's Battalion. "Battle of Carthage," *Rebellion Record*, vol. 2: Doc. 247; Lademann, "Battle of Carthage," 137.

53. Sigel has Indest commanding Company H, while Hinze and Farnham, with Peckhan list the commander as George D. Friedlein. See also note 47. *O.R.*, vol. 3: 17; Hinze & Farnham, 222; Peckham, 122.

54. The *Supplement to the Official Records* has Company I at Carthage, while Hinze and Farnham do not. Also, the *Rebellion Record* listed the commander as Captain F. E. Schreimer. "Battle of Carthage," *Rebellion Record*, vol. 2: Doc. 247; Hinze & Farnham, 221–222; Peckham, 122.

55. Company was captured at Neosho, Missouri on July 5, surrendering, according to Federal sources, 94 men. Confederate sources put the captures at 137 or "some 120 or 130 prisoners. NOTE: The disparity in numbers probably reflects the capture of some local Home Guards and/or teamsters. *O.R*, vol. 3: 19; *O.R.S.*, pt. 1, vol. 1: 223; Snead, 237.

56. This company was not listed in either Hinze & Farhman's Order of Battle or in the *Rebellion Record*. However, according to the *Supplement to the Official Records*, the company "was present and acting in the battle near Carthage." *O.R.S.*, pt. 2, vol. 36: 442; "Battle of Carthage," *Rebellion Record*, vol. 2: Doc. 247; Peckham, 122.

57. Number present at Carthage does not include Captain Conrad's Company which was captured at Neosho.

58. Excludes Conrad's Company, but includes the regimental staff.

General Sweeny's men from St. Louis. This left the regiment with seven companies or about 648 (926 / 10 = 92.6 x 7 = 648.2) officers and men present for duty, including the regimental staff. Allowing an additional five percent loss for sickness, etc., and per Livermore, another seven percent for non-effective men, would suggest an effective strength of 570 (648 x .88 = 570.2) officers and men for the regiment at Carthage, not the 400 that Sigel reported. The regimental staff, including the commander would number five, including commander, lieutenant colonel, major, adjutant, and quartermaster, leaving the regiment 565 (570 - 5 = 565) effective officers and men. The difference in this number and Sigel's could simply be that two of the 5th Missouri companies were not engaged at Carthage, which would reduce the strength to 404 (565 /7 = 80.7 x 2 = 161.4; or 565 - 161 = 404) effective officers and men. So which two companies were not engaged at Carthage?

Reviewing the *Supplement to the Official Records* gives rise to three of the companies who were possibly not engaged at Carthage–Company A has no stated comments one way or the other; Company C "fell in with the Rebel forces" but doesn't state that it was engaged; and Company G "marched off to meet the enemy" but doesn't state that it was engaged. The remaining companies were either engaged, suffered losses or "were in action" at the engagement on July 5. It appears that Companies C and G were not engaged at Carthage, but they were present. See Order of Battle below for the final breakdown.[59]

Note: Rounding will rise the overall regimental strength to 572, and adding in the regimental staff and rounding will yield an effective "engaged" strength of 410 instead of the 404 listed above. Also, there was no "official" breakdown of the two battalions in the 5th Missouri; however, Sigel in his Official Reports provides a listing of Salomon's 2nd Battalion when the command protected the crossing at Dry Fork Creek during the retreat of Sigel's command. This in turn would give the companies that comprised the First Battalion, using the process of elimination.[60]

5th Missouri Inf. (Three months–Colonel Charles Salomon):[61]:
Staff : EFF = 5 (5) [no losses].
    1st Bn. (Lt. Col. Christian Wolff):
    Co. A (Capt. N. Cole) EFF = 81 (E–81) [unknown].
    Co. C (Capt. Fred Salomon) EFF = 0 (E–81)
    [unknown–probably 0].
    Co. D (Capt. Charles Mehl) EFF = 81 (E–81) [unknown].
    Co. F (Capt. Alfred Arnaud) EFF = 81 (E–81) [1 K, 1 W, 0 M]].[62]
        Bn. EFF = 243 (E–324) [1K, 1 W, 0 M–Losses incomplete].

59. *O.R.S.*, pt. 2, vol. 36: 490–495; Britton, 54; Livermore, 69.
60. *O.R.*, vol 3: 18.
61. Hinze & Farnham have Company B in the Battle of Carthage, while *Supplement to the Official Records* have them stationed in Springfield for the battle on July 5. *O.R.S.*, pt. 2, vol. 36: 490; Hinze & Farnham, 222.
62. *O.R.S.*, pt. 2, vol. 36: 492.

2nd Bn. (Col. Charles E. Salomon):
Co. G (1st Lt. Nicholas Fuester)[63] EFF = 0 (E–81)
[unknown–probably 0].
Co. E (Capt. Carl Stephani or Stephany)[64] EFF = 81 (E–81)
[unknown].
Co. I (Capt. C. Meisner) EFF = 81 (E–81) [unknown].
2nd Bn. EFF = 162 (E–243) [Losses unknown].
Regt. Total = EFF 410 (E–572)
[1 K, 1 W, 0 M–losses incomplete].

* * * * * * *

Backof's Artillery Battalion. Backof's Battalion consisted of three batteries commanded by Captains Christian Essig (Company A–four guns), Theodore Wilkins (Company B–four guns) and John A. Neusteedter (Company C–three guns). This would suggest t it took 23 (253 / 11 = 23) officers and men to man each gun. Further, this would mean that Company A and B totaled 184 (23 x 8 = 184) officers and men. Allowing a battalion command staff of four, including the commander, would give each battery 90 (184–4 = 180/ 2 = 90) officers and men per battery, for Companies A and B, without any loss on the march due to sickness or other causes. Allowing a loss of five percent for the march and another seven percent for non-combatants, as defined by Thomas L. Livermore would give each company 79 (90 x .88 = 79.2) effective officers and men per company.[65]

Within the literature surrounding the engagement at Carthage, Thomas L. Snead, as well as others, explain part of the difference between Sigel's reported strength and others–Snead has 125 men for the artillery while Lademann puts the artillery at 200, and still others place it at 150 officers and men. And for those commentators who placed Sigel's command at 1,100, they were clearly signaling that the batteries represented 150 officers and men. [66]

---

63. Stark was noted as both the company commander and Regimental Quartermaster on the 3rd Missouri for the Battle of Carthage, in the *Rebellion Record*; as such Company G's second in command, 1st Lieutenant Nicholas Fuester would have commanded the company, while Stark was elevated and served as the Brigade Quartermaster not the Regimental Quartermaster. The Regimental Quartermaster was 1st Lieutenant Sebastian Engert, who commanded the brigade train. Hinze and Farnham have Stark as part of the force that covered Sigel's retreat across Dry Fork Creeek, citing Sigel's report on the engagement; however, a close reading of Sigel's report has Stark's Company covering the retreat, but not stating who commanded the unit. See also "Teamseters" below. *O.R.*, vol. 3:18; "Battle of Carthage," *Rebellion Record*, vol. 2: Doc. 247; Hinze & Farnham,147; Peckham, 124.

64. The *Rebellion Record* has the commander as Captain Richardson. "Battle of Carthage," *Rebellion Record*, vol. 2: Doc. 247.

65. *O.R.S.*, pt. 2, vol. 36: 136,138; Livermore, 69; United States Pension Office, *Organization of Missouri Troops*, 218.

66. Lademann, "Carthage," *Missouri Republican*, March 26, 1887; Schrantz, 31; Snead, *Fight for Missouri*, 225.

Backof's Artillery Battalion (Maj. Frank Backoff):[67]
Staff: EFF = 4 (E–4) [losses ubknown].
   Company A (Christian Essig) 4 guns: 4, 12-lb how.EFF = 79 (E–79)
   [unknown].
   Company B (Theodore Wilkins) 4 guns: 2, 12-lb how. & 2 6-lb SB
   EFF = 79 (E–79) [unknown].
   Bn. Total = 162 (E-162) [losses unknown].

* * * * * * *

Miscellaneous commands. Of the miscellaneous commands listed above under "Units not previously identified" Captain Voerester's or Foerster's Pioneer company seems to be the most definitive. The other units are not as well defined, though an educated guess is possible.

Captain Voerester's (or Voerster's or Foerster's) Pioneer Company. A review of the United States Pension Office Records shows several possibilities for Foerester's Company, as mentioned by Otto Lademann–one was a Citizens Guard Company while the other was a Provisional Enrolled Company. However, neither company had any information concerning its service or where it was raised. A further review of the Pension Office Records lists a Pioneer Company mustered into service on May 10, 1861, for three months and commanded by a Captain John D. Voerester. I suspect that Lademann's recollection of the name was simply a spelling error, resulting from a mispronunciation. Reviewing the *Supplement to the Official Records*, one finds John D. Voerester listed as commanding a Pioneer Company, known as Company A. According to the *Supplement*, a detachment of the company was assigned to General Sigel for his Expedition to Springfield, while two other detachments were assigned to other columns operating in Missouri.

On June 12, 1861, Voerester's Company was listed with 120 officers and men Present for Duty. The company, as a pioneer company, was armed, according to sources with "Sharps' rifles slung across their backs, hunting hats on their heads, and axes, shovels and picks on their shoulders." Of the three detachments, according the *Supplement.*, General Lyon's numbered 47 officers and men. This would suggest that the other two detachments each contained 37 (120 - 47 = 73 / 2 = 36.5) officers and men. Allowing a five percent loss for the march and another seven percent, per Livermore, for non-effective men, leaves Voerester's detachment with 32 (36.5 x .88 = 32.12.) effective officers and men for the Battle of Carthage.[68]

---

67. Battery guns per Lademann. Lademann, "Battle of Carthage," 132.
68. *O.R.*, vol. 3: 389; *O.R.*, Series 3, vol. 1: 794; *O.R.S.*, pt. 2:, vol. 50: 102–103; Adamson, 153; Livermore, 69; Patrick, *Nine Months in the Infantry*, 19, 25; Piston & Hatcher, *Wilson's Creek*, 74; United States Pension Office, *Organization of Missouri Troops*, 223, 231, 234;Woodard, 291.

Home Guard Cavalry or Mounted Force. From Sigel's report he stated that he had no cavalry, while other sources noted that he had some "mounted Home Guard" or "some cavalry" to support his command, having joined him at Springfield.

According to Army Regulations, each company would contain four squads, commanded by a non-commissioned officer. And in 1861, the typical Home Guard command consisted of about 100 officers and men. Two squads would represent 50 officers and men. The Home Guard joined Sigel at Springfield, as such, no loss was allowed for the march; however, seven percent is allowed for the non-effective men of the command, leaving the two squads with 47 (50 x .93 = 46.5) effective officers and men.

There are three possibilities as to which command the Home Guard squads belonged; the Greene County Independent Home Guard Company, the Lawrence County Regiment of Home Guards and the Greene and Christian County Home Guard Regiment. The Lawrence County command was mustered into the service on May 25, 1861, and accepted by Colonel Sigel on June 16. The Greene County Independent Home Guard Company was "organized under the authority of Gen. Lyon in June 1861." And the Greene and Christian County Home Guard was "unofficially" organized on June 11,1861 and later accepted by Federal authorities upon their arrival in Springfield. Of the three commands, the Lawrence County command was used, according to Frederick Dyer, as scouts, or guarding supply trains and "posts" and was mustered out on August 10, 1861 The Greene and Christian County Home Guard operated out of Springfield while awaiting the arrival of Federal troops and then served as the city's garrison until after the Battle of Wilson' Creek.

Of the three commands the most likely to have been with Sigel at Carthage was the Greene County Independent Home Guard Company which was also known as Springfield County Home Guard. The unit was commanded by Captain C. B. Holland, being organized in June 1861. Further, it had "been drilled" to some extent, being armed with "shot gun, rifle and pistol, or whatever kind of weapon" they might happen to have. This command to a member of the Greene and Christian County command was probably the best command of the Springfield Home Guard units. Additionally, this company was noted as being employed as "scouts and escorts"–the same role that Sigel used them in while under his command. It seems therefore likely that the two squads mentioned by the various sources as being with Sigel belonged to Holland's command. It should also be noted that when the Federals withdrew from Springfield, following the Battle of Wilson's Creek that the Greene and Christian County Home Guard Regiment disbanded on August 17, with the lone exception being Holland's Company which accompanied the retreating Unionists to Rolla.[69]

---

69. *O.R.*, Series 3, vol. 1: 795; Dyer, 1342; Patrick, *Nine Months in the Infantry*, 13, 15 n. 11, 16 n. 12, 27–28; United States Pension Office, *Organization of Missouri Troops*, 225; United States War

Regulars. No information on regulars, who were at Carthage, was found, with the exception of comments made by Elmo Ingenthron, R.I. Holcombe & W. S. Adams, and a period account in the Rebellion Record. In this case, I suspect that the addition of the Home Guards troops, to Sigel's command, at Springfield, were misinterpreted as regulars. However, even though there were no regulars at Carthage, there appears to have been the addition of some additional infantry or Home Guards from the Shoal Creek area that joined Sigel at the withdrawal from Dry Fork Creek. According to the *Rebellion Record* and the *Waukegan Weekly Gazette*, "the timely arrival of 200 Union men from Shoals Creek" helped Sigel's command safely cross Dry Fork Creek, losing five killed and two mortally wounded.[70]

Teamsters. There were 54 wagons in Sigel's train, according to Otto Lademann, while Hinze and Farnham put the number at 34–in this case I used Lademann's account. Allowing one driver per wagon, a wagon-master and an assistant wagon-master would suggest that 56 men were needed to drive the teams, with the original Quartermaster of the 3rd Missouri, 1st Lieutenant Sebastian Engert assigned to command of the train according to Otto Lademann Since they were not regularly organized I assume that they were unarmed and not engaged, but were present at the battle on July 5.[71]

> Miscellaneous Commands.
> Voerester's Pioneer Co. (Capt. John D. Voerester)[72] EFF = 32 (E-32) [unknown].
> Springfield County Home Guard Co.. (Probably Capt. C. B. Holland) EFF = 47 (E–47) [1 K, rest unknown].[73]
> Reenforcements from Shoal Creek (Cdr unknown) EFF = 200 (200) [5 K, 2 MW, 0 M].[74]
> Teamsters (1st Lt. Sebastian Engert)[75] EFF = 0 (E-56) [unknown–probably 0].

Department, *Revised Regulations of the United States 1861, With Full Index* (Philadelphia, PA, 1861; reprint ed., Harrisburg, PA, 1980), 21.
70. Holcombe & Adams, 7; *Rebellion Record*, vol. 2: Diary 20; "Great Battle in the South-Western Missouri," *Waukegan Weekly Gazette*, July 13, 1861.
71. Lademann in his account of the engagement mentions that the train contained 54 wagons and would later list the assistant wagon-master as a Mr. Fraser, implying that there was also a wagon-master present at Carthage. Otto Lademann, "Sigel at Wilson's Creek," *Missouri Republican*, April 9, 1887.
72. Since the train, according to Sigel, was attacked in the middle of the engagement, its assumed that the Pioneer Company, which was guarding the train would have been engaged. *O.R.*, vol. 3: 18.
73. Banasik, *Missouri in 1861*, 202; Edwards, 31.
74. "Great Battle in the South-Western Missouri," *Waukegan Weekly Gazette*, July 13, 1861; *Rebellion Record*, vol. 2: Diary 20.
75. Lieutenant Engert was included as a member of 3rd Missouri staff and not included here under the number present with the teamsters. Lademann, "Battle of Carthage," 133.

Miscellaneous Command Total = 279 (E–335)
[5 K, 2 MW, 0 M–loses incomplete]

* * * * * * *

Union Army Summary
    2nd Brigade Army of the WestStaff = 6 (6)
    3rd Missouri (Three months) Staff = 4 (6)
    1st Bn. = 316 (E–395)
    2nd Bn. = 237 (E–395)
    Unknown Bn. = 0 (E–79)[76]
    5th Missouri (Three months)Staff = 5 (5)= 405 (E–572)
    Backof's Artillery Bn. = 162 (E–162)
    Miscellaneous Commands = 279 (E– 335)
        Total 2nd Brigade = 1, 414 (E–1,950) [18 K, 53 W, 5 M][77]

Note: If you remove the Miscellaneous commands and staff from the above, excluding the artillery command, the totals would be 1,120 (1,414-279-15 = 1,117) effective officers and men engaged with an estimated 1,600 (1,950-335-15 = 1,600) effective officers and men present. Essentially, when reporting his command at Carthage, Sigel only reported the regularly enlisted volunteers that he had at the battle, excluding the Home Guards, the Pioneer Company and his teamsters. The 1,120 officers and men "engaged" would be almost identical to what most period writers and secondary authors believe that Sigel had at the battle on July 5, excluding 480 (1,600-1,120 = 480) effective regulars that he failed to employ during the engagement, as well as the total exclusion of his Pioneer Company and Home Guard commands that were present at the battle on July 5. The only legitimate command Sigel should have excluded would have been the 56-man teamster detachment, which were hired civilians who drove the wagons.

* * * * * * *

---

76. Excludes prisoners taken at Neosho on July 5.
77. See also the paragraph associated with note no.38 in Chapter 2 for additional comments on Federal losses at Carthage. *O.R.*, vol. 3: 19; *O.R.S.*, pt. 2, vol. 36: 493; Adamson, 151; Britton, 63; Dyer, 797; Engle, 65; Hinze & Farnham, 202; Ingenthron, 49; McElroy, 141; Monaghan, 155; Schrantz, 40; Snead, *Fight for Missouri*, 227.

Union Revised Order of Battle
Battle of Wilson's Creek
(August 10, 1861)

Introduction

In 2001, I put forth my version of the Union Order of Battle for Wilson's Creek in my book *Missouri in 1861*. Since that time new information has come to light that has caused me to revise the Order of Battle for the Union command. In the previous version I left out a detachment from the 13th Illinois Infantry, Voerester's Pioneer Company, Lyon's Bodyguard, and the guides, who led the two columns, as well as fine tuning the commanders of the various units. The staff is also listed below where it was indicated in the *Official Records* or elsewhere; however, it appears that with the exception of Sigel's independent command, the other three brigades had no brigade command structure, as such, none is generally listed in the Order of Battle.[78]

Voerester's Pioneer Company. According to the *Supplement to the Official Records*, following its organization the company was divided into three detachments, totaling 120 officers and men on June 12, 1861. One detachment was assigned to General Sigel, which fought at Carthage on July 5, a second detachment was assigned to General John Pope in north Missouri and the third, of 47 officers and men, accompanied General Lyon to Boonville and later to Springfield, where they linked up with te first detachment under Sigel, arriving on July 13, 1861.As shown above under the Battle of Carthage, Captain Voerester's Pioneer Company, this would suggest that Voerester's Company now contained 74 (37 + 47 = 84 x .88 = 73.9) effective officers and men, after allowing a five percent loss for the march and another seven percent, per Livermore, for non-effective men, for the Battle of Wilson's Creek.[79]

Note: Forces denoted with an "*" were three month units and their term of service had expired or were about to in the near future.

---

78. Banasik, *Missouri in 1861*, 377–378; "Battle of Wilson's Creek, MO.: Missouri 'Democrat' Narrative," *Rebellion Record*, vol. 2: Doc. 511; Dyer, 1341; Piston & Hatcher, *Soldiers' Letters*, 66; Piston & Hatcher, *Wilson's Creek*, 80, 337.

79. *O.R.*, vol. 3: 389; *O.R.*, Series 3, vol. 1: 794; *O.R.S.*, pt. 2:, vol. 50: 102–103; Adamson, 153; Livermore, 69; Piston & Hatcher, *Wilson's Creek*, 74; United States Pension Office, *Organization of Missouri Troops*, 223, 231, 234; Woodard, 291.

Lyon's Column (Brigadier General Nathaniel Lyon):
   Staff = 8 EFF [1 K, 2 W, 0 M].[80]
   Guides = 20 EFF [Losses unknown].[81]
   Bodyguard (Cdr. Unknown) EFF = 10 [1 K, 0 W, 0 M].[82]
   Voerester's Pioneer Co. (Capt. John D. Voerester) EFF = 74
      [Losses ukn.].
            HQ Total = 113 EFF [2 K, 2 W, 0 M; losses incomplete].
      First Brigade (Major Samuel D. Sturgis):
      Staff = 2 EFF [0 K, 0 W, 0 M].[83]
            1st U.S. Inf. (Cos. B, C, D; Capt. Joseph B. Plummer) EFF = 300
               [19 K, 52 W, 9 M].
            * 2nd Mo. Inf. (Cos. A, C; Maj. Peter J. Osterhaus) EFF = 150
               [15 K, 40 W, 0 M].
            * 2nd Kan. Inf. (Co. I; Capt. S. N. Wood) &
            1st U.S. Cav. (Co. D; Lt. Charles W. Canfield) EFF = 150
               [0 K, 2 W, 3 M].
            2nd U.S. Art. (Co. F; Capt. James Totten) 6 guns: 6, 6-lb SB EFF =
               84 [4 K, 7 W, 0 M].
            Brigade Total = 686 EFF [38 K, 101 W, 12 M].
      Third Brigade (Lt. Col. George L. Andrews):[84]
            *1st Mo. Inf. (Lt. Col. George L. Andrews, WIA; Capt. Theodore
               Yates)[85] EFF = 775 [76 K, 208 W, 11 M].
            1st. U.S. Inf. (Cos. B and E; Capt. Frederick Steele) &
            Co. Regular Army Recruits (Lt. Warren Lothrop) &
            Co. Regular Army Recruits (Sergt. John Morine) EFF -= 275
               [15 K, 44 W, 2 M].
            Du Bois' Battery (Lt. John V. Du Bois) 4 guns: 1, 12-lb. how. & 3,
               6-lb SB EFF = 66 [0 K, 2 W, 1 M].
            Brigade Total = 1,116 EFF [91 K, 254 W, 14 M].

80. Staff included: Major Horace Conant (Acting Quartermaster, Lieutenant Colonel I. F. Shepherd (Aid-de-camp), Captain Gordon Granger (Acting Adjutant General and Aide-de-Camp, Major John M. Schofield (Acting Adjutant General), Major William M. Wherry (Aide-de-camp), Captain Tom Sweeney (Inspector General; WIA) and Lieutenant Joseph Conrad (Assistant Commissary; WIA). Staff strength also includes General Lyon. Bodyguard per Peckham and Piston & Hatcher. *O.R.*, vol. 3: 56–57, 70, 96; Peckham, 328, 338; Piston & Hatcher, *Wilson's Creek*, 337; Wherry, "General Lyon," 80.
81. Bearss, *Wilson's Creek*, 51.
82. Banasik, *Missouri in 1861*, 149–150.
83. Mr. E. Cozzens (Aide-de-camp) was the only staff member noted by Major Sturgis as part of his command following the battle. *O.R.*, vol. 3: 70.
84. There was no indication in the Official Records that the Third Brigade had any type of command staff; indeed, George L. Andrews, commander of the brigade makes no mention of the remainder of his brigade, while the only staff member that he mentions appears to have been associated with the 1st Missouri. *O.R.*, vol. 3: 75–78.
85. Ibid., 76, 815.

Fourth Brigade (Col. George W. Detzieler, WIA):[86]
  *1st Kan. Inf. (Maj. John A. Halderman)[87] EFF = 800
    [77 K, 187 W, 20 M].
  *2nd Kan. Inf. (Col. Robert B. Mitchell, WIA; LT. Col. Charles W.
    Blair)[88] EFF = 600 [5 K, 59 W, 6 M].
  *1st Iowa Inf. (Lt. Col.. William H. Merritt) EFF = 800
    [12 K, 138 W, 4 M].
  13th Ill. Inf. Mtd. Detch. (1st Lt. James Beardsley)[89] EFF = 21
    [0 K, 0 W. 1 M].
  Dade County Home Guard (Capt. Clark Wright) EFF = 100 (E)
    [0 K, 1 W, 0 M].
  Frémont Rangers Home Guard Co. (Capt. Theodore A. Switzler)
    EFF = 100 (E) [0 K, 1 W, 0 M].
  Brigade Total = 2,421 EFF [94 K, 386 W, 31 M].
  Total Lyon's Column: 4,336 EFF [225 K, 744 W, 57 M]

* * * * * * *

Sigel's Command. In 1895, General Sigel recorded that the 3rd and 5th Missouri (Three months) totaled 912 "men" while his overall strength of his brigade was 1,118 "men," clearly excluding the officers. And Sigel's account of his overall strength also differs from most sources that place his strength at 1,200 (*Official Records*, Banasik, Bearss, Britton, Piston & Hatcher, Snead and others), with some as high as 1,500 (Burke, Moore and Wherry). Those sources that used 1,200 as Sigel's strength then used the reported strengths of the rest of Sigel's Brigade to place his infantry strength at 990 officers and men. A closer look at the numbers in the *Official Records* states that the 1,200 figure was an estimate. As both regiments together totaled roughly the strength of a normal regiment, this would suggest that the officers strength would have been about 30 captains and lieutenants, while the staff of the two regiments would have been about 8 (This assumes the loss of Major H. Bischoff and Lieutenant Colonel C. Wolff who led detachments back to St. Louis for mustering out, while the Quartermasters and Ordnance Officers, with the remaining field grade officers would give the two regiments 8 officers.). This would put the total officers and men for the two regiments, combined,

---

86. Ibid., 70.
87. The *Military History of Kansas Regiments* places the regimental strength at 644 with 75 killed, and 255 wounded. The numbers listed here come from Major Halderman's Official Report. Ibid., 72, 83; Burke, 9.
88. *O.R.*, vol.3: 84.
89. During the course of the battle the detachment guarded the prisoners, suffering the loss of Private Roland H. Stearns, who was captured, with one horse. "Battle of Wilson's Creek, MO: Missouri 'Democrat' Narrative," *Rebellion Record*, vol. 2:511, 514; G.C.C., "From Rolla," *Chicago Tribune*, August 28, 1861; G.C.C., "Gen. Lyon's Army," *Chicago Tribune*, August 14, 1861; Piston & Hatcher, *Wilson's Creek*, 80, 338.

at about 950 (912 + 30 + 8 = 950); and with Sigel's other units–85 for artillery and 121 for cavalry–would produce a total of 1,156 (950 = 85 + 121 = 1,156) or about 1,200. [90]

Sigel's two infantry commands can then be estimated based upon their relative strength as reported by General Lyon on August 4, which was 1.300–700 for the 3rd Missouri and 600 for the 5th Missouri. This would equate to 700/ 1,300 = .538 or 54 % for the 3rd Missouri and 600/ 1,300 = .461 or 46 % for the 5th Missouri. [91] Using these percentages gives the results listed below. The combined losses of 35 K, 132 W, 126 M could also be determined using the same method; however, we know from the accounts of the battle the majority of the loses fell on the 3rd Missouri when they were attacked at the James River Branch of the White River making the final determination of regimental losses a pure guess.

> 3rd Missouri 513 (950 x .54 = 513) officers and men
> 5th Missouri 437 (950 x .46 = 437) officers and men

Sigel's Column (Col. Franz Sigel):
> *3rd Mo. Inf. (Lt. Col. Anselm Albert) EFF = 513(E).
> *5th Mo. Inf. (Col. Charles E. Salomon) EFF = 437 (E).[92] Combined
>   Losses 3rd & 5th Mo. [35 K, 132 W, 126 M].
> 1st U.S. Cav. (Capt. Eugene A. Carr) EFF = 65 [0 K, 0 W, 4 M].
> 2nd U.S. Dragoons (Co. C; Lt. Charles E. Farrand) EFF = 60
>   [0 K, 0 W, 0 M].[93]
> *Backof's Mo. Art. (Lts. G. A. Schaefer & Edward Schuetzenbach)
>   6 guns: 2, 12-lb how. & 4, 6-lb SB EFF = 85 [0 K, 0 W, 0 M].[94]
>   Brigade Total = 1,156 EFF [35 K, 132 W, 130 M].
>   Total Union Army = 5,492 EFF
>   Losses = 1,319 [260 K. 876 W, 186 M]

* * * * * * *

---

90. *O.R.*, vol. 3: 96; Banasik, *Missouri in 1861*, 378; Bearss, *Wilson's Creek*, 163; Britton, 107; Burke, 6; Moore, *Missouri, Confederate Military History*, 56; Piston & Hatcher, *Wilson's Creek*, 337; Sigel, "Flanking Column," 304; Sigel's Letter, 148; Snead, *Fight for Missouri*, 310; Wherry, "General Lyon."

91. It should be noted that the bulk of the losses suffered by Sigel's infantry occurred at the James River Branch of the White River. This would further suggest that the 3rd Missouri probably suffered 80–90 percent (85 percent average) of all losses suffered by the two commands at the Battle of Wilson's Creek or 30 killed, 112 wounded with 107 missing. This would then give the 5th Missouri 5 killed, 29 wounded and 19 missing. *O.R.*,vol. 3:48; *War in the West*, 107.

92. If the losses were in the same proportion as the estimated strength, the 3rd Missouri would have lost 19 killed, 71 wounded with 68 missing, while the 5th Missouri would have lost 16 killed, 61 wounded and 58 missing. See note 92 above for additional comments on losses.

93. Piston & Hatcher, *Wilson's Creek*, 337.

94. Ibid.

Battle of Belmont, Missouri
November 7, 1861

General References:
1. Hughes, *Battle of Belmont*, 184–185, 209–215.
2. Livermore, *Numbers and Losses*, 67–69.
3. "The Latest News," *Chicago Tribune*, November 11, 1861.
4. Polk, "Belmont,"355–356.

* * * * * * *

Union Order of Battle
Battle of Belmont

Union General Information. Unit strength per Hughes, except where noted. Command staff has been added where none has been listed for army and brigades; Brigade staff includes, Adjutant, Quartermaster, Inspector General, Commissary and Ordnance officers; with commander, which gives a staff total of six. Brigade Surgeon or Chaplain were not counted. Aides are counted only if known. Excluded from the staff are any enlisted men, such as band, infirmary corps or clerks. For the purpose of brigade staff only the six officers listed above will be counted as effectives. Staff in the regiments are included in the various unit strengths.

Union Losses. Losses are normally fairly evident from the *Official Record, Supplement to the Official Records* and other reports; however, in the case of Belmont there seems to be several discrepancies, between the assorted sources. Hughes in his account on Belmont puts Grant's overall losses at between "320 and 400 wounded," with "over 100 of whom fell into Confederate hands, more than 100 were captured unwounded and about 90 were killed." Further, a lot has to do when the accounting was done–was it the day after the battle or later? Was it after the exchange of the POWs? Was it after the battlefield had been surveyed? The figures I have used come from a variety of sources, similar to what Hughes used, but oftentimes with different numbers than Hughes. Grant, in his Official Report, puts his losses at 85 killed, 301 wounded with 99 missing. "Of the wounded, 125 fell into the hands of the enemy" and would normally be counted as captured.–total loss 485. Grant's Medical Director puts the losses at 80 dead with 322 wounded and when paired with Grant's reported missing of 99 gives 501. This figure was generally accepted by the *Union Army* series and Dyer's *Compendium*.

As shown below my totals add up to 128 killed, 350 wounded and 139 missing; total 617. Hughes gives the losses as 95 killed, 306 wounded, with 205 missing; grand total of 606.[95]

---

95. *O.R.*, vol. 3:271, 275; Dyer, 799; Hughes, 164–185; *Union Army*, vol. 5:110.

Union Strength At Belmont.

Grant's Overall Strength. In Grant's original report he puts his strength at 3,114 which differs from what his brigade commanders reported–McClernand reported 2,072 or 2,086 men; Dougherty reported 1,075 men including the 7th Iowa (513 men) and the 22nd Illinois (562 men); for a grand total of 3,147 or 3,161. The difference in his number and mine are based on the numbers for the 27th and 30th Illinois Infantries, Delano's Cavalry and the staff which gives the command 3,206 men. See below for details.[96]

Twenty-second Illinois Infantry. The overall strength of the 22nd Illinois was given as 562 officers an men. Of the command's ten companies, Companies A, H, and I were part of the Boat Guard Detachment, leaving the other companies to take part in the assault on Belmont. Prorating the ten companies yields and effective strength of 56.2 (562 / 10 = 56.2) men per company. This would give the main regiment 393 men (56.2 x 7 = 393.4). The remainder 169 men (562- 393 = 169) would be in the Boat Guard Detachment. As to losses–the Boat Guard lost in Company A three wounded with two being mortal; Company H had two men slightly wounded one of whom was Corporal I. C. Anderson "of the color guard [who] was wounded in three places;" and Company I lost 5 wounded. Overall the Boat Detachment lost ten wounded, two of who were mortal. The Boat Guard numbers were then deducted from the regiment's overall losses as shown below.[97]

Delano's Adams County, Illinois. Company. Reviewing assorted sources provides no clarity as to what regiment that Delano's Company was assigned or its company designation. We know from the *Official Records* that one of the cavalry officers, Lieutenant Edwin Babcock, was from Company E, 2nd Illinois Cavalry Regiment and that Company E was noted as being at Belmont (See Dyer's *Compendium of the Civil War,* 799, 1021, which shows the unit's participation at Belmont). Further, Delano's Company was Company L, 2nd Illinois Cavalry but gives no indication that it was at Belmont. I suspect that Delano's command contained elements of both Company E and L, with the bulk of the command coming from Company E, 2nd Illinois.[98]

Delano's company like the 27th and 30th Illinois Infantry, has a difference in its reported strength for the Battle of Belmont.. The 27th Illinois had either 720 (*Official Record* and Hughes) or 724 (*Chicago Tribune*) men; the 30th Illinois had either 500 (*Official Records*) or 522 (Hughes and *Chicago Tribune*), while Delano's company had either 58 (*Official Record,* McClernand's Report) or 72

96. *O.R.*, 3:277, 287, 290; Banasik, *Missouri in 1861,* 171, 243; "General McClernand's Report," *Rebellion Record,* vol. 3:Doc. 279; "The Latest News," *Chicago Tribune,* November 11, 1861; Hughes, 209.

97. *O.R.*, vol. 3: 294; *O.R.S.*, pt. 2, vol. 8:530, 538, 548.

98. *O.R.*, vol. 3:278; *O.R.S.*, pt. 2, vol. 7:391, 393, 420, 422; Dyer, 799, 1021; "General McClernand's Report," *Rebellion Record,* vol. 3:Doc. 279.

men (*Rebellion Record*, McClernand's Report)–Hughes has no reported strength for Delano's Cavalry. In this case I chose to use McClernand's numbers from the *Rebellion Record*. I suspect that the 14 man difference were used as couriers or escort for either Grant or McClernand–regardless I believe those men were present in some capacity.[99]

* * * * * * *

District of Southeast Missouri Expeditionary Command (Brigadier General U. S. Grant):

Staff = 6 EFF [0 K, 0 W, 0 M].[100]

First Brigade (Brigadier General John A. McClernand):

Staff = 7 EFF [1 K, 0 W, 0 M].[101]

27th Ill. Inf. (Col. Napoleon B. Buford) EFF = 724 [11 K, 47 W, 27 M].[102]

30th Ill. Inf. (Col. Philip B. Fouke) EFF = 522 [9 K, 27 W, 8 M].[103]

31st Ill. Inf. (Col. John A. Logan) EFF = 610 (20 K, 63 W, 18 M].[104]

Total = 1,863 [41 K, 137 W, 53 M].

Second Brigade (Colonel Henry Dougherty; WIA, POW):

Staff = 6 EFF (E) [no losses reported or recorded].

7th Iowa Inf. (Less Cos. G, K–Col. Jacob G. Lauman; WIA)[105]
EFF = 410 [54 K, 124 W, 49 M].[106]

---

99. *O.R.*, vol. 3:277; "General McClernand's Report," *Rebellion Record*, vol. 3:Doc. 278; "The Latest News," *Chicago Tribune*," November 11, 1861.

100. *O.R.*, vol. 3:271.

101. Ibid., 277, 282.

102. Hughes has the strength as 720, the same as recorded in the Official Records. The 724 figure comes from the *Chicago Tribune* and probably includes the regimental staff with commander or could have been General McClernand simply rounding the number down. Buford recorded the loss of 11 killed, 42 wounded with 28 missing. Ibid., 277, 282, 285; "The Latest News," *Chicago Tribune*," November 11, 1861.

103. The Official Records listed the strength as 500, while the *Tribune* has it as 522. Hughes accepted the 522 number for the 30th Illinois but not the 724 number for the 27th Illinois from the same newspaper. *O.R.*, vol. 3:277; "The Latest News," *Chicago Tribune*," November 11, 1861.

104. *Supplement to the Official Records* has the loss as 8 killed, 65 wounded and 13 missing, with 3 of the wounded later dying. It would also suggest that several of the previous missing turned up dead. Fox's *Regimental Losses* has the numbers as 10 killed, 70 wounded, with 4 missing. The *Official Records* has the loss as 20 killed and 70 wounded. In this case I used Hughes numbers. *O.R.*, vol. 3:275; *O.R.S.*, pt. 2, vol. 10:343; William F. Fox, *Regimental Losses in The Civil War 1861–1865, etc.* (Albany, NY, 1898; reprint ed., Dayton, OH, 1985), 361, hereafter cited as Fox, *Regimental Losses*.

105. *O.R.S.*, pt. 2, vol. 19:711, 716.

106. On November 10, Colonel Lauman reported his losses as 51 dead, 3 mortally wounded, 49 missing or prisoner, with 124 wounded for a total loss of 227. Hughes has the losses as 31 killed, 77 wounded, with 114, missing; total 222. On November 19, 1861, Franc Wilkie, an Iowa newspaperman, recorded the loss of the regiment as 54 killed with 105 wounded. Colonel Lauman had three of those previously listed as wounded later having died, which suggest that 17 of the missing were later counted as dead. In this case I used Lauman's report, which was also in agreement with

22nd Ill. Inf. (Less Cos. A, H, and I–Lt. Col. Harrison E. Hart)
EFF = 393 [31 K, 68 W, 37 M].[107]
Total = 809 [85 K, 192 W, 86 M].
Boat Guard (Capt. John E. Detrich):
22nd Ill. Inf. (Cos. A, H, and I)[108] EFF = 169 [0 K, 10 W, 0 M].
7th Iowa Infantry (Cos. G and K)[109] EFF = 103 [0 K, 0 W, 0 M].
Total = 272 [0K, 10 W, 0 M].[110]
Unassigned:[111]
Dollin's Ill. Cav. Co. (Captain James J. Dollin) EFF = 70
[1 K, 4W, 0 M].
Delano's Adams Cty., Ill. Co. (Lt. James K. Catlin) EFF = 72
[1K, 2 W, 0 M].
Battery B, 1st Ill. Lt. Art. (Capt. Ezra Taylor)[112] 6 guns; 4 6-lb SB
and 2 12-lb How, EFF = 114 [0 K, 5W, 0 M].
Total = 256 [2 K, 11 W, 0 M].
Army Grand Total: 3,206 [128 K , 350 W, 139 M
Total Losses: 617].

* * * * * * *

Confederate Order of Battle at Belmont
November 7, 1861

General References:
1. *O.R.*, vol. 3:723.
2. Hughes, *Battle of Belmont*, 185, 211–213.
3. Polk, "Belmont," 355–356.

* * * * * * *

---

the Fox's *Regimental Losses* and *Union Army* series. *O.R.*, vol. 3:298; Banasik, *Missouri in 1861*, 243; Fox, *Regimental Losses* 407; *Union Army*, vol. 4: 142.

107. Losses exclude the Boat Guard Detachment. The 22nd Illinois in the *Supplement to the Official Records* reported the loss of 21 killed, with 9 of the wounded later dying. The wounded were recorded as 97, including .those who were mortal. This would suggest that ten of the 97 wounded (97- 9 = 88 - 78 official loss = 10) were actually slightly wounded and never included in the official accounting of loss. I suspect that the 97 figure included slightly wounded. The *Official Records* listed 23 killed, 74 wounded, with 37 Missing. Hughes has the overall loss, including the Boat Guard, as 31 killed, 78 wounded with 37 missing. *O.R.*, vol. 3:293: *O.R.S.*, pt. 2, vol. 9:523; Hughes, 184.

108. *O.R.S.*, pt. 2, vol. 9:548.

109. Ibid., 716.

110. John Seaton, of the 22nd Illinois, recalled in later years that the Boat Guard was comprised of 350 men, Seaton, "Belmont," 310.

111. There was no definitive accounting of Dalano's or Dollin's losses in the *Official Records*; however the *Chicago Tribune* does have the losses as listed above. *O.R.*, vol. 3: 275; "The Battle of Belmont," *Chicago Tribune*," November 12, 1861.

112. *O.R.*, vol. 3:290.

General Information. For the Belmont Order of Battle only selected units from General Leonidas Polk's Columbus command took part in the battle. Excluded from this Order of Battle are units that did not transport to Belmont, such as the artillery batteries that supported the battle from Columbus. Also, like the Union command the various command staff are added to the various brigades and divisions that were present at Belmont.

Command Structure. The majority of the Confederate units that took part in the Battle of Belmont were part of First Geographical Division, Western Department, commanded by General Polk. The Confederate initial deployment had various elements of Pillow's Division awaiting the Federal attack. Pillow commanded the center and left of the line and Col. R. M. Russell the far right with elements of his Second Brigade and Pillow's Third Brigade. The far left of Pillows line had elements from Pillow's First Brigade, while Col. J. K. Walker, the First Brigade commander, was still en route from Columbus.

Following the initial contact any apparent Confederate division or brigade structure broke down as the units were committed piecemeal as they arrived at Belmont. The Confederates fought by "detachments," according to E. A. Pollard, with division or brigade commanders leading whatever troops were in their immediate area; as such, the Order of Battle below was divided into two parts–the units that constituted the First Geographical Division, Western Department and the structure as they were committed to the battle. Further, you will also note that many of the rebel regiments were led by their lieutenant colonels, while their colonels commanded various brigades.

In some cases, like that of Colonel Preston Smith, who "accompanied" the 154th Tennessee in pursuit of the enemy, while taking orders, first from General B. F. Cheatham and then General Polk, while outdistancing himself from his other battalion under Lieutenant Colonel Andrew K. Blythe. And Colonel R. M. Russell, commanding Pillow's Second Brigade, was tasked to lead the 12th Tennessee of his brigade along with the 13th Arkansas, from Pillow's Third Brigade, while his other two regiments took orders directly from General Pillow. As the battle progressed the various division commanders ended up leading makeshift units as there was seemingly no divisional integrity. IE: Cheatham led the rebel counterattack at 2:00 p.m. with the 13th Arkansas the 2nd and 13th Tennessee Regiments, none of whom were in his division.

Brigade commanders who participated in the battle include Colonels Preston Smith, R. M. Russell, J. Knox Walker, and S. F. Marks. "None distinguished himself" at Belmont, while Marks, "Smith and Walker essentially fought with their own regiments," and Russell operated with only one of the three units of his brigade..Overall the services of the brigade commanders "were wasted" according to Nathaniel Hughes, with the battle being "fought at the regimental and company level."[113]

113. Ibid., 325, 344, 346; Pollard, 183; Polk, "Belmont," 355–356; Hughes, 200–201; Stewart

Confederate Strength and Losses at Belmont. Losses are per Hughes, except as noted, while the overall strength generally comes from Captain William M. Polk, General Polk's son and staff officer. Captain Polk puts the Confederate strength at 4,000, with another 1,000 arriving too late to participate in the battle. Generals Polk and Pillow have the initial Confederate force, under General Pillow, at 2,500 men, excluding the cavalry and the artillery, while the artillery and cavalry added another 200 men, according to Captain Polk and the *Memphis Appeal* newspaper. Using the two Polk's comments, on the Confederate strength, and adjusting those numbers, one can calculate the various regimental strengths. Additionally, its assumed that when the various Confederate authorities refer to the strength as "men" they mean "officers and men;" That said, this is probably a stretch as Confederates frequently excluded officers from their definition of "men" in a battle, per Thomas Livermore.

Further, if one reviews the rebel Present For Duty strength on October 31, for Pillow's First Division, one finds that the command contained 5,397 officers and men in the eight infantry regiments (The 13th Mississippi Infantry was sent to Virginia and was listed by General Polk as in the Third Brigade of Pillow's Division). This would suggest an effective strength of 5,019 (5,397 x .93 = 5,019) officers and men or an average of 627 (5,019 / 8 = 627.3) effective officers and men for each regiment, which was considerably less than Confederate sources noted as at Belmont on November 7. It should also be noted, that of all the units in Pillow's Division that had an Official Report on the battle, the 12th Tennessee Infantry reported their effective strength as 633 officers and men. However, without further information, Captain William Polk's figures will be used to calculate the various Confederate strengths at Belmont.[114]

* * * * * * *

Comments on the Confederate Command Staffs at Belmont

General Polk's Staff. General Polk proceeded to Belmont in the waning hours of the battle. Overall, including General Polk his command staff numbered 12 officers on November 7, 1861. Of that number Polk noted five members of his staff for recognition at the battle; Major H. W. Winslow of the staff was detached during the battle and served under General Pillow and is so noted below and was deducted from Polk's staff for the battle This left Polk with five members of his command staff on the field, including himself. The other members of the staff are assumed to have remained at Columbus.[115]

Sifakis, *Compendium of the Confederate Armies Louisiana* (New York, 1995), 90, hereafter cited as Sifakis, *Louisiana*.

114. *O.R.*, vol. 3: 304, 325, 723; *O.R.*, vol. 5:825; *O.R.S.*, pt. 2. , vol. 33:278, 284, 291; Livermore, 66–67; Polk, "Belmont," 348, 354–355; "Rebel Accounts of the Battle, 'Memphis 'Appeal,' Narrative,'" *Rebellion Record*, vol. 3: Doc. 296, hereafter cited as "Memphis 'Appeal' Narrative."

115. *O.R.*, vol. 3:310; Crute, *Confederate Staff Officers*, 153–156.

General Cheatham's Staff. For November 1861, General Cheatham's staff was very limited, consisting of but four men for the battle on November 7: Majors Frank McNairy and James Porter, with John Campbell and Albot or Abbot Robertson serving as volunteer aides. Another member of Cheatham's staff, Lieutenant Colonel J. A. Ashford remained in Columbus, and another, Captain R. C. Tyler, Assistant Quartermaster, has an unknown status. However, since Cheatham mentions all the staff members but Tyler, I assumed that Tyler was left back at Columbus. Any enlisted members of Cheatham's staff are excluded from this accounting, the same with all the other command staffs. This would give Cheatham an operational command of five officers, including himself.[116]

General Pillow's Staff. Pillow's command officer staff, including himself, numbered 19 officers. Of the 19, eight were at Belmont, one was known not to be present and one was a surgeon and not counted as an effective. The seven known officers, included Captain W. H. Jackson, detached from his battery; additionally Major Henry Winslow was detached from General Polk's staff to serve under Pillow, giving Pillow command staff eight members on the battlefield, or, nine total, including himself. The following nine officers were all noted as members of Pillow's staff prior to the Battle of Belmont; however, it is unknown as to whether they participated in the battle on November 7–Captains L. F. Cabler, Owen H. Edwards, John S. Hill, and James A. Wiggs with Majors Calvin M. Fackler, W. W. Guy, Richard M. Mason, Alex W. Cambell and Robert. C. Tyler. As a pure guess, half, rounded down, or four of these additional officers are considered present and effective at the battle. Including General Pillow, the command staff numbered 13 effective officers. Excluded from Pillow's staff are all the medical staff and enlisted personnel, with the exception of H. P. Woodlock, his orderly, giving his staff fourteen members[117].

Confederate Brigade Command Staffs. Colonel R. M. Russell, commanding Second Brigade, First Division has no report on the actual battle save comments to an enquiry by General Pillow in February 1862. Since his whole brigade was deployed at Belmont his entire staff is assumed to have been present, including his Adjutant, Quartermaster, Ordnance and Commissary Officers. This would give him five officers, including himself for his command staff.

Colonel S. F. Marks appears to of had a limited staff at Belmont, consisting of four, including himself with Adjutant James G. White from the 11th Louisiana, Adjutant John M. Langan and W. E. Edwards.

Colonel Preston Smith, commanding the First Brigade, Second Division, gives no indication of the staff that he had present at the battle; however, since his entire brigade was present at the battle I'll assume that his entire staff was also

116. *O.R.*, vol. 3:343, 34; Crute. *Confederate Staff Officers*, 34–36.
117. *O.R.*, vol. 3:328–329, 361; Crute, *Confederate Staff Officers*, 152–153; Memphis 'Appeal' Narrative," *Rebellion Record*, Doc. 296.

present–IE: Adjutant, Quartermaster, Ordnance and Commissary Officers. This would give him five officers, including himself for his command staff.

Colonel J. K. Walker, like Smith and Russell, has no substantial report on the Battle of Belmont save a supplement on the retaking of the Watson's Battery. Walker's entire command was eventually sent to Belmont though it is unclear as to when Walker arrived; as a pure guess. I'll say that he came with the 2nd and 15th Tennessee Regiments. And like Smith and Russell, Walker's staff, with the commanding officer would number 5 effectives.[118]

* * * * * * *

Comments on the Confederate Units at Belmont

Blythe's Mississippi Battalion and the 154th Tennessee Infantry. In his comments on the rebel units William Polk has the last two units, the 154th Tennessee and Blythe's Mississippi command numbering 1,000 men. The *Official Records Supplement* has Blyth's Battalion with only five companies before they were incorporated into what became the 44th Mississippi Regiment. The 154th Senior Tennessee Infantry contained eleven companies. Prorating the sixteen companies yields 62.5 (1,000/16 = 62.5) officers and men per company. This would mean that the 154th numbered 687 (62.5 x 11 = 687.5) officers and men while Blythe's Battalion numbered 313 (1,000 - 687 = 313) officers and men. It should also be noted that the 154th had an original enlistment of 802 This would suggest that (802 - 687 = 115 / 802 = 14) 14 percent of the command was sick, on detail, etc.[119]

Company A, Pointe Coupe Louisiana Artillery Battalion. Commanded by Captain Robert A. Stewart, the battery was part of the Second Brigade, Third Division. The division contained two artillery companies with a Present for Duty strength of 200 officers and men on October 31, 1861. Both commands had six guns, which evenly divides the strength, giving each battery 100 officers and men. This would then give Stewart's Company 93 (100 x .93) effective officers and men, per Thomas Livermore. Additionally, the battery consisted of two, 10-lb parrot rifles and four, 6-lb smoothbore cannon.[120]

W. H. Jackson (Also known as Carnes' Artillery) and M. T. Polk's Tennessee Artillery Companies. Both of these units, along with S. H. D. Hamilton's Siege Artillery, constituted the three batteries assigned to Pillow's First Division. On October 31, 1861, they numbered 396 officers and men Present for Duty. Jack-

---

118. *O.R.*, vol. 3:330, 332–333, 343–345, 355, 780;

119. *O.R.S.*, pt. 2, vol. 34:283–285; *O.R.S.*, pt. 2, vol. 67:584–588; Joseph H. Crute, *Units of the Confederate Army* (Midlothian, VA, 1987), 188, 314, hereafter cited as Crute, *Units of the Confederate Army*.

120. *O.R.*, vol. 3:724, 730; O.R., vol. 8:127–128; Larry J. Daniel and Lynn N. Bock, *Island No. 10 Struggle for the Mississippi Valley* (Tuscaloosa. AL, 1996), 29; Livermore, 68–69; "Memphis 'Appeal' Narrative," *Rebellion Record*, vol. 3: Doc. 295.

son and Hamilton's commands contained four guns each, while Polk's command numbered six guns; total 14 guns. Of the 396 officers and men, per Thomas Livermore, 368 (396 x .93 =368.2) would be considered effective or 26.3 (368 / 14 = 26.3) officers and men per assigned gun. This would give the following results: Jackson's Battery, 105 (26.3 x 4 = 105.2) effectives; Polk's Battery 158 (26.3 x 6 = 157.7) effectives; and Hamilton's Siege Battery 105 (26.3 x 4 = 105.2) effective officers and men for the Battle of Belmont. Number and type of guns are noted below under the appropriate command with the exception of Hamilton's Battery which did not transport to Belmont.[121]

Logwood's Squadron, Companies A (Memphis Light Dragoon) and B (White's Tennessee Mounted Rifles) of the 6th Tennessee Cavalry Battalion. The battalion was assigned to Pillow's Division and consisted of five companies of cavalry with a company of mounted rifles. Hughes has the battalion with five companies, but fails to mention J. S. White's Company of Mounted Rifles as part of the command; however, Hughes does note that White's command was one of the two companies that Logwood had at Belmont. On October 31, 1861, the battalion numbered 300 officers and men present for duty. And per Thomas Livermore 85 percent would be considered effective, giving the battalion 255 (300 x .85 = 255) effectives or 43 (255 / 6 = 42.5) officers and men per company. This would give Longwood's Squadron 85 (2 x 42.5 = 85) effective offices and men, including staff and Longwood.[122]

Miller's Squadron, 1st Mississippi Cavalry Battalion. The battalion consisted of six companies, two of which were posted in Belmont. The battalion was part of Cheatham's Second Division and number 162 officers and men, who were "Present for Duty" on October 31. And per Thomas Livermore, 85 percent of the total present for duty would be considered effective, giving the command 138 (162 x .85 = 137.7) effectives or 27.5 (137.7/ 5 =27. 5) effective officers men per company. For Belmont the two companies would total 55 (27.5 x 2 = 55) officers and men including any battalion staff and Miller.[123]

The Watson Louisiana Battery. The battery left New Orleans on August 15, 1861, with 150 cannoneers and 40 drivers for a total of 190 officers and men, They arrived in Columbus, Kentucky, on October 1, having recruited additional men to replace those who had left because of Captain Beltzhoover's "'rough and unfeeling treatment" of the command. From Captain Polk's comments on the initial strength of the rebel line at Belmont he makes it clear that the artillery and the cavalry numbered 200 men. As shown above, under Miller's Cavalry Battalion, we know that Miller's two squadron numbered 55 officers and men; this would suggest that the Watson Battery numbered 145 men. Given the strength of the

121. *O.R.*, vol. 3:730; *O.R.*, vol. 8:150–151; Livermore, 68–69.
122. *O.R.*, vol. 3:699, 723, 730; *O.R.S.*, pt. 2, vol. 66:126–129; Crute, *Units of the Confederate Army*, 280; Hughes, 164, 315; "Memphis 'Appeal' Narrative," *Rebellion Record*, vol. 3:Doc. 295
123. *O.R.*, vol. 3: 723, 730; Hughes, 213; Livermore, 68–69.

batteries' cannoneers of 150 officers and men when they arrived in Columbus, this would suggest an effective strength of 140 (150 x .93 = 139.5) officers and men for the battle on November 7. That said, a veteran of the Mississippi Cavalry Battalion has Tappan's strength, including cavalry and artillery, as "less than six hundred"; however, he was unclear as to whether that included officers. The numbers presented below shows Tappan's estimated force as 661 officers and men.[124]

The 13th Arkansas, 13th, 21st and 22nd Tennessee Infantries. These four commands have no regimental statements as to their strengths at Belmont; however, we can calculate their estimated values based upon the known strength of the 12th Tennessee and the overall strength of the rebel initial deployment. The Official Report of the 12th Tennessee at Belmont states that it had 633 officers and men. Gideon Pillow and William Polk have Pillow's initial deployment as "2,500 men, exclusive of a squadron of cavalry and a battery." If we accept Polk's 2,500 figure that would leave 1,867 (2,500 - 633 = 1,867) for the 13th Arkansas, 13th, 21st and 22nd Tennessee Infantries, or 467 (1,867 / 4 = 466.7) men for each of the regiments.[125]

The 11th Louisiana and 15th Tennessee Infantries. The 11th Louisiana was organized on August 13, 1861, with 857 officers and men, being comprised of eleven companies. Both of these regiments arrived in Belmont after the 2nd Tennessee Infantry With the arrival of the 2nd Tennessee, a total of 3,000 infantry, of the Confederates 5,000-man force was on the battlefield. According to Captain Polk, the last two units that arrived in Belmont comprised another 1,000 men. This would give the 11th Louisiana and the 15th Tennessee a total of 1,000 men. The 11th had eleven companies while the 15th had 10 companies. This would suggest that each company had about 47.6 (1.000 / 21 = 47.6) officers and men per company. This would give the 11th Louisiana 524 (11 x 47.6 = 523.8) officers and men while the 15th Tennessee would have fielded about 476 (1,000 - 524 = 476) officers and men. It should also be noted that the 11th Louisiana carried 550 men into the Battle of Shiloh in April 1862.[126]

The 12th Louisiana and 4th Tennessee Infantries. These two units were the last infantry commands that arrived at Belmont; however, they arrived too late to participated in the battle. Captain William Polk has the strength of these two regiments as "about 500 men each"; however, it was noted that the 12th organized with twelve companies, while the 4th Tennessee had ten companies. This would suggest that the 12th Louisiana contained 545 (1,000/22 companies = 45.4 men

124. George H. Hubbard, "In the Battle of Belmont," *Confederate Veteran* 33 (December, 1925):469; Hughes, 70; Livermore, 68–69.

125. *O.R.*, vol. 3, 325; *O.R.S.*, pt. 3, vol. 1: 461; Polk, "Belmont," 354.

126. *O.R.S.*, pt. 2, vol. 66: 674–677; Arthur W. Bergeron, Jr., *Guide to Louisiana Confederate Military Units 1861–1865* (Baton Rouge, LA, 1989), 98–99, hereafter cited as Bergeron; Polk, "Belmont," 348–349, 354–355.

per company or 12 x 45.4 = 545.4) officers and men, while the 4th Tennessee had 455 (1,000 - 545 = 455) officers and men.[127]

The 2nd Tennessee Infantry Regiment. Hughes has the strength of the 2nd Tennessee as 750; however that seems to be in conflict with Crute's and Polk's comments on the same unit. William Polk has the regiment as "numbering about 500" men, while Joseph Crute has the command with 541 effectives on July 31. It should also be noted that Hughes does not list the 750 strength of the 2nd Tennessee in his unit summaries, for those units that have known strengths at the Battle of Belmont. This would seem to say that Hughes doubts the 750 figure as being accurate. In this case I accept Polk's value of 500.[128]

* * * * * * *

First Geographical Division, Western Department (Maj. Gen. Leonidas Polk):
  First Division (Brig. Gen. Gideon Pillow)
    First Brigade (Col. J. K. Walker):
      2nd Tenn. Inf. Regt. (Lt. Col. W. B. Ross)
      13th Tenn. Inf. Regt.(Col. John V. Wright)
      15th Tenn. Inf. Regt. (Col. Charles M. Carroll)
      Polk's Tenn. Art. (Capt. Marshall T. Polk).[129]
    Second Brigade (Col. R. M. Russell):
      12th Tenn. Inf. Regt. (Lt. Col. Tyree Bell]
      21st Tenn. Inf. Regt. (Col. Edward Pickett, Jr.
      22nd Tenn. Inf. Regt. (Col. Thomas J. Freeman)
      Jackson's Tenn. Art. (Capt. William H. Jackson; WIA).[130]
    Third Brigade (Col. W. E. Travis):
      13th Ark. Inf. Regt. (Col. James Tappan)
      13th Miss. Inf. Regt. (Lt. Col. John M. Bradley)[131]
      5th Tenn. Inf. Regt. (Lt. Col. C. D. Venable).[132]
    Unassigned:
      6th Bn. Tenn. Cav. (Lt. Col. Thomas H. Logwood).
  Second Division (Brig. Gen. B. F. Cheatham):
    First Brigade (Col. Preston Smith):

---

127. Banasik, *Confederate Tales, 1861*, 155–157; Bergeron, 99–101; Polk, "Belmont," 355; Sifakis, *Louisiana*, 91.
128. Crute, *Units of the Confederate Army*, 276; Hughes, 123, 184–185; Polk, "Belmont," 354.
129. The battery was sent to Belmont but didn't land until after the battle had ended. *O.R.*, vol. 3:307.
130. Battery was sent to Belmont but was unable to unload. Captain Jackson subsequently served as a staff officer under General Pillow. Ibid., 307, 355.
131. This was Colonel William Barksdale's Regiment, which was apparently commanded by John M. Bradley, before the unit was detached, and sent to Virginia on July 11, 1861, where it participated in the Battle of Bull run on July 21. On August 31, 1861, it was in G. T. Beauregard's First Corps, Army of the Potomac. Ibid., 723; *O.R.*, vol. 5:825; *O.R.S.*, pt. 2. , vol. 33:278, 284, 291.
132. *O.R.S.*, pt.2, vol. 66: 523.

1st. Miss. Inf. Bn. (Lt. Col. Andrew K. Blythe)

154th Sr. Tenn. Inf. Regt. (Lt. Col. Wright).

Second Brigade (Col. W. H. Stephens): Not present or engaged at Belmont.

Unassigned:

1st Bn. Miss. Cav. (Lt. Col. John H. Miller).

Third Division (Brig. Gen. J. P. McCown):

First Brigade Col. S. F. Marks):

11th La. Inf. Regt. (Lt. Col. Robert. H. Barrow). Rest not present or engaged at Belmont.

Second Brigade (Col. R. P. Neely):

12th Louisiana (Col. T. M. Scott)

4th Tenn. Inf. Regt. (Lt. Col. Oyho F. Strahl)

Co. A, Pointe Coupe La. Art. Bn. (Capt. R. A. Stewart). Brigade present at Belmont not engaged.[133].

Fourth Division (Col. John D. Bowen):

First Brigade (Col. John D. Martin):

Watson La. Art. (Capt. Daniel Beltzhoover) [Detached to Belmont Camp of Observation].Rest of brigade not present or engaged at Belmont.

Second Brigade (Col. D. W. C. Bonham). Brigade not present or engaged at Belmont.

* * * * * * *

---

133. Banasik, *Confederate Tales, 1861*, 155 n. 9, 156, 158.

Confederate Order of Appearance in Belmont
November 7, 1861

Camp of Observation at Camp Johnston, Belmont. Mo. (Col. James Tappan)
    13th Ark. Inf. Regt. (Col. James C. Tappan) EFF = 467 (E)
    [12 K, 45 W, 23 M].[134]
    1st Miss. Cav. Bn. (2 Cos., Lt. Col. John H. Miller)[135] EFF = 55 (E)
    [0 K, 1 W, 0 M].[136]
    Watson La. Battery (Lt. Col. Daniel Beltzhoover) 6 guns: 4, 6-lb SB
    and 2, 12-lb how.; lost one gun of each type EFF = 140 (E)
    [2 K, 8 W & M].[137]
    Total Camp Johnston = 662 EFF [14 K, 54 W, 23 M]

First Group of Reinforcements (Arrived between 08:30–09:30 a.m.);[138]Carried by the *H. R. Hill* and the *Prince*.

General Gideon Pillow w/staff: EFF = 14 [0 K, 2 W. 0 M].[139]
    Col. R. M. Russell w/staff: EFF = 5 [0 K, 0 W, 0 M].
    12th Tenn. Inf. Regt. (Lt. Col Tyree H. Bell) EFF = 633
    [12 K, 46 W, 0 M].
    13th Tenn. Inf. Regt. (Maj. J. W. Hambleton) EFF = 467 (E)
    [27 K, 73 W, 49 M].
    21st Tenn. Inf. Regt. (Col. Edward Pickett, Jr. EFF = 467 (E)
    [13 Km 62 W, 5 M].[140]
    22nd Tenn. Inf. Regt. (Col. Thomas J. Freeman) EFF = 467 (E) ·
    [10 K, 67 W, 9 M].
    Total First Group = 2,053 EFF [62 K, 250 W, 63 M]

Second Group of Reinforcements (Arrived between 10:45 - 11:15 a.m.); Carried by the *Prince* and the *Henry Hill*.[141]

    Col. J. K. Walker w/staff EFF = 5 [0 K. 0 W/0 M].
    2nd Tenn. Inf. Regt. (Lt. Col. W. B. Ross) EFF = 500 (E)
    [18 K, 63 W, 33 M].

---

134. The *Memphis Appeal* has the loss as 13 killed 43 wounded, with 23 missing. *O.R.*, vol. 3:357; "Memphis 'Appeal' Narrative," *Rebellion Record*, vol. 3:Doc-296.
135. Colonel Miller, commanding the battalion, did not arrive until 10:30 a.m. on November 7. Prior to his arrival Captain A. J. Bowles commanded the squadron, consisting of the "Thompson Cavalry" and the "Bolivar Troop." In his report on the battle Miller implies that his command consisted of 100 men. However given the above available effective strength of the battalion I believe the calculated amount sounds more reasonable. *O.R.*, vol. 3:350–351.
136. Ibid., 351.
137. Ibid., 360.
138. Ibid., 307, 333–334, 337, 361–362.; O.R.S., pt. 1, vol. 1:461–461,
139. *O.R.*, vol. 3:328–329.
140. The *Official Records* has the report as 78 killed and wounded. *O.R.*, vol. 3:337.
141. Ibid., 331; Hughes, 122–123

Jackson's Tenn. Art. (Capt. William H. Jackson; WIA)[142] 4 guns, 2, 6-lb SB and 2, 12-lb how. EFF = 105 (E) [No losses–Not engaged].

Polk's Tenn. Art. (Capt. Marshall T. Polk)[143] 6 guns, Not Engaged. EFF = 158 (E) [No losses–Not engaged].

Total Second Group = 768 EFF [18 K, 63 W, 33 M]

Third Group of Reinforcements (Arrived between 11:30 - noon);[144] Carried by the *H. R. Hill* and the *Charm.* [145]

Col. S. F. Marks w/staff EFF = 4 [0 K, 0 W. 0 M].

11th La. Inf. Regt. (Lt. Col. Robert. H. Barrow, WIA) EFF = 524 (E) [12 K, 42 W, 0 M].

15th Tenn. Inf. Regt. (Maj. J. W. Hambletonl)[146] EFF = 476 (E) [10 K, 10 W, 0 M].

Co. A, 6th Bn. Tenn. Cav. (Capt. W. F. Taylor with Lt. Col. T. H. Logwood)[147] EFF = 43 [0 K, 0 W, 0 M]

Gen. B. F. Cheatham and ammunition supply; Carried by the *Prince* (Arrived about 1:00 p.m.)

Brig. Gen. B. F. Cheatham w/staff[148]

Staff = 5 [0 K, 0 W, 0 M]

Total Third Group = 1,052 EFF [22 K, 52 W, 0 M]

---

142. Battery sent to Belmont but never landed. Captain Jacskon subsequently was attached to General Pillow's staff where he was wounded during the battle. Battery subsequently became William Carnes' artillery and was refitted following the Battle of Chickamauga where their battery was disabled. *O.R.*, Index, 947, "Jackson, W. H." entry; *O.R.*, vol. 3:307, 328–329, 360; *O.R.*, vol. 30, pt. 2:81; *O.R.S.*, pt. 2, vol. 78: 358, 360.

143. The battery was sent to Belmont but didn't land until after the battle had ended. Gun types unknown though probably 4, 6-lb smoothbores and 2,12-lb howitzers. *O.R.*, vol. 3:307, 360; *O.R.*, vol. 10, pt.1:414, 438.

144. The captain of he steamboat *Charm* recorded that there was a delay in transporting the 11th over to Belmont, as they also loaded White's Company B, Logwood's Cavalry Battalion. The *Charm* left Columbus at 11:30 and arrived at Belmont at noon. The *Charm* was unable to land the cavalry for the lack of "stage planks," returning to Columbus where they obtained the planks and back to Belmont with the cavalry, the 1st Mississippi Infantry Battalion and the 154th Senior Tennessee Infantry. The Charm landed at 2:00 p.m. Ibid., 354–355, 359, 363.

145. The *Memphis Appeal* has the arrival time between 12:30 to 2:00 p.m.; however it's clear from the *Official Records* and Hughes' account that 11:30 to noon was closer to he truth. *O.R.*, vol. 3:307, 336, 359; Hughes, 137; 280; "Memphis 'Appeal' Narrative," *Rebellion Record*, vol. 3:Doc. 295.

146. *O.R.*, vol. 3:336, 347; Polk, "Belmont," 356.

147. Hughes, 136; "Memphis 'Appeal' Narrative," *Rebellion Record*, vol. 3:Doc. 5.

148. Seeing the confusion with his troops in Belmont, following the loss of Camp Johnston, General Polk ordered General Cheatham to proceed to Belmont to rally the troops on the western bank. Cheatham's troops were to follow once the Federal batteries in Belmont allowed the troops tp safely cross the Mississippi. *O.R.*, vol. 3, 343–345, 362.

Fourth Group of Reinforcements (Arrived between 1:30–2:30 p.m.); [149] Carried by the *Charm* and *Kentucky.*

    Gen. L. Polk w/staff EFF = 5 [0 K, 0 W. 0 M].
    Col. Preston Smith w/staff EFF = 5 [0 K, 0 W, 0 M].
        1st. Miss. Inf. Bn. (Lt. Col. Andrew K. Blythe) EFF = 313 (E)
        [0 K, 1 W, 0 M].
        154th Sr. Tenn. Inf. Regt. (Lt. Col. M. J. Wright) EFF = 687 (E)
        [1 K, 12 W, 0 M].[150]
        Co. B, 6th Bn. Tenn. Cav. (Capt. J. S. White) [151] EFF = 42 (E)
        [0 K, 2 W, 0 M].
        Total Fourth Group = 1,052 EFF [1 K, 15 W, 0 M]

Final Group of Reinforcements (Arrived about 3:00 p.m.); [152] Carried by the *Kentucky.*

        12th La. Inf Regt. (Col. Thomas M. Scott) EFF = 545 (E)
        [No losses–Not engaged.].
        4th Tenn. Inf. Regt. (Lt. Col. Oyho F. Strahl) EFF = 455 (E)
        [No losses–Not Engaged].
        Co. A, Pointe Coupe La. Art. Bn. (Capt. R. A. Stewart)[153] 6, guns, 2
        10-lb Parrots, 4 6-lb SB EFF = 93 (E) [2 K, 1 W, 0 M].
        Total Final Group = 1.093 EFF [2 K, 1 W, 0 M]

Summary of Confederate Command:
    Total Shipped to Belmont = 6,680
    Total Engaged = 5,417
    Total Losses = 119 Killed, 435 Wounded, 119 Missing[154]
    Grand Total Losses = 673

149. Ibid., 308, 345, 348; Hughes, 164–165.
150. *O.R.*, vol. 3:345.
151. White's Company landed at 2:00 p.m., suffering two "slightly" wounded during the engagement. Hughes has the total cavalry loss as one man wounded. Ibid., 363; Hughes, 165; "Memphis 'Appeal' Narrative," *Rebellion Record*, vol. 3:Doc-295. 296.
152. Captain Polk has the last group of reenforcements arriving "after Federal forces had been defeated." The Unionists broke in confusion between 2:45–3:00 p.m., making the estimate of the last Confedearte troops to arrive at Belmont as "about 3:00 p.m." Banasik, *Confederate Tales, 1861,* 155–156; Polk, "Belmont," 355.
153. The battery initially engaged the Federal gunboats, losing three men before being sent over to Belmont, where they arrived too late to participate in the land battle. It should also be noted that Hughes makes no mention of the battery being transported to Belmont in the latter part of the battle. Banasik, *Confederate Tales, 1861,* 155–156; Hughes, 66–67.
154. Watson's Battery had eight men listed as wounded or missing. I assigned two of the eight as killed and six as wounded. Nathaniel Hughes has the Confederate losses as 120 killed, 434 wounded, and 117 missing–total 671. Captain William Polk recorded the rebel losses as 105 killed, 419 wounded, with117 missing–Total 641; E. A. Pollard has the total loss as 632. Hughes, 185; Polk, "Belmont," 356; Pollard, 183

Bibliography

Books/Pamphlets/Articles

Adamson, Hans Christian. *Rebellion in Missouri: 1861 Nathaniel Lyon and His Army of the West*. Rahway, NJ: Quinn & Boden Company, 1961.

Akridge, Scott H. and Emmett E. Powers. *A Severe and Bloody Fight: The Battle of Whitney's Lane & Military Occupation of White County, Arkansas, May & June, 1862*. Searcy, AR: White County Historical Museum, 1996.

Allardice, Bruce S. *Confederate Colonels: A Biographical Register*. Columbia, MO: University of Missouri Press, 2008.

————. *More Generals in Gray*. Baton Rouge, LA: Louisiana State University Press, 1995.

Banasik, Michael E. *Confederate "Tales of the War" In the Trans-Mississippi Part One: 1861*. Unwritten Chapters of the Civil War West of the River, Volume VII. Iowa City, IA: Camp Pope Publishing, 2010.

————. *Confederate "Tales of the War" In the Trans-Mississippi Part Two: 1862*. Unwritten Chapters of the Civil War West of the River, Volume VII. Iowa City, IA: Camp Pope Publishing, 2011.

————. *Confederate "Tales of the War" In the Trans-Mississippi Part 5: 1864–1865*. Unwritten Chapters of the Civil War West of the River, Volume VII. Iowa City, IA: Camp Pope Publishing, 2019.

————. *Duty, Honor and Country: The Civil War Experiences of Captain William P. Black, Thirty-seventh Illinois Infantry*. Unwritten Chapters of the Civil War West of the River, Volume VI. Iowa City, IA: Camp Pope Publishing, 2006

————. *Embattled Arkansas: The Prairie Grove Campaign of 1862*. Wilmington, NC: Broadfoot Publishing Company, 1996.

————. *Missouri Brothers in Gray: The Reminiscences and Letters of William J. Bull and John P. Bull*. Unwritten Chapters of the Civil War West of the River, Volume I. Iowa City, IA: Camp Pope Publishing, 1998.

Banasik, Michael E. *Missouri in 1861: The Civil War Letters of Franc B. Wilkie, Newspaper Correspondent*. Unwritten Chapters of the Civil War West of the River, Volume IV. Iowa City, IA: Camp Pope Publishing, 2001.

Barney, William L. *The Oxford Encyclopedia of the Civil War*. New York: Oxford University Press, Inc., 2001.

Bartels, Carolyn. *The Forgotten Men Missouri State Guard*. Shawnee Mission, KS: Two Trails Publishing, 1995.

————. *Missouri Confederate Surrender New Orleans & Shreveport May-June 1865*. Independence, MO: Two Trails Publishing, 1991.

————. *Trans-Mississippi Men at War Volume I Missouri C.S.A.* Independence, MO: Two Trails Publishing, 1998.

————. *True Tales: Civil War in Missouri*. Independence, MO: Two Trails Publishing, 2002.

Bearss, Edwin C.. "Fort Smith Serves General McCulloch As A Supply Depot." *Arkansas Historical Quarterly* 24, (Winter 1965): 315–347.

————. *The Battle of Wilson's Creek*. Boseman, MT: Wilson's Creek National Battlefield Foundation, 1988.

Bek, William G. "The Civil War Diary of John T. Beugel, Union Soldier." *Missouri Historical Review* 40 (April 1946): 307–327.

Bell [Bull], William. "Camp Jackson Prisoners." *Confederate Veteran* 31 (July 1923): 260–261.

Bently, Charles S, Edward D. Redington, and Jared W. Young. "Samuel Henry Melcher." In *Memorial of Deceased Companions of the Commandery of the State of Illinois, Military Order of the Loyal Legion of the United States*. 70 vols., 1.13D:255–257. Chicago, IL: n.p., 1923. Reprint. Broadfoot Publishing: Wilmington, NC, 1993.

————. *Guide to Louisiana Confederate Military Units 1861–1865*. Baton Rouge, LA: Louisiana State University Press, 1989.

Bevier, R. S. *History of the First and Second Missouri Confederate Brigades 1861–1865. And From Wakarusa to Appomattox, A Military Anagraph*. St. Louis, MO: Bryan, Brand & Company, 1879. Reprint. Florissant, MO: Inland Printers, 1985.

Bishop, Albert W. *Loyalty On the Frontier or Sketches of Union Men of the Southwest With Incidents and Adventures in Rebellion on the Border*. St. Louis: E. P. Studley and Co., 1863.

Boatner III, Mark Mayo. *The Civil War Dictionary*. New York: David McKay Company, Inc., 1959.

Britton, Wiley. *The Civil War on the Border A Narrative of Military Operations in Missouri, Kansas, Arkansas, and the Indian Territory, During the Years 1861–62, Based Upon Official Reports of the Federal Commanders, etc.* Volume 1. New York: The Knickerbocker Press, 1899.

Broadhead, James O. "Early Events of the War in Missouri." In *War Papers and Personal Reminiscences. 1861–1865. Read Before the Commandery of the State of Missouri, Military Order of the Loyal Legion of the United States*. 70 vols., 14:1–28. St. Louis, MO: Becktold & Co., 1892. Reprint. Wilmington, NC: Broadfoot Publishing Company, 1992.

Brock, R. A., ed. *Southern Historical Society Papers*. 52 vols. Richmond, VA: Southern Historical Society, 1876–1959. Reprint. Wilmington, NC: Broadfoot Publishing Company, 1990–1992.

Brooksher, William Riley. *Bloody Hill: The Civil War Battle of Wilson's Creek*. Washington, DC: Brassey's, 1995.

Brown, Kent Masterson. "Secession A Constitutional Remedy for the Breach of Organic Law." *North & South* 3 (June 2000): 12–21.

Brugioni, Dino A. *The Civil War In Missouri As Seen From the Capital City*. Jefferson City, MO: Summers Publishing, 1987.

Burke, W. S. *Official Military History of Kansas Regiments During the War For the Suppression of the Great Rebellion*. Leavenworth, KS: W. S. Burke, 1870. Reprint. Ottawa, Ks: Kansas Heritage Press, n.d.

Carter, Cari, ed. *Troubled State: Civil War Journals of Franklin Archibald Dick.* Kirkville, MO: Truman State University Press, 2008.

Cater, Douglas John. *As It Was: Reminiscences of a Soldier of the Third Texas Cavalry and the Nineteenth Louisiana Infantry.* Austin, TX: State House Press, 1990.

Castel, Albert. *General Sterling Price and the Civil War in the West.* Baton Rouge, LA: Louisiana State University Press, 1968.

Connelly, Donald B. *John M. Schofield and the Politics of Generalship.* Chapel Hill, NC: University of North Carolina Press, 2006.

Connelley, William. *Life of Preston B. Plumb.* Chicago, IL: Browne, & Howell, Company, 1913

Covington, James W. "The Camp Jackson Affair: 1861." *Missouri Historical Review* 55 (May 1961): 197–212.

Craven, Avery O. *The Growth of Southern Nationalism 1848–1861.* Baton Rouge, LA: Louisiana State University Press: 1953.

Crawford, Samuel J. *Kansas in the Sixties.* Chicago, IL: A. C. McClurg & Company, 1911.

Crute, Joseph H. *Confederate Staff Officers 1861–1865* Powhatan, VA: Derwent Books, 1982.

———. *Units of the Confederate States Army.* Midlothian, VA: Derwent Books, 1987.

Daniel, Larry J. and Lynn N. Bock. *Island No. 10: Struggle for the Mississippi Valley.* Tuscaloosa. AL: The University of Alabama Press, 1996.

Dougan, Michael B. *Confederate Arkansas: The People and Politics of a Frontier State in Wartime.* University, AL: University of Alabama Press, 1976.

Duncan, Charles V. *John T. Hughes: From His Pen.* Medesto, CA; n.p. , 1991.

Dyer, F. H. *A Compendium of the War of the Rebellion*. Des Moines, IA, 1908. Reprint. Dayton, OH: The Press of Morningside Bookshop, 1978.

Eakin, Joanne C. and Hale, Donald R. *Branded as Rebels: A List of Bushwhackers, Guerrillas, Partisan Rangers, Confederates and Southern Sympathizers from Missouri During the War Years*. Independence, MO: Wee Print, 1993.

Eakin, Joanne C. *Confederate Records From the United Daughters of the Confederacy Files*. 8 vols. Independence, MO: Two Trails Publishing, 1995–2001.

———. *Missouri State Guard Doctor Leaves A Diary In 1861*. Independence, MO: Two Trails Publishing, 1999.

———. *Missouri Prisoners of War From Gratiot Prison & Myrtle Street Prison, St. Louis, Mo. and Alton Prison, Alton Illinois Including Citizens, Confederates, Bushwhackers and Guerrillas*. Independence, MO: Two Trails Publishing, 1995.

Easley, Virginia. "Journal of the Civil War In Missouri: 1861, Henry Martin Cheavens." *Missouri Historical Review* 56 (October 1961): 12–25.

Edwards. John N.. *Shelby and His Men or the War in the West*. Cincinnati, OH, 1867: Reprint. Waverly, MO: General Joseph Shelby Memorial Fund, 1993.

Engle, Stephen D. *Yankee Dutchman: The Life of Franz Sigel*. Baton Rouge, LA: Louisiana State University Press, 1993.

Etcheson, Nicole. *Bleeding Kansas: Contested Liberty in the Civil War Era*. Lawrence, KS: University of Kansas Press, 2004.

Evans, Clement A., ed. *Confederate Military History*. 13 vols. Atlanta, GA 1899. Reprint. Secaucus, NJ: Blue & Gray Press, 1974.

Evans, Clement A. and Bridgers, Robert S., eds. *Confederate Military History Extended Edition*. 19 vols. Atlanta, GA 1899. Reprint. Wilmington, NC: Broadfoot Publishing Company, 1987.

Farthing, C. M. *Chronicles of the Civil War in Monroe County (Missouri)*. Independence, MO: Two Trails Publishing, 1997.

Faust, Patricia L., ed. *Historical Times Illustrated Encyclopedia of the Civil War*. New York: Harper Perennial, 1986.

Filbert, Preston. *The Half Not Told: The Civil War in a Frontier Town*. Mechanicsburg, PA: Stockpole Books, 2001.

Fletcher Thomas C. "The Battle of Pilot Knob, and the Retreat to Leasburg." In *War Papers and Personal Reminiscences. 1861–1865. Read Before the Commandery of the State of Missouri, Military Order of the Loyal Legion of the United States.*70 vols., 14:29–53. St. Louis, MO: Becktold & Co., 1892. Reprint. Wilmington, NC: Broadfoot Publishing Company, 1992.

Fox, William F. *Regimental Losses In The Civil War 1861–1865, etc.* Albany, NY: Fort Orange Press, 1898. Reprint. Dayton, OH: Morningside Bookshop, 1985.

Frémont, John C. "In Command In Missouri." in *Battles and Leaders of the Civil War*. 4 vols. New York: Century Company, 1887–1888, 1:278–288.

Fry, Alice L. *Kansas and Kansans in the Civil War: First Through the Thirteenth Volunteer Regiment*. Kansas City, KS: Two Trails Publishing, 1996.

Fuenfhausen, Gary G. *A Guide to Historic Clay County Architectural Resources and Other Historic Sites of the Civil War also Exploits of John C. Calhoun "Coon" Thornton, a Clay County Confederate Officer*. Kansas City, MO: Little Dixie Publications, 1996..

Gerteis, Louis S. *The Civil War In Missouri: A Military History*. Columbia, MO: University of Missouri Press, 2012.

———. *Civil War St. Louis*. Lawrence, KS: University Press of Kansas, 2001.

Gibson, J. W. (Watt). *Recollections of a Pioneer*. St. Joseph, MO: The Press of Nelson-Hanna, 1912. Reprint. Independence, MO: Two Trails Publishing, 1999.

Gilmore, Donald L. *Civil War on the Missouri-Kansas Border*. Gretna, LA: Pelican Publishing Company, 2006.

Goodrich, Thomas. *War To the Knife: Bleeding Kansas*, 1854–1861. Mechanicsburg, PA: Stockpole Books, 1998.

Guernsey, Alfred H. and Henry M. Alden. *Harper's Pictorial History of the Civil War Contemporary Accounts and Illustrations from the General Magazine of the Time with 1000 Scenes, Maps, Plans and Portraits.* 2 vols. in 1. New York: Fairfax Press, 1866. Reprint. New York: n. p., n.d.

Hale, Donald R. *Branded as Rebels Volume 2.* Independence, MO: Blue & Grey Book Shoppe, 2003.

Hale, Douglas. *The Third Texas Cavalry in the Civil War.* Norman, OK: University of Oklahoma Press, 1993.

Heidler, David S. and Jeanne T. Heidler, eds. *Encyclopedia of the American Civil War: A Political, Social, and Military History.* New York: W. W. Norton & Company, 2000.

———. *Pulling the Temple Down: The Fire-Eaters and the Destruction of the Union.* Mechanicsburg, PA: Stockpole Books, 1994.

Heitman, Francis B. *Historical Register and Dictionary of the United States Army From Its Organization, September 29, 1789, to March 2, 1903.* 2 vols. Washington, DC: Government Printing Office, 1903. Reprint. Gaitherburg, MD: Old Soldiers Books Inc., 1988.

Hewett, Janet, ed. *Supplement to the Official Records of the Union and Confederate Armies.* 100 vols. Wilmington, NC: Broadfoot Publishing Company, 1994–2001.

Hickey, Donald R. *The War of 1812: A Forgotten Conflict.* Chicago, IL: University of Illinois Press, 1989.

Hinze, David C. and Karon Farnham. *The Battle of Carthage: Border War in Southwest Missouri, July 5, 1861.* Campbell, CA: Savas Publishing Company, 1997.

History of Audrain County, Missouri, Written and Compiled from the Most Authentic Official and Private Sources Including a History of Its Townships, Towns and Villages. St. Louis, MO: Historical Company, 1884.

Hodes, Frederick A. *A Divided City: A History of St. Louis 1851 to 1876.* N.C.: Bluebird Pub. Co., 2015.

Holcombe, R. I .and W. S. Adams. *An Account of the Battle of Wilson's Creek or Oak Hills*. Springfield, MO: Dow and Adams,1883. Reprint. Springfield, MO: Independent Printing, Inc., 1961.

Hubbard, George H.. "In the Battle of Belmont." *Confederate Veteran* 33 (December 1925): 469.

Hughes, Jr., Nathaniel Cheairs. *The Battle of Belmont: Grant Strikes South*. Chapel Hill, NC: The University of North Carolina Press, 1991.

Hunt, Roger D. and Jack R. Brown. *Brevet Brigadier Generals In Blue*. Gaitherburg, MD: Olde Soldier Books, Inc., 1990.

Ingenthron, Elmo. *Borderland Rebellion: A History of the Civil War On the Missouri-Arkansas Border*. Branson, MO: The Ozark Mountaineer, 1980.

Johnston, James J. "Letter of John Campbell Unionist." *Arkansas Historical Quarterly* 29 (Summer 1970): 176–182.

Kirkpatrick, Arthur Roy. "Missouri in the Early Months of the Civil War." *Missouri Historical Review* 55 (May 1961): 235–266.

———. "Missouri On the Eve of the Civil War." *Missouri Historical Review* 55 (April 1961): 99–107.

———. "Missouri Secessionist Government, 1861–1865." *Missouri Historical Review* 14 (October 1950): 124–137.

Lademann, Otto C. "The Battle of Carthage. Friday, July 5, 1861." In *War Papers Being Papers Read Before the Commandery of the State of Wisconsin MOLLUS*. 4 vols., 4:131–140. Milwaukee: 1914. Reprint. Wilmington, NC: Broadfoot Publishing Company, 1993.

———. "The Battle of Wilson's Creek, August 10, 1861." In *War Papers Being Papers Read Before the Commandery of the State of Wisconsin MOLLUS*. 4 vols., 4:433–439. Milwaukee, WI: 1914. Reprint. Wilmington, NC: Broadfoot Publishing Company, 1993.

Lademann, Otto C. "The Capture of 'Camp Jackson,' St. Louis, MO., Friday, May 10, 1861." In *War Papers Being Papers Read Before the Commandery of the State of Wisconsin MOLLUS.* 4 vols., 4:69–76. Milwaukee: 1914. Reprint. Wilmington, NC: Broadfoot Publishing Company, 1993.

———. "A Prisoner of War." In *War Papers Being Papers Read Before the Commandery of the State of Wisconsin MOLLUS.* 4 vols., 4:439–443. Milwaukee: 1914. Reprint. Wilmington, NC: Broadfoot Publishing Company, 1993.

Larimer, Charles F., ed. *Love and Valor: Intimate Civil War Letters Between Captain Jacob and Emeline Ritner.* Western Spring, IL: Sigourney Press, 2000.

Laughlin, Sceva Bright. "Missouri Politics During the Civil War." *Missouri Historical Review* 23 (July 1929): 583–619.

Lexington Historical Society. *The Battle of Lexington Fought In and Around the City of Lexington, Missouri On September 18th, 19th and 20th, 1861 by the Forces Under Command of Colonel James Mulligan, U.S.A. and General Sterling Price, M.S.G.* Lexington Historical Society: Lexington, MO, 1903. Reprint. Southern Heritage Press: Middletown, DE, 2015.

Livermore, Thomas L. *Numbers & Losses in the Civil War in America: 1861–1865.* Bloomington, IN: Indiana University Press, 1957.

Lyon, William H. "Claiborne Fox Jackson and the Secession Crisis In Missouri." *Missouri Historical Review* 58 (July 1964): 422–441.

Marvel, William. *Biographical Sketches of the Contributors to the Military Order of the Loyal Legion of the United States.* Wilmington, NC: Broadfoot Publishing Company, 1995.

McElroy, John. *The Struggle For Missouri.* Washington, DC: National Tribune Co., 1909.

McGhee, James E. *Letter and Order Book Missouri State Guard 1861–1862.* Independence, MO: Two Trails Publishing, 2001.

———. *Service With the Missouri State Guard: The Memoir of Brigadier General James Harding.* Springfield, MO: Oak Hills Publishing, 2000.

Miles, Kathleen White. *Bitter Ground: The Civil War in Missouri's Golden Valley Benton, Henry, and St. Clair Counties*. Warsaw, MO: The Printery, 1971.

Moebs, Thomas Truxtun. *Confederate States Navy Research Guide: Confederate Naval Imprints Described and Annotated, Chronology of Naval Operation and Administration, Marine Corps and Naval Officer Biographies, Description and Service of Vessels, Subject Bibliography*. Williamsburg, VA: Moebs Publishing Company, 1991.

Monaghan, Jay. *Civil War on the Western Border 1854–1865*. New York: Bonanza Books, 1955.

Moore, Frank, ed. *The Civil War in Song and Story: 1860–1865*. New York: P. F. Collier, 1889.

———. *The Rebellion Record A Diary of American Events*. 12 vols. vols. 1–6, New York: Putnam, 1861–1863. vols. 7–12, New York: Van Nostrand, 1864–1868. Reprint ed. New York: Arno Press, 1977.

Mudd, Joseph A. "What I Saw At Wilson's Creek." *Missouri Historical Review* 7 (October 1912–July 1913): 89–105.

———. *With Porter in North Missouri: A Chapter In the History of the War Between the States*. Washington, DC: National Publishing Company, 1909.

Mullins, Michael A. *The Frémont Rifles: A History of the 37th Illinois Veteran Volunteer Infantry*. Wilmington, NC: Broadfoot Publishing Company, 1990.

Musser, Richard H. "War In Missouri." In *Southern Bivouac*. 6 vols., 4:745–752. Wilmington, NC: Broadfoot Publishing Company, 1993.

Nash, Charles Edward. *Biographical Sketches of Gen. Pat Cleburne and Gen. T. C. Hindman Together With Humorous Anecdotes and Reminiscences of the Late Civil War*. Little Rock, AR: Tunnah & Pittard, Printers, 1895. Reprint. Dayton, OH: Morningside Bookshop, 1977.

Nichols, Alice. *Bleeding Kansas*. New York: Oxford University Press, 1954.

O'Flaherty, Daniel. *General Jo Shelby: Undefeated Rebel*. Chapel Hill, NC: University of North Carolina Press, 1954. Reprint. Wilmington, NC, 1987.

Parrish, William E., ed., *The Civil War in Missouri: Essays from the Missouri Historical Review, 1906–2006*. Columbia, MO: Missouri Historical Society, 2006

———. *Frank Blair: Lincoln's Conservative*. Columbia, MO: University of Missouri Press, 1998.

Patrick, Jeffery, ed. *Nine Months in the Infantry Service: The Civil War Journal of R. P. Matthews. And Roster the Phelps Regiment Missouri Volunteers*. Springfield, MO: Greene County Historical Society, 1999.

———. "Remembering the Missouri Campaign of 1861: The Memoirs of Lieutenant William P. Barlow, Guibor's Battery, Missouri State Guard." *Civil War Regiments: A Journal of the American Civil War* 5 (No. 4, 1997): 20–66.

Pearce, N. B. "Arkansas Troops in the Battle of Wilson's Creek." In *Battles and Leaders of the Civil War*. 4 vols., 1:298–303. New York: Century Company, 1887–1888.

Peckham, James. *Gen. Nathaniel Lyon, and Missouri in 1861: A Monograph of the Great Rebellion*. New York: American News Company, Publishers, 1866.

Peterson, Richard C., et al. *Sterling Price's Lieutenants: A Guide to the Officers and Organization of the Missouri State Guard*. Jefferson City, MO: Two Trails Publishing, 1995.

Phillips, Christopher. *Damned Yankee: The Life of General Nathaniel Lyon*. Columbia, MO: University of Missouri Press, 1990.

———. *Missouri's Confederate: Claiborne Fox Jackson and the Creation of the Southern Identity in the Border West* . Columbia, MO: University of Missouri Press, 2000.

Phisterer, Frederick. *Statistical Record of the Armies of the United States*. New York: Charles Scribner's Sons, 1907.

Piston, William Garrett and Richard W. Hatcher III. eds. *Kansans At Wilson's Creek: Letters from the Campaign For Southwestern Missouri*. Springfield, MO: Wilson's Creek National Battlefield Foundation, 1993.

Piston, William Garrett and Richard W. Hatcher III. eds. *Wilson's Creek: The Second Battle of the Civil War and the Men Who Fought It.* Chapel Hill, NC: University of North Carolina Press, 2000.

Piston, William Garrett and Thomas P. Sweeney. "Don't Yield An Inch: The Missouri State Guard." In *North & South* 2 (June 1999): 10–26.

———. *Portraits of Conflict: A Photgraphic History of Missouri In the Civil War.* Carl Moneyhon and Bobby Roberts. Gen. Eds. *Portraits of Conflict Series.* Fayetteville, AR: The University of Arkansas Press, 2009.

Pollard, Edward A. *The Lost Cause: A New Southern History of the War of the Confederates, etc.* New York: E. B. Treat & Co., Publishers, 1867. Reprint. New York: Bonanza, 1970.

Polk, William K. "General Polk and the Battle of Belmont." In *Battles and Leaders of the Civil War.* 4 vols. 1:348–357. New York: Century Company, 1887–1888.

Potter, David M. *The Impending Crisis 1848–1861.* Don E. Fehrenbacher, ed. New York: Harper & Row, Publishers, 1976.

Potter, Margueritt. "Hamilton R. Gamble. Missouri's War Governor." In *The Civil War in Missouri: Essays from the Missouri Historical Review, 1906–2006*: 63–107. Columbia, MO: The State Historical Society of Missouri, 2006.

Prentis, Noble L. *Kansas Miscellanies.* Topeka, KS: Kansas Publishing House, 1889.

Primm, James Neal. *Lion of the Valley: St. Louis, Missouri.* Boulder, CO: Pruett Publishing Co., 1981.

Quiner, Edwin Bentlee. *Military History of Wisconsin; A Record of the Civil and Military Patriotism of the State in the Late War for the Union, With A History of the Campaigns in Which Wisconsin Soldiers Have Been Conspicuous—Regimental Histories—Sketches of Distinguished Officers—The Roll of the Illustrious Dead—Movements of the Legislature and State Officers, etc.* Chicago, IL: Clark & Co., 1868.

Rassieur, Leo. *Civil War Regiments From Missouri*. Washington, DC: Federal Publishing Company,1908. Reprint. Pensacola, FL: eBook OnDisk.com, 2007.

Remini, Robert V. *The Battle of New Orleans: Andrew Jackson and America's First Military Victory*. New York: Penguin, Putnam, Inc., 1999.

Rowan, Steven, ed. *Memoirs of a Nobody: The Missouri Years of an Austrian Radical, 1849–1866*. St. Louis: Missouri Historical Society Press, 1997.

Ross, Margaret. *Arkansas Gazette: The Early Years 1819–1866*. Little Rock, AR: Arkansas Gazette Foundation, 1969.

Rutherford, Phillip. "The Carthaginian Wars." *Civil War Times Illustrated* 25 (February 1987): 40–47.

Ryle, Walter Harrington. *Missouri: Union or Secession*. Nashville, TN: George Peabody College For Teachers, 1931.

Scharf, J. Thomas. *History of Saint Louis City and County, From the Earliest Periods to the Present Day: Including Biographical Sketches of Represntative Men*. 2 vols. Philadelphia, PA: Louis H. Everts & Co., 1883.

Schnetzer, Wayne H. *More Forgotten Men: The Missouri State Guard*. Independence, MO: Two Trails Publishing, 2003.

Schofield, John M. *Forty-Six Years In the Army*. New York: The Century Co., 1897.

Schrantz, Ward L. *Jasper County, Missouri in the Civil War*. Carthage, MO: The Carthage, Missouri Kiwanis Club, 1923.

Schultz, Robert G., ed. *General Sterling Price and the Confederacy*. St. Louis: Missouri History Museum, 2009.

Seaton,."The Battle of Belmont." In *War Talks in Kansas MOLLUS* . Kansas City, MO: Press of the Franklin Hudson Publishing Company, 1906. Reprint. 70 vols., 15:306–319. Wilmington, NC: Broadfoot Publishing Company, 1992.

Shalhope, Robert E. *Sterling Price: Portrait of a Southerner*. Columbia, MO: University of Missouri Press, 1971.

Sifakis, Stewart. *Compendium of the Confederate Armies: Florida and Arkansas*. New York: Facts On File, 1992.

———. *Compendium of the Confederate Armies: Louisiana*. New York: Facts On File, 1995.

———. *Who Was Who in the Confederacy: A Comprehensive, Illustrated Biographical Reference to More Than 1,000 of the Principal Confederacy Participants in the Civil War*. New York: Facts on File, 1988.

———. *Who Was Who in the Union: A Comprehensive, Illustrated Biographical Reference to More Than 1,500 of the Principal Union Participants in the Civil War*. New York: Facts on File, 1988.

Sigel, F. "Battle of Wilson's Creek." *Missouri Historical Review* 1 (October 1906 –July 1907): 147–148.

———. "The Flanking Column At Wilson's Creek." In *Battles and Leaders of the Civil War*. 4 vols., 1:304–306. New York: Century Company, 1887–1888.

Simpson, Harold B. *Texas in the War 1861–1865*. Hillsboro, TX: The Hill Junior College Press, 1965.

Sinisi, Kyle S. *The Last Hurrah: Sterling Price's Missouri Expedition of 1864*. New York: Rowman & Littlefield, 2015.

Smith, William Ernest. *The Francis Preston Blair Family In Politics*, 2 vols. New York: The Macmillan Company, 1933.

Snead, Thomas L. *The Fight for Missouri: From the Election of Lincoln to the Death of Lyon*. New York: Charles Scribner's Sons, 1866.

———. "The First Year of the War In Missouri." In *Battles and Leaders of the Civil War*. 4 vols., 1:262-. 277. New York: Century Company, 1887–1888.

Snyder, J. F. "The Capture of Lexington." *Missouri Historical Review* 7 (October 1912): 1–9.

Stevens, Walter B. *St. Louis: History of the Fourth City, 1763–1909, Vol. II*. St. Louis, MO: The S. J. Clarke Publishing Co., 1909.

Swindler, William F. "The Southern Press In Missouri." Missouri Historical Review 35 (July 1941): 394–400.

Tenney, W. J. *The Military and Naval History of the Rebellion in the United States*. New York: D. Appleton & Company, 1866. Reprint. Mechanicsburg, PA: Stackpole Books, 2003.

Tucker, Phillip Thomas. *The South's Finest: The First Missouri Confederate Brigade From Pea Ridge to Vicksburg*. Shippensburg, PA: White Mane Publishing company, Inc., 1993

Tunnard, W. H. *A Southern History: The History of the Third Regiment Louisiana Infantry*. Baton Rouge, LA: W. H. Tunnard, 1866. Reprint. Dayton, OH: Morningside Bookshop, 1988.

The Union Army A History of Military Affairs in the Loyal United States 1861–1865—Records of the Regiments in the Union Army—Cyclopedia of Battles—Memoirs of Commanders and Soldiers. 8 vols. New York: Federal Publishing Company, 1908. Reprint. Wilmington, NC: Broadfoot Pub. Co., 1998.

Volo, James M. and Dorothy Denneen Volo. *Encyclopedia of the Antebellum South*. Westport, CT: Greenwood Press, 2000.

Walke, Henry. William K. "The Gunboats at Belmont and Fort Henry." In *Battles and Leaders of the Civil War*. 4 vols., 1:358–367. New York: Century Company, 1887–1888.

Ware, E. F. *The Lyon Campaign in Missouri: Being a History of the First Iowa Infantry and of the Causes Which Led up to its Organization, and how it Earned the Thanks of Congress Which it got Together With a Birdseye View of the Conditions in Iowa Preceding the Great Civil War of 1861*. Topeka, KS: Crane & Company, 1907. Reprint. Iowa City, IA: Press of the Camp Pope Bookshop, 1991.

Warner, Ezra J. *Generals in Blue: Lives of the Union Commanders*. Baton Rouge, LA: Louisiana State University Press, 1964.

Warner, Ezra J. *Generals in Gray: Lives of the Confederate Commanders*. Baton Rouge, LA: Louisiana State University Press, 1959.

Waterman, Robert E. and Thomas Rothrock. Eds. "The Earle-Buchanan Letters of 1861–1876." *Arkansas Historical Quarterly* 33 (Summer 1974): 99–174.

Webb, W. L. *Battles and Biographies of Missourians or the Civil War Period of Our State*. Kansas City, MO: Hudson-Kimberly Pub. Co., 1900. Reprint. Springfield, MO; Oak Hills Publishing, 1999.

Welch, G. Murlin. *Border Warfare In Southeastern Kansas, 1856–1859*. Pleasanton, KS: Linn County Historical Society, 1977.

Wherry, William H. "General Nathaniel Lyon and His Campaign In Missouri In 1861." In *Sketches of War History 1861–1865 Papers Prepared for the Commandery of the State of Ohio, MOLLUS*. Cincinnati, OH: The Robert Clarke Company, 1896. Reprint. 70 vols, 4:68–86. Wilmington, NC; Broadfoot Publishing Company, 1991.

———. "Wilson's Creek and the Death of Lyon." In *Battles and Leaders of the Civil War.* 4 vols., 1:289–297. New York: Century Company, 1887–1888.

Winter, William C. *The Civil War in St. Louis: A Guided Tour*. St. Louis, MO: Missouri Historical Society Press, 1994.

W. N. M. "Battle of Wilson's Creek." In *Southern Bivouac*. 6 vols., 3:49–54. Reprint. Wilmington, NC: Broadfoot Publishing, 1993.

Woodard, Ashbel. *Life of General Nathaniel Lyon*. Hartford, CT: Case, Lockwood & Co., 1862.

Woodruff, W. E. *With the Light Guns in '61–'65 Reminiscences of Eleven Arkansas, Missouri and Texas Light Batteries, in the Civil War*. Little Rock, AR: Central Printing Company, 1903.

Wooster, Ralph A. *Lone Star Regiments in Gray*. Austin, TX: Eakin Press, 2002.

Worley, Ted R. "Letters to David Walker Relating to Reconstruction In Arkansas, 1866–1874." *Arkansas Historical Quarterly* 16 (Autumn 1957):319–329.

Wright, Marcus J. *General Officers of the Confederate Army*. New York: The Neale Publishing Company, 1911.

Young, Dr. R. E. *Pioneers of High, Water and Main: Reflections of Jefferson City*. Jefferson City, MO: Twelfth State, 1997.

Government Sources:

Davis, George B. and Leslie J. Perry, and Joseph W. Kirkley. *Atlas to Accompany the Official Records of the Union and Confederate Armies*. Washington, DC: Government Printing Office, 1891–1895.

Gray, John B. *Annual Report of the Adjutant General of Missouri for 1864*. Jefferson City, MO: W. A. Curry, Public Printer, 1865.

Library of Congress. *Newspapers in Microform, United States, 1848–1983, Vol I A-O*. Washington, DC: Government Printing Office, 1984.

National Archives. Record Group 109. Confederate Muster Rolls. Assorted units. Washington, DC.

———. Record Group M393. General Order Book (October 14, 1862–April 10, 1863). Army of the Frontier.

——— Record Group M405. Union Compiled Service Records: Missouri. Assorted rolls and units. Washington, DC.

Report of the Joint Committee On the Conduct of the War. Washington, DC: Government Printing Office, 1863. Reprint. New title: *The War in the West* . Millwood, NY: Kraus Reprint Co., 1977.

United States Record and Pension Office. *Organization and Status of Missouri Troops, Union and Confederate, In the Service During the Civil War*. Washington: Government Printing Office, 1902. Reprint. Lexington, KY: Forgotten Books, 2013.

United States War Department. *Revised Regulations of the United States 1861, With Full Index*. Philadelphia, PA: J. G. I. Brown, 1861. Reprint. Harrisburg, PA: The National Historical Society, 1980.

United States War Department. *The War of the Rebellion: A Compilation of the Official Records of the Union and Confederate Armies.* 70 volumes comprising 128 books. Washington, DC, 1880–1901. Reprint. Harrisburg, PA: National Historical Society, 1985.

———. *The War of the Rebellion: Official Record of the Union and Confederate Navies.* 31 volumes. Washington, DC: Edwards Brothers, 1894–1922.

Internet Sites

www.flangan@bcl.net. "The Memoirs of Dr. Robert J. Christie."

www.geni.com, Key Word: "Judge David Walker."

www.history-sites.com. "The Arkansas in the Civil War Message Board."

www.Wikipedia.com. Key Words:"George D. Prentice." "Henry S. Geyer." "James Brown Clay." "James Buchanan Eads.""James Gutherie." "Thomas C. Fletcher." "John William Reid."

Manuscripts/Special Collections

Columbia, MO. State Historical Society of Missouri.
    Western Historical Manuscript Collection:
        Shelton, Alonzo H. Reminscences (KC166)

Little Rock, AR. Arkansas History Commission.
    Skaggs Collection:
        Coleman, William O. Letters.
        Kelly, C. S. Letter.

New York. Columbia University.
    Peter W. Alexander Collection:
        Copy Letter Book, June 1–Dec. 18, 1862, Hindman's Command.
        Special Order Book, June 1–Dec. 18, 1862, Hindman's Command.
        Book of Telegrams (June 2–October 9, 1862).

St. Louis, MO. Missouri Historical Society.
    Babcock, W. R. Collection:
        Missouri Volunteer Militia Scrapbook.
    Camp Jackson Papers:
        Coleman, John."The Riots of St. Louis, Missouri, 1861."

St. Louis, MO. Missouri Historical Society.
  Camp Jackson Papers:
    Streeter, William C. "'Volunteer' Reviews History of First Missouri
      Regiment."
  Col. B. F. Rives Papers:
    "Sketch of Colonel B. A. Rives of Ray County, Missouri."
  Ford, S. H. "Reminiscences of Capt. S. H. Ford."
  General Orders of Missouri (1862).
  Keith, Thomas C. Diary (August 1861–June 1862)
  Snead, Thomas L. Papers:
    "Acts and Deeds of Col. Burbridge's Regiment."

Newspapers

Arkansas:
  The Van Buren Press (Van Buren)
  Washington Telegraph (Washington)

Georgia:
  Daily Sentinel and Chronicle (Augusta)
  The Daily Sun (Columbus)
  Rome Tri-Weekly Courier (Rome)

Illinois:
  Chicago Daily Tribune (Chicago)
  Rock Island Register (Rock Island)
  Waukegan Weekly Gazette (Waukegan)

Louisiana:
  The New Orleans Bee (New Orleans)

Missouri:
  The Daily Missouri Republican (St. Louis)

Mississippi:
  The Daily Southern Crisis (Jackson)

North Carolina:
  The Daily Bulletin (Charlotte)

South Carolina:
  Charleston Mercury (Charleston)

Credits

Photographs and Illustrations:

Baton Rouge, LA. Hill Memorial Library: General Daniel M. Frost.

Baton Rouge, LA. Louisiana State University, Department of Archives and History: General Sterling Price,

Britton, Wiley. *The Civil War on the Border A Narrative of Military Operations in Missouri, Kansas, Arkansas, and the Indian Territory, During the Years 1861–62, Based Upon Official Reports of the Federal Commanders, etc. Volume 1*: John M. Schofield, page 363.

Carlisle Barracks, PA. U.S. Military History Institute: James Totten.

Battles and Leaders of the Civil War, 1:286: Franz Sigel.

McElroy, John. *The Struggle for Missouri*: Claiborne F. Jackson, following page 32; General Nathaniel Lyon, following page 16.

Missouri Republican, July 4, 1884: David Murphy.

Washington, DC. Library of Congress, Prints & Photograph Division, Civil War Photographs: James S. Rains (misidentified as Gabriel J. Rains) C.S.A. (LC-DIG-cwpb-07529). Civil War veterans of Grand Army of the Republic J. L. Buzzzell Post #24, Annandale, Minnesota (LC-DIG-ppmsca-56326): Cover photo.

Wikimedia Commons: James Buchanan Eads, James C. Clay, Thomas Clement Fletcher, H. S. Geyer, and George D. Prentice

Maps:

Michael E. Banasik: Battle of Belmont, November 7, 1861,

Davis, George B., et al. *Atlas of the Civil War*, plt. no. 33, 6: Battle of Dry Wood Creek. Modified by Michael E. Banasik.

Battles and Leaders of the Civil War, 1:290: Battle of Wilson's Creek or Oak Hills.

St. Louis, MO. Collections of the St. Louis Mercantile Library: Camp Jackson, May 6, 1861. Modified by Michael E. Banasik.

Index

Able, Barton, 22, 24; Bio., 22
Albert, Lt. Col. Anslem, 62–63, 65,
    83, 87, 105–108, 112, 114, 184;
    Bio., 62–63
Andrews, Lt. Col. George L., 185,
    187, 218
Arkansas Secession Convention, 153
Arkansas Troops
    Carroll's Arkansas Cavalry, 189
    McRae's Bn. 100, 122, 186
    Reid's Art., 95–100, 102
    Woodruff's Art., 102, 186
    1st Mtd. Rifles, 93
    2nd Rifles, 77, 91, 186
    3rd Inf. (State), 190
    13th Inf., 133, 196, 225, 230–231,
    233
Armed Neutrality, 27–28, 36
Arsenals
    Baton Rouge, LA, 45, 57–58, 150;
    Capture of, 45; Cargo from, 45
    Liberty, MO, 150
    St. Louis, MO 1, 7–20, 24, 35,
    37–38, 40–42, 44, 48–49, 53–56,
    62, 142–143, 156; POW's at, 56;
    Removal of weapons from, 150;
    Weapons stored at, 8
Atchison, Sen. David, 6

Backof or Backoff, Maj. Frank, 48–49,
    64, 77, 195; Bio., 48
Barlow, Capt. William, 69, 79, 121,
    126–127; Bio., 126
Battles, Engagements, Skirmishes, etc.
    Belmont, MO (Nov.7, 1861), 23,
    86, 131, 133–134, 136–141,
    194–197; 27th IL Rescued, 140;
    CSA Losses & Strength at, 226;
    CSA Cmd. Structure at, 225;
    CSA Order of Battle, 224–235;

Hunter's farm, 138; Losses, 138,
    221, 224; Importance of, 141;
    Main attack,195–197; Union
    Order of Battle, 221–224; Retreat
    to Hunter's farm, 138–139
Carthage, MO (July 5, 1861),
    68–78; Aftermath, 78–80; Buck
    Branch, 69, 73–75; Double
    Trouble Creek, 69, 72–73, 177;
    Dry Wood Creek, 128, 176–177;
    MSG Org. at, 198–206; Losses,
    80–82; Sigel's Train, 66, 72,
    80–81, 205; Spring River, 75–76;
    Union Org. at, 206–216; Union
    Home Guard at, 206, 214; Union
    odds and ends units at, 215–216;
    Union strength at, 206–208
Dug Springs, MO (Aug. 2, 1861),
    50, 53, 86, 122, 180–182
First Boonville, MO (June 17,
    1861), 20, 53, 178
Forsyth, MO (July 22, 1861), 83
Lexington, MO (Sept., 1861), 60,
    109, 111, 128–131; Losses, 129
Monroe Station, MO (July 16,
    1861), 60
Neosho, MO (July 5, 1861), 77, 83,
    155
Pea Ridge, AR (Mar. 6–8, 1862),
    108
Price's 1864 Raid, 21, 35, 52, 86,
    110, 145, 165
Second Boonville, MO (Sept. 17,
    1861), 93
Wilson's Creek, MO (Aug.10,
    1861), 17, 35, 39–40, 42, 44, 48,
    50–51, 53, 62–63, 80, 82–84,
    86–93, 95–98, 100–102, 105106,
    110–111, 114, 116, 119–122,
    124–126, 128, 155, 159–160,

172, 178179, 182, 184–187, 189, 191–193; Aftermath, 114–122; Bloody Hill, 98, 100, 126, 187, 190; Dixon house, 92, 100–101 Losses, 115–116, 124; Lyon's Col. Order of Battle, 218–219 Retreat to Rolla, 114, 117–118; Sharp's farm, 91, 100–101; Sigel's Col. Order of Battle, 219-Sigel's plan, 88–89; Skegg's Branch, 91, 96–98; Strength, 86–87, 185; Terell Creek, 91, 93, 103, 105; Union Home Guard at, 219

Beauregard , Gen. P.G.T., 36, 150
Bell, Maj. William H., 7–9, 20, 142; Bio., 8
Bencke, Lt. Henry, 56–57, 76
Benton, Sec. Thomas H., 2–5, 43, 168; Bio., 2
Bischof or Bishoff, Maj. Henry, 69, 72, 83, 210, 219; Bio., 72
Blair, Francis P., 1, 4–5, 8, 11–14, 17, 20–26, 31–32, 37, 41–43, 46, 49, 50–51, 53, 57, 78, 84–87, 156, 165; Bio., 11
Blair, Lt. Col. Charles, 188
Bledsoe, Capt. Hirman, 72, 76, 98–99,177, 186
Boats
  Confederate
    Charm, 114, 137, 234–235
    J. C. Swan, 45, 47
    Henry Hill or *H.R.W. Hill*, 137, 233–234
    Kentucky, 238
    Natchez, 45
    Prince, 233–234
  Union
    Alex Scott, 134
    Belle Memphis, 131, 134, 136, 139–141
    Chancellor, 134, 138, 140

Keystone State, 134
Lexington, 134, 138, 140; Description, 140
Tyler, 134, 138, 140
Boernstein, Col. Henry, 49, 53–54, 56, 58
Border State Convention, 27–28
Brown, Col. William, 69, 74–75, 91–93, 104, 204–205; Bio, 93
Brown, Col. B. Gratz, 11, 49, 78; Bio, 78
Brown, Gen. E. B., 176
Buchanan, Pres. James, 1, 7–9, 13, 21, 153, 164–165
Buford, Col. Napoleon B., 136–138, 140, 194–195, 227; Bio., 194–195
Burbridge, John Q., 5, 52, 202
Burke, Capt. Martin, 39–40,

Cairo, Il., 59, 86, 132–133, 136–137, 140, 183–184
Cameron. Hon. Simon, 120, 148
Campbell, Robert, 14
Camp Johnston, 138, 196–197
Camp Jackson, MO, 9, 12, 17, 20, 24–25, 31–32, 35–36, 4042, 4446, 48–58, 62, 64, 111, 120, 126, 144, 148–150, 154, 156, 171, 173; Consequences of, 32, 52–53, 120–121; Lindell's Grove, 47; Losses, 54–55; Lyon visits, 46; MacDonald challenges status, 52–53; Massacre, 54; POWs captured, 52; Riots following, 54–56, 58; Strength of forces, 52; Weapons captured at, 45, 47, 57; Weapons removed, 156 ; Why attacked, 148–151
Carr, Capt. Eugene, 89–91, 101–104, 122; Bio., 90
Carroll, Col. DeRosey, 189–190
Cawthorn, Col. James, 186–187
Champion, Capt. J. R. "Rock", 12

Cheatham, Gen. Frank, 138, 225, 227, 231, 234
Churchill, Col. Thomas, 77, 92–93, 122; Bio., 92–93
Clark, Col. John. B., Jr., 40, 69, 92,122, 177
Clark, Sen and Gen. John B., Sr., 173, 177, 187, 199, 201–202
Clarke, Marcellus, 5
Clay, Henry, 1–3, 6, 143; Bio., 2
Clay, Judge James, 3–4; Bio., 3
Clemens, Samuel, 59, 61, 137, 139
Cloud, Maj. William F., 123–124; Bio., 123
Columbus, Kentucky, 88, 132, 183–184, 196
Conrad, Capt. Joseph, 65–66, 77, 209–210; Bio., 65
Cracklin, Capt. Joseph, 123–124; Bio., 123–124
Cramer, Capt. John F., 101
Crittenden Compromise, 14
Crittenden, Hon. J. J., 14, 27–28, 142; Bio.,27
Cronenbold, Maj. F. W., 89–90
Cumby, Capt. F.M., 125, 191–192; Bio.,191–192

Davis, Dr. Phillip C., 115, 182
Davis, Pres. Jefferson, 3, 45, 112–113, 132, 150, 173; Bio., 112–113
Deitzler, Col. George W., 185, 219
Department of the West, 10, 23, 34, 63, 84, 149
Dixon, Sen. Archabald, 6
Dodge, Sen. Augustus C., 6
Dougherty, Col. Henry, 138, 223–224
Douglas, Sen. Stephen A., 2, 4, 6, 10, 30, 134
DuBois, Lt. John V., 80, 125, 186, 218

Eads, James B., 21, 164–165; Bio, 21, 164–165

Engert, Lt. Sebastian, 74–75
Essig, Capt. Christian, 64, 69, 72, 75, 176–177
Farrand, Capt. Charles, 92, 96, 101–10
Fayetteville, AR, 63, 84, 87, 91–93, 96, 100, 153, 181
Filley, Hor. Oliver D., 13, 20, 43; Bio., 43
Finkelnburg, Lt. Gustavus N., 106, 113; Bio., 106
Fletcher, Gov. Thomas C., 21, 24–26, 35, 165–166; Bio., 21, 165–166
Foerester's Pioneer Co., See Voerester's Pioneer Co.
Foote, Sen. Henry S., 3; Bio., 3
Fort Smith, AR, 77, 96–97, 168
Fort Sumter, SC, 36, 43
Franklin, Dr. Edward C., 110,127; Bio. 110.
Frémont, Gen. John C., 10, 22, 34, 63, 84–86, 88, 93, 111, 117, 120, 131–133, 182–184; Command problems, 183–184
Frost, Gen. Daniel M., 20, 47, 52, 57, 130, 144, 150; Ltr. on arsenal, 142–144

Gamble, Gov. H. R., 14, 30, 33–34, 144–146, 151, 166–168; Address to people, 151–159; Bio., 33, 165–168
Geyer, Henry S., 5; Bio., 5
Gilbert, Capt. Charles C., 122
Grant, Gen. U. S., 3, 22–23, 59–61, 110, 131–132, 133–134, 136–139, 141, 172, 194–195; Bio., 23
Gratiot, Col. John, 190
Graves, Col. John R., 177, 204
Greene, Capt. Colton, 12, 45, 122, 158
Greer, Col. Elkanah, 92, 122, 124–126, 189, 191; Bio.,191
Grimsley, Thornton, 40, 143–144; Bio., 143

Guibor, Capt. Henry, 49, 69, 72, 76, 79, 126–127
Guthrie, James, 4–5; Bio., 4

Hackman, Capt. August, 66,209
Hale, Capt. Stephen M., 125, 192; Bio., 192
Hardee, Gen. William J., 85–86; Bio., 85–86
Harney, Gen. William S., 13, 23–24, 36, 46, 150–151; Bio., 23–24; Distrusted, 23–24; Proclamation to MO, 148–151
Harris, Gen. Tom, 50, 59–61, 130, 198; Bio., 60
Hassendeubel, Lt. Col. Francis, 62–63, 65, 69, 73–75, 83, 176–177, 209; Bio., 63
Hunter, David. Maj. , 10, 1517; Bio., 15
Hurst, Col. Edgar, 177, 204

Indest, Capt. Joseph, 41, 95
Illinois Troops
   Delano's Cav. Co., 222–224
   3rd Cav., 90
   13th Inf., 59, 87, 219
   14th Inf., 59
   19th Inf., 59
   21st Inf., 23, 59
   22nd Inf., 134,137–138,141, 186, 222
   23rd Inf., 130
   27th Inf., 134, 136, 138, 140, 194, 196, 223
   30th Inf., 134, 196, 223
   31st Inf., 134, 136, 138, 195–196, 223
Indiana Troops
   26th Inf., 175
Iowa Troops
   1st Inf., 81, 83, 97–98, 117, 123, 179, 185–186, 188, 219

7th Inf., 134, 138, 196, 223
Jackson, Gov. Claiborne F., Jackson, 1, 10–13, 16, 19–20, 27, 30–34, 39, 44–45, 47, 62, 66–69, 77, 80–81, 109, 142, 144–145, 147–149, 153, 155–156, 158, 170–171, 173, 177; Bio., 19, 34; Death of, 34; Orders Militia to assemble, 47; Response to Call for troops , 147–148

Kallmann, Col. Herman, 49
Kansas Troops
   1st Inf., 83, 178, 186, 188–189, 219
   2nd Inf., 83, 106, 122–124, 178, 186, 188, 190, 218–219
Kelly, Lt. Michael, 181–182
Kelly, Capt. Joseph, 39–40, 69, 204–205; Bio., 39
Krumsleck or Krummsick or Krumsick, Lt. August G., 76–77; Bio., 76–77

Lehman, Pvt. Albert, 124, 188–189
Lincoln, Pres. Abraham, 1, 57, 16, 22, 24, 29, 34, 43, 62, 114, 154, 194
Logan, Col. John, 136–138, 195–196; Bio., 195
Louisiana Troops
   Watson's Art., 133, 196–197, 230, 232–233
   3rd Inf., 98–99, 102, 186
   11th Inf., 138, 230, 232, 234
   12th Inf. 230, 232, 235
Lothrop, William L., 51, Bio., 51
Lyon, Gen. Nathaniel, 13, 17, 19–26, 36, 41, 43, 45–46, 52, 56–58, 63–64, 82–89, 92, 95–102, 106. 110–111, 114–115, 119–127, 156, 158, 161–162, 165, 171, 173, 178–190; Arrives in St. Louis, 21–24; Bio., 17; Burial, 110–111, 119, 126–127; Commands

arsenal, 20; Commands Dept. of West, 63; Death, 17, 122–124; March to Springfield, 178–182; Pre-war activities, 24–26

Mabry, Capt. Hinche P., 125, 193; Bio., 193
MacDonald, Capt. Emmett, 52, 111, 113; Bio.,111
Magoffin, Gov. Beriah, 27
Major, Lt. Col. James P., 91–93, 99–100, 104–105, 125, 190; Bio.,93
Mann, Lt. Charles, 105–113
Marks, Col. Samuel, 119, 225, 227, 234
Marmaduke, Gen. John S., 145
Massey, Benjamin F., 156; Bio., 156
McBride, Gen. James, 187–188
McClernand, Gen. John A., 136–137, 194, 222–223; Bio, 194
McCulloch, Gen. Ben, 66–67, 77–78, 85–87, 98–100, 107–108, 115, 121, 126, 128, 158, 186; Bio., 67
McIntosh, Col. James, 77, 106–108, 122, 182; Bio., 107
McKee, William, 22, 24; Bio., 22
McKinstry, Gen. Justus, 9, 10, 13, 21, 23–27, 34; Bio., 10
McNeil, Col. John, 49–50, 78, 82; Bio., 50
McRae, Lt. Col. Dandridge, 100, 122, 186
Melcher, Dr. Samuel H., 92, 98, 110, 127; Bio., 110
Meumann, Capt. Theodore, 99–101, 104–105
Mexican War (1845–1848), 2, 10–11, 13, 15, 21, 23, 25, 49, 51, 63, 67, 85, 92, 109, 112, 123, 132-133, 141, 143, 145, 168, 191, 195; Losses, 21
Military Bill, 32, 46, 148–149, 157, 170–171

Mills, Surg. Madison, 25; Bio., 25
Missouri Compromise, 38, 40
Missouri Convention (Feb./Mar., 1861), 16, 27–28, 30–31, 166, 170–171; Amendments to Maj. Rpt., 145–147; Delegates for, 144–145; Majority Report, 30, 146–147; Minority Report, 30, 147
Missouri Convention (July 1861), 33, 43, 167, 173; Gamble elected Gov., 167; Report of, 150–159
Missouri General Assembly, 30–31, 149, 154–157, 159
Missouri, Branches, Creeks, Rivers
  Buck Branch, 69, 73–75
  Double Trouble Creek, 69, 72–73, 177
  Dry Wood Creek, 128
  Grand River, 178–180
  James River Branch, 101, 104, 220
  Osage River, 179–180
  Skegg's Branch, 91, 9698
  Spring River, 75–76
  Tyrell's or Terell Creek, 91, 93, 103, 105
  Wilson's Creek, See Battle of
Missouri Cities, Towns
  Belmont, 23, 86, 131, 133–134, 136–141, 194–197
  Bloomfield, 132
  Boonville, 50, 53, 66, 93, 97, 178, 183–184
  Carthage, 42, 44–45, 48, 62–69, 72, 74–82, 105, 111–112, 123, 172, 179–180, 192
  Clinton, 178–179
  Dug Springs, 50, 53, 84–86, 122, 180–182
  Forsyth, 82–83, 88, 90, 180
  Lexington, 60, 109, 111, 128–31, 168, 183

Little York, 78, 82, 88, 100–101, 180–181

Moody's Springs, 100, 102

Mt. Vernon, 66, 76, 78

Neosho, 64, 66, 68, 77–78, 83, 155, 173

Rolla, 10, 64, 72, 83, 87, 111–114, 118–119, 122, 127, 183, 209

Sarcoxie, 66–67, 76–78, 156, 172

Springfield, 64–66, 76, 78, 80–84, 86, 88–91, 9598, 100105, 108–115, 117–120, 122, 125, 127–128, 175, 178–181, 184; CSA occupy, 108, 118–119; Lyon's march to, 82, 97, 178–82; Sigel arrives, 64–65

St. Louis, 1–24, 26, 31–56, 58, 62–65, 72, 78, 82–86, 95, 102, 106, 109–111, 113115, 120, 126–128, 131, 133, 142–145, 147–148, 152–154, 156, 164–166, 168–176, 183–184; Committee of Safety, 20, 24, 31, 43, 56; Gratiot St. Prison, 109, 169; Jefferson Barracks, 13, 16, 18–19, 49; Minuet Men, 12, 38, 40, 55, 144; Newspapers, (*Bulletin*, 14, 109), (*Democrat*, 7, 11, 22), (*Journal*, 32, 154, 173), (*Times*, 5), (*Union*, 22, 42); Planter's House, 15–17, 35–36, 63, 178; Meeting at Planter's (June 11), 36, 178; Missouri Home Guard, 31, 42, 49, 66, 68–69, 77, 80, 91, 118, 184, 186; Riots, 54–56, 58; St. Louis Militia, 39, 40, 47, 126, 144; Wide-a-wakes or Wide Awakes, 11–13, 42

Missouri Extraordinary Session, 31–32

Missouri Troops
Missouri State Guard (MSG)

Bledsoe's Art., 72, 76, 98–99, 177, 186,200

Cawthorn's Bde., 186–187

Guibor's Art. 49, 69, 72, 76, 79, 126–127, 205

Shelby's Ranger Co., 68

1st Div., 86

2nd Div., 50, 60–61, 67, 69, 75, 81, 181–182, 186,199–200; Losses at Carthage, 201; Org. at Carthage, 199–201

3rd Div., 93, 199, 201–202, 204; Losses at Carthage, 201–203, 220; Org. at Carthage, 201-203

4th Div., 69, 82, 122, 177, 187, 198, 203–204; Losses at Carthage, 204; Org. at Carthage,203–204;

5th Div., 203

6th Div., 39, 67, 93, 104, 199, 204; Losses at Carthage, 205; Org. at Carthage, 204–205

7th Div. 187–188

8th Div. 199–200

Union
Backof or Backoff's Bn., 48, 64, 77, 105, 205, 207; 212–213, 220

Black Jaegers, 11–12, 42, 55

Clark Home Guard, 186

Essig's Art., 64, 69, 72, 75, 176–177

Sigel's Bde., 64–66,56–69, 72–76, 79, 83, 89–94, 95–96, 98–100

Union Guard, 42

Voerester's Pioneer Co., 66, 87, 206–213, 216–218; at Wilson's Creek, 217–218; strength at Carthage, 213

Wilkin's Art., 64, 72, 74–75, 105, 176

1st Lt. Art., 35, 48, 50–51, 105, 175–176
1st Inf. (Three Months), 11, 35, 41, 49–51, 106, 186–188
1st Inf. (Reserve Corps), 48, 49
2nd Inf. (Three Months), 49, 53, 83, 218
2nd Inf. (Reserve Corps), 58
2nd Inf. Bn. (Osterhaus), 106, 186
3rd Inf. (Three Months), 41–42, 44, 48–49, 54–56, 62–65, 68, 72, 74–76, 83, 89–90, 92, 95–96, 98–99, 101–102, 104, 176, 206–209; Org. & Strength at Carthage, 209–210
3rd Inf. (Reserve Corps), 49–50, 75, 78
3rd Inf. (Three Years), 42, 72, 77, 83, 95, 99, 105
4th Inf. (Three Months), 49, 55, 83
4th Inf. (Reserve Corps), 49, 64, 78, 83
5th Inf. (Three Months), 65–66, 73–75, 78, 80, 83 89–92, 96, 98, 101–102, 110, 172, 176, 206–207, 210–212; Org. & Strength at Carthage, 211–212
15th Inf., 99
17th Inf., 42, 63, 99, 101
31st Inf., 21, 165
Mitchell, Col. Robert B., 122–124, 188, 219; Bio., 123
Monroe, Lt. Col. Thomas, 68
Mulligan, Col. James, 129–131; Bio., 130
Murphy, Col. David, 35, 41, 175–176; Bio., 35; Court-martials of, 175–176

Newport Barracks, Kentucky, 9

O'Kane, Lt. Col. Walter, 98, 204

Oglesby , Col. Richard J., 132–133; Bio., 132
Omnibus Bill, 2, 6

Palmer, Col. John M., 5, 59–60; Bio., 59–60
Parsons, Gen. Mosby M., 39, 67–68, 104, 122, 176–177, 188; Bio., 67
Paschall, Nathaniel , 10, 14
Paxton, Maj. Rufus, 41
Pea Ridge, AR, 40, 44, 53, 56, 63, 67, 72, 90, 93, 99, 107–108, 111, 117, 124, 169, 191–193
Pearce, Gen. Nicholas B., 106–107, 190; Bio., 106
Phelps, Mrs. John S., 88, 91, 110–111, 127; Bio.,110–111
Pierce, Pres. Franklin, 1, 4, 6–7, 112
Pillow, Gen. Gideon J., -39, 85–86, 162, 195–196, 227, 233; Bio., 86
Palmer, Col. John M., 59–60; Bio., 5, 59–60
Plummer, Capt. Joseph, 98, 122, 186–187
Polk, Gen. Leonidas, 5, 132–133, 136–138, 183, 225, 235; Bio.,132
Pope, Gen. John, 183
Prentice, George D., 4–5, Bio., 4
Price, Gen. Sterling, 5, 16, 30, 32–33, 36, 52, 63–64, 66–67, 77, 85–86, 89, 91, 98, 104, 107–109, 111–113, 121–122, 126, 128130, 132–133, 144, 153, 158, 168–169, 173–174, 178, 186–187; CDR of MSG, 32; Description, 108; Pres. of Conv., 16, 30–31, 33; Sent to AR 67; Sieges Lexington, 128; To Lexington, 128; To Mexico, 169
Price-Harney Agreement, 35

Rains, Gen. James S., 67–69, 72 , 75, 81, 181–182, 186; Bio., 67
Rawlings, Capt. John A., 134

Redd, John T., 30, 144
Reid, Capt. John G., 95–100, 102; Bio, 96–97
Reid, Col. John W., 109–110; Bio., 109, 168–169
Reynolds, George. D., 26; Bio., 26
Reynolds, Lt. Gov. Thomas C., 11–13, 67, 78, 154, 169–171; Bio., 12, 169–171
Right to Secede, 29–30; Why secession failed in MO, 148
Rives, Col. Ben, 69, 74–75, 77, 81–82
Robinson, Lt. William G., 9–11, 13, 15, 20; Bio., 9
Rosser, Lt. Col. Thomas H., 98
Russell, Capt. Jonathan, 125, 193; Bio., 193
Russell, Col. R.M., 225, 227, 233

Salomon, Col. Charles E., 63–64, 66, 69, 73–75, 90, 100–101, 171–172, 176, 212; Bio., 171–171
Schaefer, Lt. Gustavus A., 90, 97
Schofield, Maj. John M., 22–24, 79, 89, 114, 122, 127, 183–184, 188–189
Schuettner, Col. Nicholas, 49, 55
Schuster, Lt. George, 100–101, 105–106, 113
Scott, Charles M., 131, 137–139, 141
Scott, Gen. Winfield, 14, 15, 17–19, 25; Bio., 14–15
Seminole War, 21, 23, 85; Losses, 21
Shaler, Maj. James R., 12, 45
Shelby, Capt. Joseph O., 68–69, 122, 171
Sherman, Gen. William T., 23, 133, 195; Bio., 23
Short, Capt. D.M., 125, 192–193; Bio. 192–193
Sigel, Col. Franz, 44–45, 48–49, 55–56, 57, 6266, 65–69, 72–77, 79–83-, 8793, 95–105, 112,

114–115, 118–119, 125–126, 160–161,172, 176–177, 179–180; at Carthage, 68–76, 206–208, 211, 219; at Wilson's Creek, 83, 87, 89–100; Bio., 44; Retreat from Wilson's Creek, 102–114; Strength at Wilson's Creek, 83, 87
Slack, Gen. William J., 69, 75, 122, 177, 187
Smith, Gen. Charles F., 133; Bio., 133
Smith, E. Kirby, 93, 171, 193
Smith, Col. Preston, 137, 225, 227, 231, 235
Smith, Col. Robert, 60
Snead, Col. Thomas Lowndes, 1, 8, 14, 19, 39, 46, 66, 02, 100, 109, 111, 116, 122, 124, 142, 177, 179; Bio., 109
Sokalski, Lt. George, 187
Stanley, Capt. David S., 181–182
Steele, Capt. Frederick, 114, 122, 172, 181–182, 186
Sturgis, Maj. Samuel, 101, 111, 114, 117–118, 122, 178–179, 189, 218; Assumes cmd. at Wilson's Creek, 189; to Grand River, 178–179
Strodkamp or Strodtmann, Capt. John E. 44–45; Bio., 44–45
Sturgeon, Isaac H., 1, 3–5, 7, 9–17, 19–20, 183; Bio., 1
"Sue Mundy," see Clarke, Marcellus
Sweeny, Gen. Thomas W., 32, 51, 55–57, 63–64, 66, 76, 78, 80, 82–83, 87–88, 122, 154–155, 174, 189, 211; Bio., 51

Tappan, Col. James,133
Taylor, Capt. Francis M., 125, 192; Bio., 192
Taylor, Dr. George W., 72, 80–81, 201, 206
Tennessee Troops
2nd Inf., 196, 225, 231, 233

4th Inf.230, 232, 235
12th Inf., 146, 233
13th Inf., 195–196, 225, 230, 231, 233
15th Inf., 138, 230–231, 234
21st Inf., 195, 230–231, 233
22nd Inf., 195, 230–231, 233
154th Inf., 140, 225, 229, 232, 235
Thompson, Gen. M. Jeff, 5, 85–86, 131–133;Bio., 86
Totten, Capt. James, 122, 126, 187, 190
Trask, Capt. W.L., 137
Tucker, Joseph W., 32, 40, 154, 172–174; Bio., 154, 172–174
Turner Hall, 41
Tyler, Sec. Robert, 4

Union Troops
DuBois Art., 80, 125, 186
1st Cav. (Carr's), 83, 90, 92, 107, 180–181, 220
1st Cav. (Stanley), 181–182
2nd Dragoons (Farrand's), 92, 96, 101–102, 220
2nd Art. (Totten), 218
1st Inf. (Plummer's Bn.), 98, 185–187, 218

2nd Inf. (Steele's Bn.), 114, 181, 186

Van Buren, AR, 100, 102, 169
Vicksburg, MS, 25, 35, 40, 63, 95, 99, 165, 176, 195

Walker, David, 152–153; Bio. 153
Walker, Col. J. Knox, 196–197, 225, 228, 233
Weightman, Col. Richard, 69, 76, 111, 177, 200
Western Department, 84–86
Wiatt, John, 115, 117
Wilkin, Capt. Theodore, 64, 72–75, 105, 176
Winston, Capt. T. W., 125, 191; Bio., 191
Wolf or Wolff, Lt. Col. Christian, 66, 74–75, 176, 219
Woodruff, Capt. William, 96, 102, 186
Wright, Col. John, 196
Wright, Col. Marcus, 140, 196
Wright, Urial, 52, 145

Yeatman, James, 14

www.ingramcontent.com/pod-product-compliance
Lightning Source LLC
Chambersburg PA
CBHW031946090426
42739CB00006B/102